BETWEEN DYNASTIES

Published by:
Fletcher Thomas
Adelaide, Australia

ISBN 978-0-6484330-0-2 (Paperback)
ISBN 978-0-6484330-1-9 (eBook)

www.andrewvanbuuren.com

Book design by Simon Brown, Follow the Wolves.

For Olivia River.

BETWEEN DYNASTIES

The Los Angeles Lakers
in the years between Magic and Kobe

Andrew van Buuren

Fletcher Thomas

INTRODUCTION

L AKERS FANS ARE a spoiled bunch, fortunate to experience four grand dynasties during the team's history. The great players, genius coaches, and unique personalities from these four eras are well documented. Those who saw them will never forget them and will make sure future generations hear all about them.

We can easily identify Laker dynasties. The teams and stars have books written, documentaries produced, and entire NBA-licensed DVD boxsets dedicated to them. You'll see their highlights regularly on League Pass. Banners hang in Staples Center immortalizing their championships, and their best players have their numbers retired.

Each dynasty is bookended by a corresponding black hole, the equivalent of a temporary team-wide Dark Age where something must have happened, but we see little or no evidence of it. The black holes are harder to spot. They're the connective tissue between dynasties, identifiable by their lack of banners, retired numbers, books, and documentaries. They're the years between dynasties, when the team wasn't blessed with great talent or coaching, and so get lost in the shuffle of our memories. Due to either a lack of on-court success or a lack of star talent (or both), we have selected it out of our memory.

There is no better example of this than the amount of attention black holes receives on the 47-minute documentary that complements the NBA's official 10-disc DVD set *Los Angeles Lakers: The Complete History* – only 6%. That's 16 years of Laker history told in two and a half minutes. Turns out, it isn't much of a complete history at all.

* * * * *

Dynasty #1

The league's first dynasty was the 1950s Minneapolis Lakers who were led by towering center George Mikan, the league's first star. That team won six titles in seven years in three different leagues. They were the first team in league history to win back-to-back titles and the first to three-peat.

They had six Hall of Famers – Mikan, Vern Mikkelsen, Jim Pollard, Slater Martin, Clyde Lovellette and head coach John Kundla.

This dynasty is well documented; you won't pick up a book about the history of the NBA that doesn't devote a good deal of its pages to those teams. Mikan is always in any video collage of NBA history. And for good reason. During the years when basketball was struggling to find its place in the collective American sports conscience, Mikan and the Lakers commanded attention.

Black Hole #1

Mikan retired in 1954, made a short-lived and ill-advised comeback in 1956 on a comparatively ordinary Lakers team, before retiring for good. Then, according to the way we seem to remember things, the Lakers fell into a dark hole and off the radar until they suddenly re-appeared in Los Angeles circa 1960 with superstars Jerry West and Elgin Baylor. The Lakers struggled in the years between Mikan's retirement in 1956 and West arriving in 1960. Little is talked about those teams or who played on them.

Dynasty #2

We usually give the title of Dynasty to a team that dominates the league by winning multiple championships. The Lakers of the 1960s and early 1970s are a rare exception. These Lakers were star-studded and successful, but it didn't translate into many titles.

These Lakers featured five Hall of Famers – West, Baylor, Wilt Chamberlain, Gail Goodrich, and head coach Bill Sharman. They're mostly remembered for the incredible 1971-72 season in which they won an NBA-record (at the time) 69 games. They had the longest winning streak of any team in American professional sports history by winning 33 in a row and went on to defeat the New York Knicks 4-1 in the NBA Finals.

But it was the only title they won. No team in NBA history experienced as much heartbreak as these Lakers. They made the NBA Finals in 1962, 1963, 1965, 1966, 1968, and 1969. They lost each time to the Boston Celtics. Three times they lost Game 7 by three points or less.

They advanced to the Finals again in 1970 where, for once, they didn't play the Celtics. Instead, they lost to the Knicks in seven games. After finally breaking through with their 1972 title, they made it back to the Finals in 1973 and again lost to the Knicks.

These Lakers made it to the Finals nine times and won only once. It is a wonder any Lakers fan survived these years unscathed.

Black Hole #2

If you asked 100 people what happened between West's retirement in 1974 and Earvin "Magic" Johnson being drafted in 1979, it is likely 99 of them would stare at you blankly.

The Lakers traded for Kareem Abdul-Jabbar in 1975, so the team had a bonafide superstar for all but one of those five years. But they struggled to put enough talent around him and were instead a middle-of-the-road team who averaged 46 wins per season. They made the playoffs three times, advanced out of the first round twice, but were quickly dispatched once they ran into serious championship contenders.

We only remember three things about this era. Abdul-Jabbar scored a ton of points, West was the head coach for three seasons and Kermit Washington almost killed Rudy Tomjanovich.[1]

Dynasty #3

Showtime is Lakers fans' most beloved era. It is perhaps what the franchise is best known for.

The team featured five Hall of Famers – Magic, Abdul-Jabbar, James Worthy, Jamaal Wilkes, and head coach Pat Riley. The supporting cast was an embarrassment of riches, featuring Byron Scott, A.C. Green, Michael Cooper, Norm Nixon, Kurt Rambis, Mychal Thompson, and Bob

---

[1] West was the coach of the Lakers the year before Magic's rookie season. They came very close to being player/coach.

McAdoo.[2]

They defeated the Philadelphia 76ers for the championship in 1980 and 1982. They finally broke the Celtics curse when they beat Boston in the Finals in 1985 and 1987. They became the first team to repeat as champions since the 1960s when they defeated the Detroit Pistons in seven tense games in 1988. Magic became the first rookie to win Finals MVP in 1980 and Abdul-Jabbar became the oldest player to win it in 1985.

Jerry Buss, the Lakers energetic new owner, redefined the concept of sports entertainment and turned every Lakers game into an event. The Lakers' blindingly quick, fast-breaking style became the hottest ticket in Los Angeles, and the Magic Johnson vs. Larry Bird rivalry saved the league.

Black Hole #3

Exactly when Showtime officially ended is debatable. Maybe it was when Abdul-Jabbar retired in 1989 or when Riley stood down in 1990. But the Lakers undoubtedly entered their third black hole when Magic suddenly retired in 1991. And they would stay there until they signed Shaquille O'Neal and traded for rookie Kobe Bryant before the start of the 1996-97 season.

The NBA boomed in popularity in the early to mid-1990s, led by Michael Jordan's dominance of both the league and worldwide sports marketing. But the Lakers were largely irrelevant during those boom years, stuck somewhere between nostalgia for Showtime and building for the future. These five years have turned into a mere footnote.[3]

Dynasty #4

The fourth Lakers dynasty is split into two sub-eras. Dynasty 4.1 featured superstar teammates Shaq, Kobe, and head coach Phil Jackson. It was a beautifully imperfect marriage between the best center, the best guard, and the best coach in the league. Together they won three straight

---

[2] McAdoo is a Hall of Famer too, but he's there for what he did as a superstar in Buffalo and New York, not what he did as a role-player off the bench for the Lakers at the end of his career.

[3] The *Los Angeles Lakers: The Complete History* spends one minute talking about this era and includes footage of Sean Rooks, who wasn't even a Laker during this time.

titles from 2000-2002, before dramatically imploding due to years of in-fighting.

Shaq was traded in 2004 and, after a few down years, Dynasty 4.2 was born when forward/center Pau Gasol was acquired in a lop-sided trade. Kobe, Jackson, and Gasol would win back-to-back titles in 2009 and 2010, even getting one against the Celtics for good measure.

People will be talking about these teams forever, and not just because they won five championships. Kobe, Shaq, and Jackson were transcendent talents with oversized and distinctive personalities, each polarizing in their own unique way. This era was filled with individual and team success, equaled only by the level of drama caused along the way.

Black Hole #4

The Lakers scrambled to find the right combination of players to continue Dynasty 4.2 and milk one last championship out of Kobe's twilight years. It all came crashing down on April 12, 2013, when Kobe, now in his 17th season and 34 years old, tore his Achilles tendon.

He would play three more injury-riddled seasons but was never the same. And neither were the Lakers. They had their worst ever season in 2014-15, winning just 21 games. The following season, they topped it by winning only 17. The Lakers during this time became exposed as being just another poorly coached, poorly managed NBA team without any superstar talent and seemingly no ability to attract it.

Why care about a black hole at all? After all, living in a 'championship or bust' world sounds like it has integrity – we won't accept anything less than the absolute best. But it isn't reality. There are lean years, there are times when your team can't get it done. Times when the best players in the league are on other teams, when the eyes of the sporting world are on other NBA cities.

These moments happened. These players and coaches were there. Fans filed into the Great Western Forum to cheer them on, just like they did Magic, West, and Wilt. These games were played. The team was still the Lakers. They always mattered to us. We should honor that.

CONTENTS

PART V: THE GAP BETWEEN THE AGES

BETWEEN DYNASTIES

PROLOGUE

MAGIC JOHNSON RECEIVED the ball at the top of the key from a short pass from A.C. Green and squared up his defender, Michael Jordan. He took two dribbles to Jordan's right and spun around him, unsure of what his next move would be.

He had made this move countless times over his 12-year career. He'd usually find someone wide open underneath the basket for an easy lay-up, often before they even knew they were open. It was a gift Magic always had, the kind no coach can teach. The ability to read a moving defense, spot a teammate motioning towards the basket, identify the slightest of angles between defenders, precisely feed the ball through that seam and into the waiting arms of the teammate for an easy shot. All in the fraction of a second.

But instead, he was blindsided by Scottie Pippen, who stepped in behind him and knocked the ball loose before he could do anything with it. The Bulls' Bill Cartwright picked up the loose ball and heaved it down court over his shoulder, finding a streaking Pippen with nothing between him and the basket for an easy dunk. This pushed the Bulls lead out to 70-62 with five minutes to play in the third quarter.

The Bulls had been on a run the last few minutes. Their scrambling, physical defense was forcing the Lakers into mistakes that too frequently led to easy dunks or lay-ups at the other end without much resistance. It was Game 5 of the 1991 NBA Finals. The Bulls led the series 3-1, and it was all starting to slip away from the Lakers.

To make matters worse, James Worthy and Byron Scott were in street clothes – injured and unable to play. Their limited impact on the series had meant Jordan and Pippen were free to swarm Magic on defense, suffocating his usual free-flowing game. The Bulls were making one of those pushes where they would be unstoppable for three to four minutes, the kind that would put a game out of reach for good.

It had been happening all series. The Lakers stole Game 1 in Chicago when Magic found Sam Perkins open for a three-pointer with 14 seconds left to give them a 91-89 lead. Jordan had a good look at a 17-foot potential game-winning jumper that touched every part of the ring before falling out.

Chicago came out angry in Game 2 and evened up the series with an emphatic 107-86 victory, the young and athletic Bulls making the Lakers look slow and plodding by comparison.

The series moved to Los Angeles for the next three games where the Lakers hoped the comfortable confines of home would give them control of the series. They had, after all, only lost one home game all playoffs. When an 18-2 third-quarter run gave the Lakers a 67-54 lead in Game 3, that hope seemed realistic. But the Bulls would answer with a 20-7 run of their own. Jordan's shot at the end of regulation tied the score at 92-92, and Chicago held the Lakers to four points in overtime and won 104-96.

Game 4 was an ugly affair for the Lakers, shooting a miserable 36% from the floor. Perkins, the hero of Game 1, scored just 3 points on 1-15 shooting. The Bulls defense smothered the Lakers all night, spurring them to a 97-82 victory. "They are beating us and beating us bad," Magic said.

The media had hyped the Finals as a match-up between Magic and Michael. Instead of a match-up, it turned into a passing-of-the-torch moment between superstars. Magic had dominated the NBA for 12 years, and Jordan badly wanted what Magic had. He was going to get it too.

This was an unlikely Finals match-up back when the season began. The Lakers started the 1990-91 season with fans, media, and even themselves unsure of what to expect. It had been an off-season of change with five new faces on opening night – almost half the roster. Veteran guard Michael Cooper, who had played 12 seasons with the Lakers and won five championships, had retired in August. Forward Orlando Woolridge and third-stringer Mark McNamara were traded for draft picks to free up cap space.[4] Forward Jay Vincent, who had been a teammate of

---

[4] Woolridge was traded to the Denver Nuggets in exchange for protected 1993 and 1995 2nd round draft picks. McNamara was traded to the San Antonio Spurs for a protected 1992 2nd round draft pick. All three picks were rescinded.

Magic at Michigan State, was waived.

The Lakers upgraded their frontcourt by using the newly created cap space on free agent forward Sam Perkins from the Dallas Mavericks, who took Woolridge's place in the rotation. In September, they traded their 1991 first round draft pick to the Golden State Warriors in exchange for volume shooter Terry Teagle. To fit Teagle under the salary cap, Magic agreed to re-negotiate his contract, taking $100,000 less to make room for him.

They selected forward/center Elden Campbell from Clemson University with the 27th pick in the 1990 NBA Draft and used their second-round pick on guard Tony Smith out of Marquette. The Lakers invited two unsigned rookies to training camp – Mario Elie and Irving Thomas – eventually releasing Elie before the start of the season.[5]

But the biggest change of all would be the departure of legendary head coach Pat Riley. After two and a half years as an assistant, Riley took over as head coach midway through the 1981-82 season. He'd rule the sidelines for another nine years, guiding the Lakers to four championships before stepping down to take a broadcasting job at NBC.[6]

His replacement was 36-year-old Mike Dunleavy, who had never previously been a head coach at any level. He had, however, played nine years in the NBA as a back-up point guard before retiring at age 29 in 1985 due to chronic back pain. After a stint on Wall Street at Merrill Lynch, he returned to the NBA as an assistant coach in 1989 in Milwaukee, even coming out of retirement at the age of 35 to play seven games over two seasons when injuries plagued the Bucks backcourt.

Dunleavy was a quiet and unassuming personality, a stark contrast to the brash Riley. But the coaching change was more than just a new face on the sidelines. Dunleavy bought with him an entirely new system, one that was the antithesis of Riley's famous fast-paced attack. Dunleavy's Lakers would play at a slow, patient pace and would affectionately be mocked as Slowtime. His plan was for the Lakers to use as much of the shot clock as they needed to work the ball around for a good shot. Often this meant

---

[5] After playing in the CBA, Argentina, Ireland and Portugal from 1986-1990, Ellie would go on to have an excellent 11-year NBA career. He would be a valuable role player on three championship teams in Houston (1994, 1995) and San Antonio (1999) and go onto to become an assistant coach in the NBA.

[6] Riley also played six seasons with the Lakers and was on the 1971-72 team that won 69 games and the championship.

using Magic in the post where he would find players in predetermined spots on the floor for easy shots.

There was a logic behind Dunleavy's changes. The Lakers offense in 1990-91 would be built around Magic's ability to create scoring opportunities for his teammates, just as it had been under Riley. But at 31 years old, and with 11 long NBA seasons spent playing into June almost every year, managing Magic's workload was going to be key to the team's success. They didn't have the luxury of resting him, not with two imperfect back-up options. Veteran Larry Drew was too old and too slow. Rookie Tony Smith was too green, and maybe more of a shooting guard anyhow. If they couldn't rest him, the Lakers would try to maximize Magic's mileage by making him play slower.

The Lakers struggled out of the gate with a 2-5 record by mid-November. Magic publicly preached patience but behind the scenes was worried the new playing style wasn't working. Things eventually fell into place with an eight-game win streak over November and early December and a sixteen-game win streak in early January, assuring a healthy playoff spot. They finished the season with 58 wins, third best in the league. And it was another fine season for Magic, who finished second in assists per game and second in MVP voting. Magic, along with Worthy, made the All-Star game in Charlotte. In April, he passed Oscar Robertson to become the NBA's all-time assist leader.

The season had been an undeniable success for the Lakers, yet the two teams above them in the standings – Portland and Chicago – were assumed simply too strong. The Lakers were considered merely the best of the rest.

Jordan's supporting cast in Chicago was maturing into effective role players, and Pippen was emerging as a legitimate star in his own right. After taking their lumps the previous few seasons against the Detroit Pistons in the playoffs, the Bulls were now favorites to come out of the East.

The Portland Trail Blazers were led by high-scoring guard Clyde Drexler and had a deep, versatile roster that boasted three All-Stars in 1991.[7] They were favorites in the West and winning the championship fit a nice narrative. They had lost in the Finals to the more experienced

---

[7] Drexler, Terry Porter and Kevin Duckworth all made the All-Star Game in 1991.

Detroit Pistons in 1990 and now looked ready to take that final leap.

And then there were the defending champion Pistons, who flew under the radar most of the season by winning only 50 games. On the surface they had a disappointing season, succumbing to the complacency that sometimes comes with being the two-time defending champion. A two-month injury to Isiah Thomas didn't help either. But by the start of the playoffs, they were healthy and more than capable of 'flicking the switch' like only veteran teams can – pacing themselves all season and turning it on when it mattered most.

Hakeem Olajuwon's Houston Rockets were the Lakers' first-round opponent and were swept 3-0, though the series was much closer than it appears on paper. The Lakers won the first game 94-92 at home on a game-winning shot by Scott that shouldn't have counted.[8] The Lakers eventually closed out the series sweep by taking Game 3 in Houston by four points, requiring 38 points and 7 assists from Magic to get the job done.

The Lakers got lucky with their second-round opponent as the 55-win San Antonio Spurs were upset in the first round by the 44-win Golden State Warriors. The Lakers beat the Warriors 4-1 but, again, it was closer than it appeared. The Warriors were coached by Don Nelson who was known for his odd line-ups, often playing five guards at once.[9] His small line-ups created match-up problems defensively for the Lakers, with 7'1 Vlade Divac, 6'9 Perkins, 6'9 Worthy, and 6'9 Magic forced to chase around the smaller, quicker Warriors. The Lakers won Game 3 in Oakland by three points and needed overtime in Game 5 to finish the Warriors off.[10]

Reaching the Conference Finals proved Dunleavy's system was effective and it was the right move at the right time. Waiting for the Lakers were the Portland Trail Blazers who had the more talented team and home court advantage. The Blazers were clear favorites – this was their year.

Game 1 in Portland appeared to unfold as scripted, with the Blazers taking a 92-80 lead into the fourth quarter. The Memorial Coliseum, always one of the noisiest arenas in the NBA, was at full voice. But the Lakers went on a 27-14 run before Scott's jumper with 48 seconds left

---

[8] Scott broke a tie with five seconds left but replays show he didn't beat the shot clock.

[9] Nelson was playing small-ball years before it became a thing.

[10] The highlight of the series was Game 2, a Laker loss at home. Magic finished with 44 points, 12 rebounds and 9 assists while Chris Mullin finished with 41 points.

silenced the crowd, giving the Lakers a 109-106 lead. Portland's Buck Williams missed two free throws, and Magic spread the court, determined to milk the clock. He threw a long pass to Worthy in the corner, who flipped a pass to Perkins whose dunk just barely beat the shot clock and sealed the 111-106 win. Worthy led the scoring for the Lakers with 28 points while Magic dished out 21 assists.

The Blazers nursed a four-point lead at the start of the fourth quarter in Game 2 and didn't make the same mistake twice. They took advantage of three crucial Laker turnovers in the final three minutes and evened up the series with a 109-98 win as the sound of the famous 'Beat L.A.!' chant echoed around Memorial Coliseum.

The series returned to Los Angeles for Games 3 and 4. Neither game was close, with the Lakers outhustling and outplaying the Blazers in almost every facet of the game.

The Lakers had a four-point lead in the third quarter of Game 3 before going on a 12-0 run started by Divac, the Lakers' second-year center from Yugoslavia.[11] He scored six points with two steals and a block during the run. It was a dramatic turnaround for Divac, who had been heavily criticised and openly challenged by his teammates for being outplayed by Duckworth in Game 2. He celebrated, blowing kisses to the crowd and high-fiving Jack Nicholson at his court-side seat. The Lakers ran up a 20-point lead before settling on a 106-92 victory with Magic racking up 19 assists.

Many expected the Blazers to come out swinging in Game 4. Instead, the Lakers came out on fire and led by 20 at half-time. The Forum was at fever pitch as the Lakers built the lead by ditching Dunleavy's slow tempo and outrunning the Blazers in transition in a temporary return to Showtime. The Lakers pushed the lead out to 33 in the third quarter and coasted to a 116-95 victory. Divac was again the story, scoring 20 points and convincingly outplaying Duckworth for the second straight game.

The Lakers returned to Portland holding a decisive and unexpected 3-1 series lead. The Blazers responded in Game 5, outworking the Lakers with an emphatic 30-14 second half rebounding advantage. Portland

---

[11] Divac was a true anomaly when he came to the Lakers in 1989 and still was for several years. NBA players born outside the USA made up 22% of the league's players in 2016 but it was less than 2% in 1981 and 7% in 1998. Divac was one of the first European players to play a large role on a high-profile team, years before European players transformed the NBA.

turned a three-point half-time deficit into a 95-84 victory. More troubling than the loss for the Lakers was the status of James Worthy, who badly sprained his ankle. If it was the regular season, Worthy would likely sit out a week or two to recover. But it was the playoffs, and he had to play on.

Game 6 in Los Angeles was a slug-fest. Worthy was ineffective playing on his painful ankle, managing 38 hobbled minutes but scoring just 8 points on 3-12 shooting. Magic, Perkins, and Green picked up Worthy's scoring slack, and the Lakers built a 15-point lead. But Drexler and Porter led a furious Portland rally.

The Lakers were clinging to a 91-90 lead with 12 seconds remaining when the Blazers called timeout. Drexler found Porter wide open in the corner for a jump-shot that hit the front of the rim. Magic fought off Kersey and Robinson for the rebound with four seconds left. To avoid being intentionally fouled, he threw the ball down court, placing enough spin on it that it didn't immediately roll out of bounds. It slowly bounced down court as precious seconds ticked away. The Blazers had 0.1 seconds to inbound the ball, with nothing to do but hopelessly heave it towards the basket.

The six-game victory over Portland was an upset. The Lakers overachieved by advancing to the Finals, beating a more talented team to get there by playing their best basketball of the season. But what the Lakers managed to do to Portland, they couldn't do to Chicago. They were simply out-matched against the Bulls. The Lakers could stay close to Chicago for long stretches, but there would be a few three-to-four-minute bursts every game when the Bulls ran right over them, putting the game out of reach.

That's why Pippen pushing the Bulls' lead out to eight points midway through the third quarter on yet another uncontested fast break in Game 5 felt like the tide turning yet again in favor of Chicago.

The Lakers would get back in the game with one last, short push. Magic backed Jordan down, found Perkins open in the opposite corner who drained a three-pointer, cutting the Bulls lead to five. Pippen missed a tough running jumper over Divac that Perkins rebounded. In a quick-hitting play, Smith found Magic open at the top of the key for another three-pointer. The Lakers were within two points, and the game would remain close for the next 12 minutes.

But with scores tied at 93-93 with six minutes to play, the Bulls slowly and patiently began chipping away. Defensively, the Lakers had been focused on Jordan and Pippen, always looking to funnel them into help defense. The strategy made sense, even if it didn't prove all that successful at stopping either player. The side effect was that it created plenty of opportunities for the rest of the Bulls. John Paxson scored 12 points in the final four minutes of the game, knocking down one wide-open jumper after another, each gifted to him by the Lakers' defense.

With two of his primary scoring threats injured on the bench, Dunleavy instructed the Lakers to go to Perkins down the stretch. But the Bulls were ready for the strategy and swarmed his every move. Chicago rode the hot shooting of Paxson to a 108-101 victory, a 4-1 series win, and their first championship in franchise history.

The Lakers lost three consecutive games at home in the series. Magic had been great in Game 5, recording his second triple-double of the series with 16 points, 11 rebounds, and 20 assists. But the Bulls were just better. Jordan and Pippen each scored over 30 points, and Paxson made nine of 12 shots. The Bulls players celebrated on the Forum floor. Jack Nicholson shook the Bull's coach Phil Jackson's hand. Jordan retreated to the changeroom, held the trophy for the first time and sobbed.

Laker fans had no way of knowing it at the time, but everything was about to change. The games against Chicago would be among the last Magic would play in almost five years. They were certainly the final games of significance he ever would play in a Lakers uniform during his prime. Accustomed to seeing their team routinely make the NBA Finals for over a decade, fans wouldn't see the Lakers there again for another nine years. The team was about to be on the fringe of NBA relevancy, where they would remain for five years. They were about to enter a black hole

PART I:
WELCOME TO THE BLACK HOLE

Chapter 1
EVERYTHING WAS FINE…

June 13, 1991 to November 5, 1991

U NDERDOG OR NOT, the loss to the Chicago Bulls in the 1991 NBA Finals was a tough pill for the Lakers to swallow. Yet they had reason to enter the summer of 1991 with optimism. By overachieving in the playoffs, maybe they had a better team than many had thought. The combination of players put together had, for the most part, fit well together. Mike Dunleavy's change in style had proven to work. And any team led by Magic Johnson, still one of the elite players in the game, always had a chance.

They settled in for a quiet off-season. The team had flaws, but they would only require tweaks here and there. There would be no roster overhaul, no new coach to find. "I feel we're real close," Magic said. "A horse here, a horse there, and we'll be all right."

The Lakers' frontcourt was deep, flexible, and its greatest weapon. James Worthy could cover both forward positions. Sam Perkins could play both the four and five spots. A.C. Green was pound-for-pound one of the best rebounders in the game. Vlade Divac was emerging, albeit slowly, into a legitimate NBA center. Elden Campbell, the Lakers' first round pick a year earlier, had played limited minutes during his rookie season, but took full advantage of extra opportunities afforded to him in the playoffs when Worthy was injured.[12] Like Perkins, he too could play power forward or center, and the Lakers were optimistic he could crack the rotation in 1991-92.

---

[12] After playing in 13 of the first 18 playoff games in 1991 with averages of 2.8 points in 8.5 minutes, Campbell played 27 minutes in Game 5 against Chicago and scored 21 points on 9-12 shooting.

As strong as the frontcourt was, the backcourt was their primary weakness. It featured two excellent starters in Magic and Byron Scott, but little else. The bench was skinny, offering neither an offensive punch nor a reliable back-up for Magic.

The Lakers were pleasantly surprised with rookie guard Tony Smith, who a year earlier wasn't even guaranteed a spot at training camp. Like Campbell, Smith had taken advantage of extra minutes in the Finals when Scott was unable to play in Game 5, but he still wasn't likely to make a major impact.[13] He would have to remain a third-stringer if the Lakers wanted to rest Magic without their offense falling apart every time he was on the bench.

The Lakers traded for shooting guard Terry Teagle a year earlier in search of some offensive firepower off the bench. He worked hard all season but couldn't adjust to fewer minutes, fewer touches, and a more structured offense than what he was accustomed to in Golden State. Lakers General Manager Jerry West had tried to trade Teagle mid-season to the Denver Nuggets for veteran Walter Davis, but the deal never came together.[14]

Back-up point guard Larry Drew still had a year left on his contract, but he could read the writing on the wall. He shot poorly and played limited minutes all season. "Looking at the situation realistically, I'm 33 years old, and I haven't been playing this year," he said. "You have to understand the nature of the business about bringing younger guys in to groom them." Drew was so sure he'd be released that he started making plans to spend the upcoming season in Italy, where he played one season prior to the Lakers signing him in 1989.

Another veteran player under contract but not expected to return was the 36-year-old back-up center, Mychal Thompson. A lop-sided trade had brought him to the Lakers in 1987, and he played a critical part of two championship teams. But time had caught up with him by 1991, and he was no longer physically able to contribute as he once had. Like Drew, he knew his time was probably up.

The first off-season business was to address rumors Magic was

---

[13] Smith had only played a total of 10 minutes in six playoff games in 1991 but played 30 minutes in Game 5 against Chicago, scoring 12 points on 5-6 shooting.

[14] The 36-year-old Davis was instead traded to Portland as part of a three-team trade with New Jersey that also sent Drazen Petrovic to the Nets. Davis finished the 1990-91 season in Portland before returning to Denver for one final season in 1991-92.

contemplating retirement, rumors started by Magic himself. In the lead up to Game 5 of the Finals, Magic told reporters he planned to use the off-season to assess whether he wanted to continue playing. In the heat of the Finals disappointment, it came across like he was thinking of quitting. He told reporters after the Finals that he was sure he'd be back for the 1991-92 season. A few weeks later he told the *Torrance Daily Breeze* he expected to play three more NBA seasons, maybe play a year in Europe and then become the owner of a team.

The 1991 NBA Draft came and went without the Lakers having much involvement. Their first-round pick belonged to Golden State as part of the trade for Teagle. Their second-round pick was the third-to-last selection of the draft and West used it on little-known forward Anthony Jones from Oral Roberts University.

West had secretly negotiated another trade with the Warriors in the lead up to the draft. In addition to owning the Lakers pick, the Warriors had their own – the 16th selection. West agreed to trade A.C. Green to Golden State in exchange for the 16th pick if the Warriors used it to select University of Oregon point guard, Terrell Brandon. But the deal fell through when Brandon was selected 11th overall by Cleveland, five short of Golden State's pick. "There were some players who got drafted in the wrong place for us," West said. "Naturally, we're a little disappointed."[15]

As expected, the off-season was proving to be reassuringly quiet. Worthy signed a five-year contract extension shortly after the Finals ended. He had enjoyed another fine season in 1990-91, leading the team in scoring with 21.4 points per game and was selected to his sixth straight All-Star Game. The extension would see Worthy under contract until the age of 34. Barring a trade, the contract set him up to be a Laker for life.

The off-season was so undramatic that the biggest Lakers-related story was Magic marrying his college sweetheart Earlitha 'Cookie' Kelly in a ceremony in Los Angeles in September. The summer was so dull the *Los Angeles Times* published an article detailing the success of Magic Johnson's

---

[15] The Warriors used the Lakers' 25th pick to select Shaun Vandiver from University of Colorado, who never played in the NBA. If the Lakers had the pick, they maybe would have used it to select a point guard. Randy Brown from New Mexico State and Elliot Perry from University of Memphis were both still available.

T-shirt company and how he sold more than Michael Jordan the previous fiscal year.[16]

A week after Magic was married he was named by USA Basketball to the 10-man Olympic squad, the Dream Team, set to compete in the 1992 Barcelona Olympics. FIBA had modified its rules in 1989 to allow professional athletes to compete internationally. Prior to that, both the US Men's and Women's Olympic Basketball teams were filled with college players. Once a player was drafted by the NBA, or more specifically was earning money to play basketball, they were ineligible to compete at the Olympics.

The announcement of the 1992 team was met with great fanfare. The US squad looked like a basketball fantasy with the potential to be the greatest team ever assembled. Magic and Larry Bird were named co-captains of a team littered with NBA All-Stars. Besides some controversy over a perceived snub of Isiah Thomas, the world began anticipating seeing this team in action from the moment the roster was announced. And Magic was a big reason why.

The Lakers opened training camp on October 1, 1991 at Palm Desert, California. Drew and Thompson, two players not expected to be back despite being under contract, were present at that first day of camp. "Believe me, I'm as surprised to see you guys as you are to see me," Thompson told reporters. Their presence at camp was an indication the Lakers hadn't addressed their two biggest weaknesses – guard bench scoring and a back-up for Magic.

But on the day camp opened, West was busy working on a deal that would address both concerns with the acquisition of one player. He was in discussion with the Seattle SuperSonics to acquire veteran guard Sedale Threatt.

The deal had the potential to pay off for the Lakers the same way the trade for Thompson had in 1987. Back then, the Lakers' biggest weakness was the lack of a back-up for 39-year-old Kareem Abdul-Jabbar. Thompson filled that void perfectly. Likewise, Threatt seemed like the perfect fit because he could back-up both Magic and Scott. He was a 30-year-old, little-known but well-regarded guard who was better suited to shooting guard but was more than capable of running the point. A pesky

---

[16] The article also estimated Magic owned more than 300 suits. Fascinating.

defender (his nickname was The Thief), Threatt was quick-footed and could push the ball in transition. And he was one hell of a streak shooter, capable of putting up points in a hurry when he got into a groove.

Threatt's entire NBA career was an unlikely long-shot, someone who made it despite the odds. He was, and still is, the only NBA player to come out of the obscure West Virginia University Institute of Technology. He was drafted with the 139th pick in the 1983 NBA Draft, back in the days when the draft went ten rounds instead of two. Only 16 of the 178 players selected after the second round in 1983 ever set foot on an NBA court. Threatt would go on to have a longer NBA career than all but five of the total 226 players drafted that year.

The deal came together two days after the start of camp, with West agreeing to send the Lakers' 1994, 1995, and 1996 second-round picks to Seattle. "I think we got somebody our coaches wanted," West said. "I think his versatility was pretty exciting to us." West had explored a wider deal with the Sonics, trying to secure forward Derrick McKey. But he couldn't find a way to create enough salary cap flexibility to make it happen. As it was, Threatt had to re-negotiate his contract to make the trade fit within league rules, taking less money per year but adding an extra year to his deal.

Steve Kelley vented his frustration with the Threatt trade in his *Seattle Times* column, echoing some of the complaints made about the Thompson trade in 1987. He lamented the Sonics trading Threatt to a rival Pacific Division team. "Threatt will probably add three years to Magic's career," Kelley wrote.

Drew and Thompson were finally waived to make salary cap space for Threatt. Hardly blindsided by being released, both players took it in their stride. After spending five successful seasons with the Lakers, Thompson was closing the book on his 13-year NBA career. "I'll miss these guys. They're unbelievable winners," he said. "You look for a definition of the word 'winner' in the dictionary, they should have a picture of the Lakers."[17]

The acquisition of Threatt would mean less of a workload for Magic. As a result, Dunleavy revisited his strategy of deliberately slowing the

---

[17] Both Thompson and Drew retired after being waived by the Lakers. Drew would go onto have a long career as an NBA assistant and head coach. Thompson does color commentary for Laker radio broadcasts and his son, Klay, is an All-Star with the Golden State Warriors.

pace of the Lakers' attack. With Magic getting more rest, the Lakers could run in 1991-92 and still have him fresh for the playoffs. It wouldn't be Showtime Part II, maybe more like Diet Showtime. But the idea of re-instating the running game excited the players. "I missed it. I think running does a lot for us," Scott said following a fast-paced scrimmage. "We're not as predictable. Running makes us more dangerous."

The Lakers rounded out their roster by signing back-up center Jack Haley, who was born and raised in California and played his college ball at UCLA. West held discussions with veteran center Jack Sikma but turned his attention to Haley when Sikma elected for retirement. The New Jersey Nets had fifteen days to match the Lakers' offer because Haley was a restricted free agent. They failed to do so, and he officially became a Laker on October 4. Even though he was likely destined to be a third-stringer, Haley was ecstatic to be on his hometown Lakers. Showing his trademark uniqueness, he spoke to reporters in the third person. "This is a dream come true for Jack Haley," he said.

With 11 of the 12 roster spots settled, the final spot would be fought over by six hopefuls. Rookie free-agents Tony Farmer, Roy Fisher, Jason Matthews, Keith Owens, and Demetrius Calip would each battle last season's rookie, Irving Thomas.

The Lakers flew to Boston to open their 1991-92 pre-season campaign with two games in two nights against the Celtics. The Lakers won the first game at Boston Garden 118-104, led by Worthy's 21 points and Magic's 18 points and 12 assists. Bird, who underwent off-season surgery on his lower back, played 33 minutes and scored 11 points.

The rematch was held at Worchester, Massachusetts the next night with the Celtics prevailing 117-107 behind Dee Brown's 28 points. Magic led the Lakers with 16 points and Bird was again showing no signs of pain from his back surgery. It was a pre-season just like any other, with Magic and Bird easing into the upcoming season.

But unlike any other pre-season, the Lakers then flew to Paris to take part in the two-game McDonald's Championship at the Palais Omnisports de Paris-Bercy.[18] They opened the tournament against French team Limoges CSP and cruised to an easy 132-101 victory. The game was a sort

---

[18] The McDonald's Championship was an international professional competition involving champion teams from the United States, South America, Europe and Australia.

of homecoming for Divac, who proved he was a step above his European counterparts by leading the game with 23 points and 12 rebounds.[19] Magic finished with 7 points and 21 assists in 27 minutes of action, wowing the crowd with his passing. The crowd started the night chanting *'Limoges! Limoges!'* but ended it chanting *'Magic! Magic!'*

They played the tournament final against Montigalà Joventut, the powerful Spanish club from Badalona. The Lakers had a difficult time closing out the game, winning 116-114. Magic scored 16 points, dished out 17 assists and was named MVP of the tournament. He charmed the European media after the game, complementing its players and saying the tournament was an eye-opener for what he should expect during the upcoming Olympics.

Magic may have been all smiles in front of the media, but he privately complained about the schedule. He'd never seen a pre-season like it. The Lakers had to play two games in two nights against Boston, then fly to Paris for another set of back-to-back games. They would then return to the United States for four games in five nights. It would mean six games in nine days in three nations on two continents.

Between travel, jet-lag, and the whirlwind of games, this was no warm-up. It was energy sapping. "I'm happy to get out. We want to get home to get our rest, get back on our own timetable," Magic said upon leaving Paris. "We're a tired team right now."

The Lakers flew home to Los Angeles on Sunday, October 20 and rested on the Monday before preparing for the next run of games.

First up were two games in two nights at the annual GTE Everything Pages Shoot-out at the Forum. [20] For the first game, they would be playing the Celtics for the third time that pre-season. They shook off the jet-lag with a 121-105 victory over Boston with Magic registering 16 points and 15 assists while Bird scored 24 points.

They faced the Milwaukee Bucks the following night and were run off the floor, suffering a 119-98 loss. The Bucks blew the game open with an

---

[19] It's hard to overstate how much of a superstar Divac was in Yugoslavia. Even though he was 21 years old when he was drafted by the Lakers, he had already played five years of pro ball in Yugoslavia. His wedding, held four days after he was drafted, was attended by 1,000 people and televised nationally.

[20] The GTE Everything Pages Shoot-out was a two-night pre-season tournament held yearly at the Forum. Three teams, in addition to the Lakers, would be invited to take part.

11-2 second-quarter run and never looked back. Worthy top-scored for the Lakers with 17 points and Magic produced a quiet 6 points and 5 assists in 25 minutes. "I was really satisfied last night," Dunleavy said. "I wasn't so satisfied tonight."

The Lakers enjoyed a rare day of rest before traveling to Salt Lake City to take on the Utah Jazz. The Lakers were without Magic and lost the game 107-103. The team explained that Magic returned home to Los Angeles prior to tip-off because of an undisclosed illness that had begun the previous night. According to the team, he had felt better that morning, intended to play and had traveled with the team. But the illness returned shortly after arriving in Salt Lake City and he headed home.

The Lakers were in Vancouver the next night for a game against the Seattle SuperSonics, their final of the pre-season. Magic didn't travel with the team, and the crowd of 11,725 at Pacific Coliseum booed when it was announced before tip-off that he wouldn't be playing. With Gary Payton and Shawn Kemp sitting out with injuries, Benoit Benjamin scored 30 points to lead the Sonics to a 111-102 victory. The lone bright spark for the Lakers was Threatt, who scored 27 points against his former team.

The weary Lakers closed the 1991-92 pre-season with a 4-4 record. The toll of the intense schedule obviously wore on them as they won only one of their four games after returning from Paris.

After a taxing pre-season, the Lakers welcomed five down days before opening night of the 1991-92 season, and they were in bad shape. The team explained both Magic and rookie Anthony Jones had come down with the flu. Tony Smith badly sprained his ankle in Salt Lake City and would be lost for several weeks.

Dunleavy blamed the intense schedule. "We played six games in nine days. They don't do that in the NBA (regular season)," he said. "Next year, whoever makes the schedule has to travel the schedule. I'm a little concerned at not having guys available."

Magic was attending training but not participating. The Lakers told reporters he would undergo further tests and would likely continue resting until opening night. "It's just fatigue," Magic said. "I'm just not strong. I don't feel like me."

Two days before the start of the season, the Lakers announced Magic was unlikely to play the first two games. His absence changed the team's decision-making regarding the final roster spot. Owens surprised some by winning it, and the Lakers waived Calip, Farmer, Fisher, Matthews, Jones, and Thomas.[21] Calip returned home but was recalled by the Lakers three days later as a temporary back-up when the team announced neither Magic nor Smith would be ready for opening night, leaving Threatt as the only healthy point guard.

The last thing the Lakers needed was a grueling game on opening night. But they got one in Houston, going into double overtime against the Rockets. Threatt started in place of Magic and Worthy made a three-pointer on the buzzer to send the game into overtime. In the first overtime, Campbell tied the score with a tip-in with 0.1 seconds remaining. But they ran out of steam in the second extra period, eventually falling 126-121. The double overtime game meant big minutes for tired players. Worthy scored 37 points but was forced to play 53 minutes, while Scott and Green both logged 46 each. Calip saw 15 minutes of NBA action that just a week earlier he thought he might never see, assisting on his first two possessions and scoring two points.

There was little recovery time as the Lakers flew to Dallas for a game against the Mavericks the following night, where they again went to overtime. Perkins made two free throws with 0.1 seconds remaining in extra time to give the Lakers a 114-113 win. Threatt, in the starting line-up again, almost got a triple-double with 26 points, 10 rebounds, and 8 assists. Worthy scored 30 points and dished out a career-high 14 assists but was again forced into a marathon – playing 100 minutes over the two nights. More troubling was losing Divac after just 14 minutes due to back spasms.

Returning home and with two days of rest in front of them, the Lakers confirmed Magic had been cleared to practice in lightly supervised workouts. But they also confirmed he wouldn't be ready for the next game, a cross-town matchup at the Forum against the Los Angeles

---

[21] Fisher, Matthews and Jones never played in the NBA. Fisher had a long career playing in the CBA, Israel and Spain. Matthews seems to have stopped playing basketball shortly after being waived by the Lakers and has gone on to have a successful career in real estate. Farmer spent most of his career playing in the CBA, ABA, Belgium France, Italy and Russia. He made it back to the NBA with the Charlotte Hornets in 1997-98 and the Golden State Warriors in 1999-00. Thomas, after playing 26 games with the Lakers in 1990-91, never played in the NBA again. He retired from basketball in 1999 after a career playing in the CBA, France, Italy and Spain.

Clippers. Nor was he likely to play the game after that in Phoenix. The Lakers would have to survive two more games without him, but they expected him back in uniform for the fifth game of the season, at home against the Minnesota Timberwolves.

For the first time in franchise history, the Lakers opened the season with three straight overtime games when they went into extra time against the Clippers. Divac sat out the game, still bothered by a bad back, and the Lakers lost 114-109 with second-year forward Loy Vaught taking over in overtime. Threatt again started at point guard and led the Lakers with 25 points, 7 rebounds, and 8 assists. Worthy logged heavy minutes for the third straight game, this time playing 49.[22]

The season was only three games old, and the Lakers were already tired, already injured and nursing a subpar 1-2 record. Then the team suddenly changed the timetable yet again for Magic's return. Just one day after saying he'd likely be ready against Minnesota, they were now saying he may not participate in practice for another week.

"Your legs and wind are the first things that go," Magic told reporters. "So, the good conditioning I had is now lost. Obviously, I'd like to play Sunday (against Minnesota), but I don't know if it's going to happen. If it's on me, I'd like to play tonight."

The Lakers appeared remarkably over-cautious about Magic's flu. By the time the team was due to take the floor at the Forum against Minnesota, it would have been 17 days since he suddenly returned home from Salt Lake City. More than enough time to recover from the flu.

Yet it was all easy to shrug off. The Lakers were off to a rough start, but it was nothing to worry about. At some point Magic would be back, and so would the wins.

When Thompson was waived a few weeks earlier, he was asked by reporters how he thought the Lakers would fare without him. "Let me see, they won, what, four championships before I got here?" he joked. "As long as they don't waive Magic, they'll be okay."

Thompson was right. Everything was fine.

Until, suddenly, it wasn't.

---

[22] Because each game went into extra time, Worthy averaged 49.6 minutes over the first three games of the season, 1.6 minutes longer than a regular NBA game.

Chapter 2

NOVEMBER 7, 1991

October 25, 1991 to November 7, 1991

G ARY VITTI COULDN'T concentrate on the game. He was sitting in his usual spot on the Lakers bench, but he couldn't focus. His mind was elsewhere. The Lakers were playing a game against the Utah Jazz, and it was his job to be concentrating on his players. It didn't matter that it was a pre-season game, it was his job. And he was one of the best at it.

Something wasn't right, but he couldn't work out what it was. Maybe something was terribly wrong. But what could it be?

Vitti had been the Lakers' trainer since the 1984-85 season and had recently been named Trainer of the Year by the NBA's Trainers Association.[23] It was the kind of basketball job that was year-round, it didn't start and end with the season schedule. His job was to monitor his guys – the Lakers players. He would work with them to establish their individual workout routines, their diet, their sleep routines. He would formulate plans with each player for them to achieve a goal – maybe it was to get stronger, or lose weight, or improve lateral quickness. He'd work with players to overcome routine injuries like a sprained ankle, or devastating injuries like a torn ACL. He would monitor players' training activities and work with team doctors and coaches. Together they would determine when a player should be on limited minutes, when they were ready to increase their workload, when they should rest.

His job was to make sure each player was in the best possible condition whenever they were called upon by the coaching staff. He was at every training session and every game. Vitti was well respected, an author and

---

[23] Roland Lazenby described Vitti in *The Lakers: A Basketball Journey* as a shorter, Italian version of Tom Selleck. Which was an apt description of him at the time.

lecturer in his field. He had effective working relationships with his players, and he knew when something wasn't right with one of them.

Before they were due to leave for Salt Lake City, Magic Johnson told Vitti he didn't want to go on the trip. He said he was exhausted from Paris and wanted to rest. This was not a normal request from Magic, who was one of the most competitive players in the NBA and a gym rat who loved to practice. If there was a game somewhere, chances are Magic wanted to be part of it. But this had been a uniquely demanding pre-season schedule, and Magic wasn't young anymore.

Jerry West intervened and told Magic the fans in Salt Lake City were expecting him to play. Vitti brokered a compromise. Magic would go on the trip with the team but play limited minutes. Everyone agreed but no sooner had the Lakers landed in Salt Lake City than Magic was on a plane back to Los Angeles with no explanation. Superstar players never just get called home from the road, Vitti thought.

Vitti's first suspicion was Magic was playing hooky, faking an illness so he could go back home.[24] But he also knew Magic better than almost anyone and knew something like that was out of character. So, what was it then? What was so pressing that Magic had to leave the team and go home? And then it hit him – a crystal clear thought amongst the fog of confusion that caused a rush of fear to come over him.

Two weeks earlier he had given Magic a physical exam as a requirement for a new contract. Back in 1981, Jerry Buss had given Magic a $25 million, twenty-five-year contract.[25] It was an exceedingly generous and controversial deal at the time. But the average NBA salary had ballooned in the ten years since. By 1991-92, Magic was no longer one of the league's highest-paid players. He wasn't even the highest-paid player on his team anymore.[26] His salary no longer reflected that he was one of the league's great stars. Buss recognized that, but the Lakers were over the salary cap, and league rules prevented him from doing anything about it. Instead, he calculated how much money Magic had been underpaid each year of his career and took out a loan to pay Magic outside of his normal

---

[24] This is what Worthy thought at the time too. He thought Magic was 'pulling seniority' by not taking part in a meaningless pre-season game.

[25] This kind of contract would be impossible in today's NBA. In 1981 there were no maximum contract amounts or lengths like there are today.

[26] Sam Perkins was the new highest-paid player on the team.

NBA contract.[27]

To get the insurance policy, Magic needed to take a physical. Part of the physical exam was taking blood work, and the results would be due back about now. At that moment, Vitti knew what it was. Magic had HIV.

Magic was taking a pre-game nap in his Salt Lake City hotel when his sleep was broken by a ringing telephone at 2:15 pm. It was the Lakers team doctor, Dr. Michael Mellman. He told Magic he needed to see him immediately and instructed him to get on a plane as soon as he could and return to Los Angeles. He wouldn't tell Magic what the problem was, just that he needed to come home. Magic's long-time agent and friend, Lon Rosen arranged for Magic to catch a Delta Airlines flight back to L.A. Rosen was at LAX to meet Magic when he landed at 5:30 pm and together they drove to Dr. Mellman's office.

Vitti may have been worried but Magic wasn't. He figured, whatever the problem was, it couldn't be too serious. He was in the best shape of his NBA career. Rosen and Magic speculated what the news might be. Magic's father had suffered high blood pressure his whole life, so maybe the tests found something similar. In the waiting room at Dr. Mellmen's office, they discussed how Michael Jordan and his wife, Juanita, were on the front cover of the latest edition of *Ebony* magazine and how it would be nice if Magic and Cookie could be on the cover one day too.

When they finally sat down with Dr. Mellmen they both heard the news – Magic's blood work from his physical had come back, and he had tested positive for HIV, the virus that causes AIDS.

Magic didn't know much about HIV or AIDS. What he'd heard wasn't good – it killed you, and it killed you quick. Dr. Mellman explained to Magic that he had the HIV virus but didn't have AIDS. But all Magic heard was a death sentence.

His next thought was for Cookie. Had he infected her? The two had met as freshmen at college and had an on-and-off-again relationship for a decade. They became engaged in the mid-1980s, but the wedding was called off when Magic got cold feet. He finally committed to her, and they had just married just six weeks earlier. Now, this. He and Cookie found out they were pregnant while in Paris. Had he infected the baby?

---

[27] This would be illegal in the current NBA. In 2001, the Minnesota Timberwolves were fined $3.5 million and stripped of draft picks for having an 'under the table' deal with forward Joe Smith. This was pretty much the same thing, but it was legal in 1991.

Rosen drove Magic home where he had to tell Cookie the news. "I played against the best of basketball – Michael Jordan, Larry Bird. I thought that was probably going to be the most difficult thing to do," he said. "Those things were nothing. The most difficult thing in my life was driving from the doctor's office to tell my wife Cookie I had HIV."

The next day, Magic and Cookie went into Dr. Mellmen's office to both get tested – Magic to double-check the results, Cookie to find out if she and the baby were okay. Back in 1991, it took ten days for blood test results to come back. Ten long days of waiting.

On top of worrying about his health and that of his wife and baby, there was the serious issue of how to handle the news. Magic and the Lakers knew they had to wait on the results of the second blood test before announcing anything, and Magic wanted to consult with doctors, counselors, and lawyers to work out what to do. He asked Rosen to inform Vitti of the situation, though he had already guessed. Together they established how they were going to handle the situation for the next ten days.

The stories the Lakers fed to the press about Magic – that he was missing pre-season games because of the flu, sitting out training because he needed to recover, missing regular season games because he was still weak – were, in the words of Vitti, "bullshit." Magic didn't make it easy on Vitti either, appearing at a Los Angeles Raiders game when he was meant to be at home with the flu. He felt perfectly fine and assumed he would continue playing, HIV positive or not. So, he worked out regularly, wanting to maintain his conditioning for when he returned.

The press noticed and knew it didn't make sense. But Vitti and the Lakers stuck to their story. When they knew 'the flu story' was dragging on too long and becoming thin, Rosen and Vitti agreed to tell reporters Magic had 'begun light workouts under supervision.' Neither Vitti nor Rosen knew what that meant exactly, but they knew they had to come up with something.

Mike Dunleavy also knew the story didn't add up. He scheduled a meeting with Assistant General Manager Mitch Kupchak and told him, as coach of the team, he needed to know the truth. Is Magic truly going to be in the line-up again? Kupchak was evasive with Dunleavy because he had to be. This was Magic's deeply personal news, and it wasn't up to him to share it.

On November 6, 1991, the new test results came in. They confirmed Magic was indeed HIV positive. The good news was Cookie was fine, which meant the baby was also okay. If there was any good news regarding Magic's health, it was that doctors believed they discovered the virus early. Magic was symptom-free, and it was possible he could have continued life for a while, perhaps months, without knowing he had HIV. He had a head start in fighting it.

This was new territory for the medical world. Never had an athlete in peak physical condition tested positive for HIV. There was no case study for doctors to refer to, no baseline information. As a result, Magic received contradictory advice from doctors when it came to the question of his basketball career.

On the one hand, he was told the best thing he could do was stay active. Continue working out regularly, eat well, try to build muscle and strength. On the other hand, he was told there was no way to know what impact playing in the NBA would have on his immune system. It was a judgment call, but doctors advised the grind of the NBA schedule, and the intensity in which he played and trained, could weaken his immune system and make things worse. There was too much at stake regarding Magic's health for doctors to risk him being a guinea pig. No two ways about it, he would have to retire.

Doctors immediately put him on Zidovudine (AZT), the only drug available in 1991 that slowed the onset of HIV and AIDS. It wasn't a cure, but it delayed the inevitable and extended life. For the next three months, Magic fought nausea and mood swings as his body adjusted to the three-times-a-day drug schedule.

Magic and the Lakers planned to hold a press conference on November 8 where he would announce his retirement. But on the morning of November 7, Rosen received a call from a reporter from KFWB, an all-news station in Los Angeles. Rosen was asked to comment on rumors that Magic had AIDS and was going to retire.[28] Rosen phoned Magic, informed him the story had leaked and they both agreed to push the press conference forward and announce the news that afternoon.

West was informed that reporters were heading to the Lakers' training

---

[28] The issue of who leaked the story to the press doesn't come up in any of the books or articles researched for this book.

facility, where the team was preparing for the following night's game in Phoenix. The reporters were after a story. They wanted to interview players and coaches about the rumors regarding Magic's health. But the players had been kept as much in the dark as the media. West phoned Vitti at the training facility and instructed him to get everyone out. Tell them not to shower and get themselves immediately to the Forum. If players had plans for the afternoon, tell them to cancel them. Worthy remembers being told, "Don't turn on the radio, don't stop, don't do anything."

Magic gave Rosen a short list of people he wanted informed prior to the press conference. The list included opponents he was close to (Larry Bird, Michael Jordan, and Isiah Thomas), former teammates (Kareem Abdul-Jabbar, Michael Cooper, and Kurt Rambis), former Lakers coach Pat Riley and his best friend, actor/comedian Arsenio Hall.[29]

Once the players were at the Forum, Magic met privately with Dunleavy and gave him the news. The players assembled in the locker room where Magic addressed the team, telling them he was HIV positive and he couldn't play basketball anymore. Vitti remembers Magic spoke of the wars that he had gone through with these players and how much they meant to him. He told his teammates how truly sorry he was for letting them down. Magic knew this was going to be the last time he was in that locker room as a player and breaking the news to his teammates was the first time he cried since finding out he had the virus. The players hugged and cried. Bill Bertka, the always stoic long-time assistant coach, buckled at the knees when given the news. "Then we went upstairs, he wiped away his tears and told the world," Vitti said.

At 3:00 in the afternoon, Magic entered the Forum Club in front of a series of black curtains. Reporters were warned to show up a couple of hours early for the press conference because seats were going to be scarce. By the time Magic reached the podium, they had been packed into the small room for hours.

On Magic's right were Buss, West, Dr. Mellmen and Cookie. On his left were NBA Commissioner David Stern, Rosen and former Showtime teammates Abdul-Jabbar and Cooper.

---

[29] Roland Lazenby made a good point about the emptiness of fame in *The Show*. He points out that Magic's list of people who he wanted to know he was HIV positive was short for someone who hosted 500 people at his 30th birthday party, given that he was about to tell the whole world anyway.

He hadn't prepared a statement, he just spoke off the cuff. After greeting reporters, he cut right to the chase. "Because of the HIV virus I have obtained I will have to retire from the Lakers today," he said. He made it clear he had HIV, didn't have AIDS and confirmed Cookie's test was negative.[30] He acknowledged he was going to miss playing and would now become an AIDS spokesperson. He said he wanted people to know that anyone can contract the virus, people should get tested and practice safe sex. He spoke for nine and a half minutes and was composed throughout, flashing his trademark smile and being remarkably upbeat. He closed the press conference by simply saying, "I am going to go on, I'm going to beat it, and I'm going to have fun."

Suddenly, Magic became about a lot more than just basketball to the world. Bill Simmons called Magic's announcement, broadcast live nationally on CNN and ESPN, the biggest moment in NBA history that didn't happen during a game. He describes the press conference as Generation X's version of the Kennedy Assassination – the event that everyone can recall where they were and what they were doing when they heard the news.

As upbeat as Magic was at the press conference, the rest of the world didn't see it that way. If anything, Magic sounded delusional when talking about 'beating it.' Nobody beat HIV, at least that's what the world thought at the time. "I thought Magic was going to get skinny and die," said Arsenio Hall. Everybody else did too, Magic now looked like a dead man walking. The feeling around the league was one of great loss – that Magic had turned into a ghost like he had died but was still here for a time.

Chick Hearn summed up the mood inside the Lakers camp by saying, "We're lower today than we have ever been, this L.A. Lakers family." He admitted he cried like a baby when he found out.

Scott described the scene in the locker room when Magic broke the news. "Very quiet, eleven guys with a lot of heartache and tears flowing," he said. He told Magic if anyone could beat HIV, it was him. But he didn't believe his own words.

Abdul-Jabbar, ever empathic and thoughtful, said "I know what AIDS

---

[30] Magic had to be reminded by Rosen right before walking on stage to specify he had HIV and not AIDS, because few people knew the difference in 1991. Ten days earlier, neither did they.

victims go through and it isn't a very pretty life. Derision, bigotry, and fear. If he wants my help, I'll be there."

The reaction was felt across the league as the news spread. The New York Knicks hosted the Orlando Magic at Madison Square Garden only hours after Magic's announcement.[31] Riley spoke at mid-court before tip-off, choking back tears and saying, "Obviously, there has been some very bad news." He asked everyone in the stands and on the court to, "in your own voice, in your own beliefs, in your own way, pray for Earvin and for the one million people who are afflicted with this insidious disease and who need our understanding." Players and coaches from both teams huddled around Riley, who bowed his head and gently recited the Lord's Prayer. "Let's go, let's play," Riley said softly after the prayer.

The Celtics hosted the Atlanta Hawks after the announcement and Bird said it was the toughest day he had experienced since his father passed away. Bird, just as much an obsessive competitor as Magic, always wanted to play basketball. He was always ready to compete. But years later he said he had no interest in the game against the Hawks, that he wanted no part of it.

Players from the Los Angeles Clippers each wrote either 'Magic' or '#32' in gold lettering on their black shoes when they hosted the Denver Nuggets. Charles Barkley changed his number from #34 to #32 for the season, in honor of Magic.[32]

The impact of Magic's announcement was felt far wider than basketball circles. President George H. Bush was asked about it during a press conference at the White House. Bush said he watched Magic's press conference and described it as a tragedy. Senior health officials in Washington were asked to go on record about the news. Dr. Louis W. Sullivan, Secretary of Health and Human Services, said he hoped Magic's announcement would make Americans better understand that AIDS is not a remote disease that only strikes 'someone else.' "In the months and years ahead, Magic Johnson will help carry a life-saving message to young people across our nation," he said.

---

[31] Magic's press conference was held 3:00pm Pacific Time or 6:00pm Eastern Standard Time, less than two hours before the start of the Knicks-Magic game.
[32] Barkley received permission from Billy Cunningham to wear the number, as it had been retired by the 76ers in honor of him.

Calls to the Ventura County Health Department regarding HIV and AIDS increased 600% on the day after Magic's announcement. With less than a ten-minute statement, Magic had caused the national understanding of the AIDS epidemic to change completely. "If the force of a personality can have an impact in fighting this disease, then Magic Johnson can have that impact," said Stern.

Magic was a household name across the world, even in countries where basketball wasn't a major sport. The Spanish daily newspaper *El Pais* devoted two pages to Magic's announcement. Six major television networks in Japan carried the news. Newspapers in Milan, Munich, Oslo, London, and Sydney ran front page stories. It was a watershed moment in worldwide HIV and AIDS awareness.

Behind public statements of support and disbelief, there was an ugly side to the reaction to Magic's news. Shortly after the announcement, Magic and Hall attended the Comedy Store in Los Angeles. A comedian, who was a friend to both Magic and Hall, was on stage making Magic Johnson AIDS jokes with Magic in the room.

Magic was inundated with letters, phone calls, telegrams, and flowers. For every supportive message, he also received insults and blackmail attempts. Magic's brother, who worked in a factory in Michigan, had to take time off work because of harassment he experienced from co-workers. When Rosen attempted to reserve a table for Magic at his favorite restaurant in Los Angeles, he was told Magic wasn't welcome there anymore.

Magic, always an affectionate person, found that people no longer wanted to hug or touch him. He'd ask someone if they wanted to work out or play one-on-one and they suddenly always had something else to do. Discrimination against people with HIV and AIDS was real. Magic, despite his celebrity and all the goodwill offered him, couldn't escape it.

Nor could he escape the cold, hard reality he might die soon. While he spoke with an aura of confidence and optimism in public, it was a different story in private. Magic and Cookie holidayed together in Hawaii a few days after the announcement to get away from the media firestorm that had been unleashed. Before he left, he had a heart-to-heart conversation with Rosen, asking him to pledge to look after Cookie and the baby after he died.[33]

There was more fall-out when questions started about how Magic contracted the virus. The NBA had been rocked by drug and alcohol abuse scandals during the 1970s and early 1980s, but Magic was never tempted by either. There were enough examples of promising NBA careers ruined by cocaine and alcohol for Magic to know nothing positive could come of it. But Magic had a vice, just a different one – sex. And there wasn't an example of that ruining an NBA career until Magic himself became that cautionary tale. Now it was all becoming public, exposing not only Magic's behavior but that of the entire league.

Suddenly the truth was out for everyone to see. Magic privately estimated he would sleep with 300 to 500 women annually. He kept this away from the public eye because of a 'what happens on the road, stays on the road' culture in the NBA. In fact, he carried out this lifestyle with very few people outside a small inner circle of Lakers staffers and players knowing. Any new member of the Lakers staff was astounded to see what was going on behind closed doors. On the road, hotel lobbies were filled with women wanting to meet and sleep with a Lakers player – especially Magic. At home, the Los Angeles nightlife was a playground for him. In the 1980s, the Forum Club, located in the basement of the arena, has been described as a cross between Studio 54 and the Playboy Mansion after Lakers games. Magic had rules for his behavior, such as 'no sex before tip-off' and he never allowed women to sleep over because he saved that for Cookie. Even though other Lakers players had similar lifestyles, Magic was viewed as being on a whole other level entirely.

Players were not scared off by the rising AIDS epidemic in America during the 1980s. It was viewed as a disease affecting homosexual men and drug users exclusively. Vitti was smarter than that and had begun carrying condoms and distributing them to players. He would check in with players from time to time to make sure they were protecting themselves. After Magic's announcement, Vitti said he regretted not pressing the players more on the issue. But they were always going to do what they were going to do, and they never took warnings seriously. When the topic of AIDS came up at a Lakers team meeting, one member of the team laughed and said, "If Magic Johnson does not have it, you can't

---

[33] Magic dropped that impenetrable veneer in the 2010s and now openly speaks about how terrified he was back in 1991 and how difficult this time was for him personally.

get it."

The sheer number of women Magic had slept with factored into his decision to go public. Magic certainly had altruistic motivations behind publicly acknowledging he had HIV. He knew his level of celebrity could make a real difference in fighting the disease. But he also needed the women he had slept with to know, so they could get tested too. After Magic told Cookie that he had HIV, he locked himself in a room and called as many of the women he'd slept with as he could. to tell them the news. But he knew he couldn't contact all of them. Making a public announcement was the only way to ensure they all found out.

It was far from a Lakers phenomenon. Players from every NBA team navigated this same world. Hawks star Dominique Wilkins told *Sports Illustrated* the women wanted the thrill of being with an athlete. "They don't want safe sex," Wilkins said. "They want to have your baby because they think if they have your baby, they're set for life. That's the hard fact of it because if they had a life, they wouldn't be hanging around the hotel or showing up at the back door of the arena trying to pick up a player."

Other players agreed, saying women came out in force when they were on the road, hovering and waiting to meet them. A former Lakers staffer said while players act like these women are a problem for them, it's the players who perpetuate the behavior. All of this was getting dug up in the wake of Magic's announcement, and it was undeniably harmful to his public image.

Among all the fallout from Magic's shock retirement was one very big question – where exactly did it leave the Lakers?

Chapter 3
THE STREAK

November 8, 1991 to November 30, 1991

T HESE WERE STRANGE days indeed for the Lakers. A lot of serious, life-altering questions were circulating around the team which had nothing to do with basketball. When will Magic Johnson die? Will his marriage survive? Has he infected anybody? What damage has been done to the NBA brand with the league's promiscuous, hedonistic culture now exposed? What would this mean for the broader conversation about HIV and AIDS in the United States and around the world?

The Lakers received 18,000 pieces of mail in the days following Magic's retirement. The Rev. Jesse Jackson visited them during practice to offer solace.

And then there were the basketball questions. What do the Lakers do now? What trades or signings will need to be made? They're suddenly not championship contenders anymore, but are they a playoff team?

Jerry West confirmed a few days after Magic's announcement there essentially was no plan. "It would be embarrassing to start to think about player moves today," he said. "There's been so much emotion in this, we're all worn out. We're going to wait until the weekend is over and then talk it over with our coaches."

James Worthy and Byron Scott were named co-captains, taking over those duties in the void left by Magic. For the time being, Sedale Threatt would continue as the starting point guard with Demetrius Calip the back-up until Tony Smith returned from his sprained ankle.

Bigger questions, like what changes would be implemented to Dunleavy's system, would have to wait. Dunleavy had just spent an entire off-season preparing a team that had been fundamentally changed overnight. "It's going to be one of those things you have to figure out on the job. It's like on-the-job training," he said. "It's not like you have a summer or training camp to get ready for it."

The NBA schedule rolled on, waiting for nobody. Not even these Lakers who were understandably not focused on basketball. Less than 24 hours after the press conference that stunned the team, the Lakers were in Phoenix preparing to take on the Suns. Prior to tip-off, Suns forward and former Laker Kurt Rambis took to the microphone and invited A.C. Green to lead the teams and fans in prayer for Magic.[34] Green's words reduced Scott to tears, and he remained like that throughout the rendition of the national anthem.

Then the officials blew their whistle. Elden Campbell and Suns center Andrew Lang competed for the jump ball, and a new, strange life started for the Lakers. Ready or not.

And they most certainly were not ready. The Lakers were lethargic, distracted and out of synch all game. They shot a miserable 31% from the floor.[35] Worthy scored 14 points on hideous 4-22 shooting. Sedale Threatt, suddenly thrust into the role of the Lakers' incumbent point guard and replacement of a legend, was 1-6 from the floor and finished with two assists. The Suns won 113-85 and handed the Lakers their worst loss since the final game of the 1989-90 season when Riley rested the entire starting line-up in preparation for the playoffs.

Afterward, Scott admitted he couldn't focus during the game and played in a daze. He would find his mind wandering during timeouts, drifting to thoughts about Magic. He had to ask Dunleavy to repeat himself in huddles because he wasn't listening. Dunleavy knew that accepting Magic was gone was the toughest challenge for the players. It was a cold, hard reality. "We don't have Earvin, we're not going to have Earvin, and that's it," he told the players.

It was a lifeless performance from the Lakers. Magic brought a lot of things to the team, but one of the biggest was his passion. He possessed a joy for competing, winning, playing and practicing. That joy was torn from them in a sudden, painful way. The game against the Suns, and the preparation for it, were done dutifully but grudgingly. It wasn't joyous, it

---

[34] A.C. Green will be remembered for 4 things – rebounding, playing in an NBA record 1,192 consecutive games, winning four championships with the Lakers, and remaining a virgin for his entire 16-year NBA career because of deeply held religious views.

[35] The 31.6% shooting (31-of-98) was an all-time franchise low for a game.

was work. "I think for the next two weeks, probably two months, that's basically how everybody's going to look at it," Scott said. "It's just a job. You have to go there and do a job. It's not going to be fun for a while."

Worthy took his teammates aside following the loss and told them the future wasn't going to wait for them to grieve for Magic. He said they had to start playing now, not in February or March, and the team cannot become emotionally controlled by everything that had happened to them.

Whether it was due to the speech or not, the Lakers were about to do something entirely unexpected under the circumstances – go on a season-long win streak.

One

Following three days off, the Lakers hosted the struggling Minnesota Timberwolves at the Forum. This was the game fans had circled in their calendars a week earlier as Magic's likely first game of the season. Now, it was the first home game of this unwanted new era.

A non-sell-out crowd gave the Lakers a standing ovation as soon as the team came to the bench. Worthy walked to the middle of the floor before tip-off and read a message from Magic. The note acknowledged the support he and his family had received from fans and the media over the previous four days. "I most want to tell you that this is the first day of the rest of our lives," the statement read. I say this to you fans because we, the Lakers, need your support more than ever before. I say this to all of my teammates. Starting now, it's winnin' time. And I'm saying it to myself because this is an important battle to fight and in this battle, you are all my teammates."

Then the Lakers took to the floor and did what they were supposed to do, even without Magic – beat a bad Timberwolves team. The Lakers took an 18-point lead in the third quarter and got their first win in the post-Magic era, 96-86, behind Threatt's 27 points and 14 assists. Worthy didn't shoot well for the second straight game but almost recorded a triple-double with 12 points, 9 rebounds, and 9 assists. Dunleavy praised his players after the emotionally draining win. "They played their hearts out," he said.

The system changes following Magic's retirement were still a work-in-progress and would remain so for a while. Dunleavy was forced to make a change to every play he called during the game to accommodate not having Magic, who had been the centerpiece of every Laker play.

Besides getting the win, the Lakers had good news regarding injured players Vlade Divac and Smith. Divac returned against the Timberwolves after sitting out eight days with back spasms, scoring two points in limited minutes. He was out of shape, and his strength was low after a week of no activity. But at least the injury seemed headed in the right direction.

Following the game, Smith was taken off the injured list and cleared to play. To make room for him, Calip was waived for the second time in two weeks. Calip could have taken Magic's vacant spot on the team, but league rules dictated only staff and players were permitted to sit on the bench during games. The team wanted to offer that opportunity to Magic, so kept him on the active roster.

Two

The Lakers traveled to Oakland for a match-up with the Golden State Warriors, who were off to a fast start and owned the league's best record. The Lakers got a 115-112 win and survived a scare when a broken play led to Golden State's Chris Mullin, one of the league's best outside shooters, missing a wide-open three-pointer in the dying seconds. Threatt and Worthy led the Lakers in scoring with 21 points, while Divac contributed 19 points off the bench in a stronger showing in his second game back from injury.

Three

With their loss to the Lakers, Golden State was knocked off their perch atop the league and replaced by the Houston Rockets – who were at the Forum the following night. For the second time in two nights, the Lakers beat the team at the top of the standings.

The Rockets were held to seven fourth-quarter points, an all-time franchise low for a Lakers opponent.[36] Houston went scoreless over the final seven minutes, the Lakers scored the final 13 points of the game and got an 86-74 victory. Worthy's shooting improved on both nights of the back-to-back, Threatt dished out 10 assists, and Terry Teagle delivered some much-needed scoring off the bench.

---

[36] Houston's 26 second-half points were also a franchise low for a Laker opponent.

If the Lakers hadn't yet rediscovered any joy after Magic's retirement, they had found a use for basketball in the healing process. The game was becoming therapy, or at least a distraction, for the emotional pain the team was experiencing. The results were obvious, with wins on two nights against two tough opponents. "I don't think their emotions have changed," Dunleavy said. "I think they're just channeling it in the right direction. All I can say is, I'm very proud of them."

Four

Two nights later at the Forum, the Lakers were hosting the Atlanta Hawks, and the normal pre-game routine was being played out. The starting lineups were introduced, and players were taking off their warm-ups. With no announcement and dressed in a double-breasted black suit, Magic walked across the floor to the Lakers bench. It was his first public appearance since the press conference and fans spontaneously erupted into a standing ovation. With his trademark beaming smile, Magic clapped his hands, returning the applause to the fans as a gesture of thanks.

Hawks star Dominque Wilkins led his team in a straight line over to the Lakers bench. Each player embraced Magic before moving aside to allow the next teammate in line to do the same. The ovation lasted almost two minutes, ended only by the opening tip. The sole piece of commentary Chick Hearn delivered during the ovation to his TV and radio audience was a simple line: "If this doesn't make you cry, nothing will."

Magic watched the game from the Lakers bench but was hardly a passive observer – leaping out of his seat, slapping high-fives, shouting to his former teammates during the game and yelling advice during timeouts. His presence clearly brought life to the team as the Lakers outscored the Hawks by 30 points over the final three quarters en route to a 111-89 victory, their fourth in a row.

Keeping Magic on the roster so he could sit on the bench was a supportive gesture by the Lakers to their former star. But it came at the cost of an active player and was hardly a sustainable option. Dunleavy would, at some point, need to have a full squad of 12 players at his disposal. The team compromised by keeping Magic on the roster but moving him to the injured list, freeing up a roster spot. To fill this spot the Lakers, once again, turned to Calip and signed him to another contract.

Within the space of six weeks, he had signed three contracts with the Lakers and been waived by them twice. Calip's yo-yo early pro career was the surest sign that Lakers management were being forced to make it up as they went along in the aftermath of Magic's shock retirement.

Five

Next up was a home game against the Phoenix Suns, the team that flattened the Lakers by 28 points less than two weeks earlier. The trajectory of both teams had changed dramatically since then. The Lakers had won all of their games, and the Suns had lost all of theirs since their last meeting. The Lakers continued the Suns' losing streak, breaking open a close game in the fourth quarter and snatching a 103-95 victory.

Teagle led the fourth-quarter charge, scoring 10 points in the quarter. It had been a quick and dramatic turnaround for him. Less than a month earlier he was stranded on the Lakers bench and averaged only three minutes per game in the pre-season. With an underwhelming performance the previous season, and with Threatt likely to steal most of his minutes in the new one, Teagle looked likely to be waived. But Magic's retirement created an opportunity for more minutes, one he had taken advantage of by averaging 15.8 points over the previous four games, all victories.

Six

The win streak, one hardly considered likely two weeks earlier, grew to six against San Antonio at the Forum. The Spurs owned the NBA's best record at 7-2, the third time in six games the Lakers faced the league's leading team. The Lakers entered the fourth quarter with a 13-point lead, but the Spurs tore off a 14-6 run to get back in the game. They even snatched a two-point lead on a Willie Anderson three-pointer with two minutes to play. Green answered with a three of his own on the following possession, giving the Lakers the lead back for good. The Lakers would go on to win 98-96 when David Robinson was called for traveling while attempting a potential game-tying shot in the dying seconds. "We're like a team of recovering substance abusers," Dunleavy said. "They say 'take it one day at a time.' We're taking it one game at a time."

The good mood quickly changed when the team learned Divac would require surgery on his ailing back. He had been playing off the bench since his return, with Dunleavy aiming to ease him back into the lineup as his conditioning improved. But the back spasms that forced him to sit out two games in the first week of the season had never fully gone away, and flared back-up dramatically after the Spurs game. The team was still at a loss as to the cause or how to treat it. To find out, Divac would undergo a myelogram. Dye would be shot into his spinal column so doctors could look for any structural damage. While the team still had no answers, it was likely he would be out of the line-up for a long time. Campbell would continue as the starting center, keeping Green as the Lakers' primary sixth man.

Seven

The Lakers hosted the Milwaukee Bucks at home a few days later, where they seemingly did everything they could to snap their own win streak. They were badly outrebounded without Divac. Turnovers to end both the second and third quarters ended in buzzer-beating three-pointers. To top it off, they trailed by 11 points in the fourth quarter.

But a 13-2 run gave the Lakers a three-point lead, and the Bucks had a chance to tie in the dying moments when Threatt stripped Dale Ellis of the ball. Larry Krystkowiak picked up the loose ball, but Threatt stripped him of it too. This time Threatt secured the ball, and with it the win. Threatt could see the play unfolding because he had played alongside Ellis in Seattle and guarded him every day in practice for three and a half years. In that time, he got to know Ellis' pet moves. "If he ever goes left," Threatt said. "He's going to come back right." And with that, another Laker win, 102-97.

The Lakers on-court success in the wake of Magic's retirement had been remarkable, with one courageous performance after another. But the schedule had been kind. They had played some tough opponents, but they had also spent eleven consecutive days at home. No airports, no hotel rooms, no unfamiliar rims, no screaming opposition fans. Rarely does an NBA schedule provide such a wide window of comfort.

After five consecutive games at home, their longest home-stand of the season, the Lakers would begin their longest road trip of 1991-92. The trip would see them play seven games in seven cities in eleven days – starting in Florida and ending in New Jersey.

The road trip was going to test their seven-game win streak, especially with Divac on the sidelines. They would have to do it without Magic's support too. He continued to attend home games, sitting on the Lakers bench as a combination of injured player, cheering fan and assistant coach. But Magic wouldn't travel with the team on the road.

Eight

The first stop on the road trip was Orlando. The expansion Orlando Magic were struggling to keep their heads above water, nursing a 5-4 record in their third season in the league.[37] The Lakers held them to 16 first-quarter points to build a lead they would hold the entire game. The result was never really in doubt, and the Lakers got a comfortable 98-87 win. The Lakers outrebounded their opponent for only the second time all season as Green, Campbell, and Perkins crashed the boards and grabbed 30 between them.

Nine

Next up was Florida's other expansion team – the Miami Heat. Like their expansion brother in Orlando, they entered the game one game above .500. The Lakers fell behind by 15 points in the first half, but Worthy led a third-quarter charge. He scored on a finger-roll lay-up and followed that with a dunk. He then made steals on the Heat's next two possessions, assisting Threatt on the first and Scott on the second.

With scores knotted at 87-87, Dunleavy called timeout with eight seconds on the clock. He drew up a play for Perkins, but Threatt saw that Heat coach Kevin Loughery had switched Bimbo Coles to defend him. Even though he was only 1-4 from the field all game, Threatt liked his chances against Coles and took him one-on-one. He launched a 17-foot jumper that hit the front of the rim and then the backboard. Just as the buzzer sounded, it dropped through the basket for a Lakers win, their ninth in a row. Scott could even take a moment to appreciate what the

---

[37] The NBA had recently expanded to 27 teams. By 1991-92, the Charlotte Hornets and Miami Heat were only three seasons old, while the Minnesota Timberwolves and Orlando Magic were just two seasons old. They were still being referred to as 'expansion teams' until the mid-1990s.

team had achieved over the previous few weeks. "Damn, we're playing ball," he said.

Boston

Perhaps fittingly, it was in Boston that the Lakers came crashing back to earth. This was the place where Magic and the Showtime Lakers re-wrote Lakers history and banished the Celtics curse that had hung over the franchise for twenty years. A Lakers-Celtics clash at Boston Garden would usually be a marquee match-up, but this game felt entirely different.

Though heated rivals, begrudging respect had developed between the two teams as well as a genuine friendship between Magic and Larry Bird. The Celtics had chosen this game to retire Dennis Johnson's number at half-time but postponed the ceremony so it wouldn't muddy the narrative of the night – which was now all about the Lakers' first visit to Boston without Magic.

Both teams were incomplete for the game. The Lakers were missing Magic and Divac, and the Celtics had Kevin McHale, Dee Brown and Brian Shaw sidelined with injuries. But the Celtics still had Larry Bird, who had 22 points, 10 rebounds, and 7 assists. The Lakers held a seven point lead in the third quarter before the Celtics went on a 13-2 run and never looked back, cruising to a 114-91 victory. To Bird, it just wasn't the same battling the Lakers without Magic. "It's a lot different," he said. "But there is not much you can do about it. It's just like he's still over there and he's going to be back sooner or later. He just didn't show up."

The Lakers closed out November the following night with a 93-91 win in Philadelphia, beating a 76ers team that was minus Charles Barkley due to injury. Dunleavy made a change to the rotation, starting Jack Haley and moving Campbell to the bench. Haley had played sparingly to that point but scored 11 points and grabbed 10 rebounds, doing most of his damage when matched up against 7'7 center Manute Bol.

The Lakers finished the month with an unexpected 11-4 record. They were in top spot in the West and had the second-best record in the league. Remarkably, it was an improvement on the 7-5 record they had at the same time a year earlier. Dunleavy was named Coach of the Month for guiding the Lakers through four weeks of chaos.

Mark Heisler described the Lakers' nine-game win streak in the *Los Angeles Times* as being less about artistry and more about grit. And he was right. The streak gave a small window into how the team would have to play if they had any hope of being successful without Magic. It wouldn't be done with the flashy offense of the Showtime era but with hardnose, grind-it-out defense. During the streak, the Lakers averaged 99.8 points per game – seven less than they averaged the previous season and eleven less than the year before. But they held their opponents to a paltry 91.4 per game.[38] "We have a long way to go, but we're a solid defensive team," Dunleavy said. "Our defense keeps us hanging around."

When the buzzer sounded at the end of the game in Philadelphia, it closed the door on the most bewildering month in Lakers history. At the start of it, the Lakers were a championship caliber team. Certainly not the favorite, but undoubtedly one of the contenders. By the close of the month, they had seen their leader snatched away from them in the cruelest of fashions, with genuine fears that he may not survive the illness. This was a heartbroken team, fighting through an NBA schedule that gave them no time to heal. Yet through it all, they managed to win a lot of games, even though they were often the less talented team on the floor.

"I think the level of play during those nine games was incredible," Dunleavy said. "The intensity, the concentration was unparalleled in anything I've been around. I've played with a lot of teams and a lot of good teams. This was the most focused I've ever seen a team."[39]

It won't ever show up on a highlight reel, but the Lakers' nine-game win streak after Magic's shock retirement is a Rocky-type story. One that doesn't get talked enough about.

---

[38] For context, the Detroit Pistons finished the season with the league's best defense, allowing 96.9 points per game.

[39] The win streak is even more impressive when considering the Lakers have had longer winning streaks in only 6 seasons since 1991-92: 1997-98 (11 wins), 1998-99 (10 wins), 1999-00 (streaks of 16, 19 & 11), 2003-04 (streaks of 10 & 11), 2007-08 (10 wins) and 2009-10 (11 wins.) The 2008-09 team, who won 65 games and the championship, didn't even have a longer streak.

Chapter 4

AFLOAT

November 24, 1991 to February 5, 1992

T HE LAKERS HAD been on the road for a week. This was exactly the moment when a superstar player is even more of an asset than normal. The tail end of a long road trip, when fatigue has set in and living out of a suitcase has lost whatever charm it may have had, is when a superstar talent steps up. With that superstar, the weary road team can continue snatching wins from well-rested home teams they probably have no right to take. But these Lakers didn't have a player like that anymore.

Instead, the road trip continued with a 32-point loss in Milwaukee. Then they gave up 47 points in the fourth quarter in Charlotte, allowed the Hornets to score on their last 21 possessions, and lost 124-106.

They ended their longest road trip of the season with a respectful 4-3 record, good enough to preserve their spot atop the West. Sedale Threatt had filled in admirably at point guard, averaging 13.9 points and 7.4 assists in 39.4 minutes over the first 17 games of the season. But clearly West didn't believe the current state of play was sustainable because he spent a lot of November looking for a replacement point guard.

Hamstrung by being over the salary cap, the Lakers got some relief from Magic's retirement. League rules dictated half of a retired player's salary would not count against the salary cap. Magic would earn $2.5 million for the season, meaning the Lakers suddenly had a $1.25 million salary spot. It wasn't enough to return them to where they had been with Magic. "In this day and age, $1 million isn't very much for a basketball player," West admitted. Even if it were, almost all players who could have a true impact were already under contract with other teams. But they might be able to land someone who could help.

West attended a Mavericks-Rockets game in Dallas, building speculation he was interested in acquiring Mavericks veteran point guard Derek Harper. Other rumors suggested he was trying to work a three-team deal with Miami and Boston to land Brian Shaw.[40] West was talking to teams, trying to find a deal but kept coming up against the same roadblock – the insistence from other teams A.C. Green be included in any trade. West had almost dealt Green to Golden State in the off-season, but the Lakers' early season rebounding struggles had changed West's willingness to part with him. The Lakers were 25th in the league in rebounding by the end of November and West couldn't part with his best rebounder. And their rebounding wasn't going to get better any time soon. Vlade Divac's season had never really gotten started due to back problems. He underwent surgery on November 27 for a herniated disc and would be missing from the line-up for at least six weeks.

The Lakers tendered a contract offer to the best free agent still on the market – Sherman Douglas. The 25-year-old point guard had been impressive during his first two years in the league, averaging 18.5 points and 8.5 assists in Miami. Contract negotiations between Douglas and the Heat had been at an impasse all off-season. Douglas rejected a $2.3 million-per-year offer, holding out for a better deal. He was a restricted free agent, meaning the Heat had the right to match any offer he received.

West's offer was aggressive – $17 million over seven years, a player option after two seasons, veto power over any trade and a 15% trade kicker. West hoped the contract was something Miami wouldn't match, especially since the Heat were off to the best start in their short history and already had Steve Smith and Bimbo Coles in the backcourt. Dunleavy confirmed he would, if the deal went down, initially use Douglas as a back-up to Threatt. But Douglas had enough talent to be the Lakers starting point guard.

The Heat would have two weeks to match the offer, but Douglas made it clear where he wanted to be. "I hope they won't match," Douglas said. "With the things they put me through, I can't stay with them. My feeling is, I want definitely to be a Laker. I'm going to be very happy in L.A."

West had urgent roster moves he needed to make while waiting for Douglas. Once the road trip was over, the Lakers placed Divac on the injured list and used his roster spot to sign third-year forward Chucky Brown to a minimum contract. Frustrated by a lack of minutes, Brown

---

[40] Both Harper and Shaw eventually did play for the Lakers. Harper finished his career as the starting point guard on the 1998-99 team at the age of 37. Shaw played his last four seasons as back-up point guard for the Lakers from 1999-2003, winning three championships and eventually becoming an assistant coach with the team.

asked the Cleveland Cavaliers to waive him, and upon his release, he received interest from both the New York Knicks and the Lakers. He ultimately chose to sign with the Lakers because he had grown up in New York and wanted to experience life in L.A.

The team also waived Calip for the third and final time and signed 33-year-old veteran point guard Rory Sparrow to take his spot as Threatt's back-up.[41] Sparrow, known as one of the league's steadiest guards during his 12-year career, had started the season in Chicago but was released when the Bulls traded for Bobby Hansen.

The Lakers picked up some cheap wins against struggling teams to stay atop of the West, beating Dallas at home and Sacramento twice. They then started a mini three-game road trip up north, starting in Chicago where they took on the Bulls for the first time since their Finals loss. The Bulls were cruising through the first two months of the season with an 18-3 record. Not wanting to miss the match-up, Magic traveled with the Lakers for the first time and watched from the bench.

Michael Jordan came out hot, hitting five of his first six shots, and the Bulls led 45-41 at the half. But he would go on to miss 13 of his last 14 shots, including an uncontested double-clutch dunk. The Lakers rolled off 61 second-half points and beat the league-leading Bulls 102-89. Jordan finished with 21 points and shot an uncharacteristic 6-20 from the field. Dunleavy credited the win to the Lakers' defense. "There are a lot of teams out there who are more talented than we are," he said, "but when we play this hard on defense, we're hard to beat."

Magic caused a stir in the lead-up to the Bulls game when he was asked by a reporter if he would consider playing for the Lakers in the playoffs. "I haven't ruled anything out," he said. "If I was sick, then you rule out everything. But I'm not. So that's the difference. Now my mind is open to everything." Rosen would clarify the next day, saying Magic's quote was misinterpreted and he was indeed staying retired on advice from his doctors. He had been retired less than six weeks, and already there was a rumor of a comeback. It sure wouldn't be the last.

In an unexpected twist, Kareem Abdul-Jabbar said the next day he too

---

[41] Calip never played in the NBA again. He played in the CBA until 1995 and starred in *Blue Chips* and *Eddie*, two basketball related movies, in 1994 and 1996. He also appeared in an episode of *Diagnosis Murder* in 1997, playing EMT #1.

was contemplating a comeback. The 44-year-old was scheduled to take part in an upcoming pay-per-view one-on-one exhibition game against Julius Erving in Atlantic City. Kareem said if he held his own in the game, he would consider returning to the Lakers after more than two years on the sidelines. "It's something that's crossed my mind," Abdul-Jabbar said. "When I heard the news about the HIV positive test, it really affected me, and I wanted to do something to help my friend. And the thing I do best is play basketball." He underscored these words with a pledge to use each game of his comeback to raise money for AIDS research.[42]

It was December 18, 1991 and the Lakers were still defying expectations by being in first place in the West with a 16-7 record. But they were about to start a run of seven games that would see them topple out of the top spot for good. It would then require all their energy over January simply to stay afloat.

Two days after beating the league's best team on their own floor, the Lakers squared off against the league's worst. The Minnesota Timberwolves had a hideous 3-18 record and were on a nine-game losing streak. Things were so bad in Minneapolis that fans unveiled a banner before the game that read, 'On Track for Shaq', hoping the league's worst record would reward them with the top spot in the draft and the right to select LSU's Shaquille O'Neal.

In the two days since the win over the Bulls, Dunleavy hadn't stopped talking about the risk of a let-down against Minnesota. Yet the Lakers came out flat anyway. The Timberwolves shot out to a 10-2 lead to start the game, eventually building a 55-39 lead. The Lakers spent the second half playing catch-up, and a long jumper by Sparrow got them to within 88-84. But they missed their last nine shots and lost 96-85 as former Laker Tony Campbell wound up top scoring with 23 points.

The next night the team was in Detroit, where the Pistons were struggling with a 12-14 record and would be playing without the injured Isiah Thomas. Worthy started the game shooting 4-5 but developed pain in his left knee. He kept playing but shot just 1-11 the rest of the game. The

---

[42] The game was held February 28, 1992 and Abdul-Jabbar won 41-23. It was a ratings flop, with an estimated 0.3% of the nation's 18.3 million pay-per-view homes tuning in. Abdul-Jabbar never did come out of retirement and no evidence of him announcing a final decision was found when researching this book. In fact, there doesn't seem to be any evidence that it ever came up again.

Pistons outscored the Lakers by 17 points in the second half and flogged them 112-93. The losing streak then grew to three with a 12-point loss at home to the Phoenix Suns.

With their offense sputtering in recent weeks, the Lakers could have used some good news regarding their offer to Douglas. But they didn't get it. The Heat, using all fifteen days allotted to them, matched the Lakers offer at the eleventh hour. As West had hoped, the Heat were indeed content with their guard rotation without Douglas and had no interest in bringing back the disgruntled player. But they didn't want him to walk away without getting something in return. The Heat spent the two weeks trying to find a trade partner. When they couldn't find one, they bit the bullet and matched the Lakers' offer anyway. Indeed, they did find one week later, trading him to Boston in exchange for Brian Shaw.

Unbeknownst to Laker fans at the time, West pulled off a major trade that made Charles Barkley a Laker. But unfortunately, it was only for three hours. The Lakers and Philadelphia 76ers had agreed on a trade that would have sent Worthy and Campbell to Philadelphia in exchange for Barkley and small forward Ron Anderson. Barkley was unhappy in Philadelphia, where the Sixers hadn't been legitimate championship contenders in the six years since Erving retired. He publicly demanded a trade and the Sixers were working on potential deals with Portland, Phoenix, and the Lakers. Barkley received a call from his agent informing him he had been traded to the Lakers. He was so happy with the news that he went out to lunch to celebrate and started drinking. "I was excited to get the hell out of Philly," he said. Three hours later he received another call from his agent who said the Sixers had backed out of the deal.[43] Now with a few drinks in him, he was a Sixer again and had to play that night. And the Lakers were still without that superstar to build their team around.

With Magic retired, Douglas still in Miami and Barkley staying in Philadelphia, the Lakers would have to make do with what they had. As the losses kept coming, the reality of life without Magic started to sink in.

The next loss came at home to the 17-10 Portland Trail Blazers, their

---

[43] Barkley was traded five months later to the Phoenix Suns for Jeff Hornacek, Andrew Lang and Tim Perry in an infamously lop-sided trade that re-made the Suns into championship contenders and sent the 76ers spiralling into years of struggling.

first match-up since the playoffs the previous year. The Lakers struggled offensively, shooting just 35% from the floor and lost 98-88. Worthy top-scored for the Lakers with 21 points but again played on aching knees and shot 7-19 from the field. Threatt had been struggling since the Lakers tendered the contract offer to Douglas, his potential replacement in the starting line-up. He averaged just 5.0 points and 5.7 assists on 31% shooting in the three games following the offer. He didn't perform much better knowing Douglas wasn't going to be a Laker, scoring 9 points on 4-14 shooting.

The Lakers lost at home again two days later to the Golden State Warriors. This time their defense was just as suspect as their offense, and they lost 114-99. Tim Hardaway, who had missed all seventeen shots he took three nights earlier against Minnesota, went 13-21 and scored 30 points against the Lakers. Dunleavy called it the worst beating the team had taken all year and the lowest they had been since he took the head coaching job. The loss to the Warriors ended a miserable month for the Lakers, who had a 6-8 record in December. It was their first losing month since March 1979, before Magic was drafted.[44]

But if Dunleavy thought the Warriors game was as low as the Lakers could sink, he was wrong. The Lakers ushered in 1992 by losing 114-87 at home to the Indiana Pacers. The Pacers entered the game with a 2-12 road record, a 12-18 overall record and the second-worst defense in the league. But against the Lakers, they looked like world beaters. It was the Lakers' worst loss at home in eighteen years and their fourth consecutive loss at the Forum, tying a franchise record.[45] They shot 33% from the floor and failed to score 100 points for the seventh consecutive game.

The patience of fans, who had been loudly supportive at home games since Magic's retirement, finally ran out. They rained boos down on the Lakers at half-time. West gave the team a spray in the press, calling their effort 'disgraceful' and saying he would consider trade offers for any of his players. "Maybe some players have been around here too long," he said.

The Lakers had lost six of their seven games since beating Chicago. They had fallen from first place in the West all the way to fifth. And they

---

[44] That is a remarkable stat – the Lakers did not have one losing month during Magic's 12 years with them.

[45] The previous biggest home loss was a 124-101 drubbing by the Buffalo Braves on November 3, 1974.

were now in a battle with the sixth-place Clippers to even stay that high. Dunleavy tried his best to turn the situation into a rallying call. He said a lot of people assumed this was going to happen when Magic retired. Now the question was, are the players going to let it happen? Will they let the league walk over them?

"I feel for them," Magic said. "A lot of times, you want to go out there yourself and play. What we used to do to teams for 12 years, the last five-six games, they've been doing to us. It's tough when you don't have Vlade who gave us somebody to go to down low, or myself. You're asking this team to do a lot."

The bitter taste of the loss to the Pacers was clearly still in the mouths of fans as 5,000 seats remained empty at the Forum two nights later against Miami. The Forum being almost 30% empty for a Lakers game was unheard of just a year earlier. Yet the Lakers would be improved over the rest of January with a run of games against below-.500 teams. It wasn't so much recovery as stabilization. They would fortify their spot in the middle of the playoff chase, unable to climb but determined not to fall further.

The turnaround was no small part due to Dunleavy shaking up the rotation, starting Green at power forward over Elden Campbell and moving Perkins to center. He also increased Smith's role with the second unit and moved Terry Teagle to small forward. Essentially, he was implementing small-ball before it became a common strategy in the NBA, and it would pay dividends as the quicker defense created easy shots at the other end. After failing to break the century mark in almost three weeks, they scored over 100 in three straight wins against Miami, Minnesota, and Denver.

The win over the Nuggets at the Forum came on an especially unique day for Sedale Threatt. Earlier that morning Threatt and his wife, Nicole, welcomed the birth of their first child, Tyler Sedale, an 8-pound, 87-ounce baby boy. After the game, he stopped at a gas station across the street from the Forum to use a pay phone when he was robbed at gunpoint. The thieves got away with $1,000 cash and Threatt's new Mercedes Benz. In 24 hours, Threatt had welcomed a new child into the world, scored a double-double for the Lakers and been held-up at gunpoint – all in all, not a day most people ever experience.

The Lakers picked up two victories at home against expansion teams, a comfortable 112-99 win over Orlando and a 95-93 win against Charlotte on a buzzer-beater by Perkins. They split a home-and-away series against the Seattle SuperSonics, but Worthy's painful left knee finally got to the point where he needed to sit out. He had been playing magnificently through the pain, averaging 24.5 points on 52% shooting the previous week. But he looked slow and awkward in the second game against Seattle, where he scored just 13 points on 4-13 shooting. He would sit out a week in the hope some rest would give the knee a chance to heal.

It was bad timing for Worthy to be out. The Lakers visited the surging Portland Trail Blazers and were routed 131-92, the second-worst loss in franchise history. But despite the big loss, the recovery continued as they won their next four games. And all of them were like something out of the Twilight Zone.

The weirdness started with their second home-and-away series in less than a week, this time against the Sacramento Kings. Worthy would miss both games, and Dunleavy inserted Campbell back in the starting line-up.

The first game was in Sacramento, and it was, well, eventful. The free throw count in the first half was 19-1 in favor of the Lakers. "I know I'm not great at math," Kings forward Wayman Tisdale said, "but something was wrong in that first half." Rex Hughes, the Kings' head coach since Dick Motta was fired 25 games into the season, was furious. He was called for two quick technicals after arguing too vehemently with an official and was ejected. He left the court in spectacular fashion, pushing a camera out the way before giving an angry wave to another. All to the enthusiastic cheers of Kings fans. The Lakers won 108-105 on free throws from Threatt, who also top-scored for the Lakers with 29 points, and Mitch Richmond missed a potential game-tying three-pointer on the buzzer.

Incredibly, the second game of the series held the following night in Los Angeles ended exactly the same way. Threatt made two free throws to give the Lakers a 95-92 lead with one second remaining and Richmond missed another potential game-tying three-pointer on the buzzer.

Things continued to get strange five days later when the Lakers hosted the Golden State Warriors who were playing without Sarunas Marciulionis, Rod Higgins, Alton Lister, Tom Tolbert and Jud Buechler due to injury. Things got worse for Warriors head coach Don Nelson when Tim Hardaway and Vincent Askew were ejected following a tussle with Green in a third quarter that saw eight technical fouls called. They got worse still when Billy Owens and Jaren Jackson fouled out. With the Warriors playing the fourth quarter with a one-man bench the Lakers ran out 112-99 winners.

Then the Lakers won a game they maybe shouldn't have when they beat the Denver Nuggets on the road 106-96. In the dying moments and with the game still not decided, Scott made a three-pointer that replays show he clearly didn't get off before the shot clock expired. Reggie Williams rightly protested the call and was charged with a technical that sent Scott to the line. Scott's free throw turned his three-pointer that shouldn't have counted into a four-point play that sealed the win for the Lakers.

The Lakers started February by hosting the Chicago Bulls, who they had shocked on national TV in their first match-up in December. Worthy returned from injury and Dunleavy temporarily ditched his small-ball line-up against the long and athletic Bulls. He even played Worthy at guard for a few minutes. The Lakers led by two with seven minutes to play in the fourth quarter, but that was merely setting the stage for one of 'those' games from Michael Jordan.

He made a seven-foot jump hook over Perkins to tie the score. He then made a 17-foot jumper. On the following possession, he froze Scott with a head-and-shoulder fake for another 17-foot jumper. He assisted to Grant for a jump hook in the lane, made a 12-foot jumper, ball-faked Worthy almost out of his shoes for a lay-in and finished the run with a 19-foot jump shot. In the end, the Bulls got the 103-97 win and Jordan finished with 33 points, 8 rebounds, and 11 assists. "They surprised us in Chicago and spanked us pretty good," Jordan said. "So, we didn't underestimate this team. We knew how feisty this team is."

Following a nine-point loss in Phoenix, Threatt came up big two nights later when the Lakers played the Clippers at the Forum. The Clippers had earlier in the day named Larry Brown as their head coach after parting ways with Mike Schuler. Threatt had 14 points, 11 assists, and seven rebounds but it was his defensive effort that forced turnovers on the final two Clipper possessions that gave the Lakers a 100-95 win.

After falling off a cliff in late December, the Lakers had steadied. They were 11-5 since their horrid home loss to the Pacers and had a healthy 28-18 record. It was good enough, though just barely, to hold the fifth spot in the West. It may not have felt much like success, but the Lakers had prevented the bottom from falling out of their season. At least for now.

Chapter 5

A FAREWELL WITH NO GOODBYE

February 9, 1992 to March 29, 1992

T HE ROAD FROM Magic Johnson's retirement in November 1991 to the All-Star Game in February 1992 was anything but straight. All-Star fan ballots are prepared at the very start of the season, and Magic's name was on the ballot by the time he retired three games into the season. Perhaps as a gesture of solidarity, or maybe as an act of healing, fans voted him in despite having not played a game all season.[46] When voting results were released in mid-January, Magic immediately stated his intention to play. The reaction was mixed.

His old teammates A.C. Green and Byron Scott were opposed to the idea. Scott wanted Magic to rest and look after himself, Green felt the All-Star game should be for active players only. Charles Barkley thought it wouldn't be fair for Magic to take the spot of an active player who had earned the right to play. Some players expressed fear about the risk of contracting HIV through on-court contact.[47]

But fear of Magic playing in the game was more of a rumble than a loud roar. Most of the debate was kept away from the public, primarily because David Stern wanted it that way. The league took advice from doctors that there was little risk of Magic spreading the virus through on-court contact. "We were being told that couldn't happen," Stern said. "It had to be open-sore-to-open-sore, and even then, it was unlikely." Stern was prepared to follow the expert advice and gave Magic the green light to play.

There were dissenting voices behind closed doors. A worried owner told Stern he was getting the league "too far out in front of the issue."

[46] Magic received 658,211 votes, second in the West to Clyde Drexler's 759,550 votes.
[47] Mark Price, Jerome Kersey, Chris Dudley, Sarunas Marciulionis and Rockets head coach Don Chaney all went on record with their concerns.

Another told Stern he hoped he knew what he was doing because it was a huge risk for the league to let Magic play. But Stern wouldn't be talked off the idea. The league undertook an education campaign for players and the media to quell any concerns. Stern even found an obvious solution to Green and Barkley's concerns about Magic taking someone's spot on the team: he simply permitted the West to carry an extra player.

It was when Magic announced his intention to play at the Olympics that the criticism became loud and overt.

Dr. Brian Sando, the senior medical director of Australia's Olympic basketball program, recommended a boycott against the United States team if Magic played. He acknowledged the risk of Magic infecting another player was minuscule, but because it couldn't be completely ruled out he maintained that playing against him was too high a risk.[48]

Sando had the support of several Australian players. "If it was a choice of playing for gold or staying off and taking silver," Australian center Ray Borner said, "I'd take silver." Fellow center Mark Bradtke called for compulsory HIV testing for all Olympic competitors. Team captain Phil Smyth said he wanted proof there was no danger of transmission before he agreed to play – as opposed, it seems, to requiring evidence of risk.[49]

Adrian Hurley, head coach of the Australian team, tried to say the right thing but ended up showing a lack of leadership. He said the decision to play against Magic was up to each individual player to decide. He doubted Magic would play anyway but believed there might be "political reasons" why he might be allowed to. According to Hurley, the lobby groups and politicians might force it to happen.[50]

Comments from the Australian team caused international debate and controversy, while Smyth became the poster-boy for intolerance. A cartoon of him wearing a condom on his head appeared on the front page

---

[48] Jacques Haguet, President of the Medical Council for the International Basketball Federation, estimated in 1992 the actual risk of infection through on-court contact was one-in-a-million.

[49] Smyth told Australian writer Bret Harris in 1992 that he was angry his words were twisted by the United States media, saying he never threatened to refuse to take the court.

[50] There were opposing views within the Australian team. Shane Heal, a guard on the Australian team who would go on to have a brief NBA career, published an article in Melbourne's The Age stating Borner and Smyth didn't speak for him and he would have no problem playing against Magic.

of *The Canberra Times*. Kevin Hepworth wrote in the *Times* that a quest to "enshrine Johnson's civil rights" was being undertaken by politicians and Olympic bureaucrats at the expense of free speech.[51]

When asked by Australian media about the controversy, Magic said he was prepared to sit out any game against Australia. "We're going to beat Australia anyway, with or without me," he said. "It just means we won't beat them as bad as if I was playing."

Australian Foreign Affairs Minister Gareth Evans intervened, saying the players had embarrassed the country with their "half-baked and wrongheaded comments." Basketball Australia attempted to bridge the divide and invited Magic to bring a team of his own to Australia to play their national team. Sando eventually backed off his comments, claiming he never suggested a boycott.

By the time Magic took the floor at Orlando Arena for the All-Star Game, he had been the center of controversy for over a month. Nobody knew what to expect from the game. How would players and fans react to him? Would fans still cheer for him? How rusty would he be after not playing for months? Had HIV damaged his health so much that he could only play a few minutes?[52]

The event looked and felt like no other All-Star Game before or since, but not in the way the storm of negativity before it may have suggested. This was assumed to be Magic's final NBA game, his farewell to fans and theirs to him. And it turned into a giant leap forward in enlightenment. A HIV-positive athlete competed against the world's best basketball players in a game broadcast in 90 countries and with more than 960 journalists present to cover it. It was two hours where people living with HIV or AIDS around the world could feel some representation in an often-hostile media, social and political landscape.

The pre-game player introductions were the first major step forward, with Magic receiving a lengthy standing ovation from the crowd. Then the East team, led by Isiah Thomas, walked the length of the court and greeted Magic the same way Hawks players had done in Magic's first appearance at the Forum. One by one they embraced him. Magic and Thomas kissed

---

[51] *The Age* published a three-page spread about the issue, with "*AIDS in Sports*" plastered across an entire page.

[52] Seriously, people thought like this in 1992. These were real questions heading into the game.

each other on the cheek, just as they always did before a game. These were not small gestures. The world noticed a person with HIV being accepted by his peers and the thousands of fans in attendance.

The game didn't get off to a perfect start, Magic secured the ball from the opening tip, but Thomas picked off his first pass.[53] But from there, Magic showed the world he had lost none of the qualities that made him one of the greats. In fact, he was remarkably sharp. He went coast-to-coast for a lay-up less than two minutes into the game. Three minutes later he converted a picture-perfect skyhook over Thomas. By the end of the first quarter, he had 10 points on 4-5 shooting. In the second quarter, he sliced between Reggie Lewis and Brad Daugherty for a reverse lay-up. Later, he found himself matched up with Dennis Rodman, who had promised to guard Magic tough and not let him score on him. The two tussled for position in the post before Magic scored a sky-hook over top of him.

Magic headed to the bench in the second quarter where he was interviewed by Steve Jones who asked him how he was feeling and if there had been any residual effects from playing. Magic patiently and politely told him he didn't need to worry about that.

In the fourth quarter, Magic dazzled the crowd with his trademark passing. He hit Tim Hardaway in transition on a no-look, round-the-back pass. He attacked the basket and handed off to Robinson for a lay-in. He fired a bullet pass through the defense to Dan Majerle for an open lay-in.

Then with three minutes to go, he really put on a show. He took a pass out of the post and hit his first three-pointer of the game. On the next possession, he charged up court before stopping at the three-point line, gave Thomas a ball fake and rattled in his second straight three-pointer.

With one and a half minutes to play, Thomas took the ball at the three-point line and waived off his teammates. To the delight of the crowd, he went one-on-one with Magic, dribbling between his legs, trying to shake him off before launching a long jumper that missed badly. The crowd rose to its feet for a standing ovation less than a minute later when Jordan did the same. Jordan waved off his teammates and went one-on-one with Magic – eventually taking a half-hearted jumper that rimmed out.

On the West's final possession, Magic backed Thomas down from

---

[53] Tim Hardaway was third in fan voting amongst West guards and would have started if Magic had elected not to play. Hardaway voluntarily gave up his spot in the starting line-up to Magic.

center court, turned to his right and launched a high arching fade-away three-pointer that was nothing but net. The crowd went into a frenzy, celebrating like it was a game-winning shot of a playoff game and not a shot in an All-Star game that pushed the West's lead out to 40. There were 14 seconds left, but Jordan refused to inbound the ball. He knew Magic had delivered a perfect ending to the game.[54] Magic high-fived his teammates after the game. Kevin Willis hugged him, as did Thomas. The sight of an athlete, drenched in sweat, being embraced skin-to-skin by other players was yet another meaningful moment for HIV and AIDS awareness.[55]

Magic played 29 minutes and finished with 25 points on 9-12 shooting, five rebounds, and nine assists. The West won 153-113 and Magic was named MVP.[56] The game may have been considered a farewell, but NBC's Ahmad Rashad asked Magic immediately after it if he was coming back for the playoffs. "I don't know, we'll just have to wait and see," he answered. "I'm just savoring this moment right now."

A week after Magic's farewell game in Orlando, and despite the fact he was clearly open to the possibility of a comeback, the Lakers retired his jersey during a half-time ceremony when the Boston Celtics were in town.

The ceremony was about more than just honoring Magic. It was a moment of closure and healing for fans who had been grieving the cruel loss of their superstar player all season. Some of Magic's former teammates were there. The four other players whose jerseys hung on the Forum wall – Kareem Abdul-Jabbar, Jerry West, Wilt Chamberlain and Elgin Baylor – were there too.[57] Larry Bird made the trip even though he was sitting out the game injured, ignoring doctors' advice he shouldn't travel with his bad back.

---

[54] The game was almost perfect but for two things. Larry Bird couldn't play because of his ailing back. And it never came together for Magic and Worthy, who scored nine points, to have one last signature play together.

[55] In 1992, many people were unsure if the virus could be transmitted via sweat.

[56] It's been written in several places that the game wasn't fun to watch because it was so obvious the players were scared to defend Magic. But it doesn't really look like that. Rodman and Ewing certainly wrestled for position with him freely. And it's an exhibition game where no serious defense is ever played. After all, the teams combined to score 266 points that day.

[57] Gail Goodrich and Jamaal Wilkes were retired by this point but hadn't yet had their numbers retired by the team.

Magic was bombarded with goodwill and fought hard to maintain the tough, resilient exterior he had presented to the world since the announcement. He didn't break when West gave him a framed #32 jersey and called him the greatest and most unique player he had ever seen. He stayed strong when Charles Grantham, Executive Director of the Players Association, quoted Martin Luther King Jr. on courage. Worthy presented Magic with a bust made in his likeness, and he still remained composed. Larry Bird presented Magic with a framed piece of the famed Boston Garden parquet floor and told him he would always be a part of the Celtic family. And still Magic kept it together.

Then Abdul-Jabbar took to the microphone. Known as a stoic and sometimes joyless player in the 1970s, he described how Magic helped him realize he was actually having fun, making him understand the gift he had as a basketball player. He said Magic showed him how special it was to entertain people and what a privilege it was to share his skill with the world. Magic could keep his composure no more, and tears streamed down his face as Abdul-Jabbar spoke. The two former teammates hugged after the speech. After a few moments, Abdul-Jabbar motioned to break free, but Magic just squeezed him tighter.

It was a moving ceremony, but it was also a strange one. And not because Magic caused a high-quality cringe moment when he said Norm Nixon taught him all his bad habits with women.[58] Yes, the ceremony was a moment of closure and healing for fans. But in other ways, it reinforced the uncertainty of Magic's playing career. Fans were saying goodbye to a player who could clearly still play after performing so well in Orlando. And he still wanted to play, reiterating four times during the ceremony that he remained committed to competing at the Olympics. He closed his speech by saying, "I hope that if I do decide to come back, you won't be upset if we did this all over again." It was a farewell with no goodbye.

The Lakers were awful for much of Magic's big night at the Forum against the Celtics. They shot 39% and trailed 63-47 at half-time. Chick Hearn hosted the half-time ceremony and started by promising to keep it short, so they could get back to the game. The crowd booed, not wanting to return to the horror show. "I know how you feel," Hearn told them. "It

---

[58] Before Magic came to the Lakers, Nixon was the greatest playboy on the team. Magic was considered Nixon's 'understudy' when he was a rookie.

wasn't exactly a boat ride where I was sitting." They would go onto lose 114-107, their third loss in a row.[59]

Magic's jersey retirement happened in the midst of the Lakers playing a stretch of games in which they would perform so poorly it would threaten their entire season. At the end of it, the likelihood of qualifying for the playoffs would be brought into question for the first time in sixteen years.

The losing streak grew to four games in Oakland with a sixteen-point loss to Golden State. Then it pushed out to five games at the Sports Arena with a 125-94 flogging by the Los Angeles Clippers. It was the first time the Lakers had lost more than four games in a row since March 1979. They were so pitiful that the Clippers' new coach Larry Brown thought it was an empty win. "That's not a Laker team right now with the problems they've had," he said.

Then it got embarrassing. Scores were tied with 1.7 seconds remaining in Seattle when the SuperSonics called a timeout. On his way back out on the floor, Ricky Pierce boasted that he was going to make the game-winning shot. Eddie Johnson then inbounded to Pierce, who had shaken Scott and was left wide open. As promised, he made a buzzer-beating 20-footer for a 105-103 win. "I was surprised how wide open I was," Pierce said. Mike Dunleavy probably was too.

They were given several chances to end their losing streak when they hosted the Golden State Warriors. Trailing 126-124, the Lakers got three offensive rebounds in the final 20 seconds. But Worthy missed a driving 10-footer, Threatt missed a long jumper, and Teagle missed a baseline 15-footer. It was their second two-point loss in a row and their seventh consecutive loss overall, their longest losing streak since 1958.

"You know it is discouraging," Perkins said. "You go home and think about it. No one likes to lose or accepts losing, especially the way things used to be. But you have to face reality."

The defense that had been the Lakers' redeeming quality all season had failed them badly during the losing streak. Over the seven games, they gave up an average of 113 points. But the defense was temporarily back when they hosted the New York Knicks. The game marked Pat

---

[59] Between the All-Star Game and Magic's jersey retirement, the Lakers lost to the Utah Jazz in Salt Lake City and then gave the Washington Bullets their first win at the Forum since 1987.

Riley's first time at the Forum as an opposition coach, and he received an unprompted ovation as soon as he walked onto the floor. But the game wasn't fitting for the occasion. In fact, it was one of the ugliest in Laker history. The Knicks scored only 12 first-quarter points, their starters managed just 36 points between them, Patrick Ewing shot 4-18, and the Lakers won 81-68. It may have been an eyesore but, when you're on a seven-game losing streak, a win is a win.

Divac returned against New York after spending three months on the sidelines. The Lakers activated Divac from the injured list and replaced him with Keith Owens, who had a well-timed bruised right elbow.[60] He would be back long-term too, signing a six-year, $19.5 million extension the day after returning. West would normally wait for the off-season to re-sign players, but Divac was getting serious offers from European clubs, and he needed to act quickly.

The Lakers gave the Cleveland Cavaliers their first win at the Forum since 1985 when they fell 101-90. The loss meant the Lakers closed out February 1992 with a 3-10 record, their second losing month of the season. After ending November with the best record in the West, they closed February barely holding on to seventh place. They were now in a three-team battle with the Clippers and Houston Rockets for the final two playoff spots. Three teams, two spots, two months left on the schedule. They would need to right the ship, and quickly if they wanted to keep their playoff hopes alive.

The Lakers opened March by losing 105-97 at home to the Houston Rockets.[61] Worthy played the first half, scoring six points, but the pain in his left knee flared up, and he couldn't play in the second half. "It's been bothering him for some time," Dunleavy said. "Last game, he came in with his knee swollen. I wasn't sure he was going to play that game against Cleveland. Same thing today. He made it through the first half, the doctors looked at it and said he couldn't go." Worthy would have to sit for the next two weeks as the Lakers hoped a long spell of rest would give the knee time to recover. Without him they dropped two games at the Forum,

---

[60] Before the 2011-12 season when the NBA expanded the size of active rosters, it was common that the 12th guy on the team would suddenly get an injury (usually back spasms) at the exact time a rotation player had healed from his.

[61] Vernon Maxwell scored 30 points and made an all-time Laker opponent high (at the time) six three-pointers.

losing by four to Portland then by five to Detroit.

Things were bleak. The Lakers had lost eleven of their last thirteen games, including six of eight at home. They were in a battle to keep their playoff hopes alive, and they didn't have Magic or Worthy. And the schedule was about to turn rough, with a five-game road trip featuring two sets of back-to-back games against four likely playoff teams.

The road trip started in New York where the Lakers and Knicks couldn't have played a more different game than the one they played at the Forum. This time they played at a furious pace, the Lakers trailing 57-55 at the half. Then Threatt caught fire, scoring 22 points in the third quarter by making seven of his eight shots, all but one outside 15 feet. The Knicks led 104-103 in the dying seconds when Threatt, who finished with a career-high 42 points, drove to the basket and drew the Knicks defense. He flicked a pass out to Perkins who made a three-pointer with two seconds to play that put the Lakers up 106-104. Xavier McDaniel hit a long jumper at the other end, but it wasn't clear if it was a two, if it was a three, or if it even beat the buzzer. Officials conferred and eventually ruled the shot was too late, giving the Lakers the win. Madison Square Garden erupted in boos, but replays suggest the ruling was correct.

The Lakers won back-to-back games for the first time in a month with an 11-point win in Atlanta against a Hawks team who had been in a spiral since Dominique Wilkins tore his Achilles tendon five weeks earlier. The road trip continued with losses in both Cleveland and Indianapolis. They did manage to get a 92-89 win in Washington, but the game was borderline unwatchable. The Lakers shot 36%, handed out only eight assists and made a season-low 27 shots in the win.

Yet despite some ugliness, the trip was a marginal success. The Lakers won three of five games and Divac, who had struggled with his conditioning since returning, was more productive with each game. Yet they were now in a worse predicament in the standings than before the trip. The Clippers had won three of four during the same stretch and drawn into a tie with the Lakers for the final playoff spot.

They returned home and lost by five to the Portland Trail Blazers.[62] The loss saw them tumble out of the top eight and for the first time the reality of potentially missing the playoffs began to sink in. To rub salt in

---

[62] Earlier in the day Haley and his wife Stacey welcomed the birth of their first child, Jack Tyler. Haley got one minute of playing time.

the wounds, they would be hit hard by injury. Worthy had sat out the last nine games but had been cleared to practice the day before the Portland game. The pain in his knee returned during the training session, proving the two and a half weeks of rest had done little to alleviate the problem. It gave Worthy no other option than to have exploratory surgery on the knee, knocking him out for the remainder of the season.

As if that wasn't enough, Perkins strained his right shoulder against Portland. He was at risk of damaging his rotator cuff if he continued playing, a serious injury that can take a minimum of six months to recover. The Lakers had little choice but to be conservative with the injury, and they shut Perkins down for the remainder of the season.

With playoff contention on the line, the Lakers would not only be without Magic, but also down their leading scorer Worthy and their second-leading scorer and second-leading rebounder Perkins. The deep and talented frontcourt that was a huge part of the Lakers' surprise success a year ago had been decimated. It now only featured Green, a limping and out-of-shape Divac, an all-too-green Campbell, and ring-in Brown. Dunleavy would run the rest of the season with Teagle as the lone regular rotation player on the bench. "It's been a crazy season. We've never experienced anything like this before," Scott said. "You start saying, 'who's next?'"

In need of frontcourt reinforcements, the Lakers signed 32-year-old veteran forward Cliff Robinson. He had been out of the NBA since 1989 when he suffered career-threatening injuries in a car accident during his 10th season. He bounced around Europe and the CBA before the Lakers brought him back to the NBA. "I had to go all around the world to come back home," he said.

The schedule, for at least the next 10 days, would be kind. Three out of their next four games would be at home, each against non-playoff teams. They beat a struggling Minnesota Timberwolves team 131-121.[63] Then they easily beat the almost-as-bad-as-the-Timberwolves Dallas Mavericks, who were 5-37 since Christmas and on a 14-game losing streak. They upset the Utah Jazz, who were favorites to win the Midwest Division, and returned home to thump the struggling Philadelphia 76ers 117-89 behind a career-high 32 points from Divac.

---

[63] It was A.C. Green's 456th consecutive game, breaking Michael Cooper's old franchise record.

The four straight victories saw them claw back into the playoff picture with a two-game lead over the Houston Rockets for the eighth and final playoff spot. But it had been a painful two months. The Lakers had said goodbye to their superstar floor leader, lost their two leading scorers to season-ending injuries and suffered through a 3-10 record in January. Yet, beyond all reason, they were still alive. A big reason for that was Threatt, who averaged 17.2 points and 7.6 assists in March to keep their playoff hopes alive.

"We're still breathing," Bill Bertka said. "Until they pronounce you dead, you've got to keep kicking."

Chapter 6

THE PUSH

March 31, 1992 to April 19, 1992

I F MARV ALBERT was commentating, he would have used his trademark phrase, "So, it has come down to this." There were 19.8 seconds remaining in overtime of the final game of the regular season for the Lakers and Clippers. Usually, it would be safe to assume the Lakers were heading to the playoffs and not the Clippers. But this hadn't been a normal season. The Clippers were in the playoffs for the first time in 16 years while the Lakers were still fighting to get there.

A miraculous set of circumstances had made it possible for the Lakers to even still be alive in the playoff hunt. They had started the season hoping to compete for a championship. Now, with their roster in tatters, they were in a must-win game with the Clippers on the final night of the season. Win, and they sneak into the playoffs. Lose, and they fail to qualify for the first time in 16 years. And they were clinging to a one-point lead.

Following a timeout, the Clippers' Danny Manning was trying to inbound the ball through the waving hands of A.C. Green. Manning found a passing lane to Doc Rivers, but he threw it a foot too wide and too high. Rivers had to long jump almost to half court just to catch it, and he almost traveled when his feet hit the court.

The Lakers frantically switched everything on defense in the hope of protecting their lead. Rivers passed to Manning at the three-point line, and Threatt left Rivers to double-team him. Manning fired the ball back to the wide-open Rivers. Byron Scott left Ken Norman unguarded in the corner to scramble to stop Rivers taking an easy shot.

Rivers passed to the open Norman who drove to the basket. Green left Manning and hustled from the other side of the key to stop Norman from getting a lay-in. Norman picked up his dribble, pump-faked Green into the air, pivoted to his left and launched a contested short jumper over the outstretched hand of Tony Smith. He tried to bank the shot in, but the ball ricocheted off the backboard and hit the right side of the rim.

Manning had done exactly what coaches tell players to do in a situation like that – he went to the front of the rim. He outjumped Campbell for the rebound and tapped the ball. It hit the back of the rim, bounced up, hit the front of the rim, and then fell through the basket. Clippers 108, Lakers 107 with 10.3 seconds remaining in one of the wildest seasons in Laker history.

The Lakers began their push for the playoffs two games in front of the Houston Rockets for the eighth and final playoff spot in the West. There would be 12 games to hold Houston off – six at home, six on the road, and eight against likely playoff teams. And they would have to do it without Magic Johnson, James Worthy, and Sam Perkins. "I don't think anybody expects us to make the playoffs," Terry Teagle said. "Not with Sam and James out and the things that have happened to us."

Then there was the question of whether the Lakers should even try to make the playoffs at all. They could shut down veterans Sedale Threatt and Scott for the last 12 games, increase young Tony Smith's role, and play for a spot in the lottery. If they made the playoffs, the highest pick they could hope for at the upcoming draft was 15th, behind the 11 lottery teams and three playoff teams in the East with worse records than the Lakers. If they missed the playoffs the lowest pick they would receive would be 11th, with a chance they might pick even higher in a draft expected to carry several transcendent talents.

The Lakers needed a roster upgrade in the wake of Magic's retirement and the upcoming crop of free agents looked skinny. There would be some fine players available, but none were franchise-altering.[64] The Lakers were over the cap anyway, making trades difficult and free agency almost impossible. The draft was their best bet to improve their roster but making the playoffs limited the opportunity. And that could be wasteful, especially since they were riddled with injuries and likely to be bounced in the first round anyway.

And of course, there were the believers in Laker exceptionalism, the theory that the basketball gods always smiled on the Lakers. "Personally,

---

[64] Xavier McDaniel, Nate McMillan, James Edwards, and Gerald Wilkins were the best of the upcoming free agents.

I hope they make the playoffs," Sacramento Kings General Manager Jerry Reynolds said. "I don't want them in the lottery. I know if they've got one ball out of the 66, they'll get Shaquille O'Neal. I have no doubt. I don't even worry about it."

Yet it was clear the Lakers weren't in the business of tanking at a longshot of drafting Shaq. They were striving to make the playoffs. There was defiance to it, a refusal to allow tragedy and injury to humiliate them. They were going for it. "We've got to fight and claw to win every game," Dunleavy said.[65]

Lakers: 3.0 Game Lead

The playoff push couldn't have started in a more perfect place – in Houston against the very Rockets team they were trying to hold off for that final playoff spot. The Rockets were in a state of disarray with Hakeem Olajuwon coming off a suspension handed down by the team on accusations he was faking an injury as a power play for a contract re-negotiation. Olajuwon would play against the Lakers but reluctantly, openly demanding to be traded. It was an ugly scene as the hometown Rocket fans booed their star player at the start of the game.

The make-shift frontcourt of Divac, Green, and Elden Campbell combined for 60 points and 33 rebounds, and the Lakers found themselves with a 103-101 lead with one minute to play. After Threatt missed a lay-up, Green sealed the win by tapping the missed shot in with five seconds remaining. The Lakers won 107-101, their fifth win in a row that pushed their lead over Houston to three games. "This was a huge game, and the difference was our front line," Dunleavy said. "Green, Campbell and Divac played super inside."

Lakers: 2.5 Game Lead

The Lakers were in San Antonio the next night to play a Spurs team reeling from the loss of All-Star David Robinson. He strained ligaments in his left thumb a week earlier, and he would not return to the line-up, not even for the playoffs. But Terry Cummings more than made up for Robinson's absence in the middle, scoring 35 points and hauling down 14

---

[65] In the modern NBA, there is no way a team in the Lakers' situation would attempt a push for the playoffs. They'd tank, no question about it.

rebounds as the Spurs thrashed the Lakers 104-86. The Lakers were returning home, but half a game had been shaved off their lead for the eighth spot.

Lakers: 1.5 Game Lead

The Lakers lost a full game in their lead over the Rockets when they committed a season-high 25 turnovers against the Seattle Supersonics at the Forum. "We played dumb, and we played careless," Dunleavy said. "And that's not a good combination." Eddie Johnson and Shawn Kemp combined for 46 points off the bench, and the Sonics beat the Lakers 96-91 at the Forum. The loss came despite 28 points from Threatt and a season-high 18 points from Smith.

Lakers: 1.5 Game Lead

The next day the Rockets defeated the Orlando Magic in Houston, meaning the Lakers needed to win their next game, a home game against the Phoenix Suns, to maintain their 1.5 game lead. They found themselves down by 16 points in the second quarter but ran off a 52-25 run over the third and fourth quarters. The rally was led by Scott and Divac who combined to score the Lakers' first 26 points of the third quarter. The run was good enough for a 109-104 win. Divac led the Lakers with 30 points and 13 rebounds while Teagle scored 22 off the bench on 11-17 shooting.

Lakers: 0.5 Game Lead

The Lakers traveled to Seattle to play the SuperSonics for the second time in four nights, a game that turned on a dime, and not in the Lakers' favor. Threatt made a driving lay-up in the fourth quarter to cut the Sonics' lead to seven points. He was grabbed and bumped before making the shot and wound up on the floor. When no call was forthcoming, Dunleavy was sent into a rage, chewing out the official before receiving two technical fouls and being ejected. Dunleavy was so angry at the no-call that straight after the ejection he went outside to the broadcaster's truck and watched the replay over and over. The Sonics were unstoppable from that point on, racking up 40 points in the fourth quarter for a 117-88 win. While the Lakers were losing to the Sonics, the Rockets were in San

Antonio defeating the Spurs 95-92 for their third win in a row, cutting the Lakers' lead down to just half a game.

Rockets: 0.5 Game Lead

The Lakers tumbled out of the playoff picture two nights later at the Forum where they failed to do what the Rockets had just done: beat the Robinson-less Spurs. The Lakers lost to San Antonio for the second time in just over a week, going down 102-94 as Sean Elliott carved up their defense with 33 points on 14-19 shooting. The loss pushed the Lakers into ninth place, 0.5 games behind Houston when the Rockets defeated the Timberwolves 117-102 for their fourth win in a row.

The loss to the Spurs came after Magic was named earlier in the day as the recipient of the 1991-92 J. Walter Kennedy Citizenship Award for his work raising awareness about HIV and AIDS.[66]

Rockets: 0.5 Game Lead

The Lakers received a huge gift from the universe when the Rockets dropped their next game 99-92 to the pitiful Dallas Mavericks who had lost 19 of their previous 21 games before facing the Rockets. But the Lakers failed to capitalize at home against the Utah Jazz. Trailing by three with 13 seconds to go, the Lakers' final possession turned into chaos. Green was forced to attempt a three-pointer that was blocked out of bounds by Malone. The Lakers then attempted to inbound the ball with three seconds remaining, but Teagle's pass went awry, rolling into the backcourt where the best Green could do was launch a 60-foot hook shot that had no chance of going in.[67] The Rockets survived their disaster against the Mavericks and maintained their 0.5 lead for the eighth spot.

---

[66] The award has been given annually since 1975 to a player, coach, or staff member who shows outstanding service and dedication to the community. The award is named in honour of James Walter Kennedy, the second commissioner of the NBA.

[67] Prior to the game Magic gave each player, coach and manager a $500 fax machine as a thank you gift for taking part in his jersey retirement ceremony. He spent $10,000 on fax machines – a very early-90s moment.

Rockets: 0.5 Game Lead

The schedule provided the Lakers with another gift – a home-and-away series against the Denver Nuggets who were on a 10-game losing streak, had a 6-31 record in the second half of the season and were without center Dikembe Mutombo.

The first game was at the Forum where the Lakers blew a 20-point lead before Dunleavy changed tactics by inserting a small line-up featuring three guards, and the Lakers struggled to a 100-93 victory. But the next night the Rockets recovered from their loss to the lowly Mavericks and defeated the Portland Trail Blazers, the best team in the West. The Rockets maintained their 0.5 game advantage on the Lakers, with four games left in the season for the Lakers and three for Houston.

Rockets: 0.5 Game Lead

The second game of the home-and-away series was played in Denver, where the Lakers went up by 13 in the second quarter and by 10 in the third. The Nuggets rallied over the third and fourth quarters and took a 108-105 lead with 33 seconds remaining on a three-pointer by rookie Mark Macon. Scott drove the lane looking for a foul, but only got a lay-up that cut the lead to one. The Lakers were forced to foul on their next two defensive stands and got lucky when Reggie Williams and Winston Garland each only made one of two. The Lakers were down 110-107 but, just like they did against Utah, they would falter on their final possession. A shambolic attempt at bringing the ball up the court resulted in Green being forced to take a wild shot from half court at the buzzer that missed.

At the same time as the Lakers' loss, the Rockets were busy in Utah working on a loss of their own – a 130-98 defeat to the Jazz. Stalemate, the Lakers still trailed the Rockets by half a game.

Rockets: 1.0 Game Lead

The season officially reached death's door the following night when the Lakers lost again, this time to the struggling Sacramento Kings on the road, 102-94. It was their fifth loss in a row, right at the time of year they needed wins more than ever. And it put them a full game behind the Rockets, with two games remaining on the schedule for both teams. The

Lakers would be officially eliminated from the playoffs with their next loss or Houston's next victory.

"Basically, it comes down to miracles," Dunleavy said. So, what exactly were the Lakers' chances of making the playoffs from this position? "Five percent," he estimated. Not exactly a vote of confidence.

Tied

In a terrible omen for the Lakers, the next night the Rockets faced the Dallas Mavericks for the second time in six days. The Mavericks had won just eight of their last 53 games, one of which was against the Rockets a week earlier. It was hard to believe it could happen again. The Rockets only had to beat the Mavericks, and the Lakers' playoff hopes would be officially over. It seemed a mere formality.

The Lakers were in Portland preparing to play the Trail Blazers the next night. Half of the team went to a bar to watch the Rockets-Mavericks game, a sort of vigil as their playoff hopes officially passed before them. Scott, Threatt, Smith, and Haley stayed behind in Brown's room and played video games. Haley's wife Stacey watched the game on TV back in Los Angeles and provided play-by-play over the phone to Haley and the others.

The Rockets' Hakeem Olajuwon scored 33 points, and 13 rebounds, and his basket tied the game at 106-106 with 33.8 seconds remaining. Olajuwon then fouled the Mavs' Herb Williams, who made one of two free throws. But the Rockets committed a cardinal sin of basketball by allowing the Mavs to rebound their own free throw miss. It forced them to foul Mike Iuzzolino to stop the clock. He made both his free throws, giving the Mavs a 109-106 lead.

The Rockets called timeout and set-up a play. Sleepy Floyd attempted a game-tying three-pointer, but it was blocked by Doug Smith. The ball found its way to Kenny Smith, who launched a three-pointer at the buzzer that also missed. The Mavericks had beaten the Rockets – again.

The Lakers were still alive. But they would have to beat the Portland Trail Blazers, the West's best team who they hadn't beaten all season, on the road to stay that way. A loss in Portland would negate the gift they received from the Rockets' loss to Dallas and end their playoff hopes.

In a twist of fate, they received a reprieve precisely because the Blazers were the best team in the West. Clyde Drexler and Jerome Kersey had been nursing nagging injuries, and head coach Rick Adelman decided to rest them against the Lakers because his team wasn't playing for anything. They already had the number one seed wrapped up, and it was more important to have both players fresh for the playoffs than it was for them to play a meaningless game against the Lakers.

Divac wound back the clock to the Conference Finals a year earlier when he had a coming-of-age performance against Blazers' center Kevin Duckworth. He registered 25 points, nine rebounds, and three blocks – frustrating Duckworth into collecting two technical fouls and an ejection in the third quarter. The Lakers hit 10 of their first 13 shots in the third quarter, went on an 18-7 run and held on for a 109-101 victory.

They were still alive. "Everybody's been throwing a lot of dirt on us. It's up to about here [drawing a line under his nose] right now, but we've still got a chance," Dunleavy said. At least a better chance than five percent it seemed.

D-Day

Both the Lakers and the Rockets played home games against playoff teams on the final day of the regular season. The Rockets were facing the fourth-placed Phoenix Suns, while the Lakers played the seventh-placed Los Angeles Clippers. The Rockets would be playing on one day's rest, the Lakers playing the second night of a back-to-back.

Two scenarios would see the Rockets eliminate the Lakers and qualify for the playoffs. If they beat the Suns, they would make the playoffs, no matter what the Lakers did against the Clippers. If both teams lost, Houston would still make the playoffs because they owned the tie-breaker against the Lakers. On the other hand, only one scenario would get the Lakers into the playoffs. They needed the Rockets to lose, and they needed to beat the Clippers.

The Rockets-Suns game turned into a nail-biter, and Olajuwon was at his best. He had 39 points, 16 rebounds, and 7 blocks and scored 11 of Houston's final 14 points. His basket cut the Suns' lead to a single point with less than a minute remaining. The Rockets fouled Kevin Johnson to stop the clock and Johnson made two free throws for a 100-97 lead. Sleepy Floyd, who had his potential game-tying three-pointer blocked two nights earlier against Dallas, had a chance at another one against Phoenix. He got a good look at another game-tying three-pointer, but it missed. The Rockets lost, and the Lakers had one final chance to clinch a playoff spot. Their fate in their own hands.

When Dunleavy called a timeout following Manning's tip-in with 10.3 seconds remaining in overtime, the Lakers' season hung in the balance. The Clippers led 108-107. The Lakers would either find a way to score one last basket and advanced to the playoffs, or their season would be over.

With the sold out Forum crowd on their feet, Scott inbounded the ball to Threatt at center court. Doc Rivers, one of the league's best defenders, crouched into a low defensive stance ready for Threatt to move either to his left or to his right. Threatt took three steps towards Rivers and used a quick burst of speed to cut left sharply. Rivers hustled to stay between him and the basket and the two players briefly made contact. Rivers flopped, falling backward in the hope of drawing an offensive foul. The official, wisely, didn't buy it and swallowed his whistle. "I love it when that happens to a defender who does a flop-a-roo," said Chick Hearn.

Rivers' flop left Threatt momentarily open at 16-feet. He stopped his dribble and rose to shoot, just as Ron Harper left Scott to hustle across the key and contest the shot. Harper almost got a finger on it, but the shot arched over his hand and fell in the basket, barely making the net move. There were 4.5 seconds remaining, the Lakers led 109-108.

The Clippers called a timeout, and the players returned to the benches for the coaches to draw up one final play. Rivers went one-on-one at the top of the key against Scott. He drove, and Scott forced him to pick-up his dribble at the free throw line. Careful not to pick up a foul, Scott stood his ground. Rivers pivoted and took a twisting shot at the buzzer that hit the back of the rim and bounced off. The Lakers won, they were moving on.

The crowd exploded in cheers as the bench players ran onto the court. Divac hugged Campbell underneath the basket. A fan proudly held up his hand-made sign that read, 'Sedale Threatt for President.'[68]

No team in NBA history had been on a ride like these Lakers had been

---

[68] Mark Heisler ended his article on the game in the *Los Angeles Times* with the line "Goodbye Shaquille O'Neal." Heisler was lamenting, perhaps in jest, that the Lakers had blown what little chance they had for the #1 pick in the draft by qualifying for the playoffs. They had missed their chance to get Shaq, for now.

on in 1991-92. Through no fault of their own, they had been left a shell of their former selves. Yet through hard work, perseverance and a ton of good fortune, they had achieved far more than anyone would have expected.

The Lakers didn't have Magic, Worthy, or Perkins for their playoff push in April. Instead, they had to find a new cast of characters to lean on. Threatt, who was given the thankless task of replacing Magic as the Lakers' starting point guard, averaged 17.1 points and 7.7 assists in April. Teagle averaged 16.7 points and shot 49% from the field during the push. Campbell, forced into the starting role in a critical part of the season in just his second year in the league, averaged 11.4 points and 7.1 rebounds for the month.

After the win over the Clippers, Threatt, whose game-winning shot gave him 24 points for the night, was asked if this game and this season was a miracle. "Yeah, I think so," Threatt said. "Nobody expected us to win."

Jerry West, who very much prescribed to a championship-or-bust philosophy, couldn't fail to see the magnitude of this team's comparatively meager achievements. "I don't think I've ever been more proud of a Laker team," he said. "With what has happened to us, it's a great tribute to all of the players and coaches. Amazing is a word that's used a lot, but it really is amazing."

In total, the Lakers had lost a total of 186 games to injury or retirement in 1991-92.[69] Their preferred starting line-up of Magic, Scott, Worthy, Perkins, and Divac didn't play a single game. Their Plan B starting line-up of Threatt, Scott, Worthy, Perkins, and Divac played just two. For 80 of the 82 games, the Lakers had a starting five that was, at best, a Plan C line-up.

"I remain highly optimistic of achieving the ultimate goal in professional basketball, winning an NBA championship," Dunleavy wrote in *Streets & Smiths* at the start of the season. But all of that changed the moment Magic retired. Without him, they went from 58 wins in 1990-91 to 43 in 1991-92. Their scoring dropped from 106.3 to 100.4 per game. Their field goal shooting went from being 11th best in 1990-91 to 24th in 1991-92. Their offensive rating fell from fifth best in the league a year

---

[69] Magic 82, Divac 46, Worthy 28, Perkins 19, Smith 6, Brown 3, Campbell and Sparrow 1.

earlier to 13th. Without their 6'9 point guard gobbling up rebounds, they became the second-worst rebounding team in the league.[70] In December they had their first losing month for 13 years, and in March they had another. Yet, the regular season ended, and they were still alive.

"Portland – here we come," said Hearn.

---

[70] The Lakers played a much slower pace in 1990-91, making these numbers kind. They're much uglier when compared with Riley's last year as coach in 1989-90. The Lakers' scoring dropped by 7 points a game, their shooting dropped 4%, their assists per game dropped by 5, their rebounding by 3.

Chapter 7

AS L.A. BURNS

April 23, 1992 to May 3, 1992

M IKE DUNLEAVY CALLED a timeout during the fourth quarter of Game 3 against the Portland Trail Blazers. The Lakers were facing elimination at home in a must-win game. They would either win and keep their season alive, or they would lose and start the summer earlier than anyone imagined back at training camp. The score was tied, and Dunleavy wanted to draw up a play.

He did what he had done countless times during his two seasons as Lakers coach – crouched in front of his players with his whiteboard to illustrate what he wanted them to do. But he could tell the players were distracted.

It was not unheard of for a player at the Forum to have a momentary lapse of concentration during a timeout. Maybe Jack Nicholson just walked past the bench on the way to his courtside seat. Or a player turned his head to quickly confirm that, yes, that is Ice Cube sitting next to Dyan Cannon. But this was different, the players looked worried.

Dunleavy is one person who doesn't get distracted. He heard the PA announcer's voice at the Forum say something, but didn't hear what. What he did hear was the reaction from the crowd, and it wasn't one he was accustomed to hearing at a basketball game. He stood up to look around the stadium to see what was going on. The PA announcer repeated the message, and this time Dunleavy heard him loud and clear.

"Do not go east on Manchester. You must go west on Manchester toward the beach or north on Prairie toward Culver City."

If Dunleavy didn't know immediately what that meant, Byron Scott did. He grew up in Inglewood, and his childhood home was within walking distance to the Forum. He was a huge Lakers fan as a kid but never had any money for tickets. As a teenager, he would sneak in to watch Jerry West, Elgin Baylor, and Wilt Chamberlain rip up opponents on their home floor. He was a local kid in every sense of the word. He knew the community that lived around the Forum because he was a part of it. And he knew exactly what the message from the PA announcer meant. He knew it had gotten bad outside. And a lot of people would be getting hurt.

To say the Portland Trail Blazers was a bad first-round match-up for the Lakers would be an understatement. The Blazers were considered front-runners in 1991 to make it back to the NBA Finals when the Lakers stopped them in the Conference Finals. They were considered even greater front-runners in 1992.

The deep, flexible, athletic line-up they had in 1991 remained intact. But they were even stronger in 1992 because of the spectacular play of Clyde Drexler. He had been a star in Portland for six years but upped his game further in 1991-92. His increased his scoring average by four points on the previous year to 25.0 a game while maintaining his rebounds and assist numbers. He would finish second to Michael Jordan in MVP votes. "You used to be able to count on spells of inconsistency from him," Bill Bertka said of Drexler. "I don't see those now, and I wish I did." The Blazers finished the season with a 57-25 record, best in the West and second only to Chicago in the league.

These were not the same Lakers who upset the Blazers a year earlier. They squeaked into the playoffs by the thinnest of margins with a roster that looked more like a M*A*S*H unit than a basketball team. The top three scorers for the Lakers in the series against Portland in 1991 weren't there in 1992.

Look at these numbers from the six-game series against the Blazers in 1991:

Magic: 20.7 points, 8.0 rebounds, 12.7 assists
Worthy: 18.7 points, 3.3 rebounds, 4.0 assists
Perkins: 17.5 points, 8.2 rebounds, 2.0 assists

That's what the Lakers were missing one year later – 56% of their scoring, 54% of their rebounds, 79% of their assists. "I felt like I had a little more firepower last year at this time," said a grinning Dunleavy.

"Obviously this is not the same team that knocked us out," Blazers coach Rick Adelman said. "I think we really respect the Lakers. Just what they've done this year – you've got to give (Dunleavy), his coaching staff and his team tremendous credit. No one expected them to be here. Their veterans stayed with it. They fought their way down the stretch, and they deserve to be here."

But the consolatory language from Adelman didn't extend to the Portland players. Maybe it was the veterans on the team trying to conjure motivation for a series that was a foregone conclusion. Or maybe it was genuine. But talk from the Blazers players was of revenge.

"Them beating us last year, I think it's really appropriate that we play the Lakers," Buck Williams said. "We need to beat them and put that scenario behind us. This year we get a chance to go back and right a wrong, take care of business this year we should have taken care of last year." Jerome Kersey wouldn't be giving the Lakers any concessions either. "You can't feel sorry for them because they don't have all their guys," he said. "We're not out there to babysit." If teams throughout the league had grown tired of losing to Magic and the Lakers for 12 years, they had their prime opportunity to beat up on them now.

The Blazers also had injury concerns of their own. Drexler had been bothered by a painful right knee for two weeks, and Kersey had a sore left shoulder and right ankle. Both players were rested over the last week of the season, participated in training, and said they were ready to go.

In terms of strategy, Dunleavy had few options. He would be forced to play whatever warm bodies he had on the bench. That included Chucky Brown, Cliff Robinson, and Rory Sparrow, who had played sparingly and were only on the roster because of injuries. Portland was the best rebounding team in the league, while the Lakers were one of the worst. To stay competitive, Dunleavy knew the Lakers would have to slow the Blazers' pace and keep them off the offensive boards. "If you don't do those two things, then they just walk away with it," Dunleavy said. "They'll destroy any team they play if they own the boards and the break." It was a big ask.

Game 1 in Portland wasn't pretty. The Blazers ran up a 36-point lead in the first half before eventually winning 115-102. The Lakers were hit by a freight train. They trailed by 10 points midway through the first quarter, then 20 points early in the second quarter, and by 36 within 23 minutes. Dunleavy's hope of stopping the Blazers' transition game and keeping them off the glass was for naught. The Blazers outscored the Lakers 25-0 on fast break points, and out-rebounded them 26-10, in the first half. "Everything we were afraid of happened," Dunleavy said. "Basically, the game was over after the first half." Teagle scored 12 of his 22 points in the fourth quarter and led a late rally. But the best the Lakers could do was make the final score something vaguely respectable.

Scott top-scored for the Lakers with 22 points and Green added 19 points and 10 rebounds. However, the Lakers were dominated by a foursome of Blazers players, proving powerless against Drexler, Williams, Clifford Robinson, and Terry Porter.[71] The Divac-Duckworth match-up that was so pivotal a year earlier was irrelevant in Game 1, with Divac scoring five points and Duckworth scoring eight.

After the game, the Lakers marched onto the team bus only to find their driver had been drinking. Scott wasn't sure if the guy was a happy Blazers fan who had a few too many celebratory drinks or a Lakers fan who had drowned his sorrows. Either way, the team took cabs back to the hotel.

At practice the next day, Dunleavy sounded like he had all but conceded the transition game. "This team, in a footrace, beats any team in the league," he said. Instead, he put the emphasis back on rebounding, pointing out that the Lakers had outrebounded the Blazers in three of their five clashes during the season. So, it could be done. "We used to have a saying here when we had all the great teams – 'no rebounds, no rings,'" Scott said. "It still applies."

If Game 1 was ugly for the Lakers, Game 2 was hideous. The Blazers led 89-62 early in the fourth quarter, but this time they didn't take their foot off the accelerator. They continued the onslaught, winning 101-79 as the Lakers looked powerless to do anything to stop them. The Blazers had dominated both games in Portland for a 2-0 series lead. The Lakers backs were now officially against the wall, on the brink of elimination after just two playoff games, a very new experience for the franchise.

If the Lakers could take solace from anything in Game 1, it was that they shot 50% from the floor despite the sizeable loss. Not so in Game 2, where they shot 28% in the first quarter and 38% for the game. Despite the emphasis on it, they lost the rebound count 55-35. Scott had 16 points, and

---

[71] Robinson had 24 points, Drexler added 22 points and 10 assists, Williams had 21 points and 13 rebounds, and Porter had 20 points, 7 rebounds and 8 assists.

Teagle added 15. But they were the only two players to register anything on the box score that looked vaguely like NBA offense.

They became even more banged up too. Scott came down with the flu before Game 2 but suited up anyway. Green had banged his hip during the first game, and it bothered him throughout Game 2, limiting him to just two rebounds in 27 minutes. "A.C.'s not a complainer. He's going to go out and battle," said Dunleavy. "But I know at the half when he's played 19 minutes and gets one rebound, he's hurt." Teagle banged his right knee during Game 2 and winched in pain when ice was applied later. "I'm ready to go home," he said. "It's been a long, long week."

The second game was a bruising affair, with the Blazers bullying the Lakers from pillar to post. Dunleavy complained about the officiating, saying the Lakers didn't stand much of a chance if the officials weren't going to call the game straight. Dunleavy's comments were dismissed as gamesmanship and went largely unnoticed. But Divac's comments drew criticism for revealing a lack of mental preparedness for playoff basketball. "They play so physical, so angry because they have lost to the Lakers before," Divac said. "They think this is the same team as last year. It's not. They want to fight with us, I don't know why."[72]

Divac's comments seemed to only further annoy the already irritated Blazers. Duckworth, who manhandled Divac with 19 points and 9 rebounds in Game 2, entered the playoffs in a bad mood. After making the All-Star Game in 1991, he had a disappointing 1991-92 season. His play had been a source of frustration with Blazers fans who didn't hide their feelings throughout the season. He drew a standing ovation after Game 2, but didn't care – he couldn't forget that same crowd had booed him several times during the year. "This doesn't make up for nothing," he said "I'll never forget it. I know that people aren't true, making me feel all great one moment and then talking about me behind my back the next."

So, Duckworth wasn't in any mood to be empathetic to Divac's complaints, especially after he was criticised for letting Divac outplay him in the Conference Finals a year ago. "He tends to get to me when he does all this flopping, and the referees go with it," Duckworth said. "Now I just don't care. If he flops, he just flops." Duckworth told Kerry Eggers from *The Oregonian* that Divac was a wimp.

---

[72] Can you imagine how much Magic would have chewed Divac out behind closed doors for comments like that if he was still on the team?

Divac was hurt by the comments. "I was so mad," he said. "I couldn't believe he called me that. I never could say that, even if he was, let's say, a wimp." While virtuous of Divac to avoid being overtly mean, it wasn't exactly an attitude that typically worked in playoff basketball where a little nastiness usually went a long way. Divac heard another round of criticism for his passive play and his inability to deal with playoff physicality. "The way people perceive Vlade, if they can beat him up early and get to him early and pound him and pound him, then he's not going to have a good game," Dunleavy said. "He's got to get through that."

In fairness, it wasn't only Divac who struggled with the Blazers' bruising style of play. The whole team had wilted in Game 2. Dunleavy showed the team footage of them begin shoved, pushed and bullied in the hope of sparking a reaction. Third-stringer Jack Haley figured himself the perfect solution to the problem, believing he would bring a different attitude to the team if given the opportunity to play. After all, he was once pulled into David Stern's office to explain why he had registered flagrant fouls in eight consecutive games with the New Jersey Nets.

"When I'm on the floor, there will be no lay-ups, there will be no pushing and shoving around," Haley said. "The difference between me and the other players on our team, I'm not going anywhere if anything wants to erupt or if someone wants to push or shove me. I'd be more apt to retaliate rather than just yell at the referee."

The Blazers didn't mind the suggestion from Haley, who averaged 1.6 points in 8 minutes per game on the season, that he should see more minutes as an enforcer. "Do us a favor," Danny Ainge said. "Play Haley 40 minutes."

Dunleavy switched things up for Game 3. He started Teagle at small forward, moved Green back to his natural power forward spot, and used Campbell as the sixth man. He thought he was conceding the battle on the boards by returning to small ball, but it had the opposite effect. The three-guard line-up outrebounded the Blazers, and they raced out to a 14-point lead in the first quarter. "That's why I'm a coach," Dunleavy said. "I don't know those things." The Blazers whittled the deficit down to 53-47 at the half and tied it up midway through the third quarter. From there the game remained close.

With less than a minute remaining in the game, Divac poked the ball free from Duckworth and Threatt found Scott streaking to the basket for a dunk and a 102-99 Laker lead. Porter was left wide-open on the next play and tied the game with a three-pointer. Scott's jumper down the other end hit the rim four times before falling out. Drexler secured the rebound and instead of calling a timeout, elected to push the ball with the Lakers on their heels. He found Williams for a contested but makeable lay-up that he missed at the buzzer.

Overtime was a shootout, and the lead changed hands on seven consecutive possessions. Kersey made a steal and was fouled, making one of two free throws for a 116-114 Blazers lead with 38 seconds remaining. Following a timeout, the Lakers went to Campbell who was posting up against Kersey. Divac slipped Williams on the weak-side, and Campbell found him with a bullet-pass under the basket. Williams and Kersey swarmed Divac but fouled him on the way up for his shot. Divac converted the lay-up and the free throw, completing the three-point play for a 117-116 lead.

The teams exchanged free throws on their next few possessions, and the Lakers held a 121-119 lead with 5.5 seconds to play. Drexler launched a three-pointer over Threatt that went in-and-out, the buzzer sounded, and the Lakers were somehow still alive.

After averaging 18.5 points off the bench in the two losses in Portland, Teagle scored a team-leading 26 on 9-14 shooting as a starter in Game 3. Threatt had 24 points on 8-13 shooting, and Scott added 22 points. But the game belonged to Divac. Just as he had done a year earlier, he answered criticism of his toughness with a more aggressive game, finishing with 18 points and 7 rebounds. The Lakers overcame an unstoppable performance from Drexler who scored 42 points, shot 14-23 from the field, grabbed 9 rebounds and dished out 12 assists.

The Lakers sold 16,690 tickets for Game 3, but the crowd was estimated to be somewhere between 14,000 and 15,000. There was a good reason why there were so many empty seats.

On the afternoon of the game, Scott drove to the Forum as he normally would on game day to begin his preparation. As he drove that afternoon, he heard about the acquittals of the four California Highway Patrol (CHP) officers accused of beating Rodney King.

A year earlier, members of the CHP had attempted to pull King over on the 210 freeway in the San Fernando Valley. King was on probation for an armed robbery charge, feared being sent to prison, and led the police on a high-speed chase. When he eventually pulled over, four CHP members beat King with a baton 56 times, kicked him six times and tasered him twice. The incident was caught on camera, and the four officers were charged with assault and use of excessive force. It appeared to be an open-and-shut case, but after a two-month trial, the officers were found innocent.

The verdicts were handed down in an already tense environment. Six months earlier, Soon Ja Du, a convenience store owner, was found guilty of manslaughter for the shooting death of Latasha Harlins, a fifteen-year-old African-American girl. Du thought Harlins was attempting to steal orange juice and shot her in the head. The jury in the case recommended the maximum prison sentence of 16 years. Instead, the judge sentenced her to five years' probation, community service, and a $500 fine. The sentence heightened racial tensions in the city, and the not-guilty verdicts in the King case were the final straw.

The verdicts were handed down at 3:15pm, about four hours before the Lakers-Blazers game was due to begin. Once Scott arrived at the Forum, he found every television tuned to news coverage of protests unfolding in front of the County Courthouse and police headquarters. Players watched television in silence. At 6:15pm they got dressed and went to work trying to keep their season alive.

None of the players, coaches or early arriving fans could know just how quickly the unrest would spread. At 6:46pm, the Forum was busy. The carpark was full, and around 14,000 fans were either comfortably in their seats or lining up outside with tickets in hand, waiting to file into the arena. At that same time, just four streets away, Reginald Denny was forced to stop his dump truck in the middle of a busy intersection. Denny was brutally beaten within an inch of his life in a sickening attack shown live on TV.[73] It was a turning point of the riots, the moment it became clear the unrest had turned deadly. Less than an hour later Fidel Lopez was dragged out of his truck at the exact same intersection. He was beaten so badly that his left ear was almost severed off and as he lay unconscious his chest, torso, and genitals were spray-painted black.

Fans at the Forum had little knowledge that surrounding neighborhoods of the arena were ablaze. It was 1992, there was no mobile internet and few people had cell phones. The focus of Forum staff shifted

---

[73] Denny's skull was fractured in 91 places and pushed into his brain. His left eye was dislocated so badly that it almost collapsed into his sinus cavity.

to getting fans home safely after the game. The Forum received over 1,000 calls from concerned families who had no other way to reach their loved ones at the game. If staff knew where the person was sitting, they would tell them they needed to phone home. Many fans managed to call home from Forum offices or arena pay phones, and family members told them of the events unfolding nearby.

Inglewood police were concerned more than 14,000 people might be about to drive into the middle of the chaos, and were in constant communication with Jerry West. It was imperative fans be given information about safe routes home, and the information be corrected and changed based on what was happening outside.

By half-time, there were several patches of empty seats at the Forum. Fans who stayed for the second-half left quickly after the game. There was usually a lot of activity around the Forum after a game, but players walked out to a ghost town when they headed to their cars. Green was no more than half a block away from the Forum when he saw emergency lights and heard gunfire. "That's when I put the windows up, turned the radio off and tried to get out of there and off the streets as fast as I could," he said. "I didn't know what would happen next."

Talk from the Lakers following Game 3 was not about their gutsy overtime win against the Blazers, it was about their city. Scott was the most vocal of the players in condemning the verdicts. He seemed weary from the history of racism in the city that could enable such a ruling to happen. Scott had little faith in the system because it had let down his community too many times. "I'm upset by the verdict," he said. "I thought it was pretty obvious what they did was unjustified. Then again, it's been happening here in L.A. for so many years, it's no surprise to me."

Scott refused when asked to condemn the actions of the rioters because he understood what they were doing and why they were doing it. "All the things leading up to the Rodney King case and them being acquitted, I think it builds up inside you, and sooner or later you have to let it out some way or somehow," he said.

The challenge for Scott and the Lakers was to somehow put the civil unrest out of their minds and concentrate on basketball. "I'll try to keep the TV off as much as possible. It makes it tough. My family's scared.

Every neighbor around us is a little frightened," Scott said. [74]

Game 4 was meant to take place two nights later, but there was no way it could go ahead at the Forum. The unrest continued for several days, and the National Guard instituted a dusk-to-dawn curfew. The Lakers and the league began looking around for the closest, largest site that was available. Eventually, they negotiated to hold the game at the Thomas & Mack Center in Las Vegas.[75]

It had been a unique season for the Lakers from the start, unlike anything any NBA team had been through before. They started it by losing their superstar leader because he had tested HIV positive and they had endured an almost endless run of injuries. Now they would be bringing what was left of their roster to play a home game in Las Vegas because of civil unrest in Los Angeles. "You can sit here and say, 'What else could happen?'" Dunleavy said. "It's been from start to finish a tough year."

The riots had taken any sense of joy the team or the fans could have felt from the remarkable Game 3 win. Sport was secondary to what was taking place in L.A., even for the players. And it had robbed the team of their sense of purpose. "The whole thing about the playoffs comes down to pride in your city," Dunleavy said. "But I think all that's negated by what's going on. It basically turned this into something that's almost meaningless."

It had been an especially difficult season for Divac, both professionally and personally. He had back surgery that sidelined him for more than half of the season, the first major injury of his career. Civil war broke out in his native Yugoslavia, drawing a wedge between him and his native basketball family. New Jersey's Drazen Petrovic and Boston's Stojko Vrankovic had been teammates of Divac on the Yugoslavia national team for years. So too were Dino Radja and Toni Kukoc, who would both soon be in the NBA. They won silver together at the 1988 Olympics in Seoul and won the European Championship the next year in Yugoslavia.

Divac and Petrovic had been roommates in Seoul and had formed a tight bond. As rookies during the 1989-90 season, they would call each other almost daily. Divac would share his joy of playing alongside Magic

---

[74] Magic was angry too. "They should have gotten something," he said. "Not guilty on this, not guilty on that, but not guilty on every charge? Come on."

[75] The Clippers had to move Game 4 of their series to the Anaheim Convention Center. The Lakers were criticised for moving their game out of L.A. while the Clippers were prepared to play in a smaller venue if it meant keeping the game in the metro area.

in Los Angeles while Petrovic would vent his frustrations about being glued to the bench in Portland. They helped each other settle into their new lives in the United States, and the fact that Divac was from Serbia and Petrovic was from Croatia was never an issue.

But their relationship began to break down immediately after they won the FIBA World Championship in Argentina in 1990. Ethnic tensions between Serbians and Croatians had been building since the end of the Cold War, and a separatist movement in Croatia was gathering momentum. The Yugoslavian team had been instructed to ignore any demonstrations by Croatian separatists during the tournament, but there was an incident when the team was celebrating the championship win. A fan ran onto the court waiving a Croatian flag and made a derogatory comment to Divac. He should have walked away, but Divac was insulted by the comment and forcibly took the flag from the man. He said he would have done the same if the man was holding a Serbian flag. To him, the championship hadn't been won by Croatia or Serbia – it had been won by Yugoslavia. The incident made Divac a bigger hero in Serbia than he was already, and a villain in Croatia.

Now, Petrovic and Vrankovic would make small talk on the court with him before a game, but it was just for the cameras. Neither player would talk to him off the court. Ten years of friendship had been broken. It was painful for Divac, he had spent more time with Petrovic than he had his own brother. He wanted to share the frustrations of his injury, the loss of Magic as a teammate, the pain of having his toughness questioned in the playoffs. But he couldn't. Now, his adopted American city was tearing itself apart too.

Most of the 15,478 in attendance for Game 4 were Lakers fans. The Lakers wore their home gold uniforms, while the Blazers were in their black road uniforms. But the game felt, at best, like an exhibition or, at worst, a road game. Both teams were in unfamiliar territory – different lighting, different baskets – so, there was no true home-court advantage.

The game itself resembled the two in Portland more than the one at the Forum. The Blazers unleashed their quick transition game, and the Lakers were once again powerless to stop it. A 16-2 second-quarter run by the Blazers blew open a close game, putting them in the driver's seat. The Lakers would score just 33 first-half points and trail by 16 at the break.

Threatt would top score for the Lakers with 17; Scott continued to fight with 15 points; and Green hustled the best he could with 11 points and 14 rebounds.[76] But it was all for naught. The Lakers were outscored in every quarter as the Blazers blitzed them, running them off the floor just like they had done in Portland. The Blazers took the game 102-76 and won the series 3-1.[77] Like that, the weirdest Laker season in franchise history was mercifully over.

After the game, Dunleavy told the team how proud he was of them for the effort they put in all year. "Not very many teams start the season in Paris and end it in Vegas," he told them. "I was proud to be part of it."

Green called the season a year of turbulence that tested the nerve, character, and faith of the team. A 43-win season and a first-round exit would hardly have seemed like a successful season for the Showtime Lakers. But this wasn't Showtime. For this team, with everything they had been through, making the playoffs and winning a game against the best team in the West was an enormous achievement.

Order would be restored in Los Angeles within days of the series ending. At the end of the unrest, 55 people were dead, 2,400 people were injured, and 12,000 people were under arrest. More than 5,000 buildings were damaged or destroyed, 3,100 businesses were affected by looting, and property damage totalled more than $1 billion. The process of rebuilding, both from the physical damage and the collective psychological trauma, would take a long time.

Green reflected that the same strength of will that bought these Lakers to the playoffs would be needed from the Los Angeles community for a brighter future. "You can say, 'We've been dealt a bad hand,'" Green said, "but just because you're short-handed, that's still not a reason to take things in your own hands. We had to do things collectively. I don't think any one individual could have done it. We needed one another. I guess the message to the people of L.A. is – we need one another."

---

[76] For the record, Haley didn't make it onto the floor in Game 4 after promising to fight the Blazers players. He received a 'Did Not Play – Coach's Decision' for Games 3 and 4.

[77] After eliminating the Lakers, Portland would make it all the way to the NBA Finals where they lost in six games to the Chicago Bulls.

PART II:
GHOSTS OF SHOWTIME

Chapter 8

THE WAITING IS THE HARDEST PART

May 4, 1992 to September 29, 1992

I T WAS AN unhappy summer for Jerry West. In early August, he was robbed at gunpoint in the Forum carpark. He had just parked his car and was walking toward the Forum at around 9:00am when he was accosted by two men. One pulled a handgun, demanded West's wallet and the diamond-encrusted 1985 NBA championship ring he was wearing. West owned one championship ring as a player and five as an executive, but he only ever wore the 1985 ring. It was the year the Lakers finally beat the Boston Celtics for the championship after they had broken his heart so many times as a player. The thieves were never caught, and he never got the ring back.

He was also in a bind. It was the earliest the Lakers had entered the off-season in years. Crawling their way through tragedy and injury to sneak into the playoffs, West thought the 1991-92 season had been one of their most gratifying. But he couldn't figure out all season what this team really was. Nobody could. They were never healthy long enough to tell.

But it was clear the roster as currently constructed wasn't going anywhere special. Not without Magic Johnson. The preferred starting line-up was an average of 30 years old, which would be fine if they were pushing for a title. But they weren't. The reality was they were in the bottom quarter in the league in almost every statistical category. They needed everything – scoring, rebounding, playmaking, defense, quickness, youth, and a marquee player. West had some assets, but they each had flaws limiting their return in a trade.

James Worthy was an All-Star and averaged almost 20 points a game in 1991-92. Pat Riley, for one, would have loved to bring him to New York. Byron Scott had been a starter on three championship teams, a pedigree that would make him in demand. Sam Perkins was a big body, a decent rebounder, and a stretch four back when they were a rarity. But all three were 31 years old, and each had seen their efficiency plummet without Magic setting them up for easy baskets. It would be a challenge to find a trading partner willing to part with a young player to acquire them.

The best trade assets were Vlade Divac and A.C. Green, but West was hesitant to give up either. Teams would be interested in acquiring Divac despite concerns over his toughness because of the unique skill set he brought to the center position. Green's hustle, defense, and rebounding made him the kind of player every team wanted on their roster. But Divac was only 24 years old and the Lakers' best young player. And West wanted to get more of the qualities Green possessed on the roster, not less.

The approach West would take in the off-season all depended on one thing. Would Magic, who had hinted at a comeback all season, be back? The Lakers had a flawed roster but adding Magic would make many of those flaws disappear. Without him, they were an aging team struggling to make the playoffs, but with him they were a veteran team competing for a title. If Magic returned, West would only need to tweak the roster. But if Magic stayed retired, he would have to look at big, painful changes. Until Magic decided, West was stuck.

West suddenly found himself in the market for a new coach when Mike Dunleavy accepted an offer to become the Milwaukee Bucks' head coach and general manager. He had done a fabulous job his first two seasons with the Lakers, coaching the team to the Finals in his first year and holding the team together through a tumultuous season in his second. But the Bucks' offer was his dream job. Milwaukee was his basketball home, it was where he finished his playing career and started his coaching career as an assistant. Not only would he be a coach, but he'd have authority over player movement too, a level of control many coaches craved. The offer was everything he wanted, and he couldn't pass it up.

Dunleavy was still under contract with the Lakers and West didn't want to see him leave. But West couldn't in good conscience stand in his way. As compensation, the Bucks sent their 1992 and 1995 second-round draft picks to the Lakers, and West went looking for a replacement.[78]

---

[78] Dunleavy would go on to have a long coaching career in the NBA, serving as head coach of the Milwaukee Bucks, Portland Trail Blazers and Los Angeles Clippers. He was head coach of the Blazers team when they had a rivalry with the Lakers in the late 90s and early 2000s, meeting three times in the playoffs while he was coaching them.

There were several replacement options. Former Showtime sixth man Michael Cooper had long been considered a likely candidate to go into coaching. But his resume was thin, having only been a part-time assistant with the Lakers in 1991-92. Chuck Daly, coach of the Bad Boy Pistons who won two NBA titles in Detroit, was busy coaching the Olympic team and would be looking for work for the upcoming season. Mike Fratello, the former Atlanta Hawks coach, was available but maybe didn't want to leave his media job with NBC. Del Harris, the former Bucks head coach, was a long-time favorite of West but he was considered a front-runner for the Sacramento Kings head coaching job.

Sports radio was filled with rumors the Lakers already had the perfect man for the job – Magic. "I don't think the Lakers are considering it," Lon Rosen said. "And I don't think Earvin is considering it. But if the Lakers asked him, he would listen." West said he would talk to Magic about the job, though he doubted Magic would be interested in it. Magic had long expressed an interest in owning an NBA team once his playing career was over, but he had never talked about coaching. Besides, West was waiting to hear if Magic was coming back as a player, not a coach.

Ultimately, the Lakers couldn't look past long-time assistant coach Randy Pfund, and six days after Dunleavy's departure the team named him as their new head coach. Pfund had been a loyal Lakers servant for years, recruited by Bill Bertka when Pfund was an assistant coach at Westmont College. His first job with the Lakers was projectionist during film sessions, and dissecting opponent plays. Riley appointed him an assistant coach in 1985, and he was on the sidelines during three championships. He applied for the head coaching job in 1990 when Riley stepped down but was passed over when Mike Dunleavy was given the job. He could have been forgiven for feeling slighted, but he knocked back an offer to join Riley in New York a year later in favor of staying in L.A.

In Pfund, the Lakers had a technocrat – an X's and O's guy who had never played in the NBA but had climbed the coaching ranks through his technical breakdown of the game.[79] When introduced to the media as the new head coach, he said the Lakers' rebounding in 1991-92 was an embarrassment, and he wanted to toughen up the inside game. He talked about re-designing the offense by not returning to either Showtime or

---

[79] For years, technocrats like Hubie Brown, Mike Fratello and Dick Motta dominated NBA coaching. The early 1990s saw a trend away from technocrats towards hiring former players as head coaches, which has continued to today.

Slowtime. Instead, he wanted to play a '90s style offense', though he didn't specify what that exactly meant.

Pfund had his old assistant job to fill but also Jim Eyen's spot on the bench, who followed Dunleavy to Milwaukee. He hired Chet Kammerer, who had been the head coach at Westmont College for 17 years and had given Pfund his first assistant coaching job. Now Pfund, the understudy, was head coach with his former mentor his assistant. The other spot went to former Laker Larry Drew, who rumor had it was picked because Pfund felt threatened by Cooper and didn't want him too close to the top job.[80]

The Lakers entered the 1992 NBA Draft with a new coach, their first-round pick, and Milwaukee's second-round pick as part of the Dunleavy deal. Their own second-round pick had been sent to Miami four years earlier in an agreement that the Heat wouldn't select Kareem Abdul-Jabbar in the 1988 expansion draft.[81]

The Lakers would be picking 15th in the first round, their highest selection since drafting James Worthy with the first overall pick in 1982. The Washington Bullets offered their first-round pick, sixth overall, to the Lakers for Worthy. West knocked the offer back because he was working on a much bigger deal.[82] He was talking to Houston about sending Worthy, Divac, Elden Campbell, and their first-round pick to Houston in exchange for Sleepy Floyd and unhappy superstar Hakeem Olajuwon. The deal would have changed the trajectory of the franchise and the entire league, but it never came together.

In pre-draft workouts, West was enamored with two players – Pepperdine University's Doug Christie and University of Missouri's Anthony Peeler. Both were excellent athletes, offered different things on the court, but had question marks hanging over them.

Christie was the West Coast Conference Player of the Year with

---

[80] In his year away from basketball, Larry Drew worked as a speaker, fundraiser, and administrator for the Magic Johnson Foundation.

[81] Each NBA team could protect up to eight players from being selected in the expansion draft. The Lakers didn't protect Abdul-Jabbar because they wanted to protect Mike Smrek and Tony Campbell, who were both far younger. Imagine Abdul-Jabbar finishing his career in a Heat uniform. It's a disgusting thought.

[82] Washington selected Tom Gugliotta with the pick. Other players still available at that spot were Walt Williams, Todd Day, Clarence Weatherspoon, Adam Keefe, Robert Horry, Harold Minder, Bryant Stith, and Malik Sealy.

averages of 19.5 points, 5.9 rebounds and 4.8 assists his senior year. He was an all-around player who did everything well – he could score, rebound, and was an excellent passer. But there were two red flags. Two knee operations raised concerns about his durability, and he didn't have a natural position in the NBA. He was maybe a small forward, a point guard, or nothing at all.[83]

Peeler was named Big Eight Player of the Year as a senior. An excellent shooter, he averaged 23.4 points and shot 42% from three. He was undeniably talented, but several incidents brought his character into question. In the week leading up to the draft, he pleaded guilty to a felony weapons charge and two related misdemeanors after allegedly attacking a woman, putting a gun to her head. He was put on five years' probation and was, subsequently, cleared to take part in the draft. But three days before the draft he was arrested again for allegedly punching an old girlfriend in the face and wrestling her to the ground. Prosecutors chose not to press charges because of inconsistencies in the alleged victim's story, but it was more than enough to make teams nervous about drafting him.

Both Christie and Peeler were available when the Lakers picked, and the West ultimately went with Peeler over Christie.[84] With the second-round pick from Milwaukee, they selected Duane Cooper out of the University of Southern California.[85] Cooper was a local product, born in Benton Harbor Michigan, but played his high school and college ball in Los Angeles and was a huge Lakers fan growing up.

Peeler's trouble with the law made teams pass on him, resulting in the Lakers getting a player more talented than they expected with their 15th pick. "If someone had told me two years ago I'd have had a chance to draft this kid, I'd have told everybody they were crazy," West said. "Obviously, if all of this didn't happen he wouldn't have been around."

Peeler was quick to say he had learned from his mistakes and promised he had matured. But he balked at the idea he had demonstrated a pattern of poor behavior. "I don't feel it's a pattern, it's just something

---

[83] In today's more positionless NBA, this wouldn't matter at all. But if a player didn't have a clearly defined position in the early 90s, they didn't fit anywhere.

[84] Christie was picked two selections later by the Seattle SuperSonics at 17.

[85] The Lakers pick sent to Miami ended up being the 42nd selection and they selected center Matt Geiger out of Georgia Institute of Technology.

that happened," Peeler said. West's philosophy was simple. "We're going to view him as a player whose future is ahead of him and whose past is behind him," he said.[86]

Terry Teagle, who had gone from being potentially waived at the start of last season to playing a key role in the playoff push, signed a one-year, $800,000 contract with Benetton Treviso of Italy. Despite how well he played late in the season, it was unlikely the Lakers would have extended a contract offer to him. He was 32 years old, and his minutes would mostly go to young Peeler, who played the same position.[87]

West finally used the $1.25 million cap space they received when Magic retired, signing 37-year-old veteran center James Edwards to a two-year deal. Edwards was originally drafted by the Lakers in 1977 before being traded in the middle of his rookie season to Cleveland for Adrian Dantley and Dave Robisch. He would go on to play a key role on two Detroit Pistons championship teams in 1989 and 1990 before spending the 1991-92 season with the Los Angeles Clippers. Edwards replaced Jack Haley, who had reconstructive surgery on his left knee and was out for the season, as Divac's primary back-up. He may have been in his late 30s, but Edwards was a quality player off the bench and could still make his patent turn-around jump shot.[88]

West was in advanced contract negotiations with free agent Rod Strickland, who was exactly the kind of player the Lakers needed. The 25-year-old point guard was young, athletic, had plenty of upsides and averaged over 13 points and 8 assists a game the previous season in San Antonio. He was keen to come to Los Angeles, but West couldn't bring himself to finalize the offer. If Magic chose not to return, signing Strickland would be a no-brainer. But if Magic came back, Strickland would be superfluous, and any players moved to fit him under the cap

---

[86] If the Lakers hadn't made their playoff push, they likely would have had the 11th pick. Robert Horry, Bryant Stith, and Malik Sealy were all available but it's hard to imagine them going past local hero Harold Miner. He grew up in Inglewood and was a star at USC, sharing the backcourt with Lakers second-round pick Duane Cooper.

[87] Teagle came back to the NBA to finish his career in April 1993, signing with the Houston Rockets, the team who drafted him, when guard Vernon Maxwell broke his wrist. He played the final two games of the season and sparingly in the playoffs. He finished his basketball career in 1995 at the age of 35 after a season each in Italy and Argentina.

[88] Edwards looked a lot like Hightower from Police Academy, which was also a win.

would be wasted. Strickland couldn't wait on the Lakers forever and accepted a deal with the Portland Trail Blazers. West let him walk. He couldn't give up hope on Magic coming back.

Magic spent a good deal of his summer with the Dream Team. To say the US was dominant wouldn't do them justice. Billed as 'the greatest team ever assembled,' they lived up to the hype.

They took part in the Tournament of the Americas in Portland, winning by a margin of 51.5 points per game.[89] It was a team of All-Stars and, appropriately, minutes were spread evenly. Barkley led the team in scoring with 16.3 per game, Karl Malone was second with 14.8. Magic averaged 9.0 points, 4.2 rebounds, and a team-high 9.7 assists per game.

The reaction to the team in Barcelona for the Olympic Games was more like The Beatles coming to town than a team of athletes. The Dream Team were undeniably the stars of the games, with thousands of fans cramming out front of the team's hotel in the hope of getting a glimpse of the players. The US won gold with an average winning margin of 43.8 points per game. The only game that resembled a normal kind of thrashing, as opposed to an annihilation, was the gold medal game against Croatia that the US 'only' won by 32 points.

Magic suffered a hamstring injury that forced him to sit out two games and limited his minutes in two others. But he was fully healthy for the gold medal game, scoring 11 points and handing out a game-high 6 assists. The Dream Team never did play the Australian team that had caused controversy over their reluctance to play against Magic.[90] The two teams were in separate divisions during the preliminary round, and Australia was knocked out several rounds before they would have faced the United States.

Larry Bird retired following the Olympics, while Magic's future was still unclear. He was now faced with answering the question he had danced around for almost a year – would he return to the Lakers?

---

[89] The Tournament of the Americas, now known as the FIBA Americas Championship, is a qualifying tournament for the Summer Olympic Games and FIBA Basketball World Cup for teams in the Americas.

[90] Magic and Phil Smyth did eventually find themselves on court at the same time when the Magic Johnson All-Stars played five exhibition games against the Australian national team during a tour of Australia in March 1995. The tour came and went without incident and without Magic, Smyth, or the media ever bringing up the past controversy.

Magic initially intended to decide within two weeks of returning from Barcelona, but he dragged the process out for eight weeks. It drove West crazy, and he would call Rosen almost every day complaining about Magic not making up his mind. "I absolutely know nothing about it. No one has talked to us about it," West said. "I sure wish Magic would talk to us. It's important for him to talk to the press, but we would like for him to talk to us too."

Unexpectedly, Magic told reporters in Barcelona he was leaning towards a return but maybe not with the Lakers. He was interested in whatever opportunity gave him the best chance at winning, and maybe that would be reuniting with Riley in New York. He walked back his comments a few days later, saying he only talked about New York because he was concerned the Lakers were about to break up their nucleus. He also pointed out the not-so-minor detail he was still under contract with the Lakers.

Magic dragged out his decision, but in fairness he had a lot to work through. He had to consult with doctors to hear what they thought the impact of a return would have on his health now they had been treating him for ten months. The news from doctors was positive. Contrary to medical expectations in November, Magic's health had improved from when he was first diagnosed, which doctors attributed to his diet, decrease in travel, and exercise routine. He had worked out relentlessly since his retirement and put on 20 pounds of muscle. He had never been in better shape.

The doctors didn't give him the all clear to return so much as they gave him their blessing. They could only theorize what the impact would be. There was only one way for them to know for sure – Magic play, and they continue to monitor his health.

With the medical question resolved, Magic had more to consider. He knew he could still play basketball at a very high level. The All-Star Game and the Olympics were evidence of that. But what would be the reaction if he decided to come back? He had reason to believe it would be a problem. He had experienced discrimination since announcing he was HIV positive and he had encountered many people who were reluctant to play him one-on-one for fear of contracting the virus.

But he also had reason to believe it would be fine. Some people seemed to have no fear of playing with him at all. When the Miami Heat were in town to play the Lakers in January, center Ron Seikaly hit the court early to get some shots up. When he got there, he found Magic shooting around. Seikaly, who had never spoken to Magic before, challenged him to a one-on-one match. Seikaly was just as physical with Magic as he was with everybody. If Seikaly was willing to play against him despite not even knowing him, maybe others would too.

There had been dissenting voices when Magic said he would play in the All-Star Game and the Olympics. He certainly felt the awkwardness in the locker room before the first practice prior to the All-Star Game. But had he not proven it was fine when he played, with nothing terrible happening? And had he not proven it a second time in Barcelona?

Then there was his HIV and AIDS awareness and advocacy work, which he took very seriously. The Magic Johnson Foundation had been established in the weeks following his announcement and running it, along with his other business operations, was a big commitment. He had been invited by President Bush to join the National Commission on AIDS shortly after his announcement. He served from November 1991 to September 1992, when he stepped down due to frustrations with the Bush administration's failure to respond to the commission's funding requests. Magic felt he had been used as a political pawn and the White House was trying to cash in on his celebrity. The experience led Magic to become a vocal critic of President Bush. It also made it clear he needed to chart his own course via the foundation.[91]

But more than anything, Magic just missed playing. The game had been a fundamental part of his entire life. From being taught how to play by his father, winning a championship at Everett High School, an NCAA Championship at Michigan State and five NBA titles with the Lakers – basketball was central to who he was. And it had all been taken away from him in an instant.

Magic certainly didn't act like a retired player. He played full court basketball every day at Sports Club L.A. and UCLA. It was just like old times. He would still throw no-look passes, but instead of Byron Scott being on the receiving end for a wide-open three-pointer, it was a random stockbroker or lawyer.

He had spent the entire season with the Lakers. He would arrive early at the Forum before games and, dressed in playing gear, would go through his normal shooting warm-up. After using the team shower, he

---

[91] The foundation runs education and awareness programs and free HIV testing. It has raised over $20 million for charity and given out $4 million in scholarships.

would dress. But instead of putting on his uniform he would put on a suit. Instead of playing, he would sit on the bench. He knew he was fit, strong, and could still play. He knew his old teammates, and Lakers fans wanted him to. And he wanted to play. But he couldn't.

Magic had been toying with coming back all season. The first report of a possible comeback came in the lead-up to the Lakers game in Chicago in December. Behind the scenes, he made up his mind he was going to return in January. He called Rosen and told him to inform the Lakers he would be back next week. That all ended when doctors urged caution and talked him out of it. Then in March he decided to come back for the playoffs but was again talked out of it, eventually relenting when the Lakers' run of injuries took them out of serious contention. He wanted to play but was always being held back.

The 1991-92 Lakers team photo looks like any other – two rows of Lakers players flanked by the coaching and training staff, all standing at center court at the Forum. But what isn't shown is Magic shooting at one of the baskets out of frame. The players asked him to be in the photo, but he declined. It didn't feel right for him to be in the photo because he wasn't on the team. But it hurt that he couldn't take part. He still felt like a basketball player, like a Laker. But he wasn't.

That was until September 29, 1992, when Magic walked into the same room at the Forum Club where he stood 327 days earlier to announce his retirement. Reporters were once again packed into the room. He walked to the podium and cut straight to the chase just as he did a year earlier. His first words were what Lakers fans had been wanting to hear for almost a year. "I'm coming back to the Lakers," he said. "I'm playing again." The room of reporters broke into cheers and applause. Magic gave a loud sigh. "Finally," he said.

The mood of the press conference in September 1992 couldn't have been more different than the one in November 1991. For his retirement press conference, Magic stood in front of a dour black curtain wearing a black suit. At his comeback press conference, he stood in a blue suit in front of a bright blue curtain with Lakers banners pinned to it. As upbeat as he tried to be in November, it was a tragic scene. But the press conference in 1992 was a light affair, with plenty of smiles and laughs.

He joked that he bribed his wife with $1 million to let him come back, then said she was sick of him hanging around the house watching tapes of his old games anyway. He said they would have to cover up his retired jersey because he's not dead – #32 was his, and he'd be wearing it again. "I asked myself, do I really want to go through this again?" he said. "Jerry West on my back, Randy Pfund kicking me in my rear end. Do I really want that? And I said, yeah, I want all of it."

Magic was already under contract for $2.5 million for the 1992-93 and 1993-94 seasons. League rules at the time dictated a player could sign an extension only if they had two or fewer years remaining on their contract. As a result, Jerry Buss got his chance to do what he was trying to do a year earlier and increased Magic's salary to make up for the years he was underpaid. Buss gave Magic a 1-year contract extension for the 1994-95 season worth $14.6 million.[92] A balloon payment such as this was not totally unheard of. Larry Bird and Clyde Drexler both had them included in their contracts. But the amount was astounding in 1992. It was the largest single-season salary in US sports history, and 11 of the 27 NBA teams had entire payrolls lower than that figure at the time. It was a remarkable contract, especially since Magic only committed to play the upcoming season and would re-assess his situation after that.

Unlike the controversy when he announced his intention to play at the Olympics, the immediate reaction to Magic's comeback was positive. Riley, Bird and Indiana Pacers President Donnie Walsh expressed their happiness at the news. David Stern was openly supportive once again, just as he had been when Magic wanted to play in the All-Star game. Sacramento Kings first-year head coach Garry St. Jean and Scott Layden, director of basketball operations of the Utah Jazz, seemed almost pleased to have an old rival back. "I think it's great he's playing. Why not?" Philadelphia head coach Doug Moe said. "Who are we to decide whether a guy should play? If I could have played until I was 50, I would have."

Magic compromised with his doctors who were still concerned about the intensity of the NBA schedule, and that the amount of travel and fatigue could damage his health. He would play 50-60 games, sit out back-

---

[92] It is very reminiscent of the massive two-year $45.5 million contract extension the Lakers gave Kobe Bryant, three weeks into the 2013-14 season when he was on the sidelines still rehabbing his career-redefining Achilles injury. The contract received endless criticism because it tied up the team's salary cap on an injured player, making it difficult to recruit free agents. But it was consistent with the way the Buss family do business – looking after their superstars, even when it doesn't necessarily make financial sense.

to-backs and only play parts of long road trips. Magic joked at the press conference that he would make sure he would play in Boston and New York. "I'm not going to miss the good ones," he said.

The exact number of games Magic would end up playing in 1992-93 would depend on what his doctors advised. But it didn't matter. The Lakers suddenly became championship contenders again. They might not have the firepower to defeat the Chicago Bulls, who had just won their second straight title. They may not have enough to get past the suddenly powerful Phoenix Suns who had just added Charles Barkley to an already impressive line-up.

But then again, maybe they just might. The Lakers now had a far deeper, faster, and athletic roster than they had in 1990-91. It made the last season just seem like a bad dream. The fog had lifted. Anything was possible now. Magic was back.

Chapter 9
THE FIRST COMEBACK

October 9, 1992 to November 2, 1992

T HE LAKERS OPENED training camp at the University of Hawaii in Honolulu less than two weeks after Magic Johnson's comeback announcement. Six of the 12 players who were on the 1992 playoff roster were gone. Terry Teagle was playing in Italy. Chucky Brown, Rory Sparrow, and Cliff Robinson, who were all signed as injury stop-gaps during the season, had been waived. So too had Keith Owens, who made the cut as a rookie at last camp despite long odds but struggled in limited minutes during the season.[93]

The starting line-up of Magic, Byron Scott, James Worthy, Sam Perkins, and Vlade Divac that got the Lakers to the NBA Finals in 1991 would return in 1992-93.

The bench that proved anemic in 1991 was vastly improved, especially in the backcourt. Sedale Threatt would return to the role the Lakers originally intended him to play – backing-up both Magic and Scott and providing a scoring punch off the bench. Joining Threatt in the backcourt was rookie Anthony Peeler and third-year Tony Smith. The frontcourt would consist of veterans A.C. Green and James Edwards. Joining them was Elden Campbell, who had built nicely upon his rookie performance by playing bigger minutes in his second season due to injuries to Worthy and Perkins.

There was one roster spot open and three players fighting for it – Sean Higgins, Duane Cooper, and Alex Blackwell. 24-year-old forward

---

[93] Sparrow ended his 12-year NBA career after being released by the Lakers. Robinson never played in the NBA again. He finished his career playing in the CBA and Greece. Chucky Brown would go onto play for an NBA-record 12 teams in his 14-year NBA career. Keith Owens would play in France, Spain, and the CBA before retiring from basketball in 1994.

Higgins, who had been a high school star in Los Angeles, had signed in August after being waived by the Orlando Magic to free up salary for draftee Shaquille O'Neal.[94] Cooper was living a dream when he was drafted by the team he grew up watching. He told Worthy he had attended one of the Lakers' championship parades as a teenager, making Worthy instantly feel old. The long-shot was assumed to be Blackwell, an undrafted small forward out of Monmouth University.

The person with the biggest job at camp was rookie head coach Randy Pfund. He had spent three months writing over 100 pages of offensive plays that would all need to change now Magic was back. Pfund would have to start from scratch one week out from the start of training camp. But it was a problem he was pleased to have. His task was to re-organize the offense around having Magic on the floor. It wasn't easy but was a piece of cake compared to Dunleavy's job a year earlier of retrofitting the offense three games into the season because of Magic's sudden absence.

Another issue for Pfund was finding a way to ensure consistent play with Magic in-and-out of the line-up. But there were reasons to be optimistic it could work. The Celtics won 51 games in 1991-92 with Larry Bird essentially playing part-time because of back problems. And that was with Bird being limited when on the court because of injury. When Magic would be in uniform, he would be his usual self. Pfund figured they now had a year of experience playing without Magic, which should help them adjust on the nights he wasn't with them.

Managing minutes would be an issue for Pfund with all his veteran players. Worthy's workload increased to ridiculous levels without Magic in 1991-92. He averaged a career-high 39 minutes a game, far too high for a 30-year-old veteran who had as much wear and tear on his body as Worthy. It was the legacy of playing all the way to June almost every year in Riley's fast and physically punishing system. Worthy's 10 years in the NBA was the equivalent of 12 years for the average NBA player. It wasn't a coincidence the season that saw Worthy have his heaviest workload was also a season that ended in injury.

Entering camp was like coming home for Magic. "It was like old times, once we got started," he said after the first day. "I was so nervous this

---

[94] After hardly playing in San Antonio his rookie season, Higgins averaged 8.6 points in 32 games with Orlando after a mid-season trade to the Magic in 1991-92.

morning. I must have woken up three times last night, just waiting. And it finally got here, like I was a rookie again. It was great."

Magic was careful not to come on too strong on the first day and instead focused on working his way back gradually. His teammates had gotten used to him not being part of the team, even if they never wanted him to go in the first place. He also knew he needed to allow space for Pfund to assert his authority in his first practices. But Pfund was just pleased to see him back on the floor. "I didn't see any difference," he said. "About the second or third time down the floor, he threaded a pass through the whole crowd for a lay-up. That looked pretty familiar to me."

Magic made one exception when easing back in – he got right in the ear of Divac just like he used to. During Divac's first two seasons, Magic would push him to be more physical and assertive. After a lost season of development due to injury, the Lakers were hoping Divac would make a leap in 1992-93 with Magic back. But he showed up to camp out of shape.

Gary Vitti had put Divac on a weightlifting program shortly after the Lakers were eliminated from the playoffs. He was making good progress before he went to Greece to start pre-Olympic training with the Serbia-Montenegro team. But in another painful blow, Serbia-Montenegro was banned from international competition at the urging of the United Nations. Individual athletes could compete as Independent Olympic Participants and not under a national flag, but teams couldn't compete at all. Discouraged, Divac abandoned the training regime. On the bright side, he said he had given up smoking after the Lakers had been trying to get him to quit for three years.

Campbell was another player whose training dedication had proven less than perfect in the past. He was an enigma during his first two years in the league. His nickname was 'Easy' because of his laidback personality, but sometimes he was a little too casual. He would be switched on and aggressive one day, distant and uninvolved the next. But Vitti was pleased with Campbell's work in the off-season. He had bulked up to 245 pounds, up from the 217 he weighed as a rookie. "You don't want to say it's difficult, but Elden is Elden," Vitti said. "He works at a certain speed. But you've got to give him credit. I wouldn't say he's perfect, but he's much improved."

The Lakers' 1992-93 pre-season was far more ordinary than their bizarre schedule a year ago. They had eight games scheduled over two weeks, starting in Hawaii where they were already based for training camp. Besides James Edwards, who would be forced to miss the entire pre-season because of a strained Achilles tendon, the Lakers were healthy.

Magic would play in five of the games but wouldn't release a schedule for when he would play and when he would sit out. That would go for the regular season too. "If he changes it, people will assume he's sick," said Lon Rosen. "If he gets hurt, then he'd have to adjust it anyway, and people will say, 'I bought tickets.'"

The Lakers opened the pre-season against the Portland Trail Blazers in front of a sold-out crowd of 7,584 at Neal S. Blaisdell Arena near downtown Honolulu. Magic received a loud ovation when introduced to the crowd and then got to work, draining a long two-pointer on the first play of the game. From there he did what he always did so well – fuelled the Lakers' offense with spectacular passes that dazzled the crowd.

He blew past Jerome Kersey in transition before firing a pass to Perkins under the basket for a lay-up. He backed Strickland down in the post, drew a double-team and found Divac open at the top of the key for a long jump shot. He played a perfect give-and-go with A.C. Green that resulted in a bounce pass in traffic to Green for an easy lay-in. He wrapped another bounce pass around Strickland for an uncontested lay-in by Worthy.

When Scott stole the ball in the Blazers' backcourt, he found Magic at half-court. In one motion, Magic caught the ball and fired a bullet bounce pass between Kersey and Mario Elie that found Worthy streaking to the basket for a finger roll and the foul.

The Lakers won 124-112, and it was just like old times. Magic scored five points on four shots and dished out 14 assists in 27 minutes. There were easy baskets for everybody.

"I was thrilled," Scott said. "I was excited for him. I think he was excited. Everybody on the team who had played with him was excited." Worthy, always the realist, said he wouldn't believe the Lakers of old were back until they won another championship. But even he could not escape the obvious. "It's only one game, but there's a different feeling now that he's back," he said. Magic admitted to being anxious before hitting the court but was focused on the big picture. This was all about getting ready for opening night when the season started for real.

Pfund never divulged details of what he meant when he said the Lakers would play a '90s-style offense.' If the first pre-season game was any indication, the Lakers' new attack would be a mix of Showtime run-

and-gun and Slowtime grind-it-out. After being one of the slowest-paced teams in the league under Dunleavy, the Lakers under Pfund clearly intended to run.

They looked good with Magic leading them in transition. They ran on Portland turnovers, misses, and on makes too. And they looked just as good in the half-court. The extra bulk Magic had put on in the past year was immediately evident, and it made him difficult to guard. Magic was always much bigger than the average NBA point guard, but with his extra bulk, he looked more like a forward now. The sight of Strickland guarding him in the post was almost ludicrous – Strickland looked like a grammar school player against him. He would either overpower Strickland for a lay-in or draw a double-team and find the open man. [95]

There appeared no anxiety amongst any of the players about playing against Magic. Doctors briefed the Players Association about the minimal risk playing against Magic represented. Buck Williams, an influential figure in the Players Association, wrestled and held Magic like always. "I crunched him a couple of times," Williams said. "Which he expected from me. I said, 'Welcome back.'"

The Lakers faced Portland again the following night. Magic didn't play, he had flown back to the mainland to start the promotional tour for his autobiography *My Life*. While the Lakers were taking the floor at Neal S. Blaisdell Arena, Magic and Cookie were taping an episode of the Oprah Winfrey Show. The Lakers' transition game that had run the Blazers off the court in the first game was nowhere to be seen. It was hard to know if the failure to run was because of Magic's absence or a change in defensive strategy by Portland. Every time the Lakers tried to run they found multiple Blazers back waiting for them. The Lakers lost big, falling 112-83. More worrisome was Worthy's left knee, surgically repaired in the off-season, which limited him to only 14 minutes and was swollen and painful after the game.

Next up for the Lakers were two games at the annual GTE Everything Pages Shoot-out at the Forum. The first game against the Philadelphia 76ers was a homecoming for Magic, who would play at the Forum for the first time in almost exactly a year. "I'm very excited," Magic said before the

---

[95] The Lakers' pace numbers under Dunleavy were 94.1 in 1990-91 (third slowest in the league) and 92.6 in 1991-92 (second slowest in the league).

game. "To walk down that runway again, turn left, see that Forum floor, lead the troops out once again. I've been waiting on this."

The Lakers made quick work of the 76ers, getting a 138-111 win. Magic scored 12 points and handed out 14 assists in 20 minutes. "I've been lost, and I finally made it home," he said upon reflection of playing at the Forum again. "What killed me the year I was out was that I knew I could still do it. If I had an injury, or if it was my time to go, then I would've gone out. But I knew I could still do it."

Magic was the only known HIV-positive athlete in the world, and press interest in his comeback, even in pre-season, was intense. Magic held a press conference before the 76ers game, and every game for the remainder of the pre-season, to meet media demands. He always handled the media with poise and ease throughout his career, but he detested the pre-game press conferences. They interfered with his pre-game routine, and he grew tired of different reporters asking him the same questions, that were usually about his health and not basketball.

Instead of preparing for the 76ers, Magic spent the hour before the game fielding questions about an article by columnist Dave Kindred of *The Sporting News*. Kindred had claimed Magic was bisexual, that he contracted HIV through homosexual activity, and accused him of being dishonest with the public. Kindred didn't base his column on any specific information. Instead, he used statistics on the disease that said men in the United States had only a one-in-500 chance of contracting the virus through heterosexual activity.[96]

The Sporting News article was quickly followed by an article by Jan Hubbard in *Newsday* that said a prominent NBA player had been spreading rumors Magic was bisexual. Magic said the Kindred article was false. He said he knew which player was spreading rumors about him but refused to say publicly who it was.[97] "If you're going to say it, be a man, account for your action," Magic said. "I've always accounted for my actions. I'm right here." Not only was Magic hurt by the rumor being spread by a close friend, but he didn't want to be talking to the press about his sexuality. He just wanted to play basketball.

On the second night of the Shoot-out, the Lakers faced Pat Riley and the New York Knicks. They were without Magic, but also without Green

---

[96] The statistics were true for the United States, but 76% of the millions of people world-wide with the virus in 1992 had contracted it through heterosexual activity.

[97] It was Isiah Thomas.

and Smith who sat out with niggling injuries. Worthy, who also missed the game against Philadelphia, was again out because of his aching knee.

The shorthanded Lakers put up a good fight but succumbed to the Knicks, 107-104. Perkins and Threatt handled most of the scoring, but Lakers fans were mostly focused on rookie Duane Cooper. The rookie scored 12 points, including a buzzer-beater to end the first quarter that drew a chant of *"Cooop!"* from the crowd, just as they used to for Michael Cooper.

Magic, Worthy, and Green were back in the line-up two nights later at the San Diego Sports Arena against the Sacramento Kings. The Lakers improved to 3-0 with Magic in the line-up with an easy 133-117 victory. Magic, again, played great – recording 14 points, 7 rebounds, and 13 assists in 27 minutes of action. Worthy's knee was still not 100%, but he wanted to test it. In the end, he lasted only 13 scoreless minutes.

The Lakers played the Kings again four days later in St. Louis where they recorded their first victory without Magic, winning 119-112. Peeler, playing in Missouri for the first time as a pro after starring there at college, scored 17 of his 22 points in the fourth quarter and wowed the crowd with several driving dunks.

When not in the Lakers line-up, Magic continued the promotional tour for his autobiography. He found reporters covering the tour didn't want to talk about the book, just like reporters at Lakers games didn't want to talk about basketball. Magic wrote his book to tell the story of his basketball career and to educate people about HIV and AIDS. Instead of a platform to discuss safe sex and HIV testing, Magic was forced to answer questions about his sexuality.

Considering it took until 2014 for the United States to celebrate its first openly gay athlete, one can imagine attitudes towards homosexuality were far less enlightened in the early 1990s.[98] And Magic's promotional tour got ugly, degenerating into an I'm-Not-Gay tour. Magic felt compelled to openly discuss his escapades with women to deflect from speculation about his sexuality. He felt that pressure while writing his book too, which included a chapter on that very thing. It got to new, cringe-worthy levels the further the book tour went. When asked if he was

---

[98] Jason Collins became the first publicly gay athlete to play in any of the four major North American pro sports leagues when he played for the Brooklyn Nets (against the Lakers at Staples Center) in 2014.

gay on the Arsenio Hall Show he replied he wasn't, and the crowd responded with applause and cheers. It wasn't great. Magic's image had taken a hit in the aftermath of his retirement when his hidden lifestyle became public. Hearing him talk about it made it worse. He came across as a hetero-meat-head bragging about all the women he'd conquered.

It damaged him as an HIV and AIDS advocate too. It made little sense for a person promoting safe sex and abstinence to go on national TV and brag about being promiscuous. Magic was the most famous HIV advocate in the world, and whenever he spoke, he was representing the millions of people in the world with the disease. That included a lot of people in the gay community, yet he was publicly and repeatedly distancing himself from them.[99]

Tennis star Martina Navratilova was one of the many vocal critics of Magic's performance on the tour. "If it had happened to a heterosexual woman who had been with a hundred or two hundred men," she said, "they'd call her a whore and a slut." What would the reaction have been if it had happened to her, an openly bisexual athlete? "They'd say I had it coming," she said.

Rosen had never seen Magic more miserable than he was on the promotional tour. He informed Random House that Magic would discontinue his promotional efforts for the book, stating the publicity wasn't in his best interest.

Magic was back with the Lakers in Memphis where they took on the Washington Bullets. The Lakers won 110-106, improving to 4-0 with him in the line-up. The story was the same for Magic. He played well, recording 13 points and 14 assists in 31 minutes. But questions from reporters before and after the game were only about two things – how his health was holding up, and whether he was gay. He just wanted to be a basketball player again and be treated like he always had been. But it was proving to be impossible.

The Lakers rolled into Chapel Hill, North Carolina for a game against the Cleveland Cavaliers, their last of the pre-season. The game didn't get off to a good start for Magic or the Lakers. Magic posted up Craig Ehlo, attempted his patent junior skyhook, but it rolled off the rim. Moments

---

[99] Magic became a much better HIV and AIDS advocate on behalf of the gay community in the years that followed, and he was an exceptional advocate for the gay community, especially the black gay community, when his son came out in 2014.

later he attempted a long pass to Worthy that flew out of bounds.

Midway through the first quarter, he attempted to back Ehlo down again. Ehlo was reaching across Magic, trying to slap the ball free when Magic rose for a shot. Ehlo hit his right arm and was whistled for the foul. From the bench, Higgins told Vitti he thought Magic had gotten scratched. Vitti got the attention of the official who halted Magic's free throw to examine his arms. Clearly frustrated at the intrusion, Magic told the official he didn't have an injury. The official was satisfied, and the game continued.

Vitti decided to examine Magic's arm himself during the next timeout. He lifted Magic's arm and found a small scratch, no bigger than a fingernail. He just as easily could have ignored it, but league protocols dictated any open wound, even non-bloody wounds like this, must be covered. He pulled a four-by-four gauze pad out of his jacket pocket, handed it to Magic and told him to wipe away any perspiration. Vitti got a cotton-tip applicator and sprayed benzoin on it, a substance that ensures pads will stick to sweaty skin and applied it to Magic's arm.

Under league rules, Vitti should have been wearing rubber gloves but he knew to wear them would send a mixed message to players. "I didn't forget to put gloves on," Vitti explained. "I chose not to. It was a non-bloody wound in a controlled situation, one that was so small the official couldn't see it."[100]

Vitti and Magic could feel the eyes of every person in the arena on them as Magic received treatment. Vitti put a sweatband over Magic's small bandage to ensure sweat wouldn't make it fall off. When Magic re-entered the game with the band on his arm, he could see the look of terror in the eyes of the players. Magic kept playing, the Lakers lost 103-92, but nothing about the rest of the game felt normal. It showed in Magic's performance, and he finished with 8 points on miserable 1-10 shooting and 4 assists in 27 minutes.[101]

Reporters after the game asked Magic if there was a problem with the cut. "No. Nooooo," he responded. "Anybody who gets cut, not just me, anybody, you just go, get it fixed. Boom. Come right back." He quickly changed topics, talking about how he wasn't concerned about his poor

---

[100] Vitti would later be cautioned by the Occupational Safety and Health Administration for failing to follow safety protocols.

[101] Magic averaged 10.4 points and 11.8 assists in 26.6 minutes per game in five pre-season games.

shooting against Cleveland and he was ready for the regular season to start in six days' time.

The story of Magic getting scratched spread quickly in the following days. A photograph of Vitti treating Magic made national headlines. Stories about the incident often bent towards sensationalism, exaggerating the risk to Vitti and the players. The story emboldened people around the league who had secretly held doubts about the safety of Magic's return to voice their opinion. Fears that were mere whispers before the Cleveland game turned brazen after it.[102]

Ehlo said he wasn't worried about playing against Magic, before or after the scratch. But other Cavs players were. Gerald Wilkins admitted he was scared to touch Magic after the scratch. "Everybody's talking about it," he said. "Some people are scared. This could be dangerous to all of us, but you're dealing with Magic Johnson, so people are handling it with kid gloves." Chris Morris from the New Jersey Nets said, "Everyone is trying to watch out for themselves with the virus around." Phoenix Suns president Jerry Colangelo said Magic shouldn't play because other players feared his infection, saying, "Risk is risk."

All of that was a warm-up for the interview that would become the quintessential moment of the controversy. Karl Malone, a teammate of Magic at the All-Star game and on the Dream Team, rolled up his sleeves to show his arms to a *New York Times* journalist. "Look at this, scabs and cuts all over me," he said. "They can't tell you that you're not at risk, and you can't tell me there's one guy in the NBA who hasn't thought about it." He dismissed the Olympics as an example of it being safe to play against Magic. "The Dream Team was a concept everybody loved. But now we're back to reality," he said. Malone's face, with eyes appearing full of fear, was broadcast across the country. "Fact of the matter is, if you've got the AIDS virus, it would be hard for me to play as hard as I'm capable of playing," he said.[103]

---

[102] Magic received a similar scratch during the Olympics that was treated with a band-aid and nobody seemed to care.

[103] Years later, Malone was asked if he regretted making those comments now that he knows he was wrong. His response: "I don't regret saying it because it happened." Which is a fabulous philosophy. It means someone could go through life without ever learning hard lessons because, 'Hey, I did what I did.'

Three days after the Cleveland game, and three days before the start of the NBA season, Magic phoned Rosen and instructed him to inform the Lakers he was retiring again. Rosen cut back at Magic, telling him he was a coward if he was retiring because of the scratch. But it wasn't just that; Magic knew players across the league were frightened to play against him. If they were too scared to play their hardest against him, then it was not good for the NBA, and it wasn't good for him.

Magic believed his comeback had become a distraction from basketball and that wasn't what he wanted. He was always someone who played the game with unbridled joy. But the barrage of media attention his comeback garnered took all the fun out of playing and turned it into a grind. He had seen enough to know the season was going to be a circus.

It would have only gotten worse too with news breaking a few days later that Magic was being sued by a woman from his hometown of Lansing, Michigan, who said he knowingly infected her with the HIV virus. No doubt there would have been endless rounds of post-game questions about the case.[104]

The announcement of Magic's re-retirement came through a statement. "After much thought and talking it over with Cookie and my family, I've decided that I will retire for good from the Lakers," it read. "It has become obvious that the various controversies surrounding my return are taking away from both basketball as a sport and the larger issue of living with HIV, for me and the many people affected."

Magic spoke to the media for the first time at the Sports Arena before the Lakers' opening night game against the Clippers. "I play the game because I love it and because I have fun doing it," he said. "And it got to the point where I knew I couldn't have fun playing."

In a different interview, he was asked how he felt about Malone's comments. "I'm hurt, I'm hurt inside, not at him but because I won't get a chance to play because of what he said," Magic said. "I'm not going to take it out on him because I understand he has to look out for himself, but it's too bad it's at my expense."

On the other side of the world, Australian player Phil Smyth felt vindicated by the controversy. He had been criticised in the lead-up to the

---

[104] Magic admitted to having sex with the woman but denied being responsible for her being HIV positive. The woman claimed Magic infected her the one time they had sex in June 1990, 16 months before Magic retired. The case was dismissed in December 1993 with neither side confirming nor denying the dismissal involved a settlement agreement.

Olympics because of his concerns about playing against Magic. Concerns it now seems American players also shared. "All those people who said I was a fool are now the fools," Smyth said. "Now he's playing against the NBA stars things are different. Now it's they who are starting to ask the same questions. The bottom line is that in the US they are hypocrites, one minute saying it's terrific and wonderful, the next changing their story now that it's all turned around."

Magic's re-retirement was a blow for the AIDS community. His comeback was meant to be a shining example for the world that people living with HIV can live normal lives. Instead, his comeback became a very public example of the very kind of discrimination the community was speaking out against.

"It is tragic that someone as beloved and respected as Magic Johnson has had to leave his life's work because of people's unwarranted fears," said Dr. David Rogers, co-chairman of the National Commission on AIDS. Jeff Levi, director of governmental affairs for the Washington-based lobbying group, AIDS Action Council, agreed. "I think it's a commentary on how deep-seated ignorance and discrimination have been allowed to take root, and it's tragic that someone around whom there has been so much publicity could not overcome this kind of discrimination," he said.

There was a sense of finality to Magic's re-retirement. The narrative had changed, it was no longer HIV that ended his career but people's fear of it. Fans were being robbed of the joy of watching him play, and Lakers fans robbed of a title-contending team, because of the fear and bigotry of players. Magic sitting out the 1991-92 season seemed like a tragedy because he was assumed to be too sick to play. But over the course of the season, the world learned that wasn't the case. He was the same Magic as before.

Magic's re-retirement a year later was something else entirely. The comeback he had hinted at for an entire season was over before it really began because of the attitudes of players. There was no sense those attitudes would ever change either. It felt like the end of his career. Magic wouldn't be playing basketball anymore. Not because he couldn't, but because other players wouldn't let him. He was being pushed out of the league by his peers. It was an undeniable injustice.

Chapter 10
CONSISTENT INCONSISTENCY

November 5, 1992 to December 30, 1992

W HEN THE LAKERS took the floor at the Sports Arena for their opening night match-up against the Los Angeles Clippers, they expected to have Magic Johnson with them. He was at the arena, but he wasn't in uniform. Instead, as the team was busy warming up, he was explaining to reporters why he had decided to retire again.

Jerry West had again lost an entire off-season. For the second straight year, he saw his well-laid plans turn to ruin because his best player suddenly departed at the start of the season. The hope of Magic coming back dictated every move West made, or more to the point, moves he didn't make. He kept the team's core intact because he hoped they would make a championship push with Magic. Now, the goal in training camp and pre-season of competing for a championship would have to change. There was little reason to believe the Lakers without Magic in 1992-93 would be any better than they were without him in 1991-92. This was now a team in need of rebuilding.

Randy Pfund had intended to run a motion offense but threw away those plans at the start of training camp when Magic announced his return. Instead, he put in place a fast-breaking offense that had now been rendered ineffective without Magic. He would now be forced to return to the slower-paced attack the Lakers ran under Mike Dunleavy, while gradually implementing his original motion offense. All without the benefit of training camp.

With Magic now gone for good, fans begun to turn away. The team was selling one season ticket package every few days throughout the off-season. In the days after Magic announced his comeback, they were selling a package every half hour. Now many of those fans requested refunds, arguing they were misled.

The Lakers moved Magic to the voluntarily retired list, freeing up an additional roster spot. Duane Cooper, Sean Higgins, and Alex Blackwell had been competing all pre-season for a final roster spot that had suddenly turned into two spots. Higgins was an assumed shoe-in, but the Lakers made the surprise move of waiving him the day before opening night and retaining rookie free agent Blackwell along with second-round pick Cooper.[105] It was quite a turnaround for Blackwell who had been given the impression at the start of camp that he wasn't likely to make the cut. When he received his copy of the Lakers' new media guide, he asked John Black, Lakers VP of Public Relations, why he wasn't included in the player profile section. Black's explanation that they didn't include marginal players unlikely to make the team almost brought him to tears. But now he was officially a Laker.

And with that, another season of diminished expectations began. That the Lakers were once again a middle-of-the-road team wasn't in doubt; the only question was how Magic's re-retirement would play itself out. But it would quickly become clear. These Lakers would spend the first two months of the season defying the odds at every turn, and not always in a good way. They would be a bafflement, picking up impressive wins against the league's best teams and then dropping embarrassing losses to its worst.

Another worrisome trend would also soon be obvious – the diminished play of James Worthy. At some point, every NBA player crosses over into the dreaded decline years where their skills and athleticism rapidly dissipate. It's just a question of when. Worthy started to look for the first time like he was entering the early twilight of his career. He had been one of the Lakers' leading scorers and All-Stars for eight straight years, but he suddenly looked a lot older than his 31 years. It was obvious from the get-go the knee injury that ended his season in March had robbed him of his explosiveness. His shooting would be worrisome in November, before bottoming out in December.

---

[105] Higgins spent the 1992-93 season with the Golden State Warriors before playing in Greece in 1993-94. He was back in the NBA from 1994-1998, playing in New Jersey, Philadelphia, and Portland. He retired from basketball at the age of 32 after spending three years playing in the CBA, Greece, Russia, and Venezuela.

The Lakers did manage to run on opening night, getting a 114-112 win over an expected playoff-bound Clippers team on a game-winning 20-foot jumper by Byron Scott with 13 seconds remaining. But they followed the win by losing their home opener to a team not expected to finish anywhere near the playoffs. Magic sat watching from a baseline seat as the Lakers lost 124-114 to Sacramento, the first time the Kings had won at the Forum since 1974, back when they were the Kansas City-Omaha Kings.[106] Yet two nights later they got a 107-106 win over the Golden State Warriors in Oakland on a running eight-footer by Scott with 14 seconds to play. The season was only three games old, and the trend had already been established – they had two impressive road wins against teams assumed to be in the playoffs, and a home loss to a team expected to finish near the bottom of the West.

After starting the season with two strong games, Worthy started to look pained on his surgically repaired knee the next two games, both bad losses. He scored seven points on 2-10 shooting in a loss in Seattle, then another seven points on 3-13 shooting in a 26-point embarrassment to the Clippers at the Forum. He managed to score in double figures in a three-point win against Golden State, but it came on 6-17 shooting.

After battling injuries to the frontcourt in 1991-92, the Lakers backcourt was hit early by injury in 1992-93. Scott had started the season in good form, leading the team in scoring with 19.5 points per game. But he tore ligaments when he badly sprained his right ankle in the fourth quarter against Golden State. He would have to sit for six weeks, missing the next 18 games.

Tony Smith replaced Scott in the starting line-up for the next game, at home against the two-time defending champion Chicago Bulls who were 6-1 on the season. Michael Jordan put on a vintage performance, scoring a Forum opponent record 54 points along with 13 rebounds and 7 assists. The Lakers trailed by 12 points to start the fourth quarter but rallied to take a 110-108 lead with 10 seconds to go. Jordan dribbled up the court and launched an 18-foot jumper over Threatt that hit the back of the rim. The rebound hit the floor, and seven players stood and looked at it without moving, perhaps assuming the buzzer would soon sound. Scottie

---

[106] The baseline seat at the Forum next to actress Dyan Cannon became Magic's permanent spot. He was there most Laker home game for many years.

Pippen was the only player who went to the ball, picked it up and made a short uncontested jumper in the key, tying the game with 0.2 seconds remaining.

In overtime, Jordan made two free throws to tie the score with 18.3 seconds remaining. Pfund called timeout and set up a truly bizarre play. Vlade Divac inbounded the ball in front of the Lakers bench near the Bulls' basket, throwing a long high-arching pass down-court. Worthy unexpectedly faked out Horace Grant and sprinted down-court to catch the pass. He caught it near the Lakers' basket and was fouled from behind while attempting a lay-up. His two free throws gave the Lakers a 118-116 lead with 16.7 seconds remaining.

Down the other end, Jordan caught a dribble-handoff from Scott Williams. He dribbled to the far corner before draining a near-impossible jumper over Campbell while falling out of bounds to tie the score again.

With 5.5 seconds remaining Pfund called a timeout and set up another unconventional play. This time they inbounded the ball at half-court where Worthy again shook off Grant, received the pass and dribbled into the corner. He fired a perfect bullet pass to Divac who was streaking to the basket and was fouled on a dunk attempt. Divac's free throws gave the Lakers a 120-118 lead with 3.1 seconds remaining. Jordan got a good look at a straight-on three-pointer that hit the back of the rim, and the Lakers got the unlikely win.

The game against Chicago had sold out quickly as fans came out to watch Jordan play. But attendance at the average Laker game was low at the start of the season. When the Lakers beat the struggling Denver Nuggets 119-107, they did it in front of a paltry 13,841 fans. They drew almost the exact small number of fans to their next home game where they lost by two points to New Jersey – the Nets' first win at the Forum since 1978.

The Lakers went from losing to the struggling Nets at home to defeating the 7-1 Portland Trail Blazers on the road two nights later. Portland and Chicago had played each other in the 1992 NBA Finals and were the top two teams in the league over the first few weeks of 1992-93. The Lakers were the only team in the league to have defeated both. Yet they had also seen decade-long home winning streaks snapped by the Kings and Nets. "We tend to get up against big teams," Threatt said. "And the weaker teams, because we're at home, we think it's an easy game, and we don't come out the way we would against a Chicago, a Portland, a New York, or a big team."

Just like a year ago, the Lakers responded to Magic's shock retirement with a strong opening month. A win over the Mavericks saw them close out November with a 7-4 record, tied with Phoenix and Houston for third-best in the conference.[107] As healthy as their record was, it could have been even better if not for their maddening inconsistency. If they had beaten the Kings and Nets at home, they would have been tied with Portland for the best record in the league.

Worthy's shooting had dropped to 44% in November, more than 10% lower than his career average at the time. "My knee has reached a point where I can tell what it can take and what it can't take," Worthy said. "In the beginning, it was tougher to tell. I just didn't have enough games under my belt. Now the battle is to keep it strong." Threatt stepped into the void created by Worthy's subpar start and Scott's injury, averaging 17.4 points and 7.4 assists for the month. "Sedale is now a key part of Laker lore," Pfund said. "He has come in for two years now, and he's really been the glue for us as far as handling the ball and keeping us in some kind of order out there. I hate to think where we'd be without Sedale."

The Lakers opened December with a three-game road trip where Worthy's shooting would completely bottom out. They lost by seven in Sacramento, their second loss to the lowly Kings in four weeks. It was the first time the Kings had beaten the Lakers twice in a row in 14 years. Worthy finished with just 4 points on 2-14 shooting. "That was nasty," he acknowledged after the game. They grounded out a 96-89 win in Houston but Worthy struggled to 6 points on 3-11 shooting in just 19 minutes. He then scored just 6 points on 3-12 shooting in a ten-point loss in Phoenix, taking his averages on the three-game road trip to 5.3 points on 21% shooting.

But after a mixed bag of results on the road, the Lakers put together a five-game win streak that would give them the best record they would have all season. Yes, there were some cheap wins against Minnesota,

---

[107] They started well in 1991-92 because of their defense, but their good start in 1992-93 was all about their offense. The Lakers averaged 108.1 points per game in November, on-pace for top ten in the league.

Washington and Milwaukee – all lowly teams.[108] But there were impressive wins against Portland at the Forum and against the Spurs in San Antonio. Peeler received the first starts of his career during this stretch when Smith was sidelined with a strained hamstring. The rookie scored 13 points against Portland, 16 against Washington, and 21 against Milwaukee.

It was midway through December, and the Lakers were one of the surprise teams of the season just as they had been a year earlier. They were on a five-game win streak and held a 13-6 record, good enough for the second spot in the West behind Phoenix. They were the first team to defeat the Blazers twice that season – the same Lakers who had lost twice to the Sacramento Kings. But the inconsistency that had plagued them over the first six weeks of the season would come back to bite them. And it would result in a loss that would prove to be the turning point of their season.

Following the win in San Antonio, the Lakers flew to Dallas for a game the next night against the Mavericks. Dallas was off to one of the worst starts in NBA history with a 1-15 record and were on a 12-game losing streak. It wasn't by bad luck either. The Mavs had few players on their roster with legitimate NBA talent and were losing by an average of 17 points per game. Things were so bad that Jimmy Jackson, the Ohio State guard they selected with the fourth pick in the draft, still hadn't signed with them and was holding out for more money.[109] The Mavericks would end the season with an 11-71 record, winning their final two games to narrowly avoid tying the 1972-73 Philadelphia 76ers' all-time worst record of 9-73.

The Mavericks started the game with the best 18 minutes of basketball they had played all season. They made their first 10 shots and were 20-24 from the field midway through the second quarter where they held a 43-30 lead. Pfund changed tack and implemented a zone trap that effectively froze the onslaught. The Lakers seized control of the game and had a 56-

---

[108] A.C. Green played his 500th consecutive game against Minnesota. He bought up his milestone in typical iron man fashion, coming off the bench with his left arm taped from forearm to bicep to protect a partially hyper-extended elbow.

[109] There were no rookie salaries in 1992 like there are now. The rookie salary structure was implemented, in part, to stop players like Jackson holding out for better deals. An infamous case was Glenn Robinson, who threatened to hold out in 1994 and eventually negotiated a 10-year, $68 million contract with the Bucks. Big money at the time for a draftee who had never stepped foot on an NBA court before.

55 half-time lead that grew to 70-57 midway through the third. Order, it seemed, had been restored.

Then Walter Bond checked in after not playing at all in the first half. Bond's NBA career had spanned three years in which he played sparingly for three teams and spent most of his career in the CBA and Europe. But on this night against the Lakers, he was the best player on the court. He scored 21 points in 19 minutes, including an 18-foot jumper to beat the third-quarter buzzer. Peeler's frustration guarding him boiled over, and he was ejected for the first time in his career for arguing with an official. The Lakers were held to 11 points in the fourth quarter, Worthy shot just 4-12, they could never find a way to stop Bond, and lost 102-95. It was only the Mavs' second win of the season, and a humiliation for the Lakers.

"We talked in the locker room about the danger of all the talk about this team being bad. We talked about the fact that on any given night how any NBA team can beat any other NBA team," said Pfund. "Then we came out and allowed them to score 37 points in the first quarter, which is a graphic expression of the fact that talk is cheap."

The loss to the Mavericks was more than an example of the Lakers' inconsistent play. The game exposed them and their impressive record as merely smoke and mirrors that masked the fact they were a flawed team without Magic. In a big boost to their overall record, the Lakers had gone 4-0 on their recent home-stand, with a winning margin of 19.5 points. Part of those four wins could be chalked up to their offense ticking along better than it had all season. But their schedule had also been unusually kind – eight of their last nine opponents at home were playing the second night of back-to-back games. In Dallas, they had come crashing back to reality.

Things hardly improved two days later when the Phoenix Suns came to the Forum and manhandled the Lakers with a 60-36 rebound advantage. They outscored the Lakers 35-14 in the first quarter and won by sixteen. Jerry West left his seat a few minutes into the game and retreated to his office with a disgusted look on his face. He gave the Lakers a mouthful in the locker room after the game. "I don't like our fans cheated for lack of effort," he told them. He reminded the players of their obligations as representatives of the Lakers to be someone the community was proud of by playing hard every night. "We don't talk about wins and losses here, if you do those things, the wins will come."

Two days before Christmas the Lakers lost 80-79 at home against a

Seattle SuperSonics team that was vulnerable – playing on the second night of a back-to-back and without forward Shawn Kemp. Threatt suffered a concussion from a first-half collision with Sonics guard Nate McMillan. He played only a few minutes in the second half and spent Christmas at Centinela Hospital for observation and tests. He was back in uniform on Boxing Day at the Forum, but the Lakers lost 104-92 to the San Antonio Spurs.

The schedule that had gifted the Lakers many weary opponents over the first eight weeks of the season was about to get tougher with a six-game road swing, their longest of the season.

The Lakers built an 18-point lead in the first quarter in Miami, but a rally got the Heat back to within three points midway through the fourth quarter. Then rookie Harold Miner took the game by the horns. He scored a three-point play with seven minutes remaining to tie the score at 82. He then stripped the ball from Peeler and assisted to Grant Long for a fast-break lay-up that put the Heat ahead. Miner scored seven points in the last two and a half minutes, and the Heat put the game away 107-96, their first win against the Lakers in their young history.

Two nights later the Lakers were in Orlando to face rookie Shaquille O'Neal who had been taking the league by storm. Shaq had been an instant hit, averaging 22.0 points and 14.5 rebounds in his first 23 games. Between destroying two backboards with his thunderous dunks and charming fans and the media with his big personality, Shaq had revitalized the expansion Orlando Magic. "I know he's going to be the next great player in the league," Scott said. "He's going to be the next Michael Jordan. He has personality, he has charisma, he has flash in his game."

The Lakers played Shaq the same way they played Olajuwon, double-teaming him frequently and taking their chances with Orlando's outside shooters. The strategy worked about as well as it could, limiting Shaq to 11 shot attempts, though he still recorded 23 points and 23 rebounds. The Lakers nursed a two-point lead with 11 seconds remaining when Shaq wheeled around Divac and laid the ball in with 11 seconds remaining. But he was called for traveling, the basket was waived off, and the Lakers won 96-93. "Rookie call," O'Neal murmured. "Lots of rookie calls tonight."

The Lakers ended December with a 15-11 record. After surprising many by being in second place in the West in mid-December, they had fallen to fifth place by the end of the month. They had gone 2-5 since their embarrassing loss to the Mavericks.[110]

Worthy's lateral quickness seemed to be getting worse by the week, and there were serious doubts his knee would ever fully recover. In December, he suffered through one of his least productive months since his rookie year, averaging 11.9 points on 40% shooting. The Lakers were instead carried in December by Threatt and Perkins. Threatt averaged 17.7 points and 6.0 assists for the month, while Perkins put up 16.6 points and 7.2 rebounds.

Scott was back in the line-up, playing 20 minutes in each of the two games in Florida. Rookie Anthony Peeler had performed well starting in Scott's absence, averaging 12.3 points on 47% shooting, creating a reason for optimism. His performance as a starter in December had made West's gamble in drafting him look like an early winner. "I think he's been able to do a little more than I would have thought," Pfund said, "but the consistency is always the thing with the young players. He's been up and down."

As had the entire team. It was symptomatic of the void in leadership created by Magic's second sudden departure. "When you don't have a leader on the floor, you get lost," said assistant coach Larry Drew. "Earvin was one of those guys to challenge people individually. He would set the tone in practice, and once he set the tone, it was up to everybody else to follow the lead. If you didn't, he let you know."

The Lakers no longer had that on their team. And the results were predictably mixed.

---

[110] For the record, the Mavericks closed December 0-7 after they defeated the Lakers. In fact, they would go 2-42 over their next 44 games.

Chapter 11

THE COMFORTABLE PRESENT

January 2, 1993 to February 22, 1993

T HE LAKERS OPENED the New Year by continuing their road trip with a 106-91 loss in Cleveland, dropping them to 15-12 on the season. And they would still be three games above .500 when they broke for All-Star weekend seven weeks later. There would be peaks and troughs during those weeks, but they would ultimately be treading water.

The question Jerry West needed to answer was, would that be enough? For some franchises, it would. For some teams, winning 40-45 games and qualifying for the playoffs a few years in a row would be a good outcome.

There was something to be said for being in the middle of the pack. As the ninth-oldest team in the league, there was a degree of comfortability with these Lakers. They were a team of wily veterans probably good enough to make the playoffs. So, maybe this is what these Lakers should be – a team of leftovers from Showtime playing out their twilight years on respectable teams that wouldn't achieve greatness, but probably wouldn't embarrass themselves either.

It wasn't a spot the Lakers were used to being in though – they were usually aiming much higher. If it was to change, it would take a conscious decision by Jerry Buss and Jerry West to break from the past and plot a new course. And there was no way to do that without pain.

Having lost seven of their last nine games, the Lakers ventured to Chicago to take on the defending champion Bulls who were sitting atop the East with a 22-7 record. And they would once again be without Byron Scott. After being sidelined for 38 days with a sprained right foot, he returned to play the first three games of the road trip, but the injury flared up again. He would go on to miss the next two weeks. By the time he took the floor again, he had missed 23 of the last 26 games.

With Scott out, Randy Pfund went with an unconventional line-up to say the least – starting power forward A.C. Green at shooting guard. But it seemed to work, as they put up one of their better defensive performances of the season. Michael Jordan, Scottie Pippen, and Horace Grant combined for 68 points, but the Lakers kept everyone else in check. The rest of the Bulls scored only 20 points on 29% shooting.

Scores were tied 84-84 with less than four minutes to play when Pfund then switched Green on to Jordan, who never had matched-up with him for an extended time before. But Pfund wanted to give it a try. "I knew he'd play Michael with a lot of energy," he said.

Green was bigger and stronger than Jordan but quick enough to, mostly, stay in front of him. Jordan shot 14-24 before Pfund made the adjustment and 1-7 afterward. It stalled the Bulls' scoring, and Vlade Divac hit a 15-footer to give the Lakers a 91-88 lead with 12 seconds to play. Jordan bought the ball up the court, missed a three-pointer over Green, but the Lakers knocked the ball out of bounds with five seconds remaining. The Lakers swarmed all over the ensuing in-bounds play and were given a gift when Pippen was called for not getting the ball in play within five seconds.

It was now the Lakers game to win, but they seemingly tried everything to lose it. Divac turned it over trying to inbound the ball, and the Bulls charged up court before Threatt knocked a pass out of bounds with 0.9 seconds remaining. The Bulls inbounded to Jordan and Green pushed him as soon as he touched the ball, trying to prevent a game-tying three-pointer by sending him to the free throw line. But Jordan was well and truly in a shooting motion by the time Green pushed him and should have been sent to the line for three free throws that could have tied the game. But despite the contact being obvious and deliberate, no call was made, and the Lakers won 91-88. The win improved the Lakers record against the Bulls to a surprising 3-1 since Magic's retirement.

The Lakers' chartered jet experienced mechanical problems leaving Chicago, and the team didn't depart until 3:30am. They arrived in Minneapolis at 5:45am, less than 14 hours before they were due to take the floor against the Timberwolves. "I went to bed about 6:30 and I woke up about 10:00," said James Worthy. "I just tried to get ready. I jogged in place in the hotel room. I told myself, 'You've got a game to play.'" Playing their fourth road game in five nights on less than five hours' sleep was a recipe for disaster. But, for once, the Lakers didn't fall into their bad habit of playing down to the level of an inferior opponent. The Lakers held the Timberwolves to 35% shooting and roundly beat them, 98-78.

The win meant they returned home a respectable 3-3 on the road trip, about as good as they could have hoped for. Pfund kept Green in the starting line-up two days later when the Lakers finally defeated the Sacramento Kings, who had frustrated them in two earlier losses. Green, suddenly playing shooting guard for the first time in his career, averaged 13.0 points and 11.3 rebounds in the four starts. "I can't say I haven't enjoyed it," he said.

The win over the Kings put the Lakers five games above .500 and kicked off a kind schedule where they wouldn't be required to leave Los Angeles for two weeks. It was the perfect opportunity to build on their record and establish some momentum. But they would squander it.

They'd lose at home to the second worst team in the East, the 9-21 Miami Heat, the first time the Lakers had lost at the Forum to one of the four expansion teams. They were the rested team while the Heat was on a long road trip and had played the night before, yet Miami played with greater energy all game. Worthy's shooting had improved since New Year, but he missed all eight of his shot attempts and went scoreless in 31 minutes. It was the first time he had failed to score in a game since November 1987.

The Lakers blew a 17-point lead against the Clippers at the Sports Arena in a three-point loss. They improved to 3-0 against the reigning Western Conference champion by beating Portland by three at the Forum. Then they let the Rockets shoot a ridiculous 68% from behind the three-point line in a 20-point loss at home.[111] They lost their second straight game at home, this time to the Seattle SuperSonics, despite Scott making a welcome return to the line-up where he scored 14 points off the bench.

The Lakers had won just two of the six games they had played in the two weeks where they were not required to travel. Instead of building on their record, they were now in a worse position and just two games above .500 with a 19-17 record.

* * * * *

---

[111] Vernon Maxwell matched an all-time Laker opponent record (which he previously held) with six three-pointers, and the Rockets set an all-time opponent record in three-pointers made with 11 as a team.

Two weeks after finishing a long road trip, the Lakers embarked on another one that would see them play six games in nine nights. With Scott finally back to full strength, Pfund re-shuffled the starting line-up to something a little more traditional.[112] He returned Scott to starting shooting guard and rewarded Green for his strong play by keeping him in the starting line-up at his usual power forward spot. Perkins became the new starting center, and Divac was relegated to the sixth man. Divac had been struggling of late, scoring eight points against Houston and just one point against Seattle where he was badly outplayed by Michael Cage.

The Lakers opened the road trip by giving up three offensive rebounds in a key late possession and lost 98-94 to the Utah Jazz.[113] Perkins had his #14 jersey stolen in Salt Lake City and had to wear a nameless #40 jersey two nights later in Washington. Maybe it was good luck because he registered 16 points, 13 rebounds, and 10 assists in the Lakers' 112-110 overtime victory. It was his first career triple-double and the first posted by a Laker in the post-Magic era.[114]

The Lakers then lost by 15 to the resurgent New Jersey Nets before crumbling defensively in Indianapolis, where they gave up 74 first-half points in a 17-point loss to the Pacers. The loss officially made the Lakers the .500 ball club everybody thought they might be when the season started. They were now 20-20 overall and 7-13 since their dreadful loss to the Mavericks. And they had fallen to the eighth and final playoff spot in the West – exactly where they had ended the previous season.

They ended the road trip and their January schedule in Boston on Super Bowl Sunday. It was the first Laker game at Boston Garden since 1979 that didn't feature either Magic Johnson or Larry Bird. The Lakers were 21-20 while the Celtics were 22-20, both teams idling without their star players. These once-dominant franchises now had aging rosters, carrying several players left over from their past rivalry who were now struggling past their primes. Unlike the good old days, this wasn't an epic battle. Instead, this was a game featuring two run-of-the-mill teams

---

[112] Scott had been eased back since returning from his second foot injury. He had played the last four games off the bench, averaging 10.3 points in 21.0 minutes.

[113] Jim Pollard, a California native who was one of the greats from the Minneapolis Lakers teams, died on the day the Lakers played the Jazz. He was 70 years old.

[114] The previous regular season triple-double was Magic's 30 points, 12 rebounds and 10 assists in San Antonio on April 2, 1991.

struggling to stay alive in the playoff hunt.

The Lakers won 96-87, but it wasn't like the old days. Robert Parish dragged his 39-year-old body around the court for 7 points and 5 rebounds. Kevin McHale came off the bench and proved he still had some life left in his tired 35-year-old legs by scoring 14 points. Scott didn't play because of the flu and Worthy scored 10 points on an ugly 3-15 shooting.

Instead, Reggie Lewis top-scored for the Celtics with 23 points. And Peeler, who was just 14 years old in 1984 when Bird and Magic first met in the Finals, scored 16 points as the starter including a three-pointer that sealed the win. This Laker-Celtics game vanished from memory almost as soon as the final buzzer sounded.

The Lakers were a respectable 3-3 on the road trip, but January had turned into a lost cause well before the trip started. After having two losing months in 1991-92, they suffered through their first of the new season with a 7-9 record in January. They started the month in fifth place in the West and ended it in the eighth. For the second straight season, they had found their surprisingly good start was unsustainable without Magic. And they would continue to play .500 ball for the first two weeks of February.

Laker tickets were not as hard to come by in 1993 as they had been in the past, with their lowest average attendance in eight years.[115] But rookie Shaquille O'Neal's first visit to the Forum was second only to Michael Jordan's visit in terms of interest from fans. Only a handful of Lakers games had sold out that season, but the Forum was at capacity for this one.

The Magic looked like a team of the future, while the Lakers looked like an irrelevant team from yesteryear. Orlando's young stars shone brightly at the Forum, as Nick Anderson caught fire and Shaq recorded 31 points on 13-17 shooting and had 14 rebounds. "For a young team, they played with a lot of confidence," Pfund said. Worthy struggled with 5 points on 2-9 shooting and Orlando won 110-97, handing the Lakers their fourth loss in their last five home games.

Following a surprising win against Utah and a predictable 28-point

---

[115] The Lakers averaged attendance for 1992-93 was 15,455, about 2,000 less than during Showtime. The 1992-93 number was inflated due to the large number of season tickets sold after Magic's comeback announcement.

loss in Phoenix, the Lakers managed a win against the awful Dallas Mavericks at the Forum. But even that wasn't anything to feel good about. They needed two free throws by Perkins to send the game into overtime and a three-pointer from him late in overtime to seal a 108-100 win. Rarely had a win felt so embarrassing.

The Lakers got another home win over a struggling team when they beat the Denver Nuggets 111-102 despite the usually mild-mannered Green being ejected for the first time since 1988. His teammates wondered what he, a born-again Christian who never cursed, could have said to merit an ejection. "Gosh darn it, that was a terrible call, you boo-boo," was Scott's guess. Green claimed the truth was far less interesting. "Everybody wants to know what I said," he said. "My teammates thought I called him a knucklehead. Vlade said I called him stupid. I really just asked him if he was going to make a call. But they can't believe he asked me to leave because of that."

Out of the blue everything that could possibly go right did on Valentine's Day at home against Atlanta. The Lakers shot 62% and led 69-38 at half-time. Divac, who had been struggling with his play off the bench, scored 14 points and grabbed 13 rebounds. Duane Cooper had 11 assists.[116] Alex Blackwell, who had hardly played all season, hit 3-4 shots and scored 8 points. The Lakers ran the Hawks off the court and won 135-96, their biggest win since defeating the Heat by 39 points in 1990.

Magic was presented with his Olympic ring at half-time. Fans yelled for him to come back, but unlike last year he wouldn't play into it. "There will be more banners here," he told the crowd. "I wish I could be a part of those banners. But I know basketball is here to stay, and the Lakers are here to stay, and you keep supporting them."

The fact Magic couldn't be a part of the teams' future hung over the Lakers when the league broke for All-Star weekend. They had an unremarkable, but respectable, 26-23 record. After starting January three games above .500, they were in the same position six weeks later. They hadn't lost any ground, but they hadn't gained any either. They were heading nowhere.

The Lakers wouldn't have a single representative in the All-Star Game

---

[116] Cooper's 11 assists were the most by a Laker rookie since Magic in 1980.

for the first time since 1978.[117] In fact, the entire All-Star Weekend in 1993 came and went without a Laker taking part in any event for the first time.[118] Worthy had been an All-Star in each of the previous seven years. But with his creaky knees, he was averaging 14.7 points and 3.2 rebounds on 43% shooting at the break – numbers that wouldn't get him anywhere close to the game.[119]

It was the time of year teams assess where they stand, and good teams commit to doubling their effort in the stretch run to the playoffs. "Some teams with this record at the All-Star break would say, 'We're in the top 11, 12 teams in the league and if we're okay in the second half we can be a serious contender,'" Pfund said. "But that kind of approach does not get a lot of headlines in L.A. For a number of years, we were so good, to be somewhat good and be in the pack fighting is not achieving what we want to achieve."

During All-Star weekend, West finally followed through on something he likely would have done in the off-season if he wasn't waiting on Magic. He pulled the trigger on a trade involving one of the Lakers' veteran core. The Lakers traded forward Sam Perkins to the Seattle SuperSonics, signifying the beginning of a rebuilding process.[120]

Along with Threatt, Perkins had been one of the most reliable players for the Lakers all season with averages of 13.7 points and 7.7 rebounds. Pfund had frequently used him as the go-to scorer down the stretch of close games. He had played a key role in the Lakers' run through the 1991 Playoffs and, until his season-ending injury in late March, averaged career highs in scoring, rebounds, and assists in 1991-92.

Perkins wasn't exactly shocked at the news. There had been talk for

---

[117] There were extenuating circumstances in 1978 anyway. Kareem Abdul-Jabbar would have been an All-Star, but he missed the first 20 games of the season because of a broken hand he received in a fight with Kent Benson. Besides the 1978 asterisks, the Lakers had been represented at every All-Star game since they started in 1951.

[118] Jamaal Wilkes scored five points in the Legends Game, if that counts.

[119] By retiring so close to the start of the season, Magic's name was on the ballot just like the previous season. But he said at the time of his re-retirement he wouldn't play even if he was voted in. The league wouldn't have allowed it anyway, saying 1992 was a unique situation. Votes for Magic were not tabulated because they were not considered official, so we'll never know if he was actually voted in.

[120] The trade was the first roster move of the season for the Lakers, the last team in the league to make one.

weeks that West might pull the trigger on a trade and he was often the subject of those rumors. Despite being a reserved introvert who liked time on his own, he enjoyed living in fast-paced Los Angeles.[121] And he liked being a Laker. But he was joining a much more talented team in Seattle, one that was expected to have far greater post-season success than the Lakers. The trade was a personal loss for Worthy, who had been friends with Perkins since being teammates and roommates at the University of North Carolina where they, along with Michael Jordan, won the 1982 NCAA Championship.

So, what were the Lakers getting in return? One of the players the Lakers received was 28-year-old center Benoit Benjamin, nicknamed Big Ben. He had been a standout at Creighton University and was selected third overall by the Clippers in the 1985 draft. But he never lived up to expectations, proving to be an enigmatic player who would swing between playing well some games while displaying a distinct lack of passion and interest other nights.

He once missed a pre-season game with the Clippers because he only bought two left shoes with him. But not all his stories were so endearing, and he became one of the more reviled figures amongst Clippers fans. He once went on Jim Healy's radio show where he was quizzed about his troubled relationships with fans. His response? "I don't give a shit about the fans." Two years before being traded to the Lakers, almost to the day, the Clippers traded him to Seattle. At his first game back at the Sports Arena as a Sonic, a fan held up a sign that read *'Thanks Ben…for leaving.'* He responded to being booed during introductions by giving the middle finger to the crowd. Now he was back in L.A.

A starting center his first seven years in the league, Benjamin was playing just 14 minutes a night off the bench for Seattle in 1992-93, averaging a career-low 6.7 points and 3.6 rebounds. He also had one of the most unattractive contracts in the league, with three years left on a five-year deal worth $17.5 million.[122]

But the prize of the deal for West wasn't Benjamin. If anything, he was

---

[121] Perkins listed 'enjoys spending time alone' as part of the 'Personal' information in his player profile in the 1992-93 Lakers Media Guide.

[122] It seems laughable now to think 5 years at $17.5 million was a bad contract because it's almost pocket change in comparison to what players earn today. But bear in mind the salary cap in 1993 was $14 million, so Benjamin's contract represented a quarter of the cap.

the price the Lakers had to pay for the player they really wanted – 22-year-old rookie Doug Christie. West was impressed by Christie before the draft and was torn between selecting him or Peeler with the Lakers' first round pick. Now he had both players.

But Christie was still just as much an unknown as he was on draft night. That Christie was talented was never in doubt. He could play multiple positions, was a good defender, a good athlete, and a highly skilled and willing passer. But the question mark over the health of his knees still hadn't been answered, nor had the question about what position he was best suited for. And that was because he hadn't played a single game all season. Christie was one of several draftees of the era who held contract holdouts in the hope of securing better pay. The Sonics tired of the drama and moved him, this despite the fact he was born and raised in Seattle and grew up a Sonics fan.[123]

West was rolling the dice because, with Magic gone for good, he had to. In 2007, J.A. Adande named the Perkins trade as the worst move West made in his time as Lakers General Manager. But the Lakers were stuck in neutral in February 1993 and West needed to make a change. Without Magic, the team had barely qualified for the playoffs in 1992 after a terrible run of injuries. They were healthy now, but their fortunes hadn't gotten much brighter. After starting the season well, they were 11-12 since New Year.

"Obviously, we'd like to be higher in our quest to beat somebody in the playoffs," West said. "But realistically, when you look at the eighth-place team, seventh-place team, it's one round and out, and we don't want that to happen."

The Lakers could have stayed in the comfortable present with a veteran roster that would, if nothing else, have been respectable. They could have remained a middle-of-the-road team, sneaking into the playoffs the next few years.[124] Or, they could take their chances. Instead of looking backward at Showtime, they could look forward and move on.

---

[123] West was also in discussions at the time with Dallas regarding a potential swap of Divac for Jimmy Jackson – another prized rookie who was holding out for a better contract. But the deal never happened.

[124] Because the draft rewards losing, in many respects the worst thing a team can be is middle-of-the-road and over the cap, which is what the Lakers were in 1993. Middle-of-the-road won't get you high draft picks and being over the cap means you can't afford free agents. So how are you meant to improve?

The only way to do that was by finding young players. Trading Perkins was not about making the Lakers better in 1993. It was about opening themselves up to the possibility of having a future.

West had few pieces to move for a young player. Previously the best trade chip was Worthy, but his declining numbers now made the three years left on his hefty contract too high a price for most teams. The window to trade him for a young player, such as the deal West had in place for Washington's pick in the draft eight months earlier, had closed. Both Scott and Green were about to become free agents, making it unlikely a team would give up a young player to acquire either of them. Not if it meant risking them bolting at the end of the season. Perkins, unfortunately, was the one Laker who a team was willing to part with young talent to acquire.

"The Lakers have always had one or two players that have been at the top of the league in talent," West said. "In perpetuating this franchise, our next move is, where do we find another one of those guys?" Was Christie likely to be one of those guys? Probably not. But the move was a signal the Lakers were opening themselves up to the possibility of finding one – either now or down the road.

"We've played without Magic Johnson for a year and a half, and basically we've been a .500 team," Pfund said. "It's time for a change."

Chapter 12
FOR BETTER OR WORSE

February 24, 1993 to April 24, 1993

B Y TRADING SAM Perkins, the Lakers had embraced the reality of their situation without Magic Johnson, for better or worse. Showtime was over, and it was never coming back. They were looking to the future, which would unavoidably have to come at the cost of the comfortable present.

For the first three weeks after the trade, the Lakers would continue along the same trajectory they had been on for the last two months. They would continue to play slightly better than .500 basketball. But the forward-looking trade of Perkins unavoidably gave them less meaningful talent in the present, and it was a reality they couldn't hide from forever.

If Doug Christie represented the future, fans would have to wait to get a look at him. The Lakers quickly did what Seattle couldn't do and signed him to his first NBA contract. After rejecting a four-year, $2.7 million contract from the SuperSonics during the off-season, Christie signed a deal for the remainder of the season worth $685,000. He would become a restricted free agent at the end of the season, allowing the market to decide his salary once and for all. He was moved to the injured list where he would remain for the next two weeks. During that time, he would practice with the team, get into game shape and learn the offense.

Benoit Benjamin was in uniform when the Lakers were in Sacramento for their first game following the trade. Pfund kept him on the bench, preferring he acclimatized to the Lakers' system before putting him on the floor. Divac was back in the starting line-up, replacing Perkins, and the Lakers beat the struggling Kings 104-99.

Benjamin didn't play two nights later, an eight point loss to Cleveland, in the Lakers' first home game since the trade. He received a mixed reaction from Forum fans during pre-game introductions. Some of the negativity was because of Benjamin's questionable behavior as a Clipper, but some of it was fans venting their displeasure at losing Perkins. "I wanted to be prepared for the worst," Benjamin said. "I knew I wasn't going to get cheers. I'm just being patient."

Ironically Benjamin made his Laker debut at the Forum against the team whose fanbase detested him so much – the Los Angeles Clippers. He played 12 minutes off the bench, scoring eight points on 4-6 shooting. The Clippers were playing without leading scorer Danny Manning, who was suspended after a fight with Golden State's Chris Gatling three nights earlier. The Lakers won 124-112 behind 30 points from A.C. Green.[125]

The Lakers started the month of March with a 127-115 loss in Denver.[126] After the game, Nuggets center Dikembe Mutombo expressed disbelief at the Perkins trade. "Sending Sam Perkins away hurt their cause, I don't understand that trade, " he said. "How do you send away someone who can play 40 minutes for someone who plays four minutes?"

Without Perkins, the Lakers' starting frontcourt logged big minutes the next night in Oakland, with Green playing the entire game. The Lakers picked up a six-point win over a Warriors team missing injured Chris Mullin and Sarunas Marciulionis, and who lost Tim Hardaway in the second quarter to a sprained right knee.

They then returned home and needed overtime to get a six-point win over the Philadelphia 76ers, who had been struggling all season following the trade of Charles Barkley. Divac, who had 21 points and 21 rebounds, scored six points in overtime.[127] Benjamin played 20 minutes, grabbing 14 rebounds and scoring 7 points. But he shot just 2-13 from the floor.

The Charlotte Hornets overcame a 20-point deficit two nights later to beat the Lakers 105-101 at the Forum. Divac was ejected midway through the third quarter, resulting in bigger minutes for Benjamin. But he struggled, scoring 8 points on 3-10 shooting. Pfund had increased his workload the last three games, upping it to 19 minutes a game, but he had averaged just 7.3 points on horrible 27% shooting. Pfund had seen enough. After five games in a Laker uniform, he relegated Benjamin to third-stringer for the remainder of the season, giving most of his minutes to

---

[125] Green's 30 points were his highest since 1989 and the second highest of his career.
[126] The Nuggets retired Alex English's jersey at half-time.
[127] Divac's 21 rebounds were a career high and the first time a Laker player had collected 20 or more rebounds in a game since Kareem Abdul-Jabbar in 1981.

Elden Campbell.

The Lakers started a five-game road trip two nights later in Auburn Hills. It felt much like when the Lakers visited Boston earlier in the season – a vivid reminder of everything that had been lost. Two and a half seasons removed from their back-to-back titles, Detroit was struggling with a 25-32 record. Just as the Lakers weren't Showtime anymore, these weren't the Bad Boy Pistons. Pfund again played the frontcourt heavy minutes with Worthy, Green, and Divac collectively playing 86% of the game. Threatt scored 24 points and dished out a career-high 15 assists, and the Lakers overcame 41 from Joe Dumars to win 123-121 with Terry Mills missing a potential game-tying shot at the buzzer.

The next night they were in Madison Square Garden to play a Knicks team that had come into their own under Pat Riley and held a 39-18 record, one game behind Chicago for best in the East. Patrick Ewing overpowered the Lakers with 34 points and 12 rebounds, leading six Knicks in double figures, and New York won 110-104. "What happened to Showtime, Randy?" a fan bellowed at Pfund as the Lakers walked off the court. "Where's Showtime now?"[128]

After impressing Pfund in training, Christie was in an NBA uniform for the first time in Philadelphia, and the Lakers were quick to manage expectations. "Doug is a player we wanted and pursued, but he's not a savior," Mitch Kupchak said. "His minutes will be limited. All we expect is for him to learn our plays and sets and to make a contribution when he does play." Christie was talking the same way. "I don't want to come in with a lot of hype. I want to let my playing do the talking," he said. "I still don't know the plays all too well. I'm just going to try to play my game and not force anything."

Pfund had no expectations for Christie. Instead, he wanted to throw the rookie out there to determine what kind of player he was. He planned to play Christie mostly at small forward but wanted to try him at point guard too. "The one thing we need to do this season is find out what Doug Christie is," Pfund said. "Maybe he's a Michael Cooper, a three-position player. Maybe he's a starter. Maybe he's better coming off the bench. The better the idea we get, the better idea we'll have how to build this team in

---

[128] It was the first Lakers loss at Madison Square Garden since 1984.

the off-season."[129]

Christie was so nervous before the game that he feared he would forget a part of his uniform, even checking himself in the mirror before taking the court. He failed to notice the Lakers had misspelled his name on his jersey. He played his first ever NBA game with his name spelled 'Chrisite' on the back of his jersey. "I'm just happy he put it on right, and he didn't put on two left shoes," Green said in an obvious slight to Benjamin.

With Christie joining fellow rookie Anthony Peeler, the game was the first time the Lakers had two rookies selected in the first round on the roster since 1979.[130] Peeler scored 14 points in 23 minutes on 7-10 shooting, while Christie played nine scoreless minutes in the Lakers 101-95 win over the 76ers. "For the time I was out there, I thought I did a pretty good job," said Christie. "I don't think I hurt the team, but I didn't help either. I'm glad this is over with, and I'm just looking forward to the next game."

Their next stop of the road trip was Atlanta, where the Lakers were forced to hibernate in their hotel for two days. A large cyclonic storm, dubbed the 'Storm of the Century', blasted the eastern third of the United States. The storm dumped more than 18 inches of snow on Atlanta, with winds of 50 mph blowing the snow into nearly waist-deep drifts. It paralyzed metropolitan Atlanta, causing 208 fatalities and leaving more than a million people without power.

Yet the Lakers-Hawks game went ahead as scheduled. The official capacity for the game was listed as 13,628, but that was based on the number of tickets sold, not the number of people in attendance. There would have been no more than 4,000 fans at the arena, making it the smallest crowd the Lakers had played in front of since moving from Minneapolis. Dominique Wilkins scored 35 points, the Hawks shot 54% and won 117-107. Christie scored the first two baskets of his career, scoring 4 points on 2-4 shooting in 8 minutes of action. "Garbage time, though," Christie said. "So, it doesn't count."

They managed to depart Georgia on schedule despite the ongoing chaos from the storm. They concluded their road trip with a 92-87 win over the San Antonio Spurs. Christie, who had played small forward

[129] To make a roster spot for Christie, rookie Alex Blackwell was moved to the injured list. Blackwell averaged 1.3 points on 33% shooting in 4.0 minutes per game. The official reason for Blackwell being put on the injured list was 'prostate problem.'
[130] The rookies were Magic Johnson (1st pick) and Brad Holland (14th pick.)

during his first two games, made his debut at point guard after Threatt drew his third foul midway through the third quarter. He scored 3 points in six minutes of action while Benjamin was ejected in the fourth quarter for committing a flagrant foul against Sean Elliot.

The Lakers had been 7-5 since the Perkins trade and had a three-game lead over the Clippers for the seventh spot with a 33-28 record. But trading away a key rotation player for a rookie playing sporadic minutes and a center who hardly played would eventually catch up with them. With twenty games left, their season would enter a tailspin. If they were embracing the future for better or worse by trading Perkins, they would now experience the 'worse' part of that equation.

The unraveling would start during a run of six straight home games, their longest home-stand in six years. The first was against the Spurs on the second night of their home-and-away series. Trailing 101-100, the Lakers would have three chances to win the game but blew them all. Threatt missed a jumper with 16 seconds remaining, Divac missed a jumper with three seconds to play, Scott caught the rebound and launched a 12-footer at the buzzer that bounced off the ring. Christie struggled in his Forum debut, scoring 4 points on 1-7 shooting.

The Boston Celtics were in town two days later, and the Lakers' defense collapsed. The Lakers led 94-80 at the final break, but they let the Celtics score 49 points in the fourth quarter – the most points they had given up in a quarter since moving to Los Angeles – and lost 129-119.

They lost two nights later 106-101 to the Detroit Pistons, their third consecutive loss at home. Divac and Threatt each shot 10-17 from the floor but the rest of the team shot just 32%. "It used to be you weren't coming in here and winning," said Detroit's Dennis Rodman. "You were coming here to see the stars. Now you come here, and you have an opportunity to win."

Their home losing streak grew to four games when they lost 120-105 to Phoenix. The Suns were without Kevin Johnson, who was serving a two-game suspension for his part in a brawl against the Knicks the night before. But Charles Barkley was a monster all game with 33 points, 12 rebounds, and 8 assists. The lone bright spot for the Lakers was Christie having the best game of his short career, scoring 14 points in 15 minutes. His performance showcased some of the versatility the Lakers hoped he would bring when they traded for him – coming off the bench backing-up

Threatt at point guard before taking over at small forward when Worthy's tendinitis in his right ankle ruled him out late in the game.[131]

The Lakers' interior defense, suspect before the Perkins trade, was nowhere to be seen when they hosted the New York Knicks. Bruising forwards Anthony Mason and Charles Oakley feasted on the remains of the Lakers' frontcourt and won 105-95. It was their fifth straight loss at the Forum, their longest home losing streak in franchise history. They had lost eight of their last 11 games and had fallen to 33-33 on the season.

They got a much needed 92-90 win two nights later when Threatt made four consecutive shots late in the fourth quarter, including the game-winner, against the Indiana Pacers at the Forum. "I've been worried about a lot of things, but not about Sedale," Pfund said after the game. The crowd cheered the game-winning shot, but the reaction was more relief than celebration. It ended their longest home-stand in six years with a 1-5 record. It was their first win in 11 days and the first time they had outscored an opponent in the fourth quarter in nine games.

But the good feelings from the narrow win over the Pacers wouldn't last. The Lakers would lose by eight to the Clippers at the Sports Arena before losing by thirteen at home to the Minnesota Timberwolves, the second worst team in the league. The loss to Minnesota meant the Lakers had given all four expansion teams their first-ever wins at the Forum in 1992-93, and dropped them to 6-11 for March, their second losing month of the season.

Pfund had persisted with the same starting line-up in the 19 games following the Perkins trade, but it clearly wasn't working. "As much as I've hung with these guys, it might make some sense going down the wire to get a look at some other people," he said. "Maybe we can find something out that would help us in the playoffs and into next year."

He dramatically altered the rotation at the start of April, inserting Campbell into the starting line-up at power forward and moving Green to small forward. He would give increased minutes over the rest of the season to the Lakers young core of Campbell, Peeler, Christie, and Smith. It meant changes for Worthy and Scott, two key figures of Showtime.

The move relegated Worthy to a permanent bench role for the first time since 1984. It had been coming for months. Injuries had robbed him

---

[131] Green became the eighth Laker to record 5,000 career rebounds during this game.

of the phenomenal explosiveness that made him such a key part of Showtime. He had struggled all season, and his 10 points on 3-16 shooting against Minnesota was the final straw for Pfund. The truth that he was no longer capable of carrying the Lakers' offense for 35-40 minutes a night was no longer possible to ignore.

Scott would remain in the starting line-up, but his minutes would decline in April. He was about to become an unrestricted free agent, and he knew the writing was on the wall. The backcourt had become crowded with young players at a time the franchise was looking to the future. "I understand this could be my last year here," he said. "I've got three championship rings, and I've been to the Finals six times, and I've had a great career here. It's been a lot of fun. I definitely want to stay here and finish my career in this city, but I know it's very unlikely."

The new rotation was tested for the first time against the Utah Jazz at the Forum. Campbell responded with a strong game in his first start of the season, scoring 14 points. Peeler took advantage of increased minutes off the bench and scored 19. But the result remained the same for the Lakers. They struggled defensively and lost 111-99. The loss put them back into the eighth and final playoff spot, the same place they ended last season. "Now, we're not looking at seventh position," Divac said. "Because it's going to be a big fight for the playoffs."

Pfund's changes appeared better two nights later in Phoenix, where the Lakers played perhaps their best game of the season. They shot 50% from the floor and had seven players in double figures, led by Campbell's 21 points and 11 rebounds. Free throws and a three-pointer by Scott put the Lakers up by three before Dan Majerle tied the game with a three-pointer with 10.8 seconds remaining. Following a timeout, Peeler patiently backed the smaller Kevin Johnson down all the way to the free throw line before launching a fadeaway jumper that fell, giving the Lakers a 114-112 lead with 1.6 seconds remaining.

The Suns called a timeout, and Oliver Miller looked to inbound the ball. The Lakers played almost perfect defense on the play, giving Miller no passing options besides Dan Majerle who was 33-feet from the basket near half-court. Majerle caught the ball and did the only thing he could – fling it high towards the basket to beat the buzzer. "It came straight down like a rainbow," Scott said. It fell perfectly through the net, giving the Suns a 115-114 victory and the Lakers their most crushing defeat of the season.

"No matter how well you play, how hard you play," Scott said, "you show the type of character and heart we did, it's really tough to lose that way." The Suns won the season series against the Lakers 5-0, only the second time in franchise history the Lakers had failed to defeat a Western Conference team at least once in a season.

The Lakers were in Oakland two nights later where they held a three-point lead over the Golden State Warriors in the dying seconds. But Latrell Sprewell made a three-pointer to send the game into overtime, and the Lakers went on to lose 112-116. For the second straight game, they had played well enough on the road to win but were undone by a three-pointer at the end of the fourth quarter. "It was almost like the same thing that happened in Phoenix," said Scott. "Sprewell hit a great shot, but damn, how many nights in a row can it happen?"

The Lakers got almost everything they could ask for the next night at home against the Portland Trail Blazers but, again, it wasn't enough. Worthy top scored off the bench with 26 points. Green and Campbell battled hard inside with 40 points and 32 rebounds between them. Christie played 22 minutes of controlled basketball, scoring 13 points and handing out 7 assists. Mario Elie broke a tie with a three-pointer with half a minute remaining, and the Blazers won 109-105.

Things were grim. The loss to the Blazers was their sixth in a row. They had won just one of their last 12 games, and only one of their last 10 at home. Now with a 34-39 record, any hope of a winning season was almost gone.

Perkins was back at the Forum for the first time since the trade when the Seattle SuperSonics were in town. The Lakers had gone 8-16 without him while the Sonics were 17-7 since the trade and had surged to second in the West.

"It's going to be strange to play against them, no doubt about it. They were my teammates," Perkins said. He showed no obvious resentment against the Lakers for being traded. He still followed them closely and had kept track of Pfund's recent rotation changes. "I know what Randy and the guys are going through. I saw their heartbreak against the Phoenix Suns, and I just know," he said. He was diplomatic when asked to assess which team got the better of the trade. "It's kind of hard to assess the trade because Doug has only played 14 games and Benoit, well, I don't know much about that."[132]

The Lakers held close to the Sonics for three quarters but went on a scoring drought in the fourth. Threatt cut a three-point deficit to one on a jumper before stealing the ball off Perkins and scoring on a lay-in to give the Lakers a 94-93 lead with two minutes to play. Derrick McKey missed two free throws and Green outfought three Sonics to tap in a Worthy miss for a 96-93 lead.

McKey again went to the free throw line and made one out of two, trimming the lead to two with 38.7 seconds to play. Payton forced Threatt into a tough three-pointer against the shot clock that missed. Michael Cage rebounded, and the Sonics had the ball with 12 seconds remaining and a chance to tie.

They went to Perkins in the corner who was being guarded by the smaller Threatt. Perkins wanted to pass to Payton, but he couldn't get a passing lane. Instead, he was forced to take a 20-footer with 4.3 seconds remaining that bounced off the rim. Threatt rebounded the ball and, following two free throws, the Lakers let Cage dunk for two meaningless points as they got a rare win, 98-96.

They would finish the season playing marginally better, winning four of their last eight games. Unlike the previous year, there would be no drama on the last night of the season to determine their playoff fate. This time, they officially secured a playoff berth with a three-point win over the Warriors with four more games left in the season. They were 4-13 over the previous four weeks, and qualified for the playoffs not because of anything they did well. Instead they were there because Denver and Golden State had played just as poorly beneath them in the standings over the final weeks of the season.

Peeler, who had averaged 12.1 points since the change in rotation at the start of the month, sprained his right ankle in the third to last game of the season, a nine-point road loss to the Utah Jazz. The injury would take weeks to heal, meaning he would be unavailable for the playoffs. "That's a real tough blow for us going into the playoffs," Pfund said. "We've got some other guys we can go to, like Byron. But Anthony, I thought, had the

---

[132] There were reports shortly after Perkins was traded that he was suffering from depression. *Sports Illustrated* ran a piece partly about it in May 1993 in which he said he had been given leave to attend to a family issue. He said he referred to depression at the time but had never said was the one requiring treatment.

ability to come into a playoff series and explode."

They closed out the regular season with a 125-107 win at home over the Sacramento Kings. Rumors began circulating the very next day that Jerry Buss had decided to fire Pfund as soon as the playoffs ended. Radio station KMPC reported Buss had asked Magic to replace Pfund next season. Magic and Jerry West both denied the report. But West had grown increasingly displeased behind closed doors at how disorganized the team seemed.

In truth, Pfund had been up against it from the moment Magic re-retired, and his situation only became harder after the Perkins trade. The trade was made with an eye to the future, yet Buss and West still expected wins. It put Pfund in a near-impossible situation. "We're trying to do something very difficult, win and develop young players at the same time," he said. His ability to balance those two opposing philosophies would, fairly or not, be what his performance was judged on. He was asked by the media what price the Lakers had paid in the Perkins trade. "My head," he replied, semi-seriously.

Worthy publicly gave his support for Pfund, and lamented it wasn't the appropriate time for such speculation as the team prepared for the playoffs. "It's not fair to even comment on these rumors," he said. "It's not fair to Randy. You hire a guy for a season, you ought to let him coach a season. We don't need this distraction."

For the second year in a row, the Lakers finished the season in a very different place to where they started at training camp. With Magic back, they expected to be up with the best teams in the league competing for a championship. "I picked the Lakers and the Knicks beginning of the year," Jack Nicholson said. "Got the betting slips to prove it. We'd have made it too if Magic hadn't retired."

But Magic did retire, and the Lakers finished with a 39-43 record, their first losing season since 1976. They had once again qualified for the playoffs but were the only team in the league to do so with a losing record. With a 20-21 record at the Forum, it was their first season with a losing home record since moving from Minneapolis.

Threatt led the team in scoring with 15.1 points per game, the lowest average to lead the Lakers in that category in franchise history.[133] Worthy averaged 14.9 points per game, five less than the season before. It was his lowest scoring average since becoming a full-time starter in 1984. His efficiency rating dropped to 15.6, the lowest of his career. Scott's productivity had dropped too with an average of 13.7 points, his fewest since his rookie season in 1984.[134]

Peeler averaged 10.4 points in 21.5 minutes, becoming the first Laker rookie since Scott in 1984 to average over 10 points per game. Christie averaged 6.2 points in 14.4 minutes in 23 games, but his abbreviated rookie campaign didn't provide a great deal more clarity about his future role.[135]

Unlike the previous season, the Lakers were not undone by injury.[136] Instead, it was the Perkins trade that changed the trajectory of their season. They were 26-23 when they made the trade, on track for a 44-win season, but they were 13-20 after the trade. If they had played at that rate all season, they would have won around 32 games, well and truly out of the playoff picture.

The trade didn't just impact the team's record, but also their identity. Their scoring increased from 103.3 points to 105.6 per game following the trade. But their defense, never strong all season, went south without Perkins. They'd allowed 103.1 points with Perkins, reaching 10th best in the league. After the trade, they gave up 109.1 points, dropping to fifth worst in the league. They went from outscoring their opponents by 0.2 points before the trade to being outscored by 3.5 per game after it.

Yet as ugly as the final two months of the season had been, the Lakers were moving on. The playoffs represented an opportunity to wipe the slate clean. "It's over now," Worthy said. "It's a new season."[137]

---

[133] This shouldn't diminish how important Threatt was to the Lakers in 1992-93. He was the only player to start all 82 games and led the team in scoring, assists, steals, and minutes. Jonathan Abrams was quoted in Shea Serrano's book that Threatt "provided some light during the sucky years." And it was very true.

[134] The deterioration of Worthy's play, more than anything, would have made it extremely unlikely the Lakers could have made a serious championship run in 1993 if Magic's comeback came to fruition.

[135] For the record, Benjamin averaged 4.5 points and 3.4 rebounds in 10.9 minutes in 28 games for the Lakers.

[136] The Lakers lost 142 games to injury in 1992-93, but only 42 games to rotation players. Haley 82, Scott 24, Blackwell 22, Peeler 6, Smith 4, Edwards & Campbell 2, Christie 1

[137] For the second straight season, the Lakers led the league with the most wins by three points or less. In 1991-92 they won 12 games and in 1992-93 they won 13.

Chapter 13

ONE LAST STAND

April 30, 1993 to May 9, 1993

THE ONE VS eight match-up in the playoffs is, by design, never a fair fight. The reward for having the best regular season record in the conference is to start the playoffs against the team that just scraped in. And the Suns-Lakers series in 1993 was the epitome of top vs. bottom. The Suns owned the league's best record with 62 wins, while the Lakers were the only team to qualify for the playoffs with a losing record. The Suns had beaten the Lakers all five times they played each other during the regular season. One of the games was close, but the Suns won the other four by an average of 17.3 points.

The Suns had built a powerhouse in the off-season, trading for Charles Barkley and pairing him with Kevin Johnson, one of the best point guards in the league. Dan Majerle was an All-Star, an effective outside shooter, and defender. Veteran role players Danny Ainge, Tom Chambers, Frank Johnson, and Mark West gave them steady leadership. They had two young, athletic, offensive-minded small forwards in Cedric Ceballos and Richard Dumas. And their rookie Oliver Miller may have been better known for his weight problems, but the kid could play. Barkley had the finest season of his career, averaging 25.6 points, 12.2 rebounds, and 5.1 assists. He would go on to be named MVP for the first time.

It was the best team Phoenix had ever had, and they seemed like a team of destiny all season long. And they could be wildly entertaining, playing the kind of fast-paced basketball the Lakers under Pat Riley used to play. "The Lakers are a dull team. They're a half-court team, and that's about as exciting in 1993 as watching grass grow," Chick Hearn said. "The Suns play the closest thing to Showtime you can imagine."

The Suns would start the series without Johnson, who suffered ligament damage in his left knee when celebrating a Barkley game-winning shot too exuberantly in the last week of the season. It was possible he might return during the series, but most assumed the Suns would rest him for the second round. The Suns were expected to dominate the series, with or without Johnson. Third-year reserve Negele Knight would start in place of Johnson and would share point guard duties with Ainge off the bench.

The Lakers had their own injury concerns. Anthony Peeler had been ruled out for the playoffs with a severely sprained right foot. Benoit Benjamin surprised the Lakers by having surgery to remove an infected nail from his left big toe just four days before the start of the playoffs. The surgery would make him questionable for the series, though it is doubtful Pfund would have given him meaningful minutes anyhow. Surprisingly, the Lakers left rookie Alex Blackwell off the playoff roster even though he was healthy enough to be training with the team, giving them just 10 healthy bodies for the series.

Randy Pfund wanted to slow down the Suns' fast break, and the only way to do that was to play as slowly as possible. Even slower than the Slowtime Lakers. He figured they'd have a better chance of defending Barkley and limiting the opportunities for the Suns' shooters if they forced them into a half-court game. He would try defending Barkley straight up. "We have to be concerned with more than just Barkley," Pfund said.

The job of defending Barkley would fall to third-year forward Elden Campbell, a good defender when motivated. Pfund hoped the 6'11 Campbell would be able to bother the 6'6 Barkley's shot enough to give the Lakers a fighting chance.[138] "I have to try to stay with him. You've got to keep your presence there in front of him," Campbell said. "You're not going to block all his shots, but you've got to make him take the worst shots possible and make sure he's not going to just shoot open shots."

The Lakers entered the playoffs with a lot of uncertainty hanging over them. There were the rumors about Pfund's job security and question marks about the future of Byron Scott and A.C. Green, two Showtime stalwarts. Both would be unrestricted free agents in the off-season. With a crowded and young backcourt, Scott assumed the Lakers would let him walk. "I'd definitely like to go out at my best, go down fighting," he said. Green knew the Lakers wanted him back, but did he want to be part of a

---

[138] Campbell was an effective shot blocker. He averaged 2.3 blocks per 36 minutes in 1992-93, seventh best in the league.

rebuilding process? "The excitement and the hype at the Forum, it's not at the same level as it used to be a few years back," Green said. "If this is my last year with this team, I want to go out the same way I went in, playing hard and playing to win."

America West Arena was so loud at the start of Game 1 that Hearn called it the 'Jungle on Jefferson.'[139] Sedale Threatt started the game hot, scoring eight first quarter points. In the second quarter he scored eight consecutive points as part of a 23-8 run that quietened the crowd, and the Lakers took a surprising 53-46 lead into half-time.

Threatt was just as hot in the third quarter, seemingly scoring at will against either Knight or Frank Johnson. He scored on his first four shots. In one sequence he took Barkley one-on-one, tried to blow past him but was forced to pick up his dribble. He then pivoted twice, pirouetted in the air and hit a turnaround jumper with Barkley draped all over him. The Lakers entered the last break up 83-79 with Threatt having scored 12 points in the quarter on 6-6 shooting.

Phoenix fought back in the fourth quarter, holding the Lakers without a basket for three minutes. When Chambers made a jumper to give the Suns a 103-98 lead with two and half minutes to play, it seemed like the predictable was happening.

But the Lakers clamped down on defense, forcing a 24-second shot clock violation and making the Suns take bad shots to beat the shot clock two other times. Divac stole the ball off Chambers and threw a length of the floor pass to Worthy who dunked over Majerle to tie the score at 103-103 with 47 seconds remaining. With the crowd getting nervous, Ainge missed a lay-up and Green was fouled on the rebound. He made one of two free throws for a 104-103 Lakers lead with 27 seconds to play.

Then the game turned into a scramble. Ainge missed a three-pointer from the corner, and Ceballos handled the rebound. He made a sneaky pass to Majerle, who missed under the basket. Green, Campbell, and Chambers each had the rebound slip through their hands until it was knocked free by Ceballos. Green dove on the floor to secure the ball, had it momentarily but it again slipped out of his hands. Majerle jumped over Green and dove on the ball, tried to pass it, but it hit Threatt's knee. It ricocheted straight to Scott who finally secured it before having his jersey

---

[139] America West Arena is located on Jefferson Street in downtown Phoenix.

pulled by Ainge for the foul with 9.8 seconds on the clock.

Scott hit both free throws, pushing the lead out to 106-103 and Majerle tried an off-balance three down the other end but missed. Threatt controlled the rebound, was fouled and made one of two free throws for a 107-103 lead with 3.5 seconds to go. Ainge missed a meaningless three-pointer at the buzzer, and the Lakers had stunned the Suns to take a 1-0 series lead, holding the Suns scoreless over the final two and a half minutes. It was the first win by a #8 seed on the home floor of the #1 seed since 1984.

The Suns couldn't stop Threatt all game long. He led all scorers with a playoff-career high 35 points on 17-24 shooting and 7 assists. "I think it was obvious that Sedale was the best player in the world tonight," Barkley said. "He dominated the game offensively. Every time they needed a play, he and Scott made the difference." Scott added a steady 22 points on 6-11 shooting and Divac scored 12 points and had 10 rebounds.

Charles Barkley put up the kind of numbers expected of a superstar with 34 points on 12-16 shooting and 15 rebounds. But except for Chambers who had 18 points, everybody else struggled for the Suns. Majerle scored 9 points on 4-15 shooting while Ainge scored 10 on 4-13 shooting.

Although Barkley had a big game, the Lakers held him in check in the final minutes. "We just couldn't get the ball to him when the shot clock was running down," Ainge said. "They kept rotating fresh guys on him." After frustrating his players with inconsistent rotations throughout the season, Pfund did a masterful job of juggling the line-up in Game 1. "His substitution pattern was the best I've seen. He knew what was going on in the game as far as match-ups," said Scott. "I thought he did an excellent job from tip-off until the end of the game."

Suns head coach Paul Westphal had hoped to rest Kevin Johnson until the second round, but those plans changed with the Game 1 loss. They had missed Johnson's offense but mostly missed his defense, especially against Threatt. Wearing a bulky knee brace, he was back in the starting line-up for Game 2. Westphal also moved Ceballos, who struggled in Game 1, to the bench and started Dumas in his place.

The Suns led the second game 78-72 with six minutes left in the fourth quarter, but the Lakers would quickly get back within striking distance.

Threatt found Scott wide-open for a three-pointer. Then Worthy found Campbell for a powerful dunk on their next possession that cut the Suns' lead to 78-77 with four and a half minutes remaining. Both teams struggled to score on the next few possessions before Chambers hit two free throws to make it an 80-77 Suns lead with three minutes to play.

Then, just like in Game 1, the game turned into chaos. Divac mishandled a post feed and had to skirt the baseline to stop it going out of bounds. He flung the ball in desperation, heaving it high into the air. Threatt beat Ainge to the ball and fed it to Scott at the top of the key with three seconds on the shot clock. Scott drove and fed Worthy in the corner. The shot was barely out of his hands when the shot clock sounded, and the veteran drained a three-pointer in front of the Suns bench. It tied the score 80-80 with two and a half minutes to play, Worthy jogging backward down the court, pointing and hollering at the Suns bench.

The Suns had an equally wild possession down the other end. Both Ainge and Chambers separately slipped on the floor with the ball. It resulted in Johnson being forced to heave up a prayer to beat the shot clock that wasn't close. The Lakers then barely beat the shot clock for the second straight possession, Divac's hook shot over Chambers giving them an 82-80 lead with one and a half minutes remaining. Barkley then missed a tough baseline fadeaway, and Threatt fed Divac the ball in the post where he surprised Chambers by not running down the clock. Instead, he quickly spun around him towards the baseline and dunked it for an 84-80 lead with just 46 seconds to play.

America West Arena was in stunned silence for the second straight game. Chambers shot an air-ball down the other end, but Threatt fouled Barkley on the rebound and he made one of two free throws to cut the lead to three. A long jumper by Scott pushed the Lakers lead back out to 86-81.

The Suns launched two desperation three-pointers in the dying seconds that weren't close. Worthy secured the rebound and embraced the ball. As the final three seconds ticked away, he held the ball in one hand and pointed to the ceiling with the other. He slammed the ball down on the court as the buzzer sounded, turned his back and immediately walked to the change room without looking back. His celebrating teammates and a gaggle of media cameras followed behind him.[140]

* * * * *

---

[140] The Lakers won despite the lowest free throw percentage (43%, 10-23) by a team in a playoff game in league history.

The Lakers had stunned the basketball world. The Suns hadn't lost two straight games at home all season. Now the Lakers had defeated them twice on their own floor for a 2-0 series lead. They needed just one more win to produce one of the biggest upsets in NBA history. And they would have three chances to get it, including two at home.

"I couldn't believe it," said Divac. "Before this series, if somebody asked me if we were going to beat Phoenix twice, I would have said, 'No way.'" Coming into hostile territory and silencing a frenzied crowd was something the Showtime Lakers were known for. Not these Lakers. "It felt like old times," Scott said. "I can't tell you how much fun it was."

Magic Johnson commentated the game for NBC, and his performance irked Suns fans who claimed he was showing bias toward his former team – which he most certainly was, cheering on the Lakers late in the fourth quarter. When Divac made his hook shot over Chambers, he giggled hysterically. "This is unbelievable. I can't believe this," he said. "This can't be happening. No way, no way."

Barkley scored 18 points and collected 21 rebounds, but he shot 8-24 from the field. Johnson scored 14 points and collected 16 assists. Dumas played much better as the starting small forward than Ceballos did in Game 1, and Chambers again scored 18 points. But the rest of the Suns were nowhere to be seen. Majerle had his second straight cold shooting night, scoring 8 points on 3-11 shooting. Ainge, who was recruited in the off-season to provide veteran leadership, was 1-7 from the field.

Westphal made no excuses for the loss but was defiant after the game. "We're a better team than the Lakers, and we will win the series," he said. "We're going to win one Tuesday. And the next game is Thursday, we'll win there, and then we'll come back and win the series on Sunday. And everyone will say what a great series it was."

Divac had been great in Phoenix, averaging 15.5 points and 11.5 rebounds on 54% shooting over the first two games. It was his best start to a playoff series in his four-year career after facing criticism in the past during the playoffs. As a rookie in 1990, he had been badly outplayed by Suns center Mark West when Phoenix upset the Lakers in the second round. In both 1991 and 1992, he had been bullied by Blazers center Kevin Duckworth. He would turn things around in both 1991 and 1992, but this year he didn't wait to be pushed around. Instead, he started the series aggressively. "I was very, very ready for this game," he said.

* * * * *

Divac was ready for Game 3 at the Forum too, where he scored a career playoff-high 30 points. The Suns led by 14 points in the third quarter, but the Lakers slowly edged closer. Barkley made two free throws to push the Suns' lead to 101-94 with two minutes to play in the game. Threatt then used a pick by Divac to draw a double-team before passing back to him for a wide-open three-pointer that he swished from the top of the key. The Lakers ran the same play on their next possession, but instead of shooting a three, Divac drove to the basket and drew Johnson off Threatt. He fired a pass back to Threatt who sunk a wide-open three-pointer, cutting the Suns' lead to 101-100 with one and a half minutes to play.

The crowd, one of the few sell-outs of the season, was sensing history in the making and was as loud during this stretch as Hearn could remember. "In the 80s, the season ticket holders would always pick up their option to buy playoff tickets," he said. "This year, many didn't, enabling the general public to buy playoff tickets, and the result was all that noise."

Following a Suns timeout, Campbell stole the inbound pass from Majerle, and the Lakers had the ball with a chance to take the lead with 55 seconds remaining. Threatt and Worthy worked a pick-and-roll that resulted in Threatt drawing both Johnson and Barkley. Threatt fired a pass to Worthy for an uncontested mid-range jump shot. The play was executed to perfection and created an excellent shot for Worthy – but it drew the back of the iron and bounced off. "You always think they're going in," Worthy said. "It was a good play, a pick and roll, and they switched off. It was the shot that had to be taken."

Miller made two free throws to give the Suns a 103-100 lead. With one last chance to tie the game, Divac dribbled through traffic and stopped at the three-point line. He threw a pump fake and forced up a rushed, contested three-pointer that didn't hit the rim and sailed out of bounds with 8 seconds remaining. "That was a terrible shot," Divac said. Lakers fans, who had been rowdy all night, and many of whom had brought brooms in hopes of celebrating a series sweep, began filing out. Free throws settled the game, and the Suns stayed alive, winning 107-102.

Divac's 30 points led a strong game from the Lakers' starting frontcourt unit. Campbell scored 17 points, and Green recorded 14 points and 17 rebounds. But as he had done all series, Worthy struggled to put the ball in the basket and finished with 13 points on 6-18 shooting.

The Suns were led by Barkley who had 27 points and 11 rebounds. But he shot 9-23, his second poor shooting night in a row. "It would be good for me to make a shot every now and then," he joked. "That would definitely make us more effective." Westphal hardly played Chambers after he had scored 18 points in both games in Phoenix. Instead, he gave the minutes to Miller, who had 11 points and 8 rebounds in 31 minutes.

The Lakers had blown an opportunity to win the series at home. But there were positives to take away from the loss. They hadn't played well in the first half, but still had a chance to win the game in the final minute. "We should come in Thursday and play with the same effort," said Divac. "We don't have to change anything."

The first three games of the series had been exhilarating examples of white-knuckled playoff basketball. But Game 4 wasn't. The Lakers tied the game at 51-51 on a three-pointer by Scott with eight minutes to play in the third quarter. But the Suns immediately ripped off an 11-0 run and would never look back. The Lakers had been effective in the first three games by keeping the score close and then clamping down defensively in the final minutes. But there was no such opportunity in Game 4. The Lakers shot 36%, picking a bad time to match their worst shooting performance of the season.[141] The Suns won easily, 101-86, sending the series back to Phoenix for a decisive Game 5.

Barkley found his shooting touch again, getting 28 points and 11 rebounds on 13-21 shooting. Miller backed up his excellent Game 3 performance with an even better one in Game 4, scoring 16 points and grabbing 8 rebounds in 29 minutes off the bench. Divac once again top-scored for the Lakers with 17 points to go along with 12 rebounds, but he shot just 7-20. Worthy's shooting woes continued, hitting six of 16 shots for 12 points.

The Suns, who had lamented how uncharacteristically tight they had been in the first three games, were back to their old loose selves. They credited that renewed spark to Barkley making the team laugh at half-time by telling stories in the locker room that the Suns players described as 'unprintable.' They looked like their old selves again. "They have a lot of guys going now," Pfund said. "Danny Ainge and Dan Majerle and Oliver Miller are all playing well now. For a while, we had them tentative, and

---

[141] The Lakers also shot 36% in a loss to the Houston Rockets at the Forum on April 16, 1993.

now it looks like they've warmed up. It looks now like they're back to where they were at the best point of their season."

When the teams flew back to Phoenix for Game 5, the Suns were surprised to find 5,000 fans waiting for them at Sky Harbor International Airport. They were there to show their appreciation for the team winning both games in Los Angeles, but Westphal wasn't happy to see them. "If they would have told me they were planning a celebration, I would have told them not to do it," he said. "I don't want to be the jerk or anything, but we've got a job to do, and we haven't finished it."

There is nothing in the world like a deciding game in the NBA playoffs. Two teams who know each other inside out battling it out in a winner-takes-all game. "It's fun, it's scary, it's exciting," Westphal said. "It's why you play."

It would be the Lakers' first deciding game since winning Game 7 of the 1988 NBA Finals against the Detroit Pistons. Like most playoff series that go the distance, the Lakers-Suns series was going to be a great story no matter what happened in Game 5. "Either Westphal will have made a great guarantee, and the Suns come back from 2-0," said Pfund, "or we're going to be the greatest underdog of all time and come back and win. It sounds like a pretty good scenario to me."

When Scott took the floor for Game 5, he knew it might be the last time he would wear a Lakers uniform. "For the first time in a while, I've been thinking about that stuff," he said. "I thought about Game 4, that it could have been my last home game. I've still got one more game left. I hope it's more than one."

America West Arena was in full voice in the fourth quarter of Game 5. The Suns looked to be putting the series away when Johnson scored their first five points of the quarter, pushing their lead out to eleven. Following a free throw, Threatt made a lay-in to cut the deficit to nine.

Then Worthy put on a vintage, turn-back-the-clock, Big Game James performance. "He was demanding us to give him the ball," Scott said. "When he gets in that mode, it's pretty hard to stop him." The veteran forward, who had struggled with his shooting all season, posted Majerle and scored on a turnaround jumper that cut the lead to five with eight minutes to play. He then hit on another turnaround jumper, cutting the Suns lead to 85-82. With four and a half minutes to play, he hit a third turnaround jumper over Majerle, cutting the Suns lead to a single point. Johnson hit a midrange jumper, and the Lakers again went back to Worthy in the post. His turnaround missed but Green snatched the rebound and fed it back to Worthy who coolly hit a three-pointer to tie the game at 87-87.

With the crowd getting nervous, Barkley scored to push the lead back to two. The Lakers drew fouls on back-to-back possessions but squandered the opportunity to get a lead when Threatt and Green each made only one of two free throws to tie the game at 89-89.

The Lakers played tough defense on the next possession, forcing Majerle to shoot a three-pointer with the shot clock winding down. The shot missed but Barkley caught the ball in the air and eased it into the basket just as the shot clock sounded. The Lakers were incensed, sure that Barkley didn't get it off in time. The players pleaded with the official to wave it off. The entire Lakers bench waved their arms in the air like they were making the call for the official. Worthy dropped to the floor in a wide-legged squat and pleaded with the official. Replays clearly showed the ball still in Barkley's hand when the shot clock was at zero. It shouldn't have counted, but the officials didn't wave it off, and the Suns reclaimed a 91-89 lead with two and a half minutes to play.

Worthy made yet another jumper to tie the score again with two minutes remaining. For the second straight possession, the Lakers forced the Suns to throw up a desperation shot to beat the shot-clock, this time securing the rebound. Threatt went to his favorite move, a step-back midrange jumper going to his left, that hit the rim and bounced off. But Campbell came flying in from the weak side to dunk it home. The Lakers led 93-91 with one and a half minutes left.

Barkley's reverse lay-up down the other end hit almost every part of the basket before falling out. Threatt milked the shot clock before Worthy crunched Johnson with a pick that sent the guard flying. It freed up a driving lane for Threatt who scored on the lay-in for a 95-91 lead with just over a minute to play.

Barkley hit a clutch jumper over Campbell, cutting the Lakers' lead to two with 58 seconds left. Threatt again milked the shot clock and went to his trademark fade-away but missed. Barkley got the rebound and Majerle hit an off-balance jumper with 13 seconds remaining that tied the score at 95-95.

The Lakers called a timeout to set up a play. Pfund wanted to use up all the clock and take the final shot of the game. He didn't want to risk giving the Suns a chance to win at the buzzer, not after Majerle's heartbreaking buzzer-beater during the regular season. Pfund set up a good play, with Threatt milking the clock by pretending to feed the ball to Divac in the post. Threatt spent so much time trying to get Divac the ball that the Suns overcommitted, and he found Scott for an uncontested three-pointer at the buzzer. But the pass was a second late, Scott had to rush the shot to beat the clock, and it hit the front of the rim.

The deciding Game 5 of the most intensely competitive first round match-up in recent memory was going to overtime. And it was because of Worthy and Threatt, who scored 21 of the Lakers' 24 points in the fourth quarter.

The Suns scored the first seven points of extra time with Miller going on a rampage – scoring, rebounding, and blocking shots. It took the Lakers almost three full minutes to score, finally adding to their tally on two free throws by Scott with two minutes to play. They made their first basket of overtime on a jumper by Worthy with 90 seconds remaining. The shot put the Lakers in striking distance, down only three despite hardly scoring in extra time. But Campbell got lost on the next defensive play, and Miller had a wide-open dunk for a 104-99 lead.

And there was no clawing back. From there it was a series of academic free throws, the Suns finally winning 112-104 in overtime, taking the series 3-2.[142] The Lakers were painfully close to making history, but in the end, were eliminated in the first round for the second straight season.[143]

Barkley, Johnson, and Majerle all had big games. But the hero in over-time was rookie Miller, who scored nine of his 17 points and grabbed five of his 14 rebounds in the extra session. The Lakers were led by Worthy's 24 points off the bench. Threatt had 18 points and 9 assists, Campbell had 17 points and 9 rebounds, and Green was a workhorse all night, hustling for 15 points and 19 rebounds in 50 minutes of action.

After clinching the series, Westphal reflected on the guarantee he made after the Game 2 loss. "The reason I said that was because I believed we had a better team. They didn't make it easy," he said. "I'm not gloating at all. I feel very humble to be able to escape with this win. They were

---

[142] After eliminating the Lakers, Phoenix would make it all the way to the NBA Finals where they lost in six games to the Chicago Bulls. It was the second straight year the Lakers were eliminated in the first round by Chicago's eventual Finals victim.

[143] It was the first playoff series the Lakers lost after leading 2-0 since the 1969 Finals.

fantastic, and they just showed what they were made of. We are very fortunate to get past them."

The series had, if nothing else, quelled the rumors Pfund would be fired in the off-season. He made some questionable moves late in Game 5, but there was no denying he coached the Lakers extremely well during the series. In many instances, he outcoached Westphal. The series saved his job.

The Game 5 loss was bittersweet. The season came down to just a handful of moments that would have had an entirely different outcome if they had just swung a different way. If Scott got a little more lift on that final three-pointer in regulation, it might have gone in. If the officials hadn't blown the shot clock call late in the fourth quarter, maybe the Lakers would have advanced.

Winning the first two games in Phoenix was as remarkable as it was shocking. So too was taking Game 5 down to the wire. When Worthy slammed the ball down at the end of Game 2 and walked off the court, it was one last defiant stand by the leftover remnants of Showtime. These aging, proud players had seen their moment at the top of the game pass them by. In their last stand, they didn't win. They didn't overcome. There was no fairy-tale ending. But boy, did they go out swinging.

PART III:
ROCK BOTTOM

Chapter 14

GUTTED

May 10, 1993 to November 4, 1993

A MONTH AFTER the end of the 1992-93 season, Vlade Divac was holidaying in Hawaii. He was out at the pool with his wife and children when he briefly went inside to get something. The TV was still playing, and it caught his eye. It was tuned to ESPN, and he couldn't hear what the anchor was saying, but there was a picture of Drazen Petrovic on the screen.

It had been three years since Divac and Petrovic had exchanged any kind of meaningful words with each other. Once the closest of friends, they were now almost strangers. In that time, the war in Yugoslavia had only grown deadlier, and the divide between Divac and his old Croatian teammates had only gotten wider.

Petrovic had a frustrating rookie season in Portland where he hardly played. But in the years since Divac had last spoken to him, Petrovic had been traded to the New Jersey Nets where he was thriving. Given the opportunity of big minutes, he was proving he belonged in the NBA. He had led the Nets in scoring and into the playoffs each of the previous two seasons.

After the season had ended, Petrovic traveled to Berlin to join the Croatian national team to play a qualifying tournament for the 1993 European Championship. He was meant to fly with the rest of the team back to Zagreb but at the last moment decided to drive back with his girlfriend, Klara Szalantzy. Petrovic was asleep in the passenger seat as Szalantzy drove through a rainstorm on Autobahn 9. She had no way of knowing a semi-truck had broken through the Autobahn median when trying to avoid a collision and was blocking three lanes of traffic ahead of them. Szalantzy had no time to stop, and their car crashed into the truck leaving her gravely injured. The 28-year-old Petrovic, who was not wearing a seatbelt, was killed instantly.

The funeral was attended by dignitaries, politicians, celebrities, and sportspeople from around the world. But Divac wasn't welcome. He watched the funeral on TV, the most painful moment coming when he watched his former teammates act as pallbearers without him.

Divac had held hope one day he and Petrovic would sit down and talk through their differences. Their friendship had been too deep for this rift to continue forever. At that moment as he watched the news story, he knew that moment was never coming. And the loss would haunt him for decades.

Jerry Buss and Jerry West had been prepared to fire head coach Randy Pfund in the final weeks of the 1992-93 season. But Pfund's masterful coaching in the playoffs convinced them to give him another try. But West was sure he had seen enough of maligned center Benoit Benjamin. He had played disinterested basketball during his short time with the Lakers, often drifting if he went a few possessions without touching the ball. His decision to have surgery on his big toe on the eve of the playoffs was the final straw. Well, that and the three years left on his oversized five-year, $17.5 million contract.

The Lakers traded Benjamin just two days after the NBA Finals finished. West found one of the few executives left in the NBA who believed Benjamin's potential still outweighed his performance. It was Benjamin's former college coach, Willis Reed, who was now manager of the New Jersey Nets. "I definitely don't think he has reached his potential," Reed said. "I coached him for three years. I never had any difficulties with him. I don't know anything about all this bad reputation stuff."[144]

The Lakers received 31-year-old veteran center Sam Bowie in exchange for Benjamin along with the Nets' 1998 second-round pick. Bowie was best known for being selected ahead of Michael Jordan in the 1984 Draft by the Portland Trail Blazers. Bowie would go on to spend as much time on the injured list as he did on the court while Jordan would, well, go on to

---

[144] Benjamin played seven more seasons in the NBA, spending time in New Jersey, Vancouver, Milwaukee, Toronto, Philadelphia, and Cleveland. Oddly enough, he was given a second chance by the Lakers at the age of 35. He was in training camp with them prior to the 1999-00 season but was waived after pre-season.

become Jordan.[145] In Bowie the Lakers were getting a versatile player who could play center and power forward, could shoot from outside and block some shots. He may have looked more like a 35-year-old than a 31-year-old on the court, but his reputation was that of a consummate professional. "I gave up on analyzing trades," said Bowie. "I don't look at it as though I'm not wanted, I look at it like I'm just wanted somewhere else."

The Lakers had the 12th pick in the draft, the highest non-lottery position and three spots higher than their position a year earlier. They worked out a suite of eligible players and West established his plan of attack.

Plan A would be drafting high-scoring forward Vin Baker from Hartford. "Our first choice would be Vin Baker, by far," West said. "We'd be ecstatic if we could get him." Point guard Lindsey Hunter from Jackson State was West's Plan B, and Plan C would be selecting shooting guard Allan Houston from Tennessee. Both guards were tremendous scorers in college. Hunter may have been a point guard, but he played with a shooting guard's mentality and averaged 26.7 points his senior year. Meanwhile Houston was the only player in Tennessee history to get 2,000 points, 400 rebounds, and 400 assists. "Allan Houston is a very talented player, but it would be very tough to pass up Lindsey Hunter," West said.

But as the draft unfolded, West saw his Plan A, B, and C selections go before he had a chance to pick. Baker was selected eighth overall by the Milwaukee Bucks while Hunter and Houston were both selected by the Detroit Pistons at the 10th and 11th spots.[146]

Instead West selected forward George Lynch from North Carolina. It was a safe choice, but Lynch was hardly viewed as a consolation prize. He had teamed with center Eric Montross on the Tar Heels team that won the 1993 National Championship and averaged 14.7 points and 9.7 rebounds in his senior year.[147] "You know what you're getting when you take a North Carolina player," West said. "One thing I've always felt about

---

[145] Bowie played in just 34% of games during his five years in Portland, but was healthier in New Jersey, playing in 85% of games in his four seasons as a Net.

[146] There were rumours the Lakers would send Elden Campbell and the #12 pick to Milwaukee in exchange for the draft rights to Baker, but nothing ever came of it.

[147] This was the infamous game where Michigan forward Chris Webber called a timeout they didn't have trailing by two points with 11 seconds to go, resulting in a technical foul that gave North Carolina free throws that won the championship. Future Laker GM, Rob Pelinka, was on that Michigan team.

basketball is that it's a team game, and that's how Dean Smith runs his program. If a kid can play at a high level at North Carolina, there's no reason he can't play at a high level in the NBA."

Lynch had one giant hole in his game. He wasn't much of a shooter with almost no outside range. But he bought a lot of other things to the Lakers, one big one was rebounding. The Lakers were the fourth-worst rebounding team in the NBA in 1992-93, while Lynch had collected over 1,000 of them in college. He was the first player to lead North Carolina in rebounding three years in a row since Sam Perkins in 1982-84. He was a hustler, a hard worker, and a good defender.

Adding a forward to a frontcourt weakened by the Perkins trade was a bonus. But just like with Doug Christie, the only question about Lynch was what position he would play. His rebounding skills suggested he would play power forward, the position he played in college. Yet at 6'7 and 223 pounds, he was physically better suited to the small forward position in the pros. Not that he didn't have a track record of being able to bulk up. Lynch had been born two months premature and weighed less than three pounds at birth. "I was really, really scared. He was so tiny," said his mother. "We thought he wasn't going to make it. But as you can see, he grew up to be a very good son."

The Lakers had a true curiosity on their hands with the 37th pick – Nick Van Exel from Cincinnati. The intensely fiery, lightning fast (his nickname was Nick the Quick) point guard had worked out for the Lakers before the draft. West was extremely impressed and considered using the Lakers' 12th pick to select him. But West eventually cooled on him, as did the entire league. Van Exel was once considered a chance to be a top ten pick, but he had a reputation for being cocky and irresponsible both on and off the court. He led Cincinnati to the Final Four as a junior and to the East Regional Final as a senior. But he was criticised for poor shot selection throughout the tournament and for showboating in Cincinnati's loss to George Lynch's North Carolina.

Van Exel had a tough upbringing in Kenosha, Wisconsin. He learned to play basketball from his father, who was a former high school basketball star. His father was a petty street criminal who would bring his son with him to break into cars and sell the stolen goods. His father was sent to prison when Van Exel was seven-years-old, and his mother was forced to work long hours to pay the bills. As a result, he was largely left to fend for himself. "She worked second shift which meant that when I got home from school, I would maybe see her 30 minutes before she took off to work," Van Exel remembered. "So, it turned me into a loner."

He soon found himself getting into trouble. He started driving at the age of 14, even though he could barely see over the dashboard. He fell asleep while driving at age 15, crashing his aunt's car into a tree. He injured his jaw so badly he needed 70 stitches and still had a visible scar on his bottom lip.

His parents' marriage ended while his father was in prison, and his father moved to Georgia when he was finally released. When Van Exel was a teenager, his father got in contact with him out of the blue and offered him a plane ticket to Georgia to visit. "I was real excited," Van Exel said. His grandfather took him to the airport in Milwaukee to catch the flight. "When we got there, there was no plane ticket," he said. "It hurt. It hurt my feelings a lot."

Basketball became a place of solace for Van Exel, and he earned a scholarship to St. Joseph's High School in Kenosha. He was magnificent on the court, leading St. Joseph's to the state final two years in a row and becoming the second all-time leading scorer in Wisconsin high school basketball history. But off the court, he felt out of place in a school full of white kids from affluent families, and kept mostly to himself.

He wanted to play college basketball, but his grades were not good enough to qualify for a scholarship to a university with an elite program. Instead, he went to Trinity Valley Community College in Texas where he was depressed and lonely. He wanted to quit many times but stuck with it and focused on his studies. After two years, he improved his grades enough to transfer to the University of Cincinnati. But he couldn't afford tuition and attended summer school at Cincinnati in the hope of winning a basketball scholarship. With not enough money to get a place to rent, he secretly slept each night in the university gym.

Van Exel won the scholarship and played the next two years for the Bearcats. His father got back in contact after he led Cincinnati to the Final Four in his junior year, again out of the blue. He invited his father to Cincinnati to rebuild their relationship, but something in Van Exel had changed. He couldn't trust his father. "It seemed like you had a certain motive at that point knowing that, maybe, I had a chance to play in the NBA," he said of his father. "You had a chance to get yourself maybe a nice house, get yourself a nice car. It just didn't sit right with me."

Estranged again from his father, he completed his senior year and nominated for the draft.

While Van Exel's story demonstrated his tenacity and resilience, there were question marks about his attitude leading into the draft. Word spread quickly around the NBA that Van Exel had a problem with authority, stemming from his workout with the Seattle SuperSonics. He was asked by Sonics coach George Karl to run from one baseline to the far free throw line six times. He jogged the first one and Karl told him to do the next one faster. "And I did the exact same thing, the same way," Van Exel said. "He came over and kind of chewed me out a little bit."

Van Exel was disengaged from the workout because he felt the Sonics were already overloaded at guard and were not legitimately interested in drafting him. He figured he would save his energy for workouts where he stood a chance of being drafted. Regardless of his reasons, a 22-year-old essentially telling an NBA coach where to stick it made him look, at best, unprofessional and, at worst, like a punk. It also didn't help that he twice missed flights to Charlotte to work out with the Hornets. In the end, he was too much of a risk for NBA executives and every team in the league besides San Antonio passed up on the chance to draft him.[148] Some teams passed up twice.

For the second straight season, West was drafting a player with a questionable attitude. But Van Exel had simply too much talent to pass him up a second time. "We were very pleasantly surprised that he was available," West said. "It took us about two seconds to figure out what to do."

Van Exel was a true wildcard. He had a reputation in college of being able to shoot his team into a game but also shoot them out of one. Which was a metaphor for his long-term potential in the NBA. It was conceivable he might be out of the league within two years. But it was equally conceivable he might be an All-Star one day.

With the draft over and eight players off contract, the Lakers had a lot of work to do. Doug Christie quickly signed a five-year deal worth $7 million. But ever since his arrival mid-season, Scott assumed the Lakers wouldn't tender a new contract offer to him. He wanted to remain a Laker, but he was realistic. The backcourt was already crowded with young

---

[148] The Spurs never got a chance to pass up on Van Exel because they didn't have their first-round pick and they picked after the Lakers in the second round.

players before the draft, and now Van Exel had been added to it. He could no longer see where he fit as a 32-year-old veteran. Neither could the Lakers for that matter, but they refused to commit one way or the other until after the draft.

The Lakers made it official on July 21, 1993 when they announced they wouldn't be attempting to re-sign Scott. West described the decision as one of the toughest he had to make as General Manager. The Lakers were the only NBA team Scott had ever known. He grew up a Lakers fan in Inglewood and lived his dream by winning three championships as Magic Johnson's starting backcourt partner. He had his best three seasons between 1987 and 1989. Over those three years, he averaged 19.4 points, shot 50% from the field, 87% free throws, and 39% three-pointers. The Lakers won two titles and averaged 61.3 wins in those seasons.[149]

Scott released a gracious statement, filled with pride for his years with the team, nostalgia for those championship seasons, and understanding of the team's decision. "I may not be playing for the Lakers in the coming season, but in my heart and in my dreams at night, I will be wearing my Laker jersey and running the floor at the Forum," the statement read. "Kareem will be kicking the ball out to me, Magic will be giving me a no-look pass, James Worthy will be calling for the ball. I'll see you in the Forum next season, not as a member of an opposing team, but as a long-time friend who now simply works out of town."

West considered re-signing A.C. Green his top priority of the off-season, but the process would drag on for months. Green was the only player on the roster who played consistently with any kind of grit. Like Scott, he had played all eight of his years in the NBA with the Lakers. But unlike Scott, Green was in his prime in 1992-93 and had come off a fabulous playoff series against the Suns in which he averaged 14.6 rebounds against much bigger opponents.

Green would have several good teams chasing him, with his hometown Portland Trail Blazers expected to be the leading suitor. Deeply religious, he had his free agency philosophy clearly sorted out. "The money, the comfort, the commitment to winning, those are major ingredients that I'm looking for and are going to be very important for me," he said. "But

---

[149] Scott never made an All-Star team during his career but absolutely should have during this time. Especially when he led the Lakers in scoring in 1988 with 21.7 points per game when the Lakers won the title.

nothing overrides the fact that if God says no, then I'm saying no."

The Lakers made an initial offer to Green on the first day of free agency. West called the offer 'lucrative', rumored to be double what Green earned in 1992-93, and he was publicly optimistic Green would sign it. But Green's agent, Marc Fleisher, rejected the offer out of hand. West waited to hear back from him regarding Green's thoughts on a second offer, but he didn't hear from Fleisher for weeks.

By the end of July, Fleisher said Green had received offers from multiple teams, but he would not be able to decide for several weeks. According to Fleisher, some of the teams didn't have salary slots big enough to fit Green under the cap and would have to make roster moves to create sufficient space. He wouldn't say which teams were courting Green, but rumors spread quickly about several offers being made by the Phoenix Suns.[150]

A deal still hadn't been done by late August when a sort-of-war-of-words broke out between Fleisher and the Lakers. Fleisher publicly stated he wasn't optimistic Green would re-sign with the Lakers. "Everyone else out there is very aggressive going after A.C., and the Lakers aren't," he said. "I'm just getting the impression the Lakers are holding back for some reason." He went on to say Green was concerned the Lakers wouldn't be competitive in 1993-94 and were likely headed to the lottery.

John Black disagreed. "We definitely want A.C. back," he said. "Obviously, we know we are not a championship-caliber team right now. But everyone is working as hard as they can to get back to that level of play." Green walked Fleisher's comments back a few days later. "I have a great deal of interest in them, especially after eight seasons," said Green. "I can't just turn that off."

The Lakers had a distinct advantage over the other teams courting Green. NBA rules dictated a team could exceed the salary cap to re-sign their own players. Teams could only offer Green what they had available under the salary cap, while the Lakers could offer Green whatever they wanted.

But a test case was currently being assessed by the NBA that, in a way, circumnavigated those rules. New Jersey Nets free agent center Chris Dudley had just accepted a contract offer from the Portland Trail Blazers that would have paid him $10 million less than what he was offered by the Nets. The offer from the Blazers was for seven-years but had an out-

---

[150] It would later become public knowledge that the Lakers, Suns, Trail Blazers, Spurs and 76ers all offered Green a contract.

clause after one season. Dudley would accept the smaller offer from the Blazers and then opt out after one year. Under league rules, the Blazers were then permitted to sign him to a much bigger deal. Teams were not allowed to have handshake deals with players regarding future contracts, but it was obvious the Blazers had one with Dudley. Why else would he accept $10 million less? The issue for the league was proving it.

Dudley's contract was eventually declared valid, opening the door for other free agents to sign similar deals. It then quickly became known Green had been offered a similar deal by the Phoenix Suns. Following the ruling, Jerry Colangelo publicly estimated the odds of Phoenix signing Green as 75%. West was then asked what he thought the odds were that he would re-sign with the Lakers. "I guess 25%," West replied. West was joking, but there was no denying the Lakers had a big problem on their hands.

The Lakers then made the extraordinary move of pulling their contract offer to Green, believed to be worth $17.5 million over five years.[151] "We value A.C. Green very, very highly," West said. "And we like to preserve relationships with the people we have had here a long time. But this offer has been out there for more than two months,"

Feeling the pressure, West instead gave Green a new proposal that included a one-year termination clause. In a way, it gave Green the best of both worlds. It was a long-term deal on good money with the flexibility of an out-clause. But Green wasn't especially looking for flexibility, so it meant little to him coming from the Lakers. He was, after all, only entertaining the idea because it was the only mechanism to get him to Phoenix.

Finally, after nearly three months of negotiating, Green signed a contract on September 28, 1993 with the Phoenix Suns. "There's something about the Suns and that organization that really appealed to me," Green said. "I like the competitiveness of their players. I talked to the players, and they are very hungry for a championship. They want to get back to the Finals. I like that."

Phoenix offered something the Lakers used to be able to offer free agents but no longer could – the chance to win a championship. The Suns had fallen only two wins short of a title in 1993; maybe Green was the final piece of the puzzle. "We want a championship," Colangelo said at the

---

[151] Fleisher claimed those figures reported by the Lakers were inflated.

news conference welcoming Green. "We want it now."

A year earlier on September 29, 1992 Magic had announced he was returning to the Lakers, and brought with him the hope of contending for a championship. Almost exactly one year later, Green walked away. It was incredible how much could change in a year. Between letting Scott walk and now losing Green, the Lakers' roster had officially been gutted. James Worthy was now the sole holdover from Showtime, and he was undeniably in decline. "It's not the best feeling in the world to be the only one left," Worthy said. "I thought A.C. was going to be around for a while. I'm the last one."

Negotiations with other Laker free-agents dragged on for months too. Just days before training camp, the Lakers finally came to terms with Elden Campbell, signing him to a three-year deal worth $6 million. It also took months to get a deal done with Sedale Threatt, even though he publicly stated his desire to re-sign with the team when he opted out of his contract. The new deal was worth $7.5 million over three-years, a considerable pay increase from the $800,000 he was contracted to earn if he hadn't opted out.

The Lakers also agreed to one-year deals for both Tony Smith and Duane Cooper. Alex Blackwell, who had been a long shot to make the roster a year earlier, was waived. The Lakers also wouldn't be extending a contract offer to Jack Haley, who had missed all of the 1992-93 season due to injury. [152]

Looking to get some reinforcements at power forward following Green's departure, the Lakers brought back an old fan favorite from Showtime. West signed 35-year-old veteran Kurt Rambis to a one-year deal at the league's minimum. Rambis previously played with the Lakers from 1981 to 1988, winning four championships. He signed with the expansion Charlotte Hornets prior to the 1988-89 season and played a few

---

[152] Blackwell never played in the NBA again. He seems to have had a long basketball career playing in the CBA, Europe, and South America. Exact details about his career are hard to come by, but he was playing in Chile as late as 2011 at the age of 41. Meanwhile Haley would go onto be a required signing for any team that had Dennis Rodman on its roster. Rumour had it, Haley possessed the mysterious power of being just strange enough to get through to the often-troubled Rodman. He played with San Antonio, Chicago, and New Jersey after being released by the Lakers, retiring in 1998. Haley passed away from heart disease in 2015 at the age of 51.

years in Phoenix before finishing the previous season with the Sacramento Kings. Rambis was known for doing all the dirty work – setting screens, grabbing rebounds, diving on loose balls, committing hard fouls. His long blonde hair and black-rimmed glasses inspired the 'Rambis Youth', a group of young fans who attended Lakers games wearing black horn-rim glasses. "They're not youth anymore," Rambis said. "They're creaky old men with kids now."[153]

The Lakers opened training camp in Honolulu with a noticeably less talented team than a year earlier. Nine of the eighteen players at camp were assumed a lock for opening night, either because they were on multi-year contracts or they were too talented not to make it. At guard, there was Threatt, Anthony Peeler, and Van Exel. At forward there was Worthy, Campbell, Christie, and Lynch. While the centers were Divac and Bowie.

That left nine players competing for the final three roster spots. It was the closest thing to a free-for-all the Lakers had maybe ever had at training camp. Among the hopefuls were Smith and Cooper, who would have to prove themselves all over again if they wanted to continue their careers with the Lakers. Additionally, there were the two aging veterans, James Edwards and Rambis, who bought a combined 30 years of NBA experience with them to camp. It was the first time Edwards found himself fighting for a roster spot since he was a rookie 16 years ago. "I don't know what's going to happen," he said. "I'm just going to play hard in training camp and see what happens."

Also fighting for a spot was Trevor Wilson, who played his college ball at UCLA and was a second-round draft choice of the Atlanta Hawks in 1990. He was waived by the Hawks with one month to go in his rookie season and had played the last two years in Spain. There were also four undrafted rookies, each expected to be long-shots – guards Dexter Boney from UNLV and Keith Johnson from Louisiana-Monroe, and forwards Antonio Harvey from Pfeiffer and Poncho Hodges from Colorado.

The pre-season opened for the Lakers in the same place it did the previous year, the Blaisdell Center in Honolulu, with two games in two nights against the Utah Jazz. The Lakers won the first game 98-86 before

---

[153] Rambis had worn #31 during his first seven years with the Lakers. That number was already taken by Bowie, so he wore #30 during the 1993-94 season.

losing the second 81-77. [154] More importantly, they lost key members of their young core each night. Christie landed awkwardly on his left ankle while battling Isaac Austin for a rebound in the third quarter of the first game. The diagnosis was a mild sprain, but it would be severe enough to keep him out of the remainder of the pre-season. "I'm just mad more than anything," he said. "All that work for nothing. All that work to get hurt."[155] The next night Peeler experienced pain in his right knee, would be diagnosed with tendonitis and would join Christie on the sidelines for the remainder of pre-season.

For their next pre-season game, the Lakers returned to the Thomas & Mack Center in Las Vegas where they were forced to play Game 4 of their series against Portland in 1992. The Lakers shot 61% from the field and won easily over the Los Angeles Clippers, 119-99. Worthy hit all nine of his shots to top score with 19 points off the bench. Former UNLV star Dexter Boney scored 16 points in his return to his alma mater.

The Lakers started the annual two-night GTE Everything Pages Shoot-out at the Forum three nights later against the Miami Heat. Worthy scored 16 points, including six in a row in the final 44 seconds, to give the Lakers a 99-97 victory. Inexplicably, Pfund 'repaid' Boney for his strong performance against the Clippers by not playing him at all against the Heat. Van Exel had 16 points, and Lynch scored 7 points in their first ever games at the Forum. But they lost the next night, 102-98 to the Seattle SuperSonics.

Two nights later they were in Charlottesville, West Virginia to take on the Washington Bullets. Threatt, who played his college ball at West Virginia Tech, and Jerry West, who played at West Virginia University, were both honored at half-time. Threatt was still the school's all-time scoring leader with 2,468 points and was inducted into the West Virginia Tech Hall of Fame as part of the ceremony. He had 15 points with 10 assists during the game, and Divac made a free throw with 55 seconds left to give the Lakers a 105-104 win.

Just as Boney had done in Las Vegas, Trevor Wilson had a breakout game the next night in Miami. The Heat got a 106-91 win, but Wilson led the Lakers in scoring with 16 points on 6-9 shooting.

---

[154] The Jazz played both games without Karl Malone. He didn't travel to Honolulu with the team following a death in the family.

[155] Christie, who wore #35 in 1992-93, switched to #8 for the 1993-94 season. No information was found explaining Christie's reason for changing.

The Lakers concluded the pre-season with a 4-4 record when they lost 93-77 to the New York Knicks at the Thunderdome in St. Petersburg, Florida. Campbell badly sprained his left ankle in the first quarter and joined Peeler and Christie on the sidelines.

Rookie free-agents Boney, Hodges and Johnson were waived, bringing the roster down to 15.[156] Two days later Campbell and Peeler were placed on the injured list, essentially creating room to carry 14 players. The Lakers finalized the roster the same day by waiving Cooper, their second-round draft choice from a year ago.[157] Cooper became superfluous because he was a pure point guard and the Lakers already had four players – Threatt, Smith, Christie, and Van Exel – capable of playing the position.

Losing Scott and Green in the off-season and a rash of injuries in the pre-season meant the Lakers would be starting 1993-94 with perhaps their least talented team in franchise history.[158] Injuries to Campbell, Peeler, and Christie resulted in two players being on the opening day roster who were not expected to last through training camp. Trevor Wilson and forward Antonio Harvey, who had impressed in pre-season with his leaping ability and defensive skills, survived the cuts, at least for now.

West was asked by the media if this off-season was the worst he had experienced in his 12 years as the team's top basketball executive. "By far," he said with a sigh.

---

[156] It still hurts that the Lakers squandered an opportunity to have someone with a name as awesome as Poncho Hodges on the team. Hodges played professionally in France, Israel, Japan, and Turkey. He became an actor, starring in 10 feature-length films and appearing in seven TV series including *True Blood* and *Law & Order*. Boney would play in the CBA until 1996-97 when he played eight games with the Phoenix Suns. He finished his basketball career in 2002 after playing in France, Israel, the Philippines, and Venezuela.

[157] Cooper played 23 games for the Phoenix Suns in 1993-94 before playing in the CBA, Greece, and Poland until 2003.

[158] Even the worst teams in Laker history to that point had at least one player on the roster who was a legitimate star. The 1975-76 team that failed to make the playoffs had Kareem Abdul-Jabbar. The 30-win 1974-75 team had Gail Goodrich. The 1957-58 Minneapolis Lakers who won a franchise-low 26% of their games had Vern Mikkelsen and All-Star Larry Foust. The 1993-94 Lakers had nobody.

Chapter 15

LOSERS DON'T SELL

November 5, 1993 to November 24, 1993

T HE SOLD OUT crowd of 17,505 at the Forum stood and clapped in unison, as they had done for years for player introductions. "And now, the starting line-up for your Los Angeles Lakers," said Lawrence Tanner, the Lakers' court-side announcer. Fans had been spoiled in the past, usually hearing the names of some of the game's true greats. Names like Magic Johnson, James Worthy, Kareem Abdul-Jabbar, Elgin Baylor, Jerry West and Wilt Chamberlain.

But none of those great players were taking the floor on opening night of the 1993-94 season.

Instead of Magic Johnson being announced as the starting point guard, it was rookie Nick Van Exel, a player selected 37th overall in the draft. Instead of Byron Scott at shooting guard, Tanner announced Tony Smith, who had spent three seasons with the Lakers as a third-stringer. James Worthy wasn't the starting small forward. Instead, it was Trevor Wilson, a second-round draft pick of the Hawks three years earlier who had been out of the league for two years. A.C. Green wasn't announced as the power forward. Instead, it was Antonio Harvey, an undrafted rookie nobody had heard of. Vlade Divac was announced as the Lakers starting center. The project from Yugoslavia, who had been promising but inconsistent in four seasons with the Lakers, was now their best player.

There were likely two thoughts going through the minds of most fans in attendance that night. Just who the hell are these guys? And it's going to be a long season.

"We're heading off into new territory, all of us," Randy Pfund said. "We've got to attack as though there is something good on the other side. We are well aware of the stormy seas and the obstacles, but that's how we have to look at it. I think people realize what this is. It's a really young group that will have to learn quick. So, let's get on with it."

The Lakers were in uncharted territory at the start of the 1993-94 season. The expectation of teams during Showtime was to win the championship. For the last two years, expectations had been more modest – be competitive and make the playoffs. The expectations for the 1993-94 team were less concrete. The success of this season couldn't be measured only by wins, as everybody knew there wouldn't be many of them. Instead, it would be measured by the development of the new, young core. A successful season would see the young players better at the end of the season than they were at the start. And that was a new and difficult proposition for fans to accept.

"The only thing that I'm worried about is that in L.A., we've had such a rich tradition," Pfund said. "I worry can our fans embrace this challenge? We've got some good young players. But if people are trying to relive the 80s with this team and that's what they expect, unfortunately, they're in for a tough sell, because that's not it. That's not where we're at."

The reins of the Lakers' offense would be handed over to Nick Van Exel, the first rookie incumbent point guard for the Lakers since Magic in 1979. And with fresh legs running the attack, Pfund wanted to get out and run. After being the only Laker to start every game since Magic's retirement, Sedale Threatt would finally get to play the role he was intended to play when the Lakers traded for him – coming off the bench to back-up both guard positions. But instead of backing-up Magic and Byron Scott, he would be backing-up rookie Van Exel and second-year Anthony Peeler when he returned from injury. "I've been in the league 11 years, I know they need to find a young point guard," Threatt said. "It isn't about winning a job to me. My thing is to come off the bench and spark my team. I can still play and contribute a lot that way."

There was no more appropriate way for the Lakers to open the 1993-94 season than against the Phoenix Suns at the Forum. The two teams had squared off in the most dramatic first-round series in recent memory six months earlier. Now the Suns had poached A.C. Green, one of the Lakers' best players. With Michael Jordan retiring before the start of the season, the Bulls' run of dominance was assumed over. For the first time since 1991, the race for the championship was wide open, and most pundits assumed they'd see a Phoenix Suns vs. New York Knicks NBA Finals.

Elden Campbell had played admirably against Charles Barkley in the playoffs, but he was on the injured list on opening night. Pfund didn't have any good back-up options. George Lynch was too small to be effective against Barkley. Kurt Rambis was a little long in the tooth. Pfund's only real option was undrafted rookie Antonio Harvey. "From Pfeiffer College to Charles Barkley is a heck of a leap," Pfund said. "I don't know who Antonio Harvey played against at Pfeiffer, but I don't think it was anybody like Charles Barkley."

Harvey's friends, former teammates, and coach at Pfeiffer College flocked to dorm lounges and homes around Misenheimer to watch him make his pro debut as the Lakers' starting power forward. Unfortunately, though predictably, he didn't last long against Barkley, picking up five fouls in 14 minutes.

When Worthy checked-in for his first action of the season, he and Green got into a shoving match under the basket when fighting for a rebound. It was enough for fans, already feeling burned by Green, to turn on him with a chorus of boos. The two got into it again on the last play of the first quarter. Worthy shoved Green away, and several Suns stepped into Worthy's chest. Green finished the third quarter with a three-point play, and he and Worthy jawed at each other on the way to their respective benches.

While the sold-out crowd was quick to cast Green as the villain, neither Green nor Worthy were especially upset. "Just playing a game," Green said. "That's how we always played in practice." Worthy agreed. "Just having fun like we always do," he said.

The Lakers surprisingly were in control most of the game and hung on for a 116-108 win.[159] Van Exel top-scored for the Lakers, recording 23 points and 8 assists on 9-13 shooting.[160] Tony Smith started in place of Peeler and matched his career-high with 20 points in 39 minutes. With Harvey in early foul trouble, Pfund played Rambis for 26 minutes, and he scored 5 points and had 7 rebounds in his first game as a Laker in six years. "Old horses do have some kick in them now and then," Rambis said.

Rookies Van Exel and Harvey may have both started, but the Lakers'

---

[159] The Suns were without Richard Dumas who had been suspended for the entire 1993-94 season when he tested positive for cocaine use, violating the NBA's substance abuse policy. He had also sat out the entire 1991-92 season for that same reason.

[160] Van Exel's 23 points were the most by a Laker rookie on opening night since Magic had 26 against the San Diego Clippers on October 12, 1979.

first-round selection, Lynch, watched from the sidelines. After never missing a game in high school or college, he received the first 'DNP – Coach's Decision' of his career. "It was worse than weird," he said. "It was tough sitting there. I'm glad the team got the win. That was the only good thing about it."

Green played well in his first game with the Suns, registering 25 points and 8 rebounds on 11-16 shooting. But, as usual, it was Barkley who did most of the damage for Phoenix, scoring 38 points and collecting 11 rebounds. "It's kind of funky playing against the Lakers when you don't know any of their players," Barkley said.

The Lakers were in Seattle the next night for a game that was highly anticipated in that city. The Sonics had pulled off two off-season trades that transformed them into championship contenders. They acquired 24-year-old shooting guard Kendall Gill from the Charlotte Hornets in exchange for high-scoring, but 34-year-old, forward Eddie Johnson, and third-stringer Dana Barros. The trade seemed like a coup as Gill had averaged 18.8 points over the previous two seasons and it was assumed his best years were only ahead of him. Then days before the season opener, they acquired Detlef Schrempf from the Indiana Pacers in exchange for Derrick McKey and seldom-used Gerald Paddio. Schrempf was a local favorite from his days at the University of Washington, was a two-time Sixth Man of the Year and was an All-Star in 1993, averaging 19.1 points and 9.5 rebounds a game.

The Sonics had come just one win from reaching the NBA Finals in 1993. Now they were adding Gill and Schrempf to a core that included Gary Payton, Shawn Kemp, Sam Perkins, Nate McMillan, Ricky Pierce, and Michael Cage.

The game against the Lakers was the first opportunity for fans to see their new-look Sonics. And they must have liked what they saw because the Sonics shot 61% from the floor and led 98-66 at three-quarter time in a game that was never close. They routed the Lakers 129-101, destroying any monticule of false hope the win over the Suns had given fans. "That was not a good effort," Pfund said. "I don't know where to start looking for reasons."

Van Exel led the Lakers again with 19 points, but they came on 4-13 shooting. Christie played his first game since the start of the pre-season and scored 13 points in 18 minutes off the bench. "I felt okay," he said. "I didn't have any legs under my shots, especially at the end." He was booed throughout the game, proving fans still held a grudge for his contract holdout. "They still hate me up here," he said. "And the feeling is mutual."

The team had two days off before facing the Portland Trail Blazers at the Forum. The Blazers were still looking for their first win of the season, losing their first two games for the first time since 1986. The Lakers trailed by double digits three times in the second half, but closed the deficit to 101-97 when Worthy made a three-pointer with just over a minute remaining. But it was as close as they would get. Free throws from Terry Porter pushed the league back out to six, and the Blazers got their first win of the season, 109-102. Chris Dudley, whose contract paved the way for Green to leave the Lakers, took a hard fall four minutes into the game and fractured his left ankle. The injury would relegate him to the sidelines for almost the entire season.

After three games against teams expected to battle it out atop the West, the Lakers' next opponent was a team expected to be closer to the bottom like themselves, the Sacramento Kings. But the outcome was the same. They fell 112-101 at Arco Arena, their third loss in a row. "We're still learning," Worthy said. "But if we don't learn fast, this can be a long year." The lone bright spot for the Lakers was the improved play of Christie, who had 14 points on 4-5 shooting and 9 rebounds in 21 minutes off the bench.

Christie made the first start of his NBA career two nights later at home against the Denver Nuggets. He responded with one of the best games so far in his young career, scoring 21 points in 31 minutes. But it was the only good thing to happen for the Lakers all night. They shot 31% from the floor, an all-time franchise low, and lost 113-84. Worthy scored 6 points off the bench on unsightly 2-13 shooting. Smith scored 14 points, but it came on 3-15 shooting. After selling out on opening night, only 11,215 fans showed up for the Denver game, the lowest attendance for a Laker game since December 15, 1983.

The Lakers got some much-needed help the next day when they activated Peeler from the injured list. The team needed to make a roster move to accommodate him, and speculation started they would waive Wilson. "I would say that's highly unlikely, the way he has played," Pfund said. Wilson had averaged 10.2 points, 5.5 rebounds, and 49% shooting, far better than the Lakers expected from a player who was only intended as a stop-gap until Christie and Peeler were healthy.

Things were so bad for the Lakers that James Edwards, who hadn't played in any of the first five games, was openly campaigning to be the one waived. "I think they already know how I feel," Edwards said. "I'm in the last year of my contract, I spent the last 26 games of last season on the bench, and I feel I still have some good games left in me. I would rather they released me." Pfund understood where Edwards was coming from, but he wouldn't release one of his few veteran players. "I still think Buddha has a very effective game. I am in no way down on James Edwards," Pfund said.[161] "But I can't play all 12 guys." The Lakers instead delayed making a cut and placed Rambis on the injured list with a well-timed case of tendonitis in his left knee.

After a 1-4 start to the season, Pfund shuffled the starting line-up for the first time against the Cleveland Cavaliers at the Forum. He started Peeler in his first game of the season, replacing Smith who had underperformed since starting well on opening night. He also moved Harvey to the bench, electing to start Bowie in his place.

The change breathed new life into the Lakers. They shot 50% for the first time all season and beat the Cavs 107-100. They scored on 13 of their final 14 possessions, including all their last seven. Peeler sealed the victory with a three-pointer with the shot clock running down with 53 seconds to play. "I looked at the shot clock. That's the last thing I saw. I didn't pay attention to the defensive man. I just went straight up," Peeler said. "I had a good feeling it was in." Christie and Bowie led the scoring for the Lakers with 18 points each. Peeler started his second season in the league in good form, scoring 15 points on 6-11 shooting.

Campbell was activated two days later, and Wilson was placed on the injured list with yet another well-timed case of tendinitis. Campbell played off the bench against the Los Angeles Clippers at the Forum, who were playing without leading scorer Danny Manning, who was out with a cracked ring finger.

The Lakers and Clippers had become unexpected rivals the previous two seasons. Before 1992, the Clippers hadn't enjoyed a winning season in 12 years and had rarely come close to playoff contention since moving from Buffalo to California in 1978. They were perpetually the 'other team'

---

[161] 'Buddha' was James Edwards' nickname. A highly underrated nickname at that.

in Los Angeles. Yet they had winning seasons and qualified for the playoffs in 1992 and 1993, just as the Lakers were in decline. It was a sign of how far the Lakers had fallen – instead of vying with the Boston Celtics and Detroit Pistons for the best team in the league, players would instead talk up a showdown with the Clippers to decide who the best team in Los Angeles was. And it was undoubtedly the Clippers, who had a better record than the Lakers in each of the previous two seasons. But the rivalry quickly died. As poorly as the Lakers had started the season, the Clippers were even worse – returning to their old selves where they would go another 12 years without a winning season.

In this showdown, the lead see-sawed all night and Peeler made a jumper with 13 seconds remaining to tie the score 99-99 and send the game into overtime. The Lakers trailed by five with 43 seconds to go but rallied to tie the score 107-107 to force a second overtime when Divac made a three-pointer with 1.9 seconds to play. It looked like the game might be headed for a rare triple overtime with scores tied 114-114. But Campbell capped his first game of the season with a game-winning turnaround baseline shot at the buzzer. Christie, Peeler, and Divac top-scored for the Lakers with 23 points each, with Divac collecting a career-high 24 rebounds.

Bowie only lasted six minutes in his second start before getting tangled with Bob Martin under the basket and falling awkwardly, hitting his head on the floor. Gary Vitti rushed on the court and asked Bowie some basic questions to check if he was coherent. He passed the test, Campbell subbed in for him, and he took his place on the bench next to Edwards. He sat in silence for a minute before turning to Edwards and asking him, "When did we get Elden?" The question was a red flag for Vitti, who took Bowie to the locker room where he was unable to answer the questions he had no problem answering just a few minutes earlier. Bowie spent the night at Centinela Hospital Medical Center, where he was diagnosed with a mild concussion. "Obviously I've had some injuries in my career, but I've never been hit in the head," said Bowie. "When you lose your memory and all your thoughts for a moment, it's scary." With no concussion policy in 1993, Bowie would be back in uniform two nights later.

Campbell's buzzer-beater improved the Lakers' record to 3-4. There was the slightest window of hope they had survived the worst part of their season. They were fully healthy for the first time in the new season and on a two-game win streak. But there was plenty more pain to come, and their 3-4 record would represent the closest they would come to .500 all season.

The fall started two nights later against the injury-riddled Golden State Warriors in Oakland. All-Star point guard Tim Hardaway was out for the entire season after tearing ligaments in his left knee in pre-season. Chris Mullin was out for the first six weeks with a torn finger ligament he suffered in a pre-season game against Seattle. But they had a lot of young talent and had added #1 overall draft choice Chris Webber to a team that already included second-year forward Latrell Sprewell and third-year forward Billy Owens.

A circuit breaker malfunctioned when players were hitting the floor in Oakland for warm-ups, causing the main lights to go out. The entire stadium was in the dark for 30 minutes as repairs took place. Some of the players shot around anyway, doing their best to stay warm. Once the lights came back on, the Lakers trotted out their preferred starting line-up of Van Exel, Peeler, Christie, Campbell, and Divac for the first time. It started well, as they shot out to a 28-19 lead at the end of the first quarter. But it ended horribly, as they scored just 48 points the rest of the way, shot 33%, and lost 103-76. After two positive wins in a row, it was as if they didn't turn up in Oakland. "With young people come inconsistencies," Pfund said. "We've got some people who did not come to play tonight, for whatever reason."

The Lakers were back home the following night to host the Chicago Bulls for the first time since Michael Jordan's retirement. The Bulls were struggling in the early stages of the season. Jordan's replacement was Pete Myers, a sixth-round draft pick in 1986 who had been out of the league for two years. They lost their home opener to Miami by 24 points, and entered the Forum with a 3-4 record and on a three-game losing streak. Scottie Pippen, John Paxson, and Scott Williams were all out with injuries. Even the struggling Lakers were expected to beat these rag-tag Bulls. And it looked like they would. Up 86-81 with 24 seconds remaining, Chick Hearn had put the game in the refrigerator. But then the pains of having a starting rookie point guard kicked in.

Van Exel fouled B.J. Armstrong on a lay-up, who made the basket and the ensuing free throw to cut the lead to 86-84. "Of all the dumb things that happened to us, for us to foul them on a lay-up was the worst," Pfund said. "Let them have the lay-up." The Bulls pressed the Lakers on the next possession, forcing Van Exel to throw the ball out of bounds. Armstrong made a turnaround 16-foot jumper over him with three seconds left to tie the game at 86-86.

The Lakers then gave the world a perfect example of how not to execute an inbounds play. Divac tried to inbound to Christie, but the pass went askew, and Christie fell trying to reach it. The ball went out of bounds without taking any time off the clock. The Bulls got the ball back and had enough time for Steve Kerr to heave a 20-footer that bounced off the front of the rim. Horace Grant got his fingers to the rebound and tipped the ball in just before the buzzer sounded and the Bulls won 88-86.[162] Bulls coach Phil Jackson described the win as a gift.

"I'm concerned, but hey, I know what kind of a team we have," Pfund said. "I look at the box scores every day, and I see what the first and second-year players are doing, coming up with goose eggs every once in a while."

The Lakers were 3-6 despite playing six of their first nine games at home and now faced a week-long five-game road trip. It started in New Jersey against a Nets team still reeling from the off-season death of their leading scorer Drazen Petrovic. The Nets led 105-102 with 25 seconds to play when the Lakers fouled Derrick Coleman to stop the clock. Coleman had the opportunity to seal the win but gave the Lakers a gift by missing both free throws. Peeler missed a potential game-tying three-pointer with three seconds remaining, but Divac got the rebound. He fed to Threatt, who had 30 points on 15-19 shooting, for one last shot to tie. But Threatt accidentally stepped out of bounds when trying to get behind the three-point line and the Lakers lost again.

The road trip continued to the Omni in Atlanta where the Lakers again shot poorly and lost 103-94 to the Hawks. "We've got to get better. We've got to keep improving," Pfund said. "We are not the only team with new players or who is young. At some point, we have to start winning."

If the 'at some point' part of Pfund's comment didn't fill fans with a

---

[162] Laker broadcaster Chick Hearn had a lot of loveable quirks but undeniably his most loved was putting a game in the refrigerator. Whenever a game was at the point where he knew the Lakers would win, he'd say, "This game is in the Admiral refrigerator, the door is closed, the lights are out, the butter's getting hard, the eggs are cooling and the Jell-O is jigglin'." It was him declaring a victory to the Lakers, in his own unique way. The Bulls game was the first time Hearn put a game in the refrigerator too early. He contemplated dropping the trademark phrase but continued to use it.

great deal of hope, they saw why the next night in Charlotte. The Lakers played a truly horrendous defensive game in front of 23,698 fans on Thanksgiving Day. The Hornets outrebounded the Lakers 63-36, scored 43 points in the first quarter, and won 141-124. It was the most amount of points the Lakers had given up in six years. "In the true spirit of Thanksgiving, we gave Charlotte something to be thankful for," Pfund said.[163]

November wasn't even over, but it felt like the Lakers' season, for all intents and purposes, already was. They were 3-9 and off to their worst start after 12 games in 27 years. Only Dallas and Milwaukee had worse records. They were miserable on both ends of the court, shooting 43% from the field and giving up 110.4 points – dead last in the league in both categories. Their nine losses came with an average margin of 14.8 points. Before the season, Jerry Buss said losing 50 games would be "sheer torture." But they were on pace to lose 60.

The frustration was showing on the players. Christie entered the locker room after the loss in Charlotte and kicked a chair in disgust. "What the coaches are throwing out there for us is not working," he said "Our offense is stagnant. We just need to get it and go instead of coming down every time and seeing that a play is called." He then called out some of his teammates, though not by name, for not playing hard enough.

Van Exel, who was booed throughout the Charlotte game for missing pre-draft workouts with the Hornets, sounded perplexed about the team's struggles. "I really can't tell you what the problem is. I know one thing, we're not executing the full play. We do some of the play, and then we stop," he said. "It's been going on all year. It seems like we get a little rattled if a team sticks us or gets us out of whack."

Worthy took some of the players' concerns to Pfund, who acknowledged his plan to play at a faster rate wasn't working. Wanting to implement a fast-break offense was one of the reasons he elected to start Van Exel over Threatt. But playing quickly with a young roster prone to mistakes was a recipe for disaster. "My fear when playing up-tempo basketball is, do you have the talent to play fast?" Pfund asked himself.

Peeler and Christie had shown some growth from a season ago. Peeler was averaging 13.7 points and Christie 13.4 points, but they had been

---

[163] The previous high was a double over-time game on November 15, 1988 against the Denver Nuggets. Magic hit a three-pointer on the buzzer for a 148-146 win.

impressive mainly in bursts. The rookies had been a mixed bag. Van Exel looked like the steal of the draft, averaging 13.8 points and 6.3 assists in 36.8 minutes in the first three weeks. But Lynch was out of the rotation. He had appeared in only half of the games, averaging just 12.3 minutes per game when he did play. For a team looking to develop young players, fans expected to see the highest draft selection on the court. But Pfund wasn't playing him.

This moment had been coming since Magic retired in November 1991. It had only been a question of when. Fans had feared it and hoped it might somehow be avoided. But after remaining respectable for a season and a half after losing their superstar, they were out of tricks by 1993-94. "The fall from Showtime has gone past Slowtime to Notime," wrote Joe Gilmartin in *Streets in Smiths*.

The Lakers were over the salary cap, which made recruiting a marquee free agent impossible. The draft was their only pathway to add talent, and the lottery only favored the season's losers, never its winners. The Lakers struggles were a necessary evil, and enduring them represented their only hope of a better future. "We've committed to our youth. There are nights, a lot of nights, when we take our lumps. But it's something that had to be done," Pfund said. "We're better off right now, even with this record, than we were two years ago with Byron and A.C. because that thing was coming to an end."

But that was a hard sell to a fan base accustomed to excellence. The Lakers used to be one of the hottest tickets in Los Angeles during Showtime. Now there were plenty more enjoyable things to do in the vast city than watch these Lakers struggle. Attendance at the Forum had fallen from an average of 17,498 in 1990 to 12,974 in the first three weeks of the season.

"Los Angeles fans are less patient than other fans," said one Laker fan. "Maybe because there are so many distractions here. In most NBA cities, there aren't quite as many choices."

"Kareem's gone, Worthy's aging, Magic's gone, Riley's gone," another fan said. "When you say the magic's gone, that encompasses the man and the team."

A Laker game at the Forum used to be an event, now it was merely a basketball game. Some stalwart celebrities still showed up at the Forum. Jack Nicholson and Dyan Cannon were in their usual seats. Chevy Chase,

Louis Gosset Jr., Anthony Kiedis, and Flea showed up from time to time. But games of 'spot the celebrity' at the Forum ended much faster than they used to. The Lakers had the youngest starting line-up in the league, which could have been spun as a reason for excitement and optimism. But they weren't winning. And that was everything.

As Beth Harris wrote in the *Los Angeles Times*, "They're losers, and in L.A., losers don't sell."

Chapter 16
BAD HISTORY

November 26, 1993 to January 18, 1994

W HEN A GAME at Market Square Arena is decided by a 20-foot
jumper with one second on the clock, it's usually safe to assume
it was Reggie Miller making the game-winner. But not so on November
26, 1993 when the Lakers road trip continued into Indianapolis. Instead,
Sedale Threatt dribbled the clock down to seven seconds before using a
screen from Vlade Divac to drive left. He drew both defenders and flicked
a pass to Divac, who was wide-open a few steps inside the three-point
line. He launched the long two-pointer that went in, giving the Lakers a
102-100 win.

It was a badly needed victory, snapping a five-game losing streak and
giving the Lakers their first road win in six tries. It would kick off a mini-
recovery, brimming with false hope that these Lakers were about to get it
together.

They concluded the road trip by scrapping together a four-point win
over the struggling Minnesota Timberwolves, despite blowing almost all
the 14-point lead they had with two and a half to play. They returned
home to defeat the league doormat, the Dallas Mavericks, who were 1-13
on the new season. The Mavs were so bad they gave the Lakers something
they hadn't experienced all season – an easy win. The Lakers won 124-91,
their biggest ever win over the Mavericks.

The game was so in hand that Pfund tried a novel idea – give court
time to the franchise's highest draft pick in 11 years. George Lynch played
18 minutes, most of it in garbage time, and scored 16 points on 7-8
shooting. The only problem? Nobody was there to see it. Only 10,319 fans
were in attendance, the smallest crowd for a Laker home game since 1980.

They even won their next game 109-102 against the Los Angeles
Clippers at the Sports Arena. Anthony Peeler and Doug Christie both

scored career highs, Christie with 33 points and Peeler with 28. Christie was asked after the game if he thought he was 'in the zone.'[164] "I don't know," he replied. "That was my first time."

Out of nowhere, the Lakers were on a four-game win streak. It may have come from bottom feeding on the league's worst teams, but wins were wins for these Lakers. It would of course turn out to be just an aberration. The kids would continue to surprise some nights and disappoint the next. Almost every game would see one of them play well, but rarely all at the same time. And they'd keep losing. And losing. And losing.

The next slide started at home against the lowly Minnesota Timberwolves. The Lakers were clinging to a 99-98 lead after Christie made a leaning shot from the free throw line with 26 seconds to play. Minnesota's Doug West missed a 10-foot jumper with seven seconds left, but Elden Campbell and Peeler inadvertently fought each other for the rebound, knocking it out of bounds. "The rebound was the game," Pfund said. "We had it in our hands, and it got away." Marvin Williams was left wide open on the inbounds play, converted a lay-up and drew a foul. His free throw gave the Timberwolves a 101-99 victory.

After five games against some of the worst teams in the league, the Lakers hosted the 15-4 New York Knicks. Pat Riley ran into Magic Johnson before the game and jokingly asked if he could play for the Knicks that night. Magic laughed. "Don't even start," he replied. Confident they were clear of injuries, the Lakers waived Trevor Wilson before the game.[165] Wilson had spent a month on the injured list, but James Edwards had still been hoping he would be the one cut. "I was praying," a disappointed Edwards said.[166] Instead, he had to suit up and play against the Knicks.

---

[164] 'The zone' was a mythic Jedi/Zen-like state of mind and body that would see a player go stretches of a game, or an entire game, barely missing a shot. Everybody talked about 'the zone' in the 90s but at some point, we stopped talking about it.

[165] Wilson signed with the Sacramento Kings a week after being released by the Lakers. He stayed with the Kings through the 1994-95 season and signed with the Philadelphia 76ers in 1995. He was signed by the Lakers before the 1996-97 season but was waived before the start of the season. He played in Japan, Spain, and Turkey before retiring from basketball in 1999.

[166] It was understandable that Edwards felt that way. He had played in just 4 of the Lakers' first 17 games despite being healthy. If he was going to play that role at that age of 38, it is fair he would rather do it for a contending team.

The game was predictable. The Knicks' stingy defense and physical play locked down any resemblance of a Laker offense. They scored just 31 points in the first half, two points shy of a franchise low. Patrick Ewing had 29 points and 19 rebounds, the Lakers were outrebounded 61-37 and lost 92-78. Divac was limited to 11 minutes because of a hand injury he suffered in training a week earlier. He had continued to play but the injury was getting worse, and Pfund started Bowie in his place.

The Lakers then lost 117-99 in Portland before returning home to lose 100-97 to the Golden State Warriors where they managed only three offensive rebounds, one shy of a franchise low. It was the Lakers' fourth consecutive loss, nullifying any benefit they received from the recent four-game win streak. And the schedule was about to do them no favors with a six-game road trip, their longest of the season, that would keep them on the road for ten days.

The trip started in Detroit. The players boarded the team bus at their hotel to drive to the Palace of Auburn Hills when John Black told Kurt Rambis to get off. Rambis then learned he had been waived. He had been on the injured list for a month, but that wasn't why he was being let go. His minimum salary of $150,000 would have turned into a guaranteed contract for the season worth $400,000 in two days' time. The Lakers didn't want to pay it, and they ended Rambis' homecoming season after just five games in which he averaged 3.0 points and 4.0 rebounds.

On the Detroit court, Van Exel hit a step back three-pointer late in the game to seal a 99-93 win over the Pistons. He finished the game with 16 points and outplayed both of the rookie guards West targeted in the draft. Allan Houston only played 11 minutes while Lindsay Hunter had 10 points on 4-13 shooting, and struggled to contain Van Exel.

But the trip got ugly from there, firstly in New York where the Lakers were again routed by the Knicks, this time 108-85. They lost in Philadelphia to an awful 76ers team and were then thrashed 122-92 in Cleveland by a Cavs team who had been struggling to find their way under new head coach Mike Fratello.

Sitting with a miserable 8-15 record, Pfund started to talk rotation change. He speculated to the media that he might start Worthy and Tony Smith in the next game. Essentially his solution was to bench Peeler and Christie, the team's leading scorers whose development was meant to be the focus of the season. Christie was asked if he thought a line-up change was a hunt for a real solution or a scapegoat. "Probably both," Christie replied. "I'm just out there doing the best I can with what he's giving us. That's all I can do."

Pfund didn't end up making any changes but his needless public speculating about minutes and roles caused disruption among the young players. This clearly wasn't a happy team. Pfund held a clear-the-air meeting in Orlando before they took on the Magic – a team that was climbing the ranks of the East. Maybe it did some good because the Lakers played out of character by appearing like they were having fun for a change. Christie had one of his best games of the season with 31 points, and the Lakers overcame Shaquille O'Neal's 33 points and 10 rebounds for a surprising 109-102 win. "A huge win for us emotionally," Pfund said. "It gives us a chance to salvage this road trip, to go down to Miami and get another game."

But they didn't salvage anything in Miami. They finished the road trip 2-4 when they were outrebounded 57-28 and beaten 109-92 by the Heat. They were returning home to three days' rest over Christmas with their season in tatters, sitting 13.5 games out of first place in the West with a 9-17 record.

They were also going to be without Bowie. He appeared to sprain his left knee in Orlando and was unable to play against the Heat. He had played well to that point, certainly an improvement on Benoit Benjamin. He had been averaging 8.9 points and 5.2 rebounds in 25 games, upping those numbers to 13.6 points and 8.4 rebounds in five starts while Divac was injured. It would take the Lakers over a week to diagnose the problem, eventually finding bone fragments in his knee. It was a new addition to his well-chronicled history of injury. He would undergo arthroscopic surgery and sit out the remainder of the season.

The Lakers' belated Christmas present was finishing the December schedule with home games against the league's two best teams – the 22-3 Houston Rockets and 20-3 Seattle SuperSonics. The Rockets were playing on the second night of a back-to-back, and Olajuwon was held to 17 points, well below his season average. But Kenny Smith scored a career-high 41 points on 16-24 shooting, and the Rockets thrashed the Lakers 118-93.

They lost the Sonics game 99-92, but most of the attention afterwards was on the events of the final seconds of the third quarter. Ricky Pierce committed a flagrant foul on Threatt as he was attempting a lay-up.

Christie got face-to-face with Pierce and the two engaged in a brief wrestling match under the basket. Just as they were separated, Peeler entered the fray by grabbing Pierce in a chokehold from behind. Peeler was knocked from behind into, and then over, the press table along the baseline. Christie, Peeler, and Pierce were ejected, and the Lakers were forced to play the rest of the game without their two leading scorers.[167]

It was a hell of a way for the Lakers to close out December. They started the month by putting the finishing touches on a four-game win streak. They then went 2-10 the rest of the month, losing those ten games by an average of 15 points. The Dallas Mavericks had all but locked up the league's worst record with a 2-24 record. But the Lakers were 9-19 and only one loss away from being the second worst team in the league.

The Lakers ushered in January with three road games in four nights. They fell right to the bottom of the Pacific Division with a loss in San Antonio despite everything seeming to fall their way in the final seconds. The Spurs had a 94-92 lead with one second remaining when David Robinson missed the first of two free throws. He decided to intentionally miss the second, assuming the buzzer would sound by the time someone fully secured the rebound. But veteran Terry Cummings committed a silly loose-ball foul on Edwards while fighting for the rebound.

The foul sent Edwards to the free throw line with a chance at a tie with 0.6 seconds remaining. But he too missed the first. Like Robinson moments earlier, Edwards decided to miss the second free throw intentionally, hoping a Laker could tap in the miss. And it almost happened – Campbell controlled the rebound with his right hand and pushed the ball a few feet toward the rim. But the tip banked long off the glass, and the Lakers lost again. "It was right there," Pfund said. "It was one of those nights when it seemed like everything fit for us to steal one. But the key didn't fit." The loss wasted a fine performance from Peeler, who had 27 points on 10-19 shooting including 10 in the final quarter.

It took two weeks for the team to realize Bowie required surgery and he went under the knife the morning of a bad eight-point loss to the Sacramento Kings. The Lakers needed a replacement and reached out to Rambis, but management needed to mend some fences after they waived him three weeks earlier in a cost-cutting exercise. Buss agreed to pay

---

[167] Neither Peeler nor Christie were suspended for the fight and were both in uniform the next game.

Rambis the full amount he would have been paid on the old contract if he agreed to come back. And, with that, he was a Laker again. "I understand the business end of what they did and why they did it to me," said Rambis. "I just wish they could have handled it in a different way. I guess this was their way of apologizing."[168]

Oddly enough, the early career of George Lynch got a major shot in the arm when Pfund was ejected in a three-point win over the Clippers. Pfund inadvertently bumped an official in the middle of a heated exchange, was fined $3,000, and suspended one game. The coaching reins were temporarily handed to assistant Bill Bertka. The 66-year-old had been an assistant in the NBA for 17 years and on the Lakers bench since 1982. This would be his first time as head coach in the NBA.

Bertka's first game, a match-up against the Spurs at the Forum, unfortunately, wasn't a pretty one. The Lakers shot 27% in the first half, scored just 25 points by half-time and received a healthy round of boos from the 11,069 in attendance for the 95-89 loss. It set a new franchise low for points in a half and tied the third-fewest by any team since the advent of the shot clock in 1954. "It's nice being part of history," Bertka said looking at the stat sheet. "But this is all bad history."

Usually, when an assistant coach is forced to take over for a game, they'll make as few rotation changes as possible. But Bertka made one big change by doing something Pfund should have been doing from the start of the season – he played rookie George Lynch. Pfund had played Lynch just 8.6 minutes per game and failed to play him at all in 11 of the 32 games the Lakers had played that season. Bertka put Lynch on the floor with his second sub of the game and gave the rookie 22 minutes, the second most he had received all season. He scored 10 points on 3-5 shooting and grabbed 5 rebounds.

When he returned from his suspension, Pfund would be forced to continue playing Lynch because Christie went down with a badly sprained ankle during practice the day after the Spurs game. It was another unlucky blow for Christie, who was forced to sit out almost all pre-season and opening night with the exact same injury. Though inconsistent, his play was one of the few positives in an otherwise

---

[168] Since being waived, Rambis had been playing on the Magic Johnson All-Stars, Magic's touring exhibition team. He was scheduled to play with the team in Argentina but had to pull out at the last minute to re-join the Lakers.

miserable season. He had clearly developed since his rookie season, averaging 14.4 points on 47% shooting in 29.7 minutes per game before the injury. The mounting losses were vaguely easier for fans to deal with if young, promising players were given a run. But Christie's injury would see him on the sidelines for the next six weeks.

One of the reasons Pfund struggled to find playing time for Lynch was because he still didn't know if Lynch was a small forward or power forward. Christie's injury answered the question by default. Pfund would give most of Christie's minutes at small forward to Lynch until he was healthy enough to return.

Lynch went from sitting with Edwards on the end of the bench to starter for the first time in his career the next game against the Golden State Warriors. He struggled, scoring 6 points while his Warriors counterpart, Latrell Sprewell, lit him up for 29 points. But at least he was getting exposure to the NBA game, even if it came with a five-point loss. He played 40 minutes at the Forum against Charlotte who, after scoring 141 points against the Lakers earlier in the season, scored 130 in an eight-point win. But Lynch made the most of his minutes, scoring 24 points on 11-13 shooting and grabbing 10 rebounds. Unbelievably, Van Exel set a franchise record by hitting five three-pointers against Golden and then matched it the next game against Charlotte.[169]

The Lakers were next scheduled to take on the Sacramento Kings at the Forum on January 17, 1994. However, the game had to be postponed due to the Northridge Earthquake that hit at exactly 4:30 that morning. The epicenter of the magnitude 6.7 earthquake was in Reseda, a neighborhood in the north-central San Fernando Valley region of Los Angeles. The quake was so powerful it was felt as far away as Las Vegas. It resulted in 57 fatalities, over 8,000 injuries, and between $13 and $40 billion in damage. The Santa Monica Freeway, the busiest freeway in the United States, was badly damaged and repairs would cause extensive traffic congestion for months. The Sports Arena received minor structural damage, forcing the Clippers to hold their game against the Cleveland

---

[169] The fact that no Laker had previously hit five or more three-pointers in a game shows just how much the game has changed since 1994. It's not all that unusual for a player to hit that many three-pointers in a game in the modern era. Kobe Bryant set the Laker record for most three-pointers in a game when he hit 12 of them against the Seattle SuperSonics on January 7, 2003.

Cavaliers on January 21 at the Forum, which had miraculously escaped any damage.

Instead of playing the Kings, the Lakers lost their fifth straight in Seattle against a Sonics team still playing in a different stratosphere to them. The Sonics entered the game with a 27-5 record, half a game behind Houston for the best record in the league. The game was never close. The Lakers trailed 78-56 at three-quarter time before saving a modicum of dignity by outscoring the Sonics in garbage time for a 103-88 loss. Any positives for the Lakers were, again, all about Lynch and Van Exel. Lynch had 14 points and 9 rebounds in 34 minutes while Van Exel led the Lakers in scoring for the fourth consecutive game, this time with 22 points.

But the Lakers had even bigger problems because Peeler was in street clothes. Pfund criticised Peeler two weeks earlier for only making it to the free throw line once in nine games. Pfund saw it as a sign that Peeler was playing passively, not taking the ball to the basket. In reality, he had been playing with pain in his right leg all season, and it had been getting worse. He was originally diagnosed with shin splints before the Seattle game and was listed as day-to-day. Before long, team doctors would discover he had a stress fracture in his left fibula. He had unknowingly been playing a good portion of the season on a broken leg. He was placed on the injured list and would be lost for the season, forced to sit out the remaining 47 games.

In need of a replacement for Peeler and with few options available to them, the Lakers signed 26-year-old rookie guard Reggie Jordan to a 10-day contract. Jordan had played high school basketball at Proviso East High School in Maywood, Illinois before spending two seasons at New Mexico State University. He declared for the 1991 NBA Draft but wasn't selected. He returned to Illinois where he had played the last two and a half seasons with the Grand Rapids Hoops in the CBA.

It was mid-January 1994, and the Lakers were in a world of hurt. They had won only four of their last 20 games and were 11-25 overall. They were second to bottom in the Western Conference, above only the pitiful 2-23 Dallas Mavericks and had the fourth worst record in the entire league. The young players had openly questioned the coach's rotations and strategy. Their 12th man had been praying to be waived since the start of the season. Now Christie and Peeler, their two young leading scorers, were sidelined with injuries. Without them developing on the floor, there was no meaning left in the continuing defeats.

The Lakers were not used to looking up in the standings to teams like the Sacramento Kings and Minnesota Timberwolves. Yet now there they were. "I have to turn the newspaper upside down every morning," joked West, trying to find some humor in the pain.

In the middle of all the losing was Worthy. He'd seen his body betray him and turn him into a shell of the Showtime great he used to be. When he was shuffling particularly slowly and stiffly out of a practice session, he walked past a 13-year-old boy who asked, "What hurts, James?" Worthy paused for a moment before wearily giving his answer. "Everything hurts, my man. Everything."

Worthy found the losing equal parts frustrating and isolating. "Losing Earvin, A.C., Byron, it's been difficult for me personally. Not to mention how hard it's been on the court," he said. Worthy lamented the lack of spirit amongst the team, and that the locker room always emptied out much faster than it used to back in the good old days. "That's because losing creates a kind of psychological deadness," he said. "Nobody wants to talk about it. Nobody wants to even think about it. That's why everyone wants to leave so fast."

He tried his best to remain positive for the young players, imparting whatever knowledge he could to help them. But the players could see the losing was wearing on him. "You can see it in his eyes sometimes," Christie said. "He gives us all the help he can, but you can tell that, deep down, this is hurting him."

It was hurting Magic too. He had a courtside seat at the Forum to watch the disintegration of the team he once led. He ripped them in an interview with TNT's Craig Sager, going on a long soliloquy about how the young players lacked pride and were not improving. "I never thought in my wildest dreams that after I retired it would be this bad so quickly," he said. "What's so painful is the fact that I don't think the guys have pride. We had pride. We took loses hard, and I don't think I see the same thing now. I don't see it, and I'm there all the time."

It was not even three years earlier that the Lakers had reached the NBA Finals, led by one of the greatest players in league history. It felt like a lifetime ago.

"I think anyone who was around for those championship years is frustrated by this," Pfund said. "I can remember before games sometimes during those years, Pat and I would just look around at everything. Earvin and Kareem and James warming up, the packed house, feeling the electricity in the place. And Pat would kind of warn me. 'You'll probably be the head coach someday. But it might not always be like this.' He was right."

Chapter 17

A LAME DUCK

J ERRY WEST ADDRESSED the team before they took the floor at the Forum against the 26-9 Phoenix Suns. "I don't like excuses," he told them. He knew the fragile Lakers were at risk of completely checking out for the remainder of the season. It was January 20, 1994 and they were basement dwellers in the West, with little chance of making the playoffs. Already skinny on talent, they would be missing their leading scorer for several weeks and their second leading scorer was out for the season.

"Every player has to look himself in the mirror and examine his own performance every day," he told them. "One thing, when people put the name 'professional' in front of you, it means being able to handle adversity."

And there would be plenty of adversity to come. Almost every night, the Lakers would face an opponent who was more talented, more experienced, better coached and had a better record. Yet out of the darkness, they would begin to turn things around. They would become a .500 team over the next two months, but it would come by relying more on their veterans than their young players. And it wouldn't be enough to save Randy Pfund.

Charles Barkley and Kevin Johnson were out with injuries, but it hardly made it a fair fight. The Lakers were clinging to a three-point lead with 34 seconds remaining when Nick Van Exel stepped on the baseline, but Green was called for tugging on his jersey, sending him to the free throw line. Phoenix coach Paul Westphal vehemently argued the call, received two technicals and was ejected. Free throws settled the game, the Lakers winning 107-102. In the middle of their worst season in almost 20 years, they had improved to an unlikely 2-0 on the season against the reigning conference champion Phoenix Suns.[170]

Tony Smith, who had replaced Anthony Peeler in the starting line-up the last two games, suffered a sprained ankle against Phoenix and was sidelined for the next game in Portland. It left the Lakers with only two healthy guards and a bench consisting of only Worthy, James Edwards, and Kurt Rambis. Threatt played well in his first start of the season, scoring 25 points. But they were too shorthanded and lost big to the Trail Blazers, 111-93.

Byron Scott, who had signed with Indiana in early December, had his homecoming five days later when the Lakers hosted the Pacers. "One of the first things I did when I signed with this team was look at the schedule and see when we would be in L.A.," he said. Scott had been playing off the bench, averaging 9.5 points in 19.6 minutes. But Pacers coach Larry Brown started him against the Lakers, knowing how much it would mean to him to be introduced to the Forum crowd again. The Lakers commemorated Scott's return by presenting him with his old Lakers #4 jersey in a frame. The game drew only a small crowd of 11,577, but they gave the former Showtime guard a nice ovation. Vlade Divac, who made the game-winning shot when the two teams squared off in Indianapolis earlier in the season, converted a free throw to preserve a 103-99 victory. Divac admitted the sight of Scott at the Forum in a different uniform took some getting used to. "I almost made a pass to him," he said. "Almost."[171]

Two nights later, the Lakers did something they hadn't done in two months – win two games in a row. Though they tried everything they could to lose. They were on their way to a rare easy win, leading the Detroit Pistons by 32 points in the second quarter and 62-39 at half-time. They then allowed the Pistons to score 40 points in the third quarter and cut their once gigantic lead to six points in the fourth. But they did just enough to edge out a 103-97 win. "It would have been a horrible one to lose," Pfund said. Which was an understatement, especially since a loss would have wasted a fantastic game from Lynch. He had 20 points and collected 18 rebounds, the most rebounds by a Laker rookie since Magic

---

[170] The Suns starter in place of Kevin Johnson? Duane Cooper. He played 17 minutes, scored four points on 2-4 shooting, and dished out three assists. Phoenix signed him three games into the season and he'd average 2.1 points and 5.9 minutes in 23 games for the Suns in 1993-94.

[171] Scott scored 19 points on 8-18 shooting and 1-4 three-pointers in 28 minutes of action in his first game back at the Forum.

Johnson in 1980.

A three-game road trip in Texas saw the Lakers lose 112-97 to the Spurs before going down 98-88 to the Rockets. The match-up the following night against the Dallas Mavericks was a danger game. The Mavericks had already suffered a 20-game, and then a 16-game, losing streak. But they had somewhat resembled an actual NBA team the last week by picking up two wins in their last three games. But the Lakers managed an ugly 95-87 win. Divac got into a heated exchange with forward Randy White in the third quarter when the two players tussled over a rebound. After the whistle was blown, White shoved Divac and then took a swing at him that didn't connect. Divac didn't retaliate, saving himself from being kicked out, but White was immediately ejected. Even though he certainly wasn't the instigator, Divac was booed by the crowd every time he touched the ball for the rest of the game. But it didn't bother him. "It makes me feel good," he said with a smile after the game. "I'm used to it. Laker fans boo me at home."

Two days later the Lakers hosted the 30-16 Utah Jazz at the Forum in what would turn out to be one hell of a strange game. How strange? The Lakers recorded a season-low for points in a quarter by scoring 10 in the first. They then recorded a season-high by scoring 43 in the fourth.

Van Exel picked up three personal fouls in the first three minutes of the game and sat out the rest of the half. He started the second half and picked up his fourth foul within a minute. It enraged Pfund so much that he immediately subbed him out and didn't play him again. The stat line for the Lakers' starting point guard that night was 4 minutes, 0-1 field goals, 1 assist, 0 points, 4 fouls.

Divac shot 2-10 from the field and scored 5 points. But he dished out 9 assists and grabbed 23 rebounds. It was a Dennis Rodman-type stat line. "Don't be surprised if I come to the next game wearing purple hair," he said.

Worthy had been struggling through two weeks of basketball hell before the game against Utah. In his last six games, he was averaging 4.8 points in 19.0 minutes of action on an almost inconceivable 21% shooting from the field. Yet, the game against Utah saw a rare appearance of Big Game James. He scored 26 points on 12-19 shooting in 25 minutes of action.

And then there was Reggie Jordan, who had signed two 10-day contracts with the Lakers after Anthony Peeler and Doug Christie went down with injuries. The undrafted player from the CBA had hardly played since joining the team. He hadn't produced much else other than giving Laker fans a chance to live in a fantasy. Because he wore #23 and had 'Jordan' on the back of his jersey, Lakers fans could occasionally squint their eyes and pretend they had Michael Jordan on their team. But the fact he was averaging 0.5 points on 25% shooting in 2.8 minutes broke the illusion. [172]

But on this night, he was one of the best players in the world. He had six points at half-time, which was four more than he had scored in his entire NBA career to that point. He then made four of five shots in the third quarter to bring his total up to 14 points. The Jazz pulled to within three points with four minutes to play when Jordan completely took over the game, scoring 14 points down the stretch to secure the 107-90 win. The player whose biggest prior achievement was once making the CBA All-Star Game had the Lakers bench and every fan at the Forum cheering. He ended the game with 28 points on 9-12 shooting in 25 minutes. "Yeah, I surprised myself," Jordan said. "This is where you want to be your whole life since I was a kid. I'm here. Now I want to keep it alive."

The Lakers then hosted the depleted Phoenix Suns at the Forum for the second time in just over two weeks. They had their point guard Kevin Johnson back, but Barkley was still on the sidelines joined by Dan Majerle who had the flu. The Suns' offense had been carried through injuries by Cedric Ceballos, who had been playing the best basketball of his career. He was still rusty when the Lakers last saw him, freshly back on the court after missing the first 29 games of the season with a knee injury. But in the eight games since, he had averaged 30.3 points and 9.1 rebounds on 57% shooting.

The Suns built a 16-point lead in the third before the Lakers ended the quarter on a 20-4 run to tie the score at 79-79 at the final break. Neither team led by more than two points in the fourth quarter until Worthy hit a jumper from the left side that put the Lakers up 101-97 with three minutes remaining. Johnson scored a lay-up, but Worthy responded again, hitting

---

[172] Jordan had been averaging 18.8 points and 9.2 rebounds in the CBA with the Grand Rapid Hoops and Yakima Sun Kings.

a jumper from the right side for a five-point lead with 35 seconds to play. The Lakers won 107-104 after Ceballos made a meaningless lay-in at the buzzer. [173]

The Lakers were now 3-0 against the Suns for the season. It was a surprising stat, due in equal parts to the Suns' run of injuries and the Lakers coming out aggressive each time, wanting some revenge for their playoff exit the previous season. "We just reflect back to last year's playoffs," Threatt said. "We won the first two games, and they came back to win the series. I think that was on their minds. I know it was on our minds."

The Lakers were in Salt Lake City the following night for a seven-point win over the Utah Jazz. Then, before breaking for All-Star weekend, they played their rescheduled game against the Sacramento Kings that was moved because of the Northridge Earthquake. The hasty rescheduling created a quirk in the schedule that set them three games in three nights for the first time since 1985. The Lakers were exhausted, and it showed, losing 103-84.

The season was still a lost cause when the Lakers entered the All-Star break with an 18-28 record. But they had won seven of their last 10 games, by far their best stretch of the season. And it was no coincidence it coincided with their two leading scorers, Peeler and Christie, being sidelined. Injuries to the inconsistent young players forced Pfund to play his more reliable veterans bigger minutes, and it resulted in more wins. Now in his fifth season, Divac was playing the best basketball of his life, averaging 16.9 points, 15.1 rebounds, 6.0 assists, and 3.3 blocks in the last seven games.

For the second straight season, the Lakers didn't have a representative at the All-Star game. But unlike last year, they did have a player take part in one of the events held over the weekend. Christie had been selected to compete in the Slam Dunk Contest but was unable to take part because of his ankle injury. But their second-round pick, Van Exel, made the inaugural NBA Rookie Challenge, while their first-round pick, Lynch,

---

[173] After his incredible game against the Jazz, Jordan received 24 minutes of playing time against the Suns. He had 9 rebounds and 5 assists but struggled from the floor, scoring 4 points on 1-6 shooting.

didn't.[174] Some players would be thrilled to be included in the All-Star weekend but not Van Exel. "I'll probably just try to get it over with as soon as possible," he said. "All-Star games, they're no fun at all. I like to win, and it seems in these games everyone tries to go out and have fun, not win." When Pfund got wind of his rookie's comments, he quipped that "Nick always has a different slant on things."

Van Exel's distaste for exhibition games came from a good place – his fiery competitiveness, a trait the Lakers were, on the whole, missing. And the game certainly didn't pan out like something Van Exel would enjoy. His team lost 74-68, and he failed to score, missing all eight of his shots. But the most unexpected thing happened, he appeared to be having fun. "The best time of my life," he said after the game. "I'm not being sarcastic."

The Lakers came out flat following the All-Star break. They lost 113-96 in Phoenix for, surprisingly, their first loss to the talented Suns all season. After six weeks on the sidelines, Christie was back in uniform and ready to play in Phoenix. But Pfund kept him on the bench, even during garbage time. Christie was irritated, saying he would have been better off staying in Los Angeles for further treatment on his ankle if Pfund had no intention of playing him.

Christie did see action two nights later, scoring four points in 21 minutes off the bench, when the Lakers won 107-95 over the struggling Philadelphia 76ers at the Forum. Pfund mostly played him at shooting guard, partly because the Lakers needed help there with Peeler out but mainly because Lynch had played so well at Christie's small forward spot. Lynch averaged 16.1 points and 9.4 rebounds in the 16 games Christie had been on the sidelines, better numbers that resulted in more wins than when Christie was the starter. Lynch wasn't nearly as surprised by his play as Pfund was. "I was the 12th pick in the draft," he said. "I feel I'm only doing what I was supposed to do all along."

The Lakers then badly lost both games of a back-to-back. First, they lost 103-84 at Arco Arena to the slumping Sacramento Kings, then lost 126-110 to the San Antonio Spurs at home the following night.

The losses coincided with Pfund changing the rotation again, moving Smith to the bench and making Threatt a full-time starter in the backcourt

---

[174] Lynch undoubtedly would have been selected to play if Pfund didn't wait until January to start playing him.

with Van Exel. Smith was one of the Lakers' few good defensive guards, but he was hurting the Lakers on offense, shooting 37% in 14 games as a starter. Van Exel was struggling from the field too, and Pfund didn't want both his starting guards shooting below 40%. Threatt played well in both games, scoring 28 against Sacramento and then getting 15 points and 9 assists against San Antonio. And while a decent defender, the 32-year-old Threatt had lost some quickness and wasn't as effective as Smith. With the change, Pfund boosted the offense but hurt what little defense the Lakers previously had. It was a juggling act Pfund never seemed able to get right, especially since he didn't play Smith at all in either game of the back-to-back. Going from a starter to not playing left Smith dumfounded. When asked if he could explain it, he replied, "Ask the guy up there [Pfund]. He knows everything."

Jerry West made a minor roster move at the trade deadline, sending a conditional second-round pick to Milwaukee for 34-year-old back-up center Danny Schayes.[175] The son of Hall of Famer Dolph Schayes, he had been scarcely used by the Bucks that season, averaging 2.1 points and 10 minutes in 23 games off the bench. Pfund said he was looking forward to having another veteran guy who could clog up the middle, but the Lakers almost solely made the move for salary cap purposes. They had a $1.75 million open salary spot left vacant by A.C. Green, and it would have expired at the end of the season if the Lakers didn't use it. Schayes was due that exact amount for the season and would be an unrestricted free agent at the end of the year. The move meant the Lakers could let Schayes walk at the end of the season but ensure they kept the salary spot available for free agency. A roster spot was created for him by moving rookie Antonio Harvey, who hadn't played in six weeks due to a strained left hip, to the injured list.

A Lakers-Celtics match-up had bought diminishing returns the last few years as both teams struggled in mediocrity. Now both teams were amongst the worst in the league. Reggie Lewis, the star meant to carry the Celtics in the post-Bird era, passed away at the age of 27 that off-season from a cardiac arrest while shooting around at the team's practice

---

[175] It is unclear which second round draft pick West traded for Schayes. But the Lakers never surrendered one to the Bucks, so it must have been rescinded.

facility.[176] The Celtics were 20-34, and the Lakers were 19-33 – the franchises continuing to match each other, even if it wasn't in the way fans would have liked. "I can't ever remember it being like this," said Worthy. "Usually, you'd be talking about this game a week before. Now, it's just another game."

But just like always, the game was fun. "I know this rivalry is well-remembered from the days when we played the Celtics for championships," Pfund said. "But for me, the last three minutes, it didn't make a difference. It was a close game, they wanted to win, and we wanted to win. They were still in green, and we were still in gold."

An off-balance 18-footer from Threatt with 33 seconds remaining gave the Lakers a 96-95 lead. Sherman Douglas was then left wide-open on a pick and roll, and he sunk a long jumper for a 97-96 Celtics lead with 22 seconds to play. The Celtics had a foul to give and used it perfectly, forcing the Lakers to inbound with six seconds remaining. Worthy got the ball into Divac beyond the three-point line, and he shook Robert Parish off the dribble. Divac charged to the basket and banked in a leaning 10-footer over Ed Pickney with 2.5 seconds remaining. Free throws concluded the game, with the Lakers winning 100-97. Divac led the Lakers with 28 points and 13 rebounds, while Threatt scored 26.

The Lakers opened March with a four-game east coast road trip, starting in Chicago against a Bulls team who had come a long way since they last played the Lakers. When the Bulls visited the Forum in mid-November 1993, they were 3-4 and still struggling to come to terms with life after Michael Jordan. Now they were 36-19 and half a game ahead of New York for the second-best record in the East.

Van Exel hit three three-pointers in the final two minutes of the third quarter. The last came with three seconds remaining that gave the Lakers a 70-65 lead at the final break. He went to work late in the fourth quarter too, hitting a three-pointer with one and a half minutes left to play to give the Lakers a 92-84 lead. Pippen answered with a three of his own before Van Exel went one-against-four to hit a runner with 54 seconds to play that sealed a 97-89 win that was, surprisingly, the Lakers' third straight win at Chicago Stadium since Magic retired.

Divac led the Lakers with 27 points and 11 rebounds, but the hero in

---

[176] Lewis had collapsed on court three months earlier at Boston Garden during Game 1 of the Celtics' first round matchup with the Charlotte Hornets.

the clutch was Van Exel. He had 22 points, including the Lakers' last 11 points, and dished out a little payback for his costly crunch time errors against the Bulls earlier in the season. He also hit five three-pointers, matching his own franchise record for the third time.

Van Exel then broke this record by hitting six three-pointers two nights later in Boston, but the Lakers lost to the Celtics 109-99. [177] The following night they lost 124-118 to the Washington Bullets but concluded their trip with a 2-2 record when they picked up their first win in Milwaukee since 1986, beating the struggling Bucks 106-84.[178] In the city home to the largest Serbian population in the United States, Divac received a warm ovation from fans, many waving Serbian flags throughout the game.

The win against Milwaukee would kick-start a stretch of eight games that would see the Lakers play vastly improved basketball. It would be enough to make extremely optimistic fans start thinking about the playoffs and make more realistic fans hope that maybe the team might get out of this horrible season with their pride intact.

Though 'proud' probably wasn't how anyone would describe their next game against the 8-51 Dallas Mavericks at the Forum. The Lakers led 42-16 at the first break but would blow the entire lead. The Mavs edged out a four-point lead early in the fourth quarter before the Lakers righted the ship and limped to a 106-101 win. Divac got his second triple-double of the season with 22 points, 17 rebounds, and 12 assists, but few of the Lakers felt good about the victory. "Someone asked me the question if it would have been embarrassing if we had lost," Worthy said. "It's still embarrassing."

The Lakers picked up another few wins against bad teams, winning in Minneapolis before thrashing the Washington Bullets 129-94 at the Forum, where Rambis got his first double-double since April 1990 with 11 points and 10 rebounds in 13 minutes. But after outhustling the Bullets, the Lakers were outhustled themselves by the New Jersey Nets in their next game, losing 102-90.[179]

A schedule oddity saw the Lakers host two games at the Forum in two

---

[177] Danny Schayes made his first Laker debut in Boston, scoring 2 points in 8 minutes.

[178] Chick Hearn almost saw his streak of 2,665 consecutive broadcasts snapped as he lost his voice after the game in Boston but recovered just in time to cover the Washington game.

[179] Benoit Benjamin had 12 points, 9 rebounds, and shot 4-13 in his first game at the Forum since being traded in the off-season.

nights for the first time since 1981, both against the Floridian expansion teams. The Forum was sold out for the first time since opening night when Shaquille O'Neal, Anfernee Hardaway, and the 39-25 Orlando Magic came to town. Threatt made a series of big plays down the stretch as the Lakers got a surprising 97-91 win over Orlando. They then edged out an 84-81 win the next night over the Miami Heat when Bimbo Coles missed three consecutive three-pointers in the final seconds. Threatt top-scored for the Lakers with 23 points, and Christie scored 17 points on 7-14 shooting in 32 minutes off the bench. For Christie, it was a reprieve from the horrid slump he had been in since returning from injury where he had averaged just 5.1 points on 36% shooting in 14 games off the bench. "To me, it was a nice win for us," Pfund said, "but more than that, I feel great for Doug."

They had won six of their last eight games and were 27-37 on the season. They now only trailed the Denver Nuggets by five games for the eighth and final playoff spot. The upswing was very much the work of Threatt, who was averaging 19.4 points in his 16 starts, and Divac, who averaged 16.2 points, 12.3 rebounds, and 5.6 assists since the start of February.

It may not have been likely but qualifying for the playoffs was now vaguely possible with 18 games left in the season. It was something inconceivable just a month earlier. But it was an uncomfortable thought. The Lakers badly needed an infusion of talent, and a high draft pick would be their only likely way to achieve that. Making the playoffs was a guaranteed way to finish out of the top 11 draft picks. "To be honest, what they say is probably right. But as a player, that's not in my mind," Threatt said. "Because of our record, and the fact that we are rebuilding, we definitely want to go in and get a good pick. But it's tough on a guy like myself who has always been in the playoffs. I'm a winner, and I want us to go out and win every game."

Pfund agreed. "There's not a coach who doesn't try to win basketball games. That's what we try to do," he said. "I understand that mentality, of people wanting a top draft choice. But, to me, I'd rather stay on the side of doing more than people thought we would."

Pfund had operated with a cloud of uncertainty hanging over him all season. He was all-but fired last season before a strong playoff performance saved his job. He struggled over the first few months of the new season to find a rotation that worked, upsetting several players who freely took their complaints to the media. But he eventually found a rotation that enabled the Lakers to play at least competent basketball most nights.

He also seemed more relaxed over the last month. Pfund even called into Chick Hearn's pre-game call-in show, disguising his voice and claiming to be R.C from Inglewood. He played on Hearn's reputation for being a backseat coach by asking him, "Does Pfund know what to do when you don't tell him to call a timeout?" Hearn didn't realize at first he was speaking to Pfund, saying later he was relieved he said Pfund was doing a good job.

During the recent stretch of games, Jerry Buss had given Pfund a one-year contract extension. "There are certain people I feel are Laker people, and Randy is one of them," Buss said. "I offered him a year extension because I wanted to indicate to him that he would be around with us in some capacity for a long period of time."

Pfund, justifiably, took the contract extension as a shot in the arm. "That means something to me personally," he said. "I think it showed there is some confidence in our management in what I've tried to do the last year and a half."

But when Buss talked about having Pfund with the team 'in some capacity', he meant just that. Because eleven days after extending his contract, and seemingly out of the blue, he fired Pfund as coach of the Lakers.

Chapter 18

COACH JOHNSON

A T THIS POINT, the Forum Club could have been renamed the Magic Johnson Press Room. For the third time in two and a half years, Magic Johnson walked into the Forum Club where a room of reporters was waiting for him. In the same spot where he announced his retirement and his ill-fated comeback, he was introduced to the media as the new head coach of the Lakers.

He didn't wait for the inevitable question about his health. Instead, he opened the press conference by succinctly shutting down any speculation he might not be physically up to the rigors of NBA coaching. "Let me just say this to everybody before we begin," he said. "I'm fine, I'm great, don't worry about that. If I wasn't, I wouldn't be doing this. Okay? So, let me just ease everybody's mind."

For the most part, the press conference was more about the joy of having Magic back in the league than it was about the minutia of Xs and Os. He offered few specifics about changes he would make as head coach besides the need for tougher defense and a more up-tempo offense. "I don't have all the answers," he said. "But I do know what it takes to win and what it takes to be a good basketball player, and that's hard work. You have to go to work."

Magic joked that his wife told him that he was never at home anyway because he was always at the Forum, so he may as well be there coaching. He was asked how worried he was about not being up to the challenge. "There's already a lot of bad coaches," he said. "So, I'll just join the rest of them."

He was, of course, asked if he intended to become the NBA's first player-coach in 15 years. Magic joked he would probably want to tear off his suit like Superman. "I know if it gets tight, a minute to go, I'm going to look and say, 'Man, go get that #32 jersey,'" he said, drawing laughs from reporters. "That will never leave me. I love basketball." Jerry West was less light-hearted when asked about it. He told reporters Magic's playing days were over and it was bordering on annoying to continue to be asked about it.

Even though Randy Pfund's job security had been in question for over a year, he was ultimately blindsided by the firing. It did, after all, come out of the blue. There was only a month left on the schedule, and the team was on their best run of the season. But he was gracious, refusing to criticise either Jerry Buss or West publicly. Instead, he thanked them for the opportunity and thanked his assistant coaches for their support throughout the last two seasons.

The Lakers' erratic defense had irked Buss and West all season. They were giving up 103.9 points per game, the sixth-worst mark in the league. "If you're defensively coordinated, you can compete," West said. "All year long our biggest concern, especially with our younger players, was that at times we just did not defend well."

Pfund had inherited a poor rebounding team, and the trend had only worsened under his leadership. The Lakers were, for the third straight season, one of the worst rebounding teams in the league.[180] On the one hand, the poor defense and rebounding was the inevitable by-product of the noticeable lack of talent and experience on the roster. On the other hand, it was exacerbated by a distinct lack of organization from the coaching staff.

The Lakers under Pfund had become known for their lack of intensity in games and practices. There was an alarming lack of accountability, especially from the young players. Van Exel was as brazen about it as anyone could be. Following a win in Chicago where he frequently freelanced on court, he was asked if he felt empowered by Pfund to improvise. "He really doesn't allow me to do it, I just do it," he said. "It's not like I need a green light or anything. Right now, I say I'm undisciplined."

Pfund had been a lame duck coach over his final few weeks. Buss had already decided he wouldn't retain him despite the recent improved play and the fact he just signed him to an extension. But in reality, Pfund was

---

[180] The Lakers averaged 42.5 rebounds a game while giving up 46.9 in 1993-94.

a lame duck from the moment Magic ended his comeback days before the start of the 1992-93 season. He was forced to throw away his plans for the season when Magic announced his comeback and then forced to return to those plans at the 11th hour. It was never going to result in success, especially with a team that had suddenly gone from championship contenders to playoff hopefuls.

And then the team of dependable veterans was dismantled before his very eyes. James Worthy's body was breaking down, taking him from being an All-Star to a tired old veteran playing off the bench. Byron Scott, A.C. Green, and Sam Perkins were gone. All the while, Pfund was expected by Buss and West to make the Lakers a respectable playoff team while at the same time building for the future. "One of the top priorities this season will be not only to improve upon our 39-43 record of a year ago, but to also establish more consistency, both as individual players and collectively as a team," Pfund wrote in *Streets & Smiths* at the start of the season. All this while having the youngest starting five in the league. It's a trick few NBA coaches and front offices have ever pulled off, and would have been a challenge to any coach in the league.[181]

The driver behind firing Pfund seemed to be almost entirely the work of Buss, with West simply following the desires of the owner.[182] Buss had wanted Magic to be the Lakers coach almost as soon as he re-retired. The rumors that Magic had been offered the job almost a year earlier didn't come from nowhere. Magic had indeed been offered the job in April 1993, but he turned Buss down because he wasn't especially interested in coaching and would only consider doing it if it came with owning a percentage of the team.[183]

Magic had long been open about his desire to own a team after his playing days, even mentioning it in his first retirement press conference. He was a member of a consortium in 1993 that was applying for the

---

[181] Pfund never coached in the NBA again, either as a head coach or an assistant. He rejoined Pat Riley in Miami in 1995, serving as General Manager for the Heat until 2008, winning a championship in 2006.

[182] Every time West was asked to explain why the Lakers had fired Pfund, his response always started with something like "Jerry Buss decided..." or "Jerry Buss thought..."

[183] Magic did broadcasting work for NBC in 1992 and 1993. He was commentating the Lakers-Sonics at the Forum in April 1993 and frequently ranted about Divac's play. Dick Enberg interrupted one rant, joking that Magic would make a great coach one day. Magic responded by jokingly saying "next year."

expansion franchise in Toronto, which eventually went to a group headed by Toronto businessmen John Bitove.

He had been offered the Atlanta Hawks head coaching job in December 1992, just six weeks after his re-retirement. Hawks General Manager Pete Babcock and President Stan Kasten were considering firing coach Bob Weiss when the team was mired in a seven-game home losing streak. Babcock and Kasten met with Magic in Los Angeles and were impressed by him. Magic had a deep knowledge of the Hawks' roster and laid out what each player could do to maximize their strengths while hiding their weaknesses. They made a formal offer to Magic, and he was close to accepting it but ultimately walked away because he wanted to continue to pursue ownership.

Another factor that prevented Magic from taking the leap into coaching was his commitment to his substantial business portfolio. Additionally, he ran the Magic Johnson Foundation as well as the Magic Johnson All-Stars – his team of mainly ex-NBA players that toured the world playing exhibition games.[184]

But Buss wasn't letting go of the idea of Magic coaching the team. He publicly said exactly that in October 1993, when his actual coach, Randy Pfund, was busy conducting training camp. "I think it would be great for Earvin to be coach of the Lakers, but at the same time, he has a lot of very big-time businesses," he said at the time. "And whether he can devote the unbelievable number of hours weekly to one occupation to the exclusion of all others, I don't know. If he tells me he can, we're going to sit down and talk."

By March 1994, the Lakers were suffering through their worst season since 1975 and had a very un-Laker-like 27-37 record. It wasn't mathematically impossible for them to make the playoffs, but it was unlikely. The fans had, for the most part, accepted the ugly truth months ago that the Lakers were heading for the lottery. So why fire Pfund with just 18 games left in a season that, to most people, already seemed lost months ago? And why would Magic accept the job now when he didn't

---

[184] Bill Simmons compared Magic playing on the All-Stars as being like a washed-up Bono wasting a winter singing karaoke at Irish Bars. But it was the only way Magic could get his basketball fix after being exiled from the NBA. And it was a profitable way too, earning him up to $365,000 a game. He likely earned more a year doing that than he earned from his contract each year with the Lakers.

before?

A plausible explanation for the move was that it was all about ticket sales. The Lakers had sold out only two games all season. They were 24th in attendance averaging just 12,815 fans a game, their lowest attendance for 26 years. Buss knew Magic did a lot for the Lakers, and one of those things was sell tickets.[185] The Lakers denied this was the root cause of the decision. "This is not a sideshow," West said. "This is something we hope that will help our ballclub and particularly our younger players." It was unlikely to make a huge difference on the team's balance sheet anyway, not with just 10 home games remaining on the schedule. "They didn't bring me in just to fill up the Forum," Magic said. "Believe me, if I was hired just to make the Lakers some money, I'd be getting a piece of it. I'm a businessman."

Buss had decided a few weeks earlier he didn't intend to retain Pfund and he wanted Magic to coach the Lakers in 1994-95. He figured, why not offer the job to Magic now so he could try it out for the final 18 games of the season. Then he could make an informed decision about doing it full-time next season. "Somebody compared this to taking a car for a test drive," Magic said. "That's about right. I'm taking this job out to see how it handles. Mr. Buss and Jerry West are watching to see if they like the way I drive. Then we'll figure out if we've got a sale." Buss also caught Magic at an opportune time, as his next tour with the Magic Johnson All-Stars wasn't scheduled until May.

Magic agreed to take the job, in a way, as a favor to Buss. The two had a father-son relationship dating back to Magic's rookie year. And no doubt Magic believed he owed Buss for continuing to honor his sizeable player contract even though he was retired. "It is something that I'm doing because Dr. Buss asked me would I do it. I told him I would do it for him," Magic said.

But the most likely reason for the change? While neither Magic nor Buss said so publicly, it is highly likely Buss agreed to sell Magic a minority stake in the team if he agreed to help him out by coaching them. Which might explain Magic's decision to essentially do the job for free, drawing no coaching salary on top of the money he was still receiving from his player contract.

---

[185] The *Orange County Register* published an editorial cartoon on the day of the announcement of Buss preparing to shoot a basketball with Magic's name on it. The caption read, "Off the media, through the box office, nothing but net."

There was a sound reason to think Magic would make an excellent coach. He was not only one of the game's greatest players but also one of its smartest, most driven, and successful. Pat Riley would refer to him as a coach on the floor, an extension of him from the sidelines to the court.

It was a win-win situation for Buss. Best case scenario – Magic liked coaching and ended up being as good at it as Buss thought he would be. If so, he would have found his new coach. Worst case scenario – Magic didn't take to coaching or wasn't any good at it. Which left Buss in the same situation he was in anyhow.

It was also a win-win for Magic because he could test the coaching waters without making a full-year commitment. If it turned out he didn't like it, he walked away. No harm, no foul. If it turned out that he did like coaching, then he had found a way to be part of the league again.

When the Lakers fired Pfund, they also fired Chet Kammerer, his hand-picked assistant and former boss at Westmont College. The Lakers replaced him with Michael Cooper, who had wanted to be an assistant coach for the Lakers ever since Pfund was promoted to the top spot. When Pfund opted to hire Kammerer, Cooper instead became an assistant to West. Rumors persisted that Pfund made the call because he felt threatened by Cooper. Pfund may have worried Cooper would be groomed by Buss and West for the head coaching job, and he may not have wanted to be looking over his shoulder. Cooper was one of the NBA's elite defensive guards during his playing days, and Magic hoped he would provide invaluable tutelage to the not-so-defensive-minded young players.

Reaction from players was, at least publicly, a mixture of cautious optimism about Magic and empathy for Pfund. The keenest of the group were Christie and Van Exel, two young players who looked forward to learning under the leadership of one of the game's great players. Christie patterned a lot of his game growing up by watching Magic play, especially his passing ability.

Van Exel, true to character, admitted he wasn't a fan of Magic growing up. "I was from the Midwest," he said. "I hated the Lakers." But he was won over by Magic playing against him in post-draft pickup games at UCLA and the Inglewood YMCA. He noticed everyone on Magic's team was always more serious and focused than the rest of the competition. It was something that appealed to a player like Van Exel who claimed to hate All-Star games because everybody wanted to have fun instead of playing to win. "It'll be exciting, it will be a lot of fun and competitive," he said.

Worthy and Rambis had a different perspective, one that came from being veterans who had seen their fair share of change over the years. And they, along with Divac, were dealing with the surrealism of playing under a coach who used to be their teammate. They knew Magic had potential to be a good coach. "I was playing *for* him when I was playing *with* him," Rambis said. "When he was out on the floor, he was choreographing and orchestrating the offense. You'd see him waving his arm, getting players to do this and that. He'll have to learn how to do that from the bench." But they also knew it was going to be a process. Worthy preached patience while Rambis said Magic was going to take his lumps early on, just like any rookie coach must.

Magic wouldn't be able to take over as coach for another six days after the announcement. He had speaking engagements and a television taping organized before accepting the job, and he couldn't drop them at a moment's notice. As a result, Bill Bertka would coach the second and third games of his long coaching career in the interim, two games in two nights in Texas. The Lakers barely got past the Dallas Mavericks 112-109 before losing the next night 113-107 to the Houston Rockets.

Perhaps trying to answer questions about his commitment to the job, Magic arrived at the Forum at 8:00am on his first day on the job. Days earlier, Lon Rosen asked Magic what time he wanted to hold practice on his first day. "Whatever they want," Magic replied. Rosen shook his head. "No, you're the guy. This is your team, you decide" he told him. "You're Pat Riley." Magic held his first practice session later that morning – an intense three-hour-and-20-minute workout. Magic thought the Lakers were in 'walk-it-up' shape and not in the kind of shape they needed to be to run the fast-paced offense he wanted to implement. Consequently, the session included a healthy dose of running. "If he had us all season, my pants wouldn't fit," Sedale Threatt said.

Magic's first game as head coach would come the next day – a home game against the Milwaukee Bucks and his former coach, Mike Dunleavy. Magic gave his first pre-game locker room speech as coach, becoming emotional a few times as he addressed his team. Moments before confidently striding onto the Forum floor, he turned to assistant coach and former teammate, Larry Drew. "Can you believe I'm the coach of the Lakers? What have I gotten myself into?" he asked. Cooper walked onto the floor before Magic and received the familiar cheer of "Coooop!" from the crowd. Magic followed shortly after, receiving a two-minute standing ovation as he made his way to the bench for the first time.

The Forum was sold out for just the third time all season. The game had a playoff atmosphere from the start, with the crowd providing an electricity not seen since Game 3 against the Suns almost a year earlier. "It was great. It was something we had not felt all year," said George Lynch. "It was great the fans didn't come in for Shaq. They came in to see the coach and the Lakers."

On the game's first possession, Van Exel fired a pass to Campbell for an alley-oop dunk. The Lakers hit their first five shots and sprinted out to an early 12-2 lead. They hustled like they hadn't all season, playing tight defense around the rim. The Bucks drove to the basket time and again but always found a wall of Laker defenders waiting for them. They fought for rebounds, made second and third efforts at block shots and hustled for every loose ball.

They also got out running. Divac collected the rebound on a missed Bucks free throw and fired a length of the court pass to Threatt for an easy lay-in and a 16-6 lead. A few minutes later, Rambis hustled to rebound his own miss and put it in for a 22-10 lead, drawing a huge cheer from the crowd. Doug Christie checked-in and immediately made more impact than he had in months. He tipped in a missed lay-in from Smith before driving along the baseline for a beautiful reverse lay-up. The Lakers led 30-14 at quarter time, outshooting the Bucks 58% to 33%.[186]

Christie came out aggressive again in the second quarter, playing under control and scoring the Lakers' first six points. The Lakers were playing unselfishly, perhaps too much at times. Threatt, Van Exel, and Lynch over-passed and almost ruined a three-on-one fast break when none of them shot the ball. Lynch eventually forced the issue and made a short jumper for a 45-21 lead.

The Lakers grew their lead to 25 when Threatt made a steal and fired a long pass up court to Van Exel, who converted a three-pointer in transition. They pushed that lead to 30 when Worthy broke through the

---

[186] The Bucks also shot an awful 2-10 on free throws in the first quarter.

Bucks' full-court pressure to feed Christie for a fast break dunk. They would close the half up by 31 points, maintaining their 58% shooting and holding the Bucks to just 29% from the field.

Chick Hearn put the game in the refrigerator as the fourth quarter started, saying it had been in the refrigerator since warm-ups and that the Jell-O had been jiggling for an hour and a half. But the Bucks were about to make Hearn and the crowd nervous. The Lakers came out flat, and the Bucks pushed back. Todd Day, Lee Mayberry, and Derek Strong led a rally as the Bucks clawed back to trail 91-80 with six minutes to play.

Van Exel led the much-needed response for the Lakers. He penetrated the lane and dished off to Campbell for a dunk. On the next possession, he drove the lane again and found Lynch for a lay-in and foul. On the following possession, he did the same thing again, finding Lynch for another lay-in and a foul.

Divac sealed the win with an unlikely play. A double-team pushed him out to the three-point line, and he made an alley-oop pass to Lynch but accidentally threw it in the basket for a 101-83 lead. Magic laughed on the sidelines at the absurd accident, while Divac ran back down the court shrugging like Michael Jordan in the 1992 Finals.

The Lakers won 110-101. Magic was exhausted after watching the game seesaw from a Lakers blowout, to a Bucks upset, and back to a Lakers win again. "I feel like I played," he said. "I could use an ice pack for my throat." There was no denying the Lakers, at least for one game, played with an intensity under Magic they hadn't shown all season. "I enjoyed it more than I thought I would," Magic said. "To see them play as hard as they played, that was enjoyable. No matter what happens, I'll always remember this day."

Lynch scored a career-high 30 points to go along with 7 rebounds. Divac continued his good form, adding 18 points, 19 rebounds, and 7 assists. And Christie had one of his better games since returning from injury, scoring 20 points on 7-9 shooting. He had played small forward and point guard during his short career and Pfund had been playing him at shooting guard since re-joining the line-up. It wasn't his ideal position, but Magic mostly played him there too. "I'm tired of switching him around," Magic said. "I think he's confused."

Things got back to normal two nights later against Minnesota. The crowd was down to 13,588, not close to a sell-out. Most of the celebrities, except for Jack Nicholson, stayed away. To top it off, the Lakers almost lost to the horrible Timberwolves. They trailed by eight at half-time before seizing the lead in the middle of the third quarter with a 17-7 run. A dunk by Worthy at the end of the quarter gave them a six-point lead. But the Timberwolves fought back, and the teams traded leads throughout the fourth quarter. Elden Campbell tied the score 89-89 on a lay-up with 37 seconds left. The Lakers got a defensive stop, and Van Exel made a driving lay-up with 1.7 seconds left to give the Lakers a 91-89 lead. The Timberwolves called a timeout to set up a play, but Isiah Rider bobbled the entry pass and had to force up a shot at the buzzer that was short. The Lakers had improved to 2-0 under their new coach.

The Lakers played their first road game under their new coach against the powerhouse Seattle SuperSonics. The Lakers had lost all three games against Seattle by an average of 16.6 points that season. Magic got a nice ovation from the KeyArena crowd, including one from head coach George Karl. The Lakers trailed by 15 points but fought their way back and trailed 93-92 with 48 seconds to play. Campbell intercepted Gary Payton's bad pass, and the Lakers had a chance to take the lead. But they looked thoroughly confused on the biggest play of the game. They got the ball to Worthy, just as Magic wanted. But with the shot clock winding down, Worthy tried to feed a pass to Campbell that was knocked away, leading to a 24-second violation with 23.9 seconds remaining.

They got another chance when they intentionally fouled Shawn Kemp. He missed one of his free throws, giving the Lakers the ball back trailing by two. Magic drew up a play that would see Smith drive down the left side, draw two defenders and kick it out to whoever was open. Smith did his part on the floor, but the Sonics didn't. The second defender never came, and Smith was forced to take an off-balance 15-footer with 12 seconds left that wasn't close. The Sonics edged out a 95-92 win. "This hurts because I wanted this bad for them," Magic said. "I knew with this win, it would have turned the table for us."

The Lakers had a second tough opponent in a row – the 50-19 Houston Rockets who the Lakers hadn't beaten at the Forum in almost two and a half years. Both teams were rough around the edges in the first half, and the Rockets had a 42-40 lead at the major break. Then the Lakers sprinted out in the third quarter, playing some of their best basketball of the season. Worthy scored nine of the Lakers' 11 points in the final three and a half minutes of the quarter to extend the Lakers' lead to 71-61 at the end of the period. They continued the streak in the fourth quarter as Smith beat the shot clock with a three-pointer on their first possession. The Rockets never got much closer, and the Lakers pulled out a 101-88 win behind 31 points by Van Exel. "We are making great strides," Magic said. "The defense was fabulous. I mean, to hold a first-place team to that many points, we're doing a great job."

Magic had made his first change to the starting line-up following his debut against Milwaukee, starting Smith ahead of Threatt the following three games. The philosophy for the change was committing to the youth movement, but it caused Threatt to almost disappear. In the first four games Magic coached, Threatt had averaged just 2.5 points in 18.8 minutes. It was a startling drop-off from the previous month when his expanded role played a big role in the Lakers playing their best basketball of the season. "I've got to get Sedale back," Magic said. "I kind of lost him."

After beating the West's second-best team, they hosted the East's second-best team – the 50-21 Atlanta Hawks. The Lakers led by seven points at half-time and, like they did against Houston, broke the game open in the third quarter. They outscored Atlanta 28-17 in the third and never let the Hawks seriously challenge in the fourth, winning 102-89. Campbell top-scored for the Lakers with 17 points despite leaving the game with six minutes remaining in the third quarter. He was taken to the hospital suffering from double vision after being inadvertently hit in the eye. Van Exel had 16 points, his three-pointer in the third quarter giving him 107 for the season, breaking Magic's old team record for most three-pointers in a season. Not bad for a second-round draft pick.

With a 4-1 coaching record, Magic seemed almost disappointed he was enjoying coaching so much. "I'm fond of the players, they won me over," he said. "I was thinking sixteen games and get me out. It's going to be tough leaving. I thought it would be easy to do. Now I see we've come a long way. This is going to be a good team."

The Lakers hosted a Sacramento Kings team who they hadn't beaten all season. They came out lethargic defensively, confused offensively, and appeared to have completely regressed to their pre-Magic form. They trailed 80-64 with two minutes to play in the third quarter in what was, in the words of Chick Hearn, the most inept they had played under Magic.

It was a game where the officials struggled to get control right from the start, resulting in some truly bewildering calls and no-calls. In one passage of play, Duane Causwell leaped in the key to receive a pass from Spud Webb and landed on his teammate Andre Spencer, knocking him to the ground. Divac was whistled for the foul even though he was only standing nearby and clearly never moved.

This infuriated the Lakers crowd, but the confusion from the refs was evenly spread. In one sequence, Divac made a lay-in after dribbling around his back, the problem being that he clearly traveled before the nifty dribbling and committed an offensive foul in the process. But no call from the officials was forthcoming. The worst example came just minutes later when Christie pushed Randy Brown out of bounds when he was collecting a rebound, but the officials awarded the ball to the Lakers.

Late in the second quarter, Edwards would concede a lay-up to Webb and be called for a phantom foul even though he never came close to touching him. Magic was enraged and was assessed a technical for continuing to argue the call even while Webb was shooting his free throws.

In the third quarter and with the Lakers down 77-64, Edwards was blatantly being held by Wayman Tisdale in the post, but there was no call. Seconds later, Trevor Wilson pushed Worthy out of rebounding position with both hands, and still there was no call. Wilson charged up the court, converted the lay-in and drew a foul from Christie. Magic again erupted in anger on the sidelines, complaining vehemently that the officials let two calls go at the Lakers end.

Wilson converted the free throw, and Threatt was dribbling the ball up court when officials gave Worthy a technical for still arguing about Wilson pushing him. It was all Magic could take. He charged onto the court, screaming and pointing at the official before being stopped at mid-court by Lakers officials. He was quickly given another technical and ejected, continuing to holler at the official until he was led off the court by equipment manager Rudy Garciduenas to a standing ovation.

The Lakers immediately went on a run and got back in the game. Bertka, who took over coaching duties after Magic's ejection, instructed the Lakers to go to Worthy on almost every possession in the fourth quarter. And he delivered a turn-back-the-clock performance. He scored eight straight points, including a 15-foot jumper with 30 seconds remaining to give the Lakers a two-point lead.

Tisdale forced overtime with a baseline jumper, but Worthy remained the go-to guy for the Lakers. He would seal a 128-123 win with a 20-footer that just beat the shot clock and finish the game with 31 points and 8 assists. Bertka repeatedly punched the air when the buzzer sounded before shuffling off the court with a smile on his face.

With five wins in his first six games, it started to look like Magic might be as good at coaching as he was at playing. The team was undeniably playing with renewed passion since he took over the job. But any hope Coach Johnson was the answer to the Lakers' problems would quickly come crashing down.

Chapter 19

THE STREAK PART II

April 8, 1994 to April 24, 1994

T HE GAME AGAINST the Denver Nuggets at the Forum on April 8, 1994 was the most hyped of the season for the Lakers, even more than Magic Johnson's coaching debut. It was billed as the crossroad of the season that would answer the question about who this Lakers team was. Were they legitimate playoff hopefuls? Or were they the lottery team everyone assumed them to be all season?

Denver had held the eighth and final playoff spot for months. When Magic took over as coach, he was asked to assess the likelihood of the Lakers overtaking them. "It's going to be tough," he replied. "They have to go on a hell of a losing streak, and we have to go on a hell of a winning streak."

Yet it looked like that very thing was happening. The Nuggets immediately went on a four-game losing streak after Magic debuted as coach, while the Lakers won five of their first six games. The Lakers were catching ground, now only trailing by three games with ten left to play. It would be a tough schedule to finish, with five straight back-to-back sets. But they were close enough to the playoffs for James Worthy to call a team meeting to talk about the focus needed for the remainder of the season if they were to make the playoffs.

It was a must-win situation, and Magic never wished he was back on the court more than he did the day of the game. "You lived as a player for games like this," he said. "I told the players at shootaround today, 'You are the luckiest 12 guys on the face of the earth tonight.' And they are. This is what you live for."

The Lakers were about to start a streak that would define their season. Unfortunately, it wasn't the kind of streak they wanted.

One

The game against Denver drew a sell-out, and the atmosphere inside the Forum was charged from tip-off. The Lakers came out aggressive, especially at the defensive end where they held the Nuggets to 33% shooting in the first quarter. Doug Christie tapped in his own miss with one second remaining to give the Lakers a 29-23 lead at quarter time. The Lakers pushed their lead out to 10 points in the third quarter before the Nuggets started dominating the offensive boards to draw within one at three-quarter time.

But the Lakers fell apart in the fourth quarter. A three-pointer by Rodney Rogers and a basket the next possession by Bryant Stith gave the Nuggets a 92-85 lead. The Lakers then committed three consecutive turnovers, each resulting in baskets down the other end that pushed the Nuggets lead to 99-85 with seven minutes to play. In all, it was a 28-6 run from the Nuggets, and the Lakers never recovered, eventually losing 112-99.

"All the speculation, people were saying a lot," Nuggets center Dikembe Mutombo said. "Christie, or whatever his name is, was talking about they were going to kick our butts, we're scared of them. You can't talk trash like that. You can't talk trash until you take care of business."

The loss left the Lakers trailing the Nuggets by four games with just nine games remaining. While not mathematically eliminated, the loss to the Nuggets all but ended any hope for the playoffs. Magic said pretty much that after the game, calling the Lakers playoff hopes "slim to none." He also confirmed he was now leaning towards not coming back next season.

Two

The Lakers were in Portland the next night, but Magic wasn't with them. Before accepting the coaching job, he had agreed to play at Magic's Roundball Classic, a high school all-star game in his hometown of Lansing, Michigan. Attempts to change the date of the game failed, so he had to attend.[187] He made an interesting choice for a replacement, overlooking Bill Bertka and his 1,467 games as an assistant. Instead, he

---

[187] It may have appeared like Magic was jumping ship after the Lakers' loss to Denver, but the scheduling conflict was discussed openly when Magic first took over as coach.

chose Michael Cooper, who been an assistant for seven games. Magic discussed the decision with Jerry Buss, who agreed. "I want Coop to see what he can do," said Magic. "Everyone does."[188]

The Lakers were great in the first half, leading 65-56 at half-time. But the entire lead was gone within the first four minutes of the third quarter after the Blazers used a 13-2 run to take a 69-67 lead. From there, the Lakers shot just 36% and Cooper lost his coaching debut, 112-104.

Three

Magic re-joined the team the next day in Los Angeles, where he participated in training for the first time since his aborted comeback attempt. He brought the ball up court, delivered trademark no-look passes, matched up with Christie and frequently got free for easy lay-ups. Magic said he planned to train with the team more often. "I'm in shape. I shoot and play every day. I can play," he said. "You can see I'm not there missing anything. My timing's there, I can go to the basket, I can do all the things I used to. It's nice to get out there. Sometimes, talk is cheap, so now I can show them."

Christie was impressed with just how difficult it was to match-up against him. "He'd still be an All-Star," Christie said. "He'd still be the best point guard in the game. Nothing's changed."

It highlighted how ridiculous the Lakers' situation was. The guy who was the best player on the team wasn't playing but was instead their coach. Never in the history of the NBA was a team coached by a person who could wipe the floor with every player on the roster but wasn't a player-coach.

The Lakers had improved their defense dramatically under Magic, holding teams to 92.5 points during his first five games. But their bad habits started to return. After giving up 112 points the last two games, they gave up a ton to the Golden State Warriors at the Forum, losing 128-117. "The disappointing thing is the number of lay-ups," Magic said. "When you give up 38 lay-ups, you expect to lose. Golden State is not a big team, but they just pushed us around, outmuscled us." It was the Lakers' 42nd loss of the season, assuring them of back-to-back losing seasons for the first time since 1974-75 and 1975-76.

---

[188] Seeing this no doubt made Randy Pfund feel justified in being paranoid the Lakers would groom Cooper to be head coach to one day replace him.

Magic started Vlade Divac on the bench as punishment for being late to practice the day before. He moved Elden Campbell to center and George Lynch at power forward, making room to start Christie at small forward. It was his first start in over three months, and he scored 15 points in 28 minutes.

James Worthy got into a scrap with Chris Gatling late in the third quarter of the game against the Warriors when the two got tangled after Worthy attempted a jumper. Both players were ejected, but it was clear Worthy was the instigator, initiating the scuffle and connecting on a punch.

Four

Worthy traveled with the team to Phoenix for the Lakers' next game against the Suns, but was forced to return to Los Angeles before the game when he received news he would be suspended and fined for the fight with Gatling. As per league rules, he was not allowed to be at the venue for the game, even as a spectator.[189]

Divac was back in the starting line-up, and Christie was back to the bench where he scored 2 points on 1-7 shooting. The Lakers stretched their losing streak to four games with a listless 117-88 thrashing by the Suns. The frontcourt for Phoenix did whatever they wanted all night with little resistance from the Lakers. Cedric Ceballos top scored with 29 points on 13-16 shooting while Charles Barkley collected 20 points and 20 rebounds without ever appearing to get out of second gear.

Magic ripped the Lakers after the game. "One team [Phoenix] is in the playoffs and going for a world championship, and another team is already on vacation," he said. "We've quit already. As a matter of fact, we had done that the last couple of games. As soon as we didn't win versus Denver, we kind of packed it in."

Magic especially targeted the Lakers' frontcourt players, who were almost non-existent all game long. "Elden, Vlade, all them, if they don't want to play, fine. They won't play," he said. "I'm disappointed in all five of them in their effort and the way they came out and approached this game. Every time we get hit with a right hook, we submit. It's over. We go into the tank."

---

[189] In addition to being suspended one game, Worthy was fined $28,811.

Five

The Lakers' losing streak grew to five, matching their longest of the season, with a 105-100 loss at home to the Portland Trail Blazers. The loss made it official – the Lakers were eliminated from the playoffs for the first time since 1975-76 and for just the fourth time in franchise history.

With the playoff push officially over, Magic announced he would see out the remaining five games of the season but wouldn't return to coach next season. "It's not the fact of our record," Magic said. "I never wanted to be a coach. I'm just sticking by that."[190]

Buss was disappointed Magic didn't want to return but was thankful he gave it a try. "Yes, I would have preferred for him to stay," Buss said, "but I'm not disappointed, because I would not have wanted him to do something he did not want to do."

West didn't sound the least bit surprised. The decision to fire Pfund and hire Magic had clearly been Buss' move. And West sounded, just a little bit, like someone saying, 'I told you so' without ever saying it. "This is something, frankly, that I anticipated all along," he said. "This does not surprise me at all. We'll get busy immediately exploring all our options."

It was almost surreal for the Lakers not to be in the playoffs. They had been there 17 consecutive seasons, the longest active string of appearances in the league and the third-longest in NBA history. "It's a damn shame," Kurt Rambis said.

"It's very unusual," Worthy said. "There's not a lot to say. It's something I'm not accustomed to, playing 82 games and not making the playoffs."

"I know it's weird to everybody, us and the NBA," Magic said. "The other teams, you know they love it. This is their payback for all those years. But it hurts. It hurts the league. People won't say it, but it hurts not having both the Lakers and Boston in it."[191]

* * * * *

---

[190] Magic had made up his mind before the game but delayed making the announcement to avoid overshadowing Kareem Abdul-Jabbar, who was honoured at half-time of the Blazers game for the 10th anniversary of him passing Wilt Chamberlain as the NBA all-time leading scorer. Pfund was at the game to take part in the ceremony, his first time back at the Forum since being fired.

[191] The Celtics were out of the playoff hunt too, eventually finishing the season with a 32-50 record and missing the playoffs for the first time in 14 years.

Six

The Lakers were down the street the next night for a road game against the Los Angeles Clippers, a game in which Dominique Wilkins didn't believe he would play because of a sprained right wrist.[192] He badly wanted to play to get the bad taste of the Clippers' 49-point loss to the Seattle SuperSonics out of his mouth from two nights earlier. He tested the wrist in pre-game warm-ups and thought he would give it a try. The Clippers were glad he did as he scored a season-high 42 points and grabbed 11 rebounds.

The Lakers cut the Clippers' lead to 104-103 with one and a half minutes remaining after Nick Van Exel made a three-pointer and Tony Smith made a short jumper. Lynch stole a pass from Ron Harper on the next possession and the Lakers had a chance to steal the lead, but Van Exel shot an airball on a drive to the basket. "I felt it leaving my hand and slip a little bit," Van Exel said. "I didn't get the full release I wanted, so I knew it was going to be short."

Wilkins blocked a desperation shot by Rambis, resulting in a shot clock violation with 46 seconds remaining. He then drilled a jump shot on the next possession for a 106-103 lead. Van Exel missed again on the Lakers' next trip down that led to a dunk by Wilkins, sealing the Clippers' 108-103 win.

To their credit, the Lakers played with more intensity than anyone would expect for a team whose coach had publicly said he had no interest in being their coach. "I was happy about the effort," said Magic. "I told them if we had been playing like this all along, we would be in the playoffs. We fought back and played smart. That's all you can ask."

Worthy didn't play in the game, receiving just his second 'Did Not Play – Coach's Decision' of his 12-year career. "It wasn't that tough," Worthy said after the game. "I kind of understood before the game that it would be limited minutes if anything."

Antonio Harvey left the game midway through the second quarter with a rapid heartbeat. He was taken to Centinela Hospital Medical Center for observation where he would spend the next three nights. He would be given a clean bill of health, but it was a scary situation – especially with

---

[192] Wilkins had been traded from Atlanta to the Clippers at the trade deadline in exchange for leading scorer Danny Manning. Wilkins had played 11 and half seasons in Atlanta, averaging 26.5 points and 7.0 rebounds.

two athletes dying in recent years from that very thing. "I thought about those guys – Hank Gathers, Reggie Lewis," he said. "Of course, those things come to mind. That's why I said something."

Harvey wouldn't play again in 1993-94 but was told he could resume training, though doctors instructed him to wear a heart monitor all summer. He was placed on the injured list, and Reggie Jordan was put back in the rotation.

Seven

The Lakers had a shot at a moral victory of sorts when they played the Denver Nuggets at McNichols Arena three nights later and found themselves trailing 99-97 with two and a half minutes to play. They were already without Van Exel, who missed the first game of his career because of the flu, and Campbell was on the bench with foul trouble. Then Divac sprained his ankle and was forced to leave the game. From there, they had no answers for the Nuggets who would go on to get a 105-98 win and extend the Lakers' losing streak to seven games.

Even though x-rays proved negative, and Gary Vitti would label the strain as moderate, Magic decided to shut Divac down for the remaining three games of the season. There was little use in risking further injury to Divac in a lost season.

Eight

Van Exel was still under the weather, but he was back in the line-up the next night at home against the Seattle SuperSonics, though he was limited to just six minutes off the bench. With Van Exel only making a cameo and Divac injured, Magic threw out the oddest starting line-up of the season. He started Threatt and Christie in the backcourt and gave veterans Worthy and James Edwards their first starts of the season in the frontcourt along with Campbell. Threatt recorded 28 points and 7 assists, Christie had 16 points, 8 rebounds, and 7 assists, but almost everybody else struggled. The Lakers were outscored by 29 points in the fourth quarter and were routed 112-90 for their eighth straight loss.

* * * * *

Nine

The Lakers were just as listless three nights later in Oakland where they gave up 73 points in the first half and fell 126-91 to the Golden State Warriors. It was their ninth consecutive loss, a new franchise record. The win meant the Warriors had swept the Lakers 5-0 in the regular season for the first time in franchise history. The only fun part of the game for the Lakers was Jordan getting a season-high 28 minutes and using it well – scoring 15 points and collecting 8 rebounds.

Magic was asked if he was upset at the loss. "I'm already past that," he replied. "It's too late to be upset. I'm frustrated, I'm embarrassed, and I told them at half-time that I am embarrassed for them."

Magic had continued to train with the Lakers in practice and the idea of activating himself and playing in the last two meaningless games of the season had crossed his mind. "I was thinking about it," he said. "Both of these, this one and Utah."

Ten

Magic wasn't in uniform when the Lakers wrapped up the 1993-94 season against the Utah Jazz at the Forum. But he did put the veterans back in the starting line-up one last time, with Worthy, Edwards, and Rambis getting the nod. Worthy was 32 years old and banged up, Rambis was 36 and Edwards 38. Magic knew it might be the last NBA game for each of them, and if it was, he wanted to ensure they rode off into the sunset the right way. With the team eliminated from the playoffs, putting them in the starting line-up was the best he could offer. "I want them to go out with something special."

The Lakers' season at last came to an end with a 103-97 loss in front of 15,338 fans. Almost fittingly, the Lakers ended their miserable season by securing their tenth consecutive loss, the longest losing streak in franchise history.

Jordan again took advantage of extra minutes, finishing his unlikely first season in the NBA with 20 points and 8 rebounds. The veterans did their part in limited minutes – Rambis collecting 8 points and 9 rebounds, Edwards scoring 8 points, and Worthy getting 8 points on 3-7 shooting. Worthy was non-committal on whether he thought it was his last NBA game, though he knew it might well be. "It's the last game of the regular season, with no playoffs," he said. "I think about that a lot."

The Lakers finished the season with 33 wins, their fewest since the 1974-75 season. Just like they had been in 1991-92, the Lakers were decimated by injury all season, losing 216 total games to injuries.[193] But this time they didn't have nearly enough talent to stay afloat.

Magic's tenure as head coach lasted one month and two days. The early stages of his stint, when the Lakers went 5-1, was the epitome of a coaching bump. A new head coach can temporarily increase players' intensity and produce a few wins, but the team will often return to who they really are.

And it showed in the stats. Overall the Lakers were the same offensively but worse defensively under Magic compared to how they were under Pfund. They were vastly improved in Magic's first five games and considerably worse in their last ten.

Lakers under Pfund: 100.0 points per game, 103.9 allowed
Magic first six games: 104.0 points per game, 97.5 allowed
Magic's last 10 games: 98.7 points per game, 112.8 allowed
Lakers under Magic overall: 100.7 points per game, 107.1 allowed

Either the team returned to normality or simply gave up when it was clear they were not making the playoffs.[194]

Magic made it sound like his decision not to return as coach was a simple one – he never wanted to do it, so he wasn't going to continue in the role. But a lot went into the decision.

It was partly lifestyle. As much as he had retirement thrust upon him, he had become accustomed to it. And there were real perks, especially for someone with young children. He could set his own hours, concentrate on his business ventures, and head off on vacation whenever he wanted to. These things were impossible when living by the NBA's busy schedule. He might give up those perks if it meant playing again. But give them up to coach when he wasn't 100% committed? Not so much.

---

[193] Bowie 57, Peeler 52, Harvey 42, Rambis 18, Christie 16, Wilson 11, Jordan 8, Campbell 6, Edwards 2, and Divac, Van Exel and Threatt 1.

[194] The Lakers' defensive rating continued to decline after Magic retired. It was fifth best in the league in 1990-91, fell to 16th in 1992-93, and 22nd in the league in 1993-94.

Magic no longer knew where he fitted with this Lakers team anymore. It was different from when he was a player, and not just because of the new faces. With young players came a lot of losses, two things sure to change team culture. Magic couldn't connect with that new culture, even though he had only been away from the game for two and a half seasons.

It started as a slow burn. When the Lakers lost by three points in Seattle, his first loss as a coach, he walked into the locker room to find the coaches were more upset about the loss than the players. He wasn't used to that. The Showtime Lakers took losses hard, but these Lakers didn't seem to mind all that much. He wanted to instill a commitment to winning, but the players were not willing to do it. And he found that frustrating, infamously smashing a player's beeper against a wall when it went off during practice.

He struggled with the individualist culture of modern players, as opposed to the team culture he was used to. It was a generational difference, with the young players having walked into the modern NBA that Magic helped create. They were instantly rewarded with money and fame before they had proved anything. It was an issue Pfund had struggled with too. "I've heard people say I give these guys too much freedom, that I let Nick shoot too much or somebody else talk too much, that kind of thing," Pfund said in January 1994. "But these are players of the 90s. The days when a coach could completely hush his players are over."

"It's changed a lot," Magic said. "Back when I was playing, I used to love it. If you were late, those other 11 guys would just rag on you until you couldn't be late anymore. We understood how to help each other. If you had a baby, we all had a baby. Every guy was there. If you had a tragedy, every guy had a tragedy. It's just that family. Now you've got a lot of individuals. Everybody cares about me. I, I, I. 'Where's *my* minutes, where's *my* shots? What's wrong with *my* game? Why can't *I* get *my* game off? So, it's a lot of that now, and I don't like that."

"I won't say they drove him away," assistant coach Larry Drew said. "But what he wanted to accomplish and try to do just wasn't happening. He wanted to change their attitude about approaching the games. Being focused. If we lost, he wanted them to understand why we lost. That didn't happen, and those are all the factors that snowballed."

Yet the changes that had happened with the Lakers were symptomatic of a cultural shift that occurred across the entire league in the early 1990s.

Some coaches dealt with it better than others, managing to remain leaders despite the generation gap between them and the players. But Magic couldn't deal with it at all.

The two players who seemed the most willing to buy into Magic's philosophy were Lynch and Van Exel. Not so much because they were the youngest and most impressionable but because they had an inbuilt commitment to winning. Lynch was part of a winning system and culture at the University of North Carolina, while Van Exel was a natural competitor who hated losing. "If we would have had him from the beginning of the year, it would have made a difference," Lynch said. "But he came in too late to change some of the players."

It was an especially tough start to the season for Lynch, who hardly played over the first two months. He looked like a bust early in the season and a waste of the Lakers' high draft pick, averaging 4.0 points and 1.8 rebounds in his first 21 games. He didn't play in 11 of the first 32 games. But he wasn't a bust, it's just that Pfund wasn't giving him a chance. When he finally did, Lynch showed he belonged in the league with averages of 12.0 points and 7.5 rebounds over his final 49 games.

Van Exel's experience was the opposite. He was given the keys to the offense, was anointed the starting point guard in pre-season, was second on the team in minutes played, and started 80 of the team's 82 games. But all the losing was hard for him to take. "It was tough. There were a lot of games where we'd go out and see guys who really didn't want to play and were not giving their all," he said. "That really hurt the most because we know they could do better."

Almost every General Manager in the league had passed up on drafting Van Exel, some more than once. He seemed to dedicate his entire season to proving each of them wrong. He certainly showed signs of youth – appearing out of control and impatient on offense with questionable shot selection and inconsistent numbers. But he had played with a fire and competitiveness the Lakers, overall, severely lacked. He averaged 13.6 points and 5.8 assists on the season, far and away better numbers than any other player selected in the second round that year. In fact, they were better numbers than 22 of the 27 players taken in the first round, and he was voted second-team All-Rookie.

Questions about Van Exel's attitude had, at least in his first year, appeared to be misplaced. His brash image was proving to be only a half-truth. Off the court, Van Exel was quiet and unassuming, preferring to stay home to watch movies or play video games than hit the clubs. He would be quiet and appear nervous in the locker room, then turn into a maniacal motor-mouth when he hit the court. He acknowledged his approach on the court was his way of masking nervousness and insecurity. But above all, he just wanted to have fun, and it was through competition that he would have it. "To be playing basketball for a job, that's the best thing in the world that could happen to me," he said. "I live basketball. I dream basketball."

Seattle head coach George Karl, who had a run-in with Van Exel during a pre-draft workout, knew his team wouldn't take a chance on the young player but also knew the kid brought something special to the table. "We saw an individualist," said Karl. "But we also saw a winner. There's that thin line." Finding the best way to navigate that thin line would be the key part of Van Exel's development going forward.

The Lakers' two second-year players, Peeler and Christie, had both shown signs of development from their rookie seasons but were severely limited by injury.

Peeler had played well to start the season, increasing his scoring average from 10.4 as a rookie to 14.1 in 1993-94. But he played just 30 games due to injury. "I had so many expectations in the summertime. I wanted to do well for the team and myself," Peeler said. "It gets frustrating because I wanted to play real bad. Now I just try to stay mentally focused and learn a lot about what other people are doing. I try to make my game better that way."

Christie also posted better numbers, upping his scoring from 6.2 points to 10.3 in 1993-94. But he too had endured an up and down season because of injury. It started in pre-season when he badly sprained his ankle in the first exhibition game. His play was encouraging over the first three months of the season, with averages of 14.4 points and 4.5 rebounds in his first 32 games before injuring his ankle again. When he finally returned he had lost his starting small forward spot to Lynch and appeared also to lose confidence. He regressed in the final 33 games, his averages over that time slumping to 6.4 points on 38% shooting, closer to his numbers as a rookie.

Amongst all the losing, one of the bright spots in the season was the play of Divac. Now in his fifth NBA season, he was still more inconsistent than coaches and fans would have liked. But he appeared to be turning into the player people thought he might have been when he first came into the league. He started the season putting up numbers close to his career average but blossomed in the second half of the season. Over the last 41 games, he averaged 16.6 points, 11.6 rebounds, and 4.7 assists and turned into one of the best ten centers in the league. "He's about the closest thing we have to a go-to guy," Worthy said.

On the other hand, Worthy suffered through the worst season of his career. He registered career lows in minutes, scoring, rebounds, steals, blocks, and field goal percentage. He was undeniably slowing down in 1992-93, but it got to the stage in 1993-94 that it was questionable that he had anything left. The sight of him struggling night in and night out was more than just watching an athlete on the decline. It was a nightly reminder of everything the Lakers had lost since Showtime ended.[195]

After the worst season many Lakers fans had ever seen, the team shut up shop for the season when the final buzzer sounded on the game against the Jazz. The playoffs would be taking place without them. They were entering an off-season with a lot of questions, but one thing was for sure – changes were needed. Probably a lot of them. "If I were a lot of these players," West said after the final game of the season, "I don't think I'd buy a home."

---

[195] Worthy's PER had fallen from 18.1 in 1990-91 to 12.8 in 1993-94.

PART IV:
THE LAKE SHOW

Chapter 20
AN EYE ON RESPECTABILITY

April 25, 1994 to November 3, 1994

M IKE DUNLEAVY DIDN'T want it. Randy Pfund couldn't keep it. Magic Johnson didn't need it.[196] For the third time in five years, the Lakers started their summer in search of a new head coach. After nine years of stability under Pat Riley, the Lakers had cycled through three head coaches in four seasons. Jerry West wanted to break from Laker tradition and hire an experienced NBA coach who might better handle the young players. The only head coach the Lakers had ever hired who had previously coached in the league was Bill Sharman, who coached the Lakers from 1970 to 1976.

West spent the best part of a month talking to potential candidates. These included University of Kentucky head coach Rick Pitino and University of Maryland's Gary Williams. He also approached Golden State Warriors owner Jim Fitzgerald for permission to talk to Don Nelson, but was rebuffed.

In mid-May 1994, the Lakers announced the team's new head coach would be Del Harris. As would prove to be the case with every move the Lakers made that off-season, the hiring of Harris flew under the radar and few NBA pundits paid it much mind. On the surface, it appeared to be an underwhelming choice. Harris wasn't the big-named coach some hoped the Lakers would land. Instead, Harris was grey-haired and middle-aged with a not so flattering nickname of 'Dull' Harris.

Harris was a seasoned basketball veteran with a long resumé. An Indiana native, he played his college ball in the late 1950s at Milligan College, a small Christian liberal arts college in Tennessee. There he

---

[196] This was how Steve Springer summarised the Lakers' recent coaching history in the *Los Angeles Times* on May 14, 1994.

earned a degree in religious studies and history, and was eventually inducted into the Milligan College Athletic Hall of Fame. After graduation, he returned to Indiana as a high school history teacher and basketball coach.[197] He landed his first major coaching job when he was appointed head coach of the Hustlin Quakers of Earlham College. There he coached nine seasons from 1965 to 1974, taking a previously struggling basketball program to a 175-70 record during those years.

His first pro job came as an assistant to Tom Nissalke with the Utah Stars of the ABA in 1975. The Stars folded after the season and Nissalke landed the head coaching job of the Houston Rockets for the 1976-77 season, taking Harris with him. Harris served three years as an assistant in Houston before taking over as head coach in 1979-80. He coached the 42-40 Rockets to a series of surprising upsets in the 1981 playoffs, taking them all the way to the NBA Finals where they lost to the Boston Celtics in six games. Harris endured the 1982-83 season where they tanked to draft Ralph Sampson and was replaced by Bill Fitch the following season.

After a few years away from the game, Harris served as an assistant to Don Nelson with the Milwaukee Bucks in 1986-87 before taking over as head coach and Vice President of Basketball Operations the following season. He coached the Bucks to an average of 45.8 wins over four seasons, making the playoffs each year.[198] He was fired 17 games into the 1991-92 season and replaced by his assistant Frank Hamblen.[199]

Harris spent the ensuing years as a consultant to Sacramento Kings owner Jim Thomas and turned down an offer to be the Kings' General Manager because he hadn't given up hope of another coaching job. He published a book entitled *Winning Defense* in 1993 and was a finalist for the Los Angeles Clippers coaching job the previous summer, but the job eventually went to Bob Weiss.

Though West undertook due diligence by looking at several candidates, in truth he wanted to hire Harris from the get-go. West had considered Harris for the job back when Dunleavy quit but felt he couldn't in good faith look past Pfund a second time. West and Harris had been

---

[197] Harris was also a semi-pro baseball player during his teaching days.

[198] Mike Dunleavy was an assistant to Harris in Milwaukee for three seasons from 1987 to 1990.

[199] Frank Hamblen would go onto become a long-time assistant to Phil Jackson, joining him in Chicago in 1996-97 and serving as an assistant with the Lakers from 1999-00 to 2010-11. He served as interim head coach for the Lakers in the second half of the 2004-05 season.

friends for years and touched base regularly to talk basketball.

"Del has been our first choice for coach for a very long time," Buss said. "My feeling was, we should leave no stone unturned. We should go through everyone we thought conceivably might be a candidate. But quite honestly, our thoughts have been on Del for many months now." Indeed, West had complimented Harris when introducing Dunleavy as coach to the media in 1990. "He [Dunleavy] had played for two people I greatly admire from a coaching standpoint," West said at the press conference, "Don Nelson and Del Harris."

One thing West always liked about Harris was he wasn't wedded to a fixed system. His coaching philosophy was flexible, molding the style of play to the personnel on the team. He was known more for teams that specialized in defense and a half-court game, which made him appear an odd choice for the Lakers who had long been devoted to a wide-open, running style of play. But he rebuffed that reputation during his introductory press conference. "Pat Riley became categorized as a Showtime kind of coach, now he's doing just the opposite," Harris said. "I believe a master coach must find a way to win with his particular talent." An early indication of his flexible coaching style was he didn't demand to bring his own assistants, instead saying he would retain the current coaching staff of Bill Bertka, Larry Drew, and Michael Cooper.

Harris had long demonstrated an ability to connect with even the most distant and hard-to-reach players. He told a story about trying to get to know Moses Malone, long considered a difficult personality, when he was coaching him in Houston. He asked Malone what he did during the summer and Malone, never one to waste words, replied by saying, "Swimming pool." Harris responded with surprise, "Oh, you built yourself a swimming pool?" Malone shook his head. "Went swimming. Shot pool," he said. It was more than most NBA coaches got out of him.

Harris had a reputation for being dull, but it was an unfair one. He was a dead-ringer for actor Leslie Nielsen, occasionally being mistaken for him in the street and signing autographs under his name. While coaching Milwaukee, he ran into Nielsen at Chicago Stadium when the Bucks were playing the Bulls. He approached Nielsen and asked him if he would go into the Bucks locker room and pretend to be him. Nielsen walked into the locker room screaming at the Bucks players to play harder, stop dribbling and act like men for a change.

He was also a mainstay on NBA blooper reels with his most famous moment coming when coaching the Bucks at home against the Denver Nuggets. He inexplicably took three steps onto the court and Nuggets point guard Michael Adams ran right into him while trying to dribble the ball up court. He later appeared on TNT and jokingly said he was trying to set a pick, even drawing up the play to explain how much of an effective pick it was.

As promised, Buss sold a 5% share of the team to Magic for between $10 million and $15 million, making him team Vice President.[200] His responsibilities would include consulting on player matters, working with the marketing department to lure sponsors, and developing the Lakers' role in the community. Magic promised to have a lower profile at Lakers games and be less publicly critical of players than he had been in the past. "I want the team to get its own identity," he said. It was a change of tack from the final days of his coaching tenure, when he questioned the young Lakers for trying to distance themselves from his era. "I don't want Del or anybody to think I'm looking over their shoulders or anything. I think it's good for them to do their own thing. I don't want them to feel like I'm there for any other reason than to cheer for them."[201]

The Lakers' reward for their dismal 1993-94 season was the 10th pick in the draft.[202] In a sign of how much they had struggled since the retirement of Magic, it was the third straight year they had their highest draft pick since selecting James Worthy first overall in 1982.

West brought in several players for pre-draft workouts, including Carlos Rogers from Tennessee State University, Khalid Reeves from University of Arizona, and Jalen Rose from the University of Michigan. But unlike in 1992, when West agonized over the choice between two players, it was clear this time who he wanted. And unlike in 1993, when his first, second, and third choices were all selected before he could get to

---

[200] It likely wasn't a coincidence that the purchase price was in the same ballpark as the $14.6 million balloon payment Buss had agreed to pay Magic for the upcoming season.

[201] Buss also changed Jerry West's title from General Manager to Executive Vice President of Basketball Operations and Mitch Kupchak was promoted to General Manager. It is unclear what practical difference the changes made, as West was still responsible for his former duties of trades, contract negotiations, and scouting.

[202] The Lakers didn't own a second-round pick in 1994, having sent it to Seattle as part of the trade for Sedale Threatt. The pick ended up being 37th overall and Seattle used it to select Dontonio Wingfield from University of Cincinnati.

them, he got his man in 1994 – shooting guard Eddie Jones from Temple University.

Jones was an excellent defender and was named the Atlantic 10 Conference Player of the Year in 1994 with averages of 19.2 points and 6.8 rebounds his junior year. He was arguably the best athlete in the draft, a spectacular leaper, and a driver with a great first step. His offensive game reminded many of Ron Harper, but his defense reminded West of Michael Cooper. He even looked like Cooper – standing 6'6 with a thin, lanky build. "It was like looking into a mirror," Cooper said when watching him in pre-draft workouts. Jones had grown up in Florida and played college in Pennsylvania, but he had been a Lakers fan his whole life and modeled his game on Magic and Cooper. "It's a dream come true," said Jones.

The selection raised a few eyebrows because Jones was yet another guard, joining a backcourt already crowded with young players. But West wanted to acquire the most talented player he could and would figure out the rest later. "We wanted the best athlete available," West said. "We didn't care if we duplicated some position we already had. Eddie was just too good to pass up." And Jones didn't come with the kinds of question marks Peeler, Christie, and Van Exel bought with them. Jones was known as unselfish and highly coachable, with an easygoing, friendly disposition.

By drafting Jones, the Lakers added another talented player to their young core of Vlade Divac, Elden Campbell, Peeler, Christie, George Lynch, and Van Exel – who were all under the age of 25. But as talented as Jones was, he was unlikely to be the sole answer to the Lakers' problems. Despite their horrible season, they had talent on the team. But they were a team full of role players, a supporting cast without a lead. This was obvious by the fact Divac led the Lakers in scoring in 1993-94 with just 14.1 points per game, the lowest average to lead a team in the league. What the Lakers needed more than anything was a dependable scorer who could be relied upon for 18 to 20 points a night. Unfortunately for the Lakers, they had few available options to acquire one.

The Lakers were never expected to be a big player in the free agent market that off-season. They had three things to sell: year-round good weather, the big sports market of Los Angeles, and their long, proud history. But they couldn't offer money or wins, the two things most free agents coveted. They had little money to offer because they were already over the salary cap. The $14.6 million balloon payment to Magic and the

$7.2 million owed to Worthy already put them well over the $15.9 million salary cap, not to mention the $18 million they owed the rest of the players. They had the highest player payroll in the league, despite being a non-playoff team.

But they did make some minor moves early in free agency. They traded a 1995 second-round draft pick to the Golden State Warriors in exchange for the draft rights to center Anthony Miller from Michigan State University.[203] Miller was selected 39th overall, but the Warriors already had three centers on the roster. Veteran center James Edwards was a free agent and was unlikely to re-sign with the Lakers given he had spent most of the last season lobbying to be waived. Indeed, he would eventually sign with the Portland Trail Blazers that off-season. Miller would be invited to training camp with the opportunity to replace Edwards as the Lakers' third-string center behind Divac and Sam Bowie.

They then cut ties with the expendable parts of their roster. They waived center Danny Schayes, who was never part of the Lakers' long-term plan and was only on the team to ensure they didn't lose A.C. Green's vacant salary spot. The Lakers also elected not to extend a qualifying offer to Reggie Jordan, making him a free agent.[204] Kurt Rambis accepted an offer to become a Special Coach for the Lakers, ending his 13-year NBA career at the age of 35.

Armed only with the Green/Schayes $1.75 million salary spot, West called Jim Sexton, the agent for free agent forward Horace Grant, on the first day of free agency. Grant was a bruising power forward who was a good defender and rebounder, a dependable scorer, and had championship pedigree by winning three titles in Chicago. Magic tried his hand at recruiting Grant, but it was never going to happen. Grant wanted an opportunity to win and eventually signed with the Orlando Magic,

---

[203] It was the 1995 second-round pick that the Lakers received from Milwaukee as part of compensation for losing Dunleavy.

[204] Edwards would play one season in Portland and finish his career by winning a championship with the Chicago Bulls in 1995-96 at the age of 40. Schayes played another five years in the NBA with Phoenix, Miami, and Orlando before retiring in 1999 at the age of 39. Jordan played in the CBA and Greece in 1994-95 before signing with the Atlanta Hawks in 1995-96. He played four more seasons in the NBA with Portland, Minnesota, and Washington before returning to the CBA and Greece. In the 186 games he played in the NBA, his 28 points for the Lakers against Utah remained his career high.

instantly elevating them from a team of young talent to title contenders.[205]

West couldn't find a taker for the $1.75 million salary spot for most of the off-season until a perfect situation presented itself. The Lakers and Phoenix Suns swung a deal that equally benefited both teams.

In a case of the rich getting richer, the already talented Suns added two major pieces to their roster that off-season. In early September, they signed forward Danny Manning, who averaged 20.8 points and 6.8 rebounds with the Los Angeles Clippers and Atlanta Hawks in 1993-94. Less than two weeks later, they signed forward Wayman Tisdale, who had averaged 16.7 points and 7.1 rebounds the past season with the Sacramento Kings. But they had a problem – Manning and Tisdale were joining an incredibly strong frontcourt that also included Charles Barkley, A.C. Green, and Cedric Ceballos. It would also eventually include Richard Dumas who was due to return from his year-long drug suspension in March 1995. There were just not enough minutes to go around for six talented forwards.

The Phoenix Suns were willing to trade small forward Cedric Ceballos to the Lakers in exchange for a first-round draft pick to break the logjam. It was exactly the kind of deal West had been waiting for. Taken late in the second round by Phoenix in 1990, Ceballos was an athletic, 24-year-old small forward who was probably best known for winning the 1992 Slam Dunk Contest by completing a dunk blindfolded.[206] But gimmicks aside, he had proven to be an excellent rebounder and a high volume, efficient scorer who led the league in field goal percentage in 1992-93 by making 57% of his shots. He had enjoyed a breakout season in 1993-94, taking advantage of extra opportunities when the Suns were hit with injuries, and averaged 19.1 points and 6.5 rebounds while starting 43 games.

Ceballos was the kind of player who could score 20 points in a game without ever having a single play run for him. He was an opportunistic scorer with an uncanny knack for being in the right place at the right time. He did most of his damage by expertly moving without the ball or scoring off offensive rebounds. He was exactly the kind of player the Lakers wanted, not to mention he was a Californian product. He had attended Manuel Dominquez High School in Compton, California and played his

---

[205] The NBA rejected the first contract Grant signed with the Magic on the same grounds they had rejected Chris Dudley's contract a year earlier. It took two months, but Grant eventually joined Orlando before the start of training camp.

[206] Whether or not he could see through the blindfold was a serious debate at the time.

college ball at Cal State Fullerton. And he was an avid Lakers fan growing up, modeling his game on Worthy.

It was a win-win situation for Phoenix and the Lakers. With this deal, West would be able to add a scorer without giving up any of his young players. Phoenix would alleviate the pressure of minute allocation for their talented front-court without receiving a player in return. It was also a win for Ceballos. He would, at best, average 20 minutes a game off the bench in Phoenix. But with the Lakers, he would be the incumbent starting small forward on his hometown team. He also had ambitions to be an actor and musician, and there was no better place to do that than Los Angeles.

There was, however, an off-season incident at Ceballos' home that may have been the reason Suns management singled him out to be moved. On the night the Suns were eliminated by the Houston Rockets in Game 7 of the 1994 Semi-Finals, Ceballos went out with teammates Barkley and Oliver Miller to a nightclub in Scottsdale. There they met three women who they invited back to a party at Ceballos' house. One of the women contacted police shortly after leaving the party and claimed she had been raped by Miller. The woman declined to press charges, and no further legal action was taken. The incident was one of the primary reasons the Suns elected not to extend an offer sheet to Miller who was a restricted free-agent.

The one roadblock to the trade going through was the fact Ceballos was due to make $2.1 million in 1994-95, and the Lakers could only absorb $1.75 million without adding a player in the trade – something the Suns weren't interested in doing. The Suns granted permission for West to talk to Ceballos' agent and together they worked out a way to restructure his contract. Ceballos would agree to take less money for the upcoming season to fit under the $1.75 million salary spot but be given an additional fourth year to his deal. The trade became official on September 24, 1994 with the Lakers sending their 1995 first round pick to the Suns to complete the deal.

With 16 players in tow, The Lakers opened training camp on October 8, 1994, in what had become their traditional pre-season home at the University of Hawaii. None of the moves West made in the off-season drew much attention from the national sports media or NBA fans. Not hiring Harris, not drafting Jones, not trading for Ceballos. For the second straight season, they were an afterthought in the NBA. They were a bad team in 1993-94, and it was assumed – when anyone gave the team any thought – they would only be scarcely better in 1994-95.

The starting point guard was assumed to be Van Exel again, who agreed to a five-year contract extension earlier that summer. "I know the organization, and I know they take care of people," Van Exel said at the time. "I haven't caused any problems. They stuck by me and gave me a chance to start. I look at it like they're going to take care of me." The 33-year-old Threatt was expected to be used solely as Van Exel's back-up, while Peeler and Jones would battle for the starting shooting guard spot. Fitting in there, somewhere, would be Tony Smith, who had seen his role expand each of his first four seasons but had never developed a steady enough offensive game to be part of the rotation consistently.

The frontcourt was versatile but inconsistent. Ceballos was a lock for the starting small forward position, but it was anyone's guess who the starting power forward would be. Campbell was the starter most of the previous season and had continued to develop into a useful, if still inconsistent, contributor. He had increased his scoring from 7.7 in 1992-93 to 12.3 in 1993-94, and his rebounding from 4.2 to 6.8. But he was also capable of playing center, which perhaps made him an ideal sixth man. The same could be said for Lynch, who had all the skills of a power forward but played better as a small forward his rookie season. His versatility also suggested he might work well off the bench. 33-year-old Worthy, who despite rumors all off-season that he would retire, was at camp and appeared like he wanted to give it one more season.

Divac would once again be the starting center and Bowie his back-up. Bowie announced before the start of camp that the 1994-95 season would be his last in the NBA. "I still enjoy the game," he said. "But all the surgeries and injuries have really taken a toll on me. I guess next year would be a longshot for me."

There were four young players fighting for the final two roster spots, including second-year forward Antonio Harvey and rookie Miller. In addition, there were two undrafted rookies – point guard Trevor Ruffin from the University of Hawaii and forward Kendrick Warren from Virginia Commonwealth University.

A big question leading into camp was where Christie fit into the Lakers' plans. One of the biggest issues surrounding him when he entered the league was the lack of a clearly defined position. He was now entering his third season in the NBA, and the issue still wasn't resolved. The Lakers had played him at both guard positions and at small forward, but he had never found a natural home. And no matter where he played, he was part of a logjam. If he was a guard, where would Harris find minutes for him with Van Exel, Threatt, Peeler, Jones, and Smith already there? If he was a small forward, what role would he have with Ceballos, Lynch, and Worthy all capable of playing the position?

That he had talent was never in doubt, but his injury-riddled second season had seriously hurt his development. He was never on the active roster long enough to establish his role. With a new coach and a new system, this training camp and pre-season was a pivotal one for him to sort out those issues. But he wouldn't be participating. He had undergone surgery in August to remove calcium deposits on the ankle he badly injured twice in 1993-94. He was out for training camp and seemed destined to be on the injured list on opening night.

On the day of the Lakers' first pre-season game, West finally resolved the issue once and for all by trading him to the New York Knicks in exchange for a 1997 and a 1998 second-round draft pick. The trade ended Christie's career with the Lakers, one that never felt like it ever truly got started. West gave up a lot to acquire him, but it never panned out. He joined the Lakers mid-way through a season, which is tough for a veteran but especially difficult for a rookie. He then missed most of the following pre-season because of injury, played well in bursts throughout the first two months of his second season before missing six weeks due to injury. He never re-discovered his confidence, and had essentially been made redundant by how well Lynch played in his absence. Now the Lakers just had too many players ahead of him at each position he could play. "At the time we traded for him, we had a much greater need than we do today," West said.

On the bright side, Christie was going from a non-playoff team to a Knicks team that four months ago was a few John Starks made jumpers away from winning the NBA championship. But the trade still stung. "I think when I was healthy, I was playing fantastic basketball. Then I got hurt and lost some confidence, and it was tough really," Christie said. "It came down to a numbers game. I wasn't in camp to be able to defend myself, if you want to look at it in those terms."[207]

Harris had been non-committal upon entering camp about what offensive structure he would implement, preferring to assess his team's strengths and weakness first. Before long he had seen enough quickness and athleticism from his young players to convince him their greatest weapon would be a running game. "We're going to run every chance we get, I'll say that," Harris said. "Certainly, at home. On the road, I may like to slow it down a bit to take the crowd out of the game. You don't want to get in an up-and-down style in some places."

It wasn't just the injection of athleticism from new players like Ceballos and Jones that convinced Harris to run. It was also the vastly improved floor leadership of Van Exel, who had taken to heart the criticism he heard about his shot selection. "In the summer, I read a lot about how I would be a good player if I was more like a true point guard and passed more," he said. "I took that and used it in the summer. Pass first, shoot second."

He spent the summer studying tapes of what Utah Jazz point guard John Stockton and Indiana Pacers point guard Haywoode Workman did during the playoffs. How they played, how they balanced looking for their own shots with moving the ball and setting up teammates to score. "I noticed a big difference," said Drew. "I see a more mature Nick Van Exel. Knowing that his scoring opportunities will come, he likes to get the other guys involved in the offense first. He knows now that is his responsibility. He's grown up, big time."

The Lakers opened their pre-season schedule with two games in two nights against the Sacramento Kings at Neal S. Blaisdell Center in Honolulu. They won the first game 110-103 behind 24 points from Ceballos and 18 points from Lynch. [208]

They won the second game 125-120, this time behind Van Exel's 25 points and 21 from Jones. There was only one problem – nobody knew

---

[207] Christie would go onto have a long career, retiring at the age of 36 after playing for New York, Toronto, Sacramento, Orlando, Dallas, and the L.A. Clippers. He will be best remembered as the starting shooting guard and defensive specialist on the Sacramento Kings from 2000-2005, who had several memorable playoff clashes with the Lakers.

[208] Just as Christie had switched numbers after his rookie season for no expressed reason (none that could be found anyway), Lynch did as well. Lynch wore #24 his rookie season and changed to #30 for 1994-95.

where Threatt was. He scored six points in 17 minutes off the bench in the first game but didn't show up for the game the following night. He slipped a note under West's hotel door asking to speak to him. He then apparently left Honolulu that morning and returned to the mainland without explanation. West arrived back in Los Angeles the following day and was clearly furious. "I'm not looking for him," he said. "We'd like to know what is going on because we have no clue. We have tried to run him down and have gotten no return calls."

Threatt's agent, Jim Sexton, phoned West the next day and said Threatt had left Honolulu early because he was unhappy with his contract. His current deal expired at the end of the 1995-96 season, and he wanted an extension at his current pay of $2.4 million a season through to the end of the 1997-98 season. West believed Threatt's request came from seeing young players straight out of college signing big contracts, the kind he never got a chance to sign when he was young. But West wasn't having any of it. "We're not doing anything, period," he said. "He's probably the highest paid back-up guard in the league at this point in time. We're certainly not going to be held hostage by him or anyone. He's got two years on the contract, and we expect him to honor that."

Threatt still hadn't rejoined the team when they played the Los Angeles Clippers at The Pond in Anaheim. Despite the distraction, the Lakers sprinted out to an easy 120-104 win. Next was a 131-133 loss to the Seattle SuperSonics at the San Diego Sports Arena.

The Lakers started the annual two-night GTE Everything Pages Shoot-out at the Forum two nights later, with the first game coming against the Orlando Magic. Threatt was back in uniform after re-joining the team at shootaround that morning. In a bizarre twist, he told media before the game his agent had lied to West, and he hadn't walked out on the team because of his contract. He refused to elaborate much further, other than saying it was a personal issue and he had talked it out with West. He was fined an undisclosed amount for missing three exhibition games and subsequent training sessions.

Threatt got a lukewarm response from the 10,977 fans at the Forum during pre-game introductions, and the Lakers went on to lose 125-100.[209] Shaquille O'Neal top-scored for the Magic with 32 points while Jones led the Lakers with 21 points. Grant said before the game that he strongly

---

[209] Threatt played 16 minutes off the bench in his first game back with the team, scoring 2 points on 1-4 shooting and handing out 5 assists.

considered signing with the Lakers during the off-season. "Jerry West was close," he said. "I liked the organization's attitude and way of life. They take care of their people." Instead, the newest Orlando Magic scored 18 points and collected 8 rebounds in 27 minutes.

Worthy played in the game but left straight afterward, flying back home to North Carolina following the death of his mother, Gladys. Worthy would miss the remainder of the pre-season and would re-join the team before opening night. A moment's silence was observed for his mother the following night as the Lakers defeated the Nuggets 114-107 at the Forum.

Following two days' rest, the Lakers traveled to Vancouver to take on the Seattle SuperSonics for the second time that pre-season. The Lakers trailed by one point late in the game when Lynch, who scored 26 points, drained a 15-foot jumper with 22 seconds remaining to lift the Lakers to a 114-113 victory. It would turn out to be just the first of many dramatic games against the Sonics that season.

The Lakers concluded the pre-season with a 5-3 record with a 99-98 loss to the Utah Jazz in Ogden, Utah. Two of the new faces for the Lakers had been impressive. Ceballos averaged 19.5 points in the eight pre-season games. "I think he's a little bit better than even what we thought," Harris said. "His shooting is better than advertised. People saw him as a good runner and a good athlete who had a scoring knack, but he also has some of these other things that were not included on his bubble gum card."[210]

Jones averaged 13.9 points in the pre-season, where he was often the most athletic player on either team. He had struggled with his shot, shooting just 41% from the field, but Harris was impressed with his mental toughness and especially with his defense. And he had clearly outplayed Peeler, his rival for the starting shooting guard spot. Peeler was nursing a strained wrist for much of the pre-season, which clearly affected his shooting. But Harris wasn't impressed with Peeler's inability to contribute when his shot wasn't falling. "We know Anthony can shoot. The problem is sometimes when Anthony's shot isn't going well, it affects his defense and overall game. That's a real negative," he said.

The Lakers made their final roster moves in the days leading up to opening night. They waived Warren, who had averaged 1.5 points in four

---

[210] Referring to basketball cards as 'bubble gun cards' was the first time Harris sounded like a middle-aged man in his mid-50s since joining the Lakers.

pre-season games, and Ruffin, who had averaged 6.2 points in six games after getting increased minutes when Threatt went AWOL.[211] They also placed Worthy on the injured list, partially due to tendinitis in his left knee but mainly to give him a chance to get his conditioning back after sitting out the final three pre-season games. The moves meant that second-year forward Harvey and rookie Miller survived the cuts and would be on the active roster on opening night.

Before the start of the 1993-94 season, Buss proved to be an adept prognosticator. He speculated the Lakers might lose 50 games during that season and they went on to lose 49. On the eve of the 1994-95 season, Buss' prediction was much cheerier – 47 wins. Most of the national sports media paid the Lakers very little attention during the pre-season, and those that did hardly expected the Lakers to improve by 14 wins. But the players seemed to be singing a similar tune to Buss. "I just want to get to the playoffs," Ceballos said. "I don't care how many wins we get, as long as we get to the playoffs. From there, you never know what can happen."

Maybe it was the naiveté of youth or simply players wanting to say the right thing in front of the media. But it sounded very much like the first signs of a positive culture change. Harris, on the other hand, was being more cautious. "Right now, my goal is to win the first game and then go from there," he said.

---

[211] Warren never played in the NBA. He played in the CBA for several years, and in Brazil, England, Finland, France, and Sweden. Ruffin spent the 1994-95 season playing sparingly with the Phoenix Suns. He was drafted by the Vancouver Grizzlies in the 1995 expansion draft but, as a free agent, elected to play in Greece instead. He signed with a terrible Philadelphia 76ers team in December 1995 and averaged 12.8 points in 61 games. He played in France, Greece, and Turkey between 1997-2004.

Chapter 21

THE KIDS ARE ALRIGHT

November 4, 1994 to December 15, 1994

NICK VAN EXEL'S new off-season pass-first-shoot-second mentality lasted all the way to opening night against the Detroit Pistons at the Palace of Auburn Hills. There it was cast aside, if only for the one night. "It's hard when you're on fire," said Van Exel. "When the fellas on the team tell you to keep shooting, you keep putting it up." In front of 21,454 fans, he had more three-pointers than assists. He scored a career-high 35 points on 11-15 shooting that included 6-9 three-pointers.

The Lakers led 90-78 at the end of the third quarter, but a Pistons run cut the lead to 92-87 with eight minutes to play. The Lakers responded with a push of their own, punctuated by Van Exel's sixth and final three-pointer that sealed a 115-98 victory. "It was a spectacular display," Del Harris said.

The off-season battle for the starting shooting guard spot between Eddie Jones and Anthony Peeler seemed well and truly over. Jones started, scoring 8 points in 28 minutes, while Harris didn't play Peeler at all. He was the only Laker not to get any court time and received the first 'Did Not Play – Coach's Decision' of his career. "I told Anthony before the game that for now, he's not going to play much," said Harris. "Other guys are playing well, and Anthony is struggling. Until he gets his game going, he's just going to have to keep working hard. He shot 33% in the preseason, and he's a shooter. It's a circle, though. It'll come back to him as long as he works hard."

Harris also started Lynch at the power forward spot and bought Campbell off the bench, a change from the previous season. Neither Campbell nor Lynch impressed though and were both outplayed by Detroit's Terry Mills and Oliver Miller.

Cedric Ceballos, who scored 22 points and grabbed 14 rebounds in his

Laker debut, dropped by the Pistons' locker room before the game. He visited former Suns teammates Mark West, who had been traded to the Pistons that off-season, and Miller, who signed as a free agent a month later. Pistons rookie Grant Hill, who made his debut that night scoring 25 points and 10 rebounds, wasn't used to something like that happening. "If an opposing player came in the locker room before the game at Duke," Hill said, "Coach K probably would have beaten him up. But this is the NBA."

The Lakers had a tough schedule to start the new season. Six of their first seven games were on the road, and their home debut wouldn't come until a week into the season. In all, they would play 10 of their 14 games in November away from home. And for the first two weeks of the season, they would appear only marginally improved from a year earlier.

They followed their win in Detroit with a loss in Milwaukee the following night. They led 97-96 with 15 seconds to play when Van Exel decided to challenge the Bucks full court press instead of calling a timeout. He threw an ill-advised pass to Sedale Threatt at midcourt that was intercepted by Bucks center Marty Conlon. He raced upcourt and was fouled while attempting a lay-in. Conlon's free throws gave the Bucks the lead for the first time since the second quarter, good enough for a 97-96 win. "The turnovers were costly to us," said Harris. "We self-destructed."

The Lakers had a perfect opportunity to pick up a win in New York three nights later when they led 47-27 with eight minutes to play in the second quarter. But the Knicks exploded with 43 points on 83% shooting in the third quarter, including 15 points from John Starks. It was the Knicks' highest-scoring quarter since April 16, 1990. The Lakers trailed by eight late in the fourth quarter, but a three-pointer by Van Exel cut the lead to three with 14.6 seconds remaining. Their comeback attempt was over when Starks converted two free throws, giving the Knicks a 117-113 victory in a rare high scoring game for the defensive-minded Knicks.[212]

Peeler made his season debut in New York, scoring 4 points on 16 minutes. "I thought A.P. worked hard in practice," Harris said. "I wanted to give him a chance to play." Campbell, who had been underwhelming off the bench in Detroit and Milwaukee, was given his first "Did Not Play

---

[212] Christie was still on the injured list for the Knicks and didn't play. He wouldn't make his debut until December 27, 1994 and would only play 12 games in 1994-95.

– Coach's Decision" since his rookie year.[213]

Jones had played well to start the season, averaging 11 points over the first three games. And he exploded in his fourth game, scoring 31 points in 26 minutes in Minneapolis as the Lakers kept the Timberwolves winless with an easy 122-99 victory. "You know what impressed me?" Harris said. "That with that thin body, he is fearless. He goes after everything. He wasn't intimidated going into the pile." Ceballos continued his good start to the season by getting 25 points, and Campbell appeared awake for the first time that season, getting 16 points and 9 rebounds in 24 minutes off the bench.

The Lakers returned home with a 2-2 record to prepare for their belated home opener against the Denver Nuggets when the team got word James Worthy had decided to retire. He had been on the injured list to start the season, something that mandated he miss at least five games. He would be eligible to be activated after the Nuggets game but, for the first time in his highly successful career, he just didn't want to do it. "I didn't feel good physically, and I knew I couldn't make the contribution that I needed and wanted to," he said.[214]

Worthy's decline over the last two seasons had been rapid. He had gone from being an elite forward, a seven-time All-Star and Finals MVP to someone who looked far older than his 32-years. He limped through the previous season on 20 minutes a night off the bench for a bad team. "The thing that really wore on me was that I could only play one way," he said. "Some players, when they get older, they adjust and find a way to continue. I just couldn't do it. I think I may have tried it this past year, to modify, because I knew the minutes were going to decrease, but it was a forced situation."

His body may have given out before his will ever did, but Worthy was finding it impossible to recapture his old motivation. "I can remember when my alarm clock would go off and I would be right up, right to practice, ready to go. It was fun," he said. But now? "It got to the point where you hit the snooze five or six times."

---

[213] He hadn't collected a single rebound in 24 minutes of action across the first two games of the season. Not a great stat for a 6'11 power forward/center.

[214] Worthy's last ever game with the Lakers was the October 21 pre-season game against the Orlando Magic at the Forum. He scored 7 points on 2-6 shooting in 20 minutes. He averaged 7.0 points and 11.4 minutes in five pre-season outings.

Just as he had done with Magic Johnson, Jerry Buss would honor the remainder of Worthy's contract, one that owed him $7.2 million for the 1994-95 season and $5.1 in 1995-96. "You make a commitment to do something, so you do it," said Bob Steiner, Buss' spokesman.

Worthy's retirement severed the last remaining link to Showtime. Kareem Abdul-Jabbar and Mychal Thompson were retired. Pat Riley was in New York, Byron Scott was in Indiana, and A.C. Green was in Phoenix. Michael Cooper and Kurt Rambis were relegated to the sidelines as assistant coaches. Magic was in the front office. It was all gone. Magic, Abdul-Jabbar, and Cooper were at Worthy's retirement press conference, there to be part of the goodbye. "I glanced around and saw (them) standing outside, and I wished real hard those guys were 22 again," West said.

Worthy's retirement didn't alter Harris' plans for the season as the veteran was unlikely to see major minutes in the crowded frontcourt. His minutes as back-up small forward would be shared between Lynch and Jones, which was a better outcome for their development. Ceballos lamented he never got a chance to play an official game with the player he patented his game on.

In a sign the world didn't expect much from the Lakers in 1994-95, the Forum was 555 short of a sell-out for the home opener. And it wasn't pretty for the first three quarters as the Nuggets took a 90-72 lead into the final quarter. But the Lakers staged a late rally, and Sedale Threatt drained a three-pointer with 55 seconds to play that cut the deficit to 104-102. He then hit another one with 19.9 seconds remaining to tie the score at 105-105. Antonio Harvey blocked Dale Ellis' potential game-winning lay-in, and Divac grabbed the loose ball. The Lakers had a chance to win the game following a timeout, but Van Exel's 20-footer hit the front of the rim. The Nuggets would go on to win 124-117 in overtime with center Dikembe Mutombo putting on a dominating performance, recording 19 points, 26 rebounds, and 9 blocks in 53 minutes.

The Lakers had played well in each of their first five games, even in the three games they lost. But they were terrible the next night in Oakland, falling 121-99 to the Golden State Warriors. The Lakers were bad offensively, shooting just 34% from the floor, and they were worse defensively, as 35-year-old Ricky Pierce lit them up with 23 points off the bench. "We played poorly, there's no two ways around it," Harris said.

"At half-time, I said there wasn't one thing to talk about. I said our problem was basketball."

The Sports Arena was half empty with only 8,807 fans showing up for the Lakers-Clippers match-up three nights later that the Lakers won 102-92. Harris ended the experiment of starting Lynch at power forward, elevating rookie Anthony Miller into the spot. Lynch had averaged 9.3 points in 25.3 minutes as a starter in the first six games, but Harris wanted more than the 3.3 rebounds he was getting from him. Starting Miller didn't look like the answer either as he collected just two rebounds in 15 minutes.

Campbell was in the starting line-up for the first time the next night when the Lakers hosted the Knicks, and would remain the starter for the best part of the season. But fans started streaming out of the Forum with seven minutes to play, and for good reason. The Lakers shot poorly for the second time in three games, hitting 36%, and were routed 110-89.

It was two weeks into the new season, and the Lakers were 3-5 and third to last in the West. They looked at first glance to be very much like the horrible team they were a year earlier. But they were about to start a run of wins that indicated for the first time that these Lakers were indeed very different from last season.

There were just 10,177 fans at the Forum two nights later when the Lakers hosted the Cleveland Cavaliers. This looked and felt like a quintessential Cavs game – low scoring, scrappy, and with both teams shooting poorly. The Cavs held an 80-79 lead when the Lakers called timeout with 2.6 seconds remaining. Smith inbounded the ball to Threatt, who immediately gave it back to him with just enough time to get off a three-point heave. It barely beat the clock and barely beat John Williams and Chris Mills who were scrambling to block it. Smith's shot banked in at the buzzer, and the Lakers escaped with an 82-80 victory. Smith didn't intend to bank it in. In fact, he couldn't even see the basket when he got the shot off. "I couldn't see it," said Smith. "John Williams was all over my face. I couldn't see it until it was coming off the glass."

The Dallas Mavericks were a team the entire league had become accustomed to beating the last few years. But things looked like they might be changing in Dallas with their young core of Jimmy Jackson, Jamal Mashburn, and rookie Jason Kidd leading them to a 4-3 record. Ceballos was slowed by a painful left big toe, the result of an ingrown nail and infection. But it didn't show as he scored 11 of his 24 points in the fourth quarter and the Lakers got a 118-106 win. Campbell missed the game because he was in Georgia attending his uncle's funeral. Harvey, who had hardly played to that point, started in his place and scored 16 points in 43 minutes.

The Lakers started their second road trip of the young season in Atlanta. They trailed 80-73 in the fourth quarter when Ceballos made baskets on consecutive possessions, and Van Exel hit a short runner from the right side that capped a 10-0 run. A three-pointer by Van Exel and a score in traffic by Ceballos iced the 92-87 win.

They pushed their win streak to four games the next night in Washington. Nine days earlier the Bullets acquired reigning Rookie of the Year Chris Webber in a trade with the Golden State Warriors. Playing in just his third game for Washington, Webber scored 22 points and grabbed 20 rebounds, but little else went right for the Bullets. Van Exel had 22 points, and 13 assists, and the Lakers ran away with an easy 112-96 win. The win improved the Lakers record to 7-5 on the season, the first time they had been two games above .500 in a year and eight months. "They're up right now," Harris said. "Hopefully we can ride the crest. I hoped this trip would bring us together as a team. So far, it's moving in that direction."

The Lakers trailed the Nets by sixteen points with eight minutes left in the fourth quarter three nights later in East Rutherford before the game turned into a marathon. They got back in it when Harris switched to a press defense that created five straight turnovers by the Nets. Campbell tied the score at 109-109 with a dunk, sending the game into overtime. The Nets led 116-114 late in overtime before Sam Bowie tipped in Campbell's miss that forced a second overtime.

Threatt hit a three-pointer in the first five seconds of the second overtime period, then connected again on a foul-line jumper for a 121-117 lead. "I like Sedale Threatt in there to nail down the coffin," Harris said. "The guy's just cold-blooded." The Nets didn't score a field goal until 23.4 seconds were left in the second overtime. Back-to-back baskets by Ceballos, who had 34 points in all, sealed a 129-120 win.[215] "A tremendous win," Harris said. "For a young team to come back like that, we've done it a couple of times, and each time it adds maturity, particularly when the last rites have been administered."

[215] The win came despite the Nets attempting 50 free throws compared to 15 by the Lakers.

The Lakers looked like you'd expect the next night after three games on the road and a double overtime win the night before – exhausted. The Cleveland Cavaliers were the beneficiaries, trouncing the Lakers 117-79. "They were very precise and put on a clinic," Harris said. "They beat our butts really bad."

The road trip may have ended with an ugly 38-point loss, but overall it had been a success. Their five-game win streak was their longest in almost two years. They returned home with an 8-6 record, holding on to the seventh spot in the West. It wasn't necessarily setting the basketball world on fire, but it was a considerable turnaround from where they were a year earlier. The toughest part of the schedule was now behind them, and they faced a much friendlier six home games, six away games in December.

But if they wanted to recover quickly from the bad loss to the Cavs, they would have to do it at home against the defending NBA champion Houston Rockets. Center Hakeem Olajuwon had elevated his game from All-Star to legendary in 1993-94, leading the Rockets to the championship and winning the regular season MVP, Finals MVP and Defensive Player of the Year in the process. And he hadn't skipped a beat so far in 1994-95, averaging 27.6 points, 11.6 rebounds, and 3.9 blocks entering the game against the Lakers. Neither had the Rockets, who were sitting atop of the Western Conference with an 11-3 record.

But the season felt like it pivoted in the Lakers' direction at the Forum on December 2, 1994. They opened the game with a 22-8 run and had a nine-point lead over the Rockets after one quarter. They then doubled the margin by half-time and tripled it by the end of the third quarter. It was a route from the opening tip with the lead blowing out to 89-61 early in the fourth quarter. The Lakers ran out winners 107-89. "This was one of those out-behind-the-shed butt-kickings," Rockets coach Rudy Tomjanovich said. "They just trounced us right from the jump ball."

Ceballos, who top scored with 25 points to go along with a career-high 16 rebounds, joked after the game that the Lakers were well rested. "We didn't really play at Cleveland, we kind of had three days off." Divac had 22 points, 9 rebounds, 8 assists, and managed to outplay Olajuwon. Jones, who'd had a rough two weeks averaging just 5.8 points on 34% shooting before the game, rewarded Harris for keeping him in the line-up by adding 17 points.

* * * * *

The Lakers next hosted the Golden State Warriors who had been in a slide since trading Webber in mid-November. Even though Webber hadn't suited up for the Warriors at any point in the season, they were 6-1 before he was traded and just 2-6 since. Before the game, Van Exel said he overheard a Warriors player calling the Lakers' big victory over Houston four nights earlier a fluke. With a point to prove, he went out and recorded 20 points and a career-high 14 assists. The Lakers ran out to a 36-17 lead late in the first quarter and cruised to a 113-101 win. "I'm sure if we would have lost, teams would have said, 'same old Lakers, they fell back again,'" Van Exel said. "We're here to let people know we're going to stay at this place." Ceballos led all scorers with 28 points, and Jones backed up his slump-breaking performance against Houston with 18 points on 7-12 shooting.

The Lakers had won seven of their last eight games and boosted themselves to the fourth spot in the West. But Lakers fans obviously needed more convincing this team was for real, as evidenced by the more than 6,500 empty seats at the home game against the awful 1-16 Los Angeles Clippers. It was probably for the best that few fans were there to see the game as the Lakers came out flat against the worst team in the league. They committed 11 turnovers in the first quarter, scored just 35 points in the first half and trailed the Clippers 67-35 early in the third quarter. "This is not an April Fool's story folks," Chick Hearn said when repeating the scoreline. They staged a fightback in the third quarter, but the damage was well and truly done, and the Clippers got a 109-84 win.

The next night the Lakers started a week-long, four-game road trip in Salt Lake City. It didn't look like an auspicious way to start a road trip for the Lakers, not with the embarrassing loss to the Clippers the night before. Nor with Van Exel in street clothes, being held out as a precaution after he lightly sprained his ankle the previous night. But instead, Threatt made his first start of the season, played 40 minutes, handed out 8 assists, hit 13-19 shots, and scored 38 points. "I'm just filling in," Threatt said nonchalantly after the game. Ceballos chipped in 27 points, and they looked like a totally different team from the previous night, beating the Utah Jazz 120-113.

Van Exel's injury also resulted in a Peeler sighting, who played 26 minutes off the bench and scored 11 points including two three-pointers. Peeler had well and truly been in the doghouse, playing in only 13 of 18 games and averaging just 3.2 points in 8.4 minutes on horrendous 31% shooting. He had fallen a long way since being the incumbent starting shooting guard a season earlier. Harris told the media after the game that it was wonderful to have Peeler back. "I've been sitting down there," Peeler said. "Maybe he just couldn't see me."

Van Exel was back in uniform three nights later when he picked up against the Dallas Mavericks where Threatt left off against the Utah Jazz. He tied his career high by scoring 35 points, hit a Lakers franchise-record eight three-pointers and dished out 10 assists. "I guess you could say I was in a zone," he said. "It seemed like every time I touched it, it was going in. It feels good knowing everybody in the gym is oohing and aahing when you're hitting the shots." The Lakers were clinging to a 101-100 lead late in the fourth quarter when Van Exel took over the game. He hit three three-pointers in four possessions, setting up the 115-108 victory.

Two nights later the Lakers were in Houston to square off against the Rockets for the second time in two weeks. Ceballos scored eight of the Lakers' 12 points in a mini-run midway through the fourth quarter that gave them a 94-87 lead. The Rockets responded with their own run, capped by Robert Horry banking in a short jumper to cut the Lakers' lead to 96-94 with 38 seconds left.

Threatt launched an ill-advised three-pointer on the Lakers' next possession, and the Rockets had a chance to tie or take the lead. Olajuwon missed a 17-foot shot with seven seconds to go, and Van Exel was fouled securing the rebound. He hit the first free throw, giving the Lakers a 97-94 lead, but he missed the second. The Rockets had one last chance to send the game into overtime, and Horry got a good look at a three-pointer. But it didn't drop, and the Lakers got their second victory of the season over the defending champions. Ceballos was fantastic against the Rockets two weeks earlier at the Forum, and he was great again at the Summit. He hit 15-22 shots, grabbed 10 rebounds and led all scorers with 36 points.

"This was the biggest win we've had all year," said Bowie. "I was afraid we weren't ready, they would come out and try to beat us bad after the way we embarrassed them at our place. But we were ready." Bowie played an important role in that, with Harris always keeping two of his tallest players – Divac, Campbell, or Bowie – in the game at the same time to bother Olajuwon. "He's the MVP of the league," Bowie said. "We needed the 21 feet of defense to slow him down."

By the middle of December 1994, the Lakers had entirely flipped the script and were in the exact opposite place they were a year earlier. After the first 20 games of the 1993-94 season, they were sitting third to last in the West with a 7-13 record. One year later and they had a 13-7 record and were sitting third from top, behind only Phoenix and Utah. They were yet to find the consistency to be competitive every night, with bad losses to Golden State, New York, Cleveland, and the Clippers. But they had won 10 of their last 12 games, beating the defending champions twice, and won six games on the road.

The quick tempo Harris had the team playing was a perfect fit for the young and athletic roster. It was creating the most fun Lakers team to watch since Showtime. What was perhaps missed in all the high-flying dunks from Jones and the pull-up transition threes from Van Exel was that their offense was fuelled by their defense. Harris used all the young legs on his roster to implement a variety of presses and traps that created fast-break opportunities down the other end. "I think guys are beginning to trust each other more," said Harris. "That's such a key word in team defense – trust. If I run over to cover Player A, I want to make sure somebody will watch my back and cover Player B."

The two new faces in the starting line-up were making a bigger difference than anyone could have expected. Ceballos had built upon his break-out season in 1993-94 and was putting up All-Star caliber numbers, averaging 21.6 points and 9.0 rebounds.

Jones seemed mature beyond his years and was averaging 11.5 points in 25.0 minutes in the first 20 games of his NBA career. But it wasn't just about numbers with Jones, it was also about his character. He had already endured a shooting slump but never pouted; instead, he worked hard on defense and found other ways to contribute. He fought his way through the slump without letting it shake his confidence and had averaged 14.8 points over the last six games.

Snagging Van Exel in the second round was one of the few positives for the Lakers a year ago. And his production had jumped exponentially to start the new season. His shot selection, the most criticised part of his game as a rookie, had improved markedly. And he was balancing his own scoring better with getting his teammates involved, averaging 16.8 points and 7.7 assists per game.

"I think Nick and Eddie Jones have got to be the most exciting backcourt in the league," Harris said. "I mean these kids are 23 years old and they are like salty veterans. We are really blessed."

Divac, perhaps to the relief of Lakers management, had continued to build on his good play that begun around the All-Star break the previous season. He had been playing under control throughout the first six weeks of the season, averaging 15.0 points and 9.9 rebounds. His development appeared to have momentum for the first time in his career.

These Lakers were a breath of fresh air after being, for the most part, difficult to watch since trading Sam Perkins almost two years earlier. "It's about attitude now," Van Exel said. "We had a lot of chances to be a pretty good team last year. But everybody had coach problems. Everybody was having a problem with playing time. This year, we threw all that out."

Chapter 22
CLOSING THE GARDEN

December 20, 1994 to February 1, 1995

T HE CROWD HAD been restless all night as they watched their Lakers struggle to put away the miserable Minnesota Timberwolves. "This is nothing to write in your memoirs," said Chick Hearn with the Lakers leading by four points with 30 seconds remaining in the third quarter. But then the game became something worth remembering.

It was December 20, 1994 and Cedric Ceballos had 32 points at three-quarter time. He had done it in quintessential Ceballos fashion – Harris hadn't called a single play for him. He had scored on a few one-on-one plays, but he mostly stuffed the stat sheet by displaying his uncanny ability to be in the right place at the right time. "He is a scavenger. He lives on other people's plays," Harris said. "Opponents know when we're running a play for one of our big guys, they cheat over on them. Cedric knows that, too. He cheats into the gaps and transfers the ball from his hands into the net more quickly than anybody I've ever seen."

He had eight points in the first quarter, six on wide-open shots around the basket from teammates feeding him. By half-time, he had 21 points and the Lakers ran away with the game in the fourth quarter.

Ceballos scored his 36th point when he missed a lay-up and beat three Timberwolves players to the rebound to lay it back in. Later, when Minnesota center Sean Rooks was busy tapping the rebound to himself, Ceballos flew out of nowhere to steal the ball o and lay it in. He tied his career high when he got his 40th point by cutting to the basket and getting a pass from Divac from the post for a lay-up. He received a beautiful pass from Nick Van Exel on the next possession for another lay-up. He got his 46th point by going one-on-one for a short leaner in the paint.

With the crowd egging them on, the Lakers targeted Ceballos on every possession. But as a result, the offense became predictable, Ceballos began to tire, and the Lakers became sloppy. Ceballos committed an offensive foul while trying to get post position and committed two turnovers when trying to force the issue against double and triple teams. Divac was so anxious to set Ceballos a screen to get him open that he was called for an offensive foul.

He scored his 47th point by going one-for-two at the free throw line. But it looked like he would run out of time to get his 50, especially when Antonio Harvey elected to shoot a long two-pointer that missed with 26 seconds remaining, drawing boos from the crowd. After a three-pointer down at the other end with 13.6 seconds remaining, Ceballos had one final chance. Threatt bought the ball up court and found Ceballos partially open behind the three-point line. He threw up a high arching three-pointer with 7.5 seconds remaining that was nothing but net for his 50th point. "I don't know how I made that shot," Ceballos said. "I don't know. [Pat] Durham was on me, I don't even know how I got it off. Someone was looking out for me. It went in. It was a fitting ending."

There were a ton of empty seats in the arena, but the 11,101 fans who were there cheered like it was a game-winning shot. Ceballos scored his 50 points on 21-31 shooting in 46 minutes. It was the first time a Laker player scored 50 points in a game since Gail Goodrich in March of 1975.[216]

Ceballos and the rest of the Lakers were clearly gunning for the 50. The game was all but over, the Lakers eventually won 108-95, and Harris would have ordinarily taken him out. After all, Hearn had put the game in the refrigerator when Ceballos still had 46 points. "I was going to take him out," Harris said. "But the players said, 'Leave him in, let him get the 50.'"

The shot that brought up Ceballos' 50 broke an unwritten rule of basketball that says if the winning team has the ball with less than 24 seconds left in the game, they don't run the lead up by looking to score. In the name of sportsmanship, Ceballos should have dribbled out the clock instead of shooting. Surprisingly there wasn't a reaction from the Timberwolves, who just took the embarrassment without making a scene. Harris sensed Timberwolves coach Bill Blair was annoyed by it, but he didn't care. "I'm sure there will be a night when he'll have to choose

---

[216] It's odd to think the Lakers went almost 20 years without a player scoring 50 points. Especially since they had some good teams with great players in those years from 1975-1995.

between me and his player," Harris said. "And I'm sure he'll take his player every time."

Ceballos backed up his 50-point game with 21 points in a win against Sacramento three nights later, and was named NBA Player of the Week, the first Laker to receive the honor since Magic Johnson in April 1991.

Following a loss in Oakland, the Lakers returned home to kick off their second five-game win streak of the season. They had one in November that saw them recover after an ordinary start to the season. The one in December would catapult them to a position where the rest of the league took notice.

The Forum was sold out for the first time all season against the Seattle SuperSonics, who had swept the Lakers 5-0 last season. The Sonics held a three-point lead with one and a half minutes to play when Ceballos drew the Lakers to within one on a driving lay-up. Payton missed two free throws and Campbell scored on a short bank shot on the baseline to give them a 96-95 lead with 45 seconds remaining. The Sonics wouldn't score again, and the Lakers got the one-point win. Ceballos led the Lakers with 35 points on 13-18 shooting, but it was Campbell who came up big down the stretch. He had 28 points, including six of the Lakers' last eight points and the game winner.

The Lakers' last game of 1994 was Ceballos' first game back in Phoenix following the off-season trade. He didn't talk about it with anyone before the game, but his teammates knew he badly wanted to beat his old team. The Suns had stocked up in the off-season and were off to an imposing start, sitting atop the West with a 21-6 record. Ceballos got a warm welcome from the crowd when introduced and went out to torch his old team with 37 points on 13-25 shooting. Van Exel backed him up with 21 points and 16 assists, and the Lakers ran over the Suns for a 127-112 win. Especially gratifying for Ceballos was the fact Wayman Tisdale and Danny Manning, essentially the two players whose acquisition forced him out of Phoenix, struggled all night. Tisdale scored just two points while Manning missed eight of his 10 shots, scoring four points in 31 minutes.

The Lakers would bring in 1995 without Sedale Threatt, who the team discovered had a stress fracture in his right foot. It had likely developed over the last two weeks of December. He played two minutes against Phoenix, but Harris took him out because it was clear something wasn't right. "The last three or four games, it definitely hurt," Threatt said. "But you feel at the time that you can play through the pain." Threatt would go on to miss all but one of the Lakers' 14 games in January.

His loss was a big blow to the Lakers. Threatt, one of the few steady and trusted veterans on the team, had played a bigger role in the first two months than originally intended. Harris' original vision was to use the combo-guard strictly as Van Exel's back-up. But with Peeler unexpectedly in the doghouse, Threatt resumed his role as back-up for both guard positions. He was playing 25.6 minutes a night, averaging 10.4 points and 4.2 assists while shooting 51% from the floor.

The Lakers placed Threatt on the injured list and signed 35-year-old point guard Lester Conner to a 10-day contract. Conner was a 12-year NBA vet who had spent two years playing under Harris in Milwaukee.[217] He played 11 games for the Indiana Pacers towards the end of the 1993-94 season when point guards Pooh Richardson and Vern Fleming went down with injuries, staying with the team through the playoffs. He had spent the last few months with the Magic Johnson All-Stars and was brought in mainly as an insurance policy. "I don't want to take any playing time away from the guys we already have," Harris said. "They've been waiting their chance. The guys we have will get the priority."

With Threatt out, Harris played Van Exel all 48 minutes in the first game of the New Year, a 105-96 victory over the Detroit Pistons at the Forum. Threatt's absence didn't result in more minutes for Peeler. Instead, he didn't play at all and Threatt's minutes went exclusively to Tony Smith who played 26 minutes, scoring 13 points.

Ceballos was forced out of the Lakers' next game at home against the Milwaukee Bucks because of back spasms, leaving the team with 10 healthy players. But that didn't result in many more minutes for Peeler either. Jones had his second excellent game in a row, hitting 9-11 shots for 26 points; Smith scored 14 points in 38 minutes; Peeler logged only four minutes; and the Lakers won 106-98.

The Lakers pushed their win streak to five in a home game against the Miami Heat. Ceballos was again out, but it didn't matter – Divac's triple-double of 21 points, 11 rebounds, and 10 assists ensured an easy 122-105

---

[217] Conner had what was perhaps the most unfortunate nickname – The Molester. He got the nickname for being such a tenacious defender. But still.

win.[218] "You would think that all the injuries would be a reason for us to open the floodgates for all the excuses," Sam Bowie said. "But as you can see, this is a lot different than last year." The lop-sided victory freed up 31 minutes of playing time for Peeler, and he made the most of it, top scoring with 23 points.

A week into January 1995 and the Lakers were the most surprising team in the league. They were 20-9 and tied with Utah for third in the West. They had won 17 of their last 21 games, including two wins in two nights against the Seattle SuperSonics and Phoenix Suns, two power-houses of the West. Out of the blue, they were on pace for 56 wins. "At the beginning of the season, I didn't know what to expect," Harris said. "I really thought it would take longer. But it's a very competitive, a very bright bunch of guys."

Ceballos had been named the NBA's Player of the Month for December with averages of 27.8 points and 9.0 rebounds. It was the first time a Laker had received the award since Magic in February 1990. This new Generation X brand of Laker basketball was starting to look like it might be for real. "I think everyone is more surprised than we are," Van Exel said. "We knew what we could do. It was just a matter of going and doing it."

But the Lakers were about to enter a strange fortnight where they would revert to some bad habits from a season ago. Yet in the middle of the bad run would come one of the most memorable regular season moments in franchise history.

The bad run started with a complete implosion in Portland where the Trail Blazers handed them a 129-83 loss. It was the biggest loss in franchise history, but that wasn't the only concern. Their offense was ticking along nicely in the first half, but they were dreadful defensively and trailed by 11 at the main break. Harris was frustrated at the lack of defensive intensity and went, in his own words, "goofy" at half-time. He went on a rampage in the locker room – shouting and screaming at the team, turning over a table, and throwing cups of water at some of the players. "There's no other words for it," Peeler said. "He went nuts." Harris was trying desperately to spark life into the team. But it backfired badly. Instead of

---

[218] James Worthy was in attendance, appearing at the Forum for the first time since retiring earlier in the season. He got a long ovation from fans when he was shown on the scoreboard.

coming out inspired, the players came out angry at their coach and were mere passengers in the game for the second half. They were outscored 41-15 in the third quarter and 64-29 for the half.

Van Exel was the most upset about Harris' half-time performance. He refused to take the court and spent the entire second half on the bench. The incident would be explained away by the Lakers as a 'failure to communicate.' But it was the first sign the coach and point guard were not on the same page, something that would become an issue increasingly over the ensuing years.

The one positive for the Lakers was that Ceballos was back in the starting line-up for the game. But he didn't look right, scoring just 2 points on 1-4 shooting in 21 minutes. "His pain is gone," said Harris. "But his timing is also gone."

The top team in the West were not the ideal next opponent for a Lakers team feeling vulnerable after their meltdown in Portland. But that's what they got when the Phoenix Suns visited the Forum, which sold out for just the second time that season. Van Exel led the Lakers back from a 20-point deficit, no doubt proving a point after the controversy in Portland. "It's like you take a kid's toy from him," Ceballos said. "He cries, but the next day he's forgotten all about it." He scored 19 of his game-high 35 points in the second half including 11 consecutive points as part of a 20-0 run that tied the score. But the Suns steadied down the stretch and won 118-108.

They picked up two wins at home against the Warriors and Clippers before starting their first road trip since November, with four games in six nights.[219] It began in Indianapolis where they trailed by one point with 4.3 seconds left when Van Exel, who scored 16 of his 30 points in the fourth quarter, drove the lane. Former Laker Byron Scott cut him off, leaving Smith open at 14-feet. "The only thing I could hope was Tony would be Tony and miss it," Scott said. And he did. The shot banged off the ring, and the Pacers survived for a 106-105 win.

It was their third loss in five games, and Ceballos had endured a rough ten days after sitting out two games with back spasms. He hadn't been playing well, averaging 14.8 points per game since coming back. And he played poorly in Indianapolis, scoring 7 points on 3-10 shooting. Harris benching him in the final six minutes coincided with the Lakers going on a run that got them back in the game. And he sounded depressed

---

[219] The Lakers beat the Clippers despite trailing in the fourth quarter. Van Exel had a good quote after the game – "I knew it would slip away from them. It's the Clippers, man."

following the loss to the Pacers. "I haven't been having fun the last five games," he said. "I'm dreading coming to games. I'm dreading coming to practices."

Conner's ten-day contract was about to expire, and Jerry West intended to sign him to another one. But he abruptly announced he was retiring from the NBA after having an epiphany during the game against the Warriors five days earlier. Sitting on the bench, he watched Ryan Lorthridge play in his first NBA game, scoring 8 points in 23 minutes for the Warriors. Lorthridge had played at Jackson State but had gone undrafted. He spent the pre-season with the New Jersey Nets, didn't make the cut and had been playing in the CBA before being called up by Golden State. "He must have been elated to be there, even on a 10-day contract," Conner said. "I figured I must be in the way of somebody else who just wanted the chance to be able to say they played in the NBA."[220]

But Conner's retirement wouldn't result in an opportunity for a young player. The Lakers instead signed 32-year-old point guard Danny Young to a 10-day contract. Young had been a back-up point guard for nine years in the NBA, mostly with the Seattle SuperSonics and Portland Trail Blazers. He played the previous season with Limoges CSP in France before averaging 1.1 points in seven games earlier in the 1994-95 season with the Milwaukee Bucks.[221]

The Lakers-Celtics game on January 20, 1995 wasn't the final basketball game played at Boston Garden. After 49 years of calling the Garden home, the Celtics would play there 21 more times that season before moving to the new Fleet Center. But this was the last time the Lakers would ever play there. After the game, only the memories of the famed battles between the two teams at the Garden would remain. Most of those memories were painful for the Lakers. Entering the game, they were 44-94 at the Garden and 10-22 in the playoffs. It was the scene of

---

[220] Lester played five minutes across two games with the Lakers, scoring 2 points. He finished his playing career in the CBA before having a long career as an assistant coach in Boston, Philadelphia, Milwaukee, Indiana, Atlanta, and Denver.

[221] Young was with the Bucks because point guard Erik Murdock started the season on the injured list with an eye injury but was waived when Murdock was activated. Young played six minutes for the Bucks in the Lakers one-point loss in Milwaukee in early November, scoring 3 points.

some of their most crushing loses, all part of losing eight NBA Finals to the Celtics. "Will I miss the Boston Garden?" Kurt Rambis, now a coach on the Lakers, said. "I'll miss it like I'd miss my bald spot."[222]

The game itself wasn't exactly a masterclass of defense. The Lakers struggled to defend the Celtics pick and roll all night. And the Celtics had no answer for Ceballos, who had 31 points; Campbell, who had 30 points; or Van Exel, who had 29 points and 10 assists. But it was a fun, high-tempo game that, appropriately, went down to the wire.

The Lakers led 117-116 with a minute to play, but they couldn't score. Van Exel drove the lane and turned it over trying to pass out to Bowie. On the next possession, Smith blocked Rick Fox's three-point attempt and sprinted down the other end. He received a length of the court pass from Van Exel but blew a very makeable lay-up.

The Lakers forced a turnover with 12 seconds left, but David Wesley quickly stripped the ball from Van Exel. As the two players scrambled for the ball, Wesley knocked it out of bounds. But the officials called it out on Van Exel, giving the Celtics the ball back with a chance to win the game. Dino Radja then missed a hook shot in the lane but got his own rebound and scored, giving the Celtics a 118-117 lead with 2.4 seconds to go. The Garden erupted.

Following a timeout, Harris had Bowie in position to make the inbounds pass but quickly replaced him with Jones. It was an odd choice because 7'0 Eric Montross was guarding the inbounds pass and the taller Bowie had a much better chance of seeing over him. But Jones threw a head fake to get Montross leaning one way, then threw the ball the other way. Van Exel caught it near the Celtics bench and was inches away from stepping out of bounds. Smothered by Wesley, Van Exel was out of options and out of time. "I just wanted to get it up," he said. "I thought I might travel. Then I thought I was out of bounds. Then when I didn't hear a whistle, I just threw it up."

With his back to the basket and his feet almost out of bounds, he leaped forwards, twisted in mid-air and heaved a shot at the basket as he was falling out of bounds. "As I released it, it was straight," he said. "But as far as going in, I didn't think it would."

But it did. The shot barely beat the buzzer giving the Lakers a 120-118 victory in front of 14,890 fans standing in stunned silence. The entire team

---

[222] The Lakers of course did get their moment of redemption when they finally defeated the Celtics in the Finals in 1985, winning Game 6 at the Garden for good measure.

embraced Van Exel, lifting him up on their shoulders. "L.A., Boston, last game at the Garden," Van Exel said. "It wasn't for a championship but having the last game come down to the last second will make fans remember this game for a long, long time."

"Closing out a lifetime of experiences in Boston Garden. This box score is going on the wall," Bill Bertka said. "I'm going to have Nick sign it."

The win at the Garden was a nice moment, but it wasn't enough to lift the Lakers out of their rut – even though it looked like it for much of the following night in Philadelphia. Jones, who played at Temple University in the Cecil B. Moore neighborhood of Philly, drew cheers from the crowd when he produced two spectacular dunks, both over 7'6 Shawn Bradley. And the Lakers led by sixteen in the fourth quarter before Dana Barros took over the game. Barros had been having a remarkable season that would see him win the Most Improved Player award for 1994-95, upping his averages of 9.2 points and 2.7 assists over the previous five seasons to 20.6 points and 7.5 assists.

Barros hit two three-pointers as part of a 15-2 run that cut the Lakers' lead to 99-93. A few minutes later he would hit another two three-pointers as part of a 10-0 run. His flurry sent the game into overtime where the Lakers lost 117-113 and Barros finished with a career-high 41 points on 14-23 shooting, including seven three-pointers.[223]

A week after beating Boston at the buzzer, Van Exel added to his resume of clutch performances in Seattle. He was struggling when he checked back into the game with four minutes left in the fourth quarter. He had just 7 points on 2-6 shooting and two assists, but he caught fire when it mattered most. The Sonics led 111-103 with two minutes to play when Van Exel made a floater in the lane. After Divac forced a turnover, he hit a three-pointer in transition. He then hit another three-pointer to tie the score at 111-111 and force overtime. He followed that by making a lay-up and hit a three-pointer in extra time to seal a 128-121 win. "As soon as you give him an opportunity, he's going to run all over you," Ceballos said.

The Lakers returned home with the most favorable part of their schedule ahead of them. Twelve of their next 18 games would be at the

---

[223] The 7 three-pointers by Barros were an all-time high for a Laker opponent.

Forum. First up were the Chicago Bulls, who had surprised many in 1993-94 by winning 55 games after Michael Jordan's sudden retirement. But with Horace Grant now in Orlando, the reality of life after Jordan started to set in. They were sitting in the sixth spot in the East with a 21-21 record, the first time they entered the Forum with a worse record than the Lakers since February 1991. Not that it was evident from the game as the Bulls shot 55%, Scottie Pippen had 34 points and 13 rebounds, and the Bulls ran out winners 119-115. The loss wasted a strong team offensive game, including 27 points and 16 assists from Van Exel, because the Lakers couldn't get any stops in the second half.

They gave up a ton of points the next night too, losing their second game in a row 118-109 in Phoenix. The Lakers had reached the midway point of the season with a 26-15 record. The loss to the Suns knocked them out of the fourth spot in the West and put them in a tie with the Houston Rockets for fifth. After being one of the surprise stories of the season by winning 20 of their first 29 games, they had been 6-6 over the last three weeks. Considering they were 14-27 at the same time a year earlier, playing .500 basketball still felt like a success. Yet there was something undeniably missing from their game in recent weeks.

Bad habits, especially defensively, were starting to creep in. "Success probably hurts you some," Harris said. "Defense is not a lot of fun sometimes. The stats just show you we are not as good of a defensive team in January as November and December. Determination and desire create good defense. These are things we need to get back into our minds and our basketball hearts to be a good team. Good teams play good defense all the time."

With three months left in the season, there was plenty of time to correct those bad habits and turn the last three weeks into more of a blip on the radar. But that would get a whole lot harder because of what was coming next.

Chapter 23
THE BUG

February 3, 1995 to March 19, 1995

O NE OF THE proving tests for a team in the NBA is how well they play with injuries. "It tests the mettle of a team, and it tests their style and their system," Del Harris said in early January when Sedale Threatt was sidelined with a stress fracture in his foot. He was right, but he hadn't seen anything yet.

Threatt was activated on January 31 and played limited minutes against Chicago and Phoenix. But he was immediately replaced on the injured list with Sam Bowie, who injured his right thumb against Seattle the night before. Bowie jammed the thumb on the bottom of the rim when attempting to block a shot. X-rays revealed the injury was just a sprain and he wouldn't need surgery. "I'm just glad surgery's not the direction this time," said Bowie. "In the past, there was always some sort of hardware that needed to be inserted into my leg." But he would be sidelined for two and a half weeks.

The loss of Bowie was a bigger blow than it may have appeared on the surface. His role fluctuated in November and December, but he had since become a mainstay in the rotation. His numbers in January of 4.2 points, 6.0 rebounds in 21.3 minutes didn't tell the whole story. He provided a defensive presence off the bench at center and power forward, something the young Lakers badly needed. It wasn't a coincidence the Lakers defense went south in the first two games he sat out.

The Lakers would also temporarily be without Elden Campbell, their starting power forward. He sprained his left ankle in the loss to Chicago and would miss five games. Campbell had been the unsung hero of the Lakers' resurgence. After starting the season on the bench, he had been in the best form of his career since rejoining the starting lineup in mid-November. In the 32 games he had started, he averaged 14.1 points and

6.5 rebounds in 31.9 minutes. He was one of the few rim protectors on the team, averaging 2.3 blocks a game. Antonio Harvey started in place of Campbell against Phoenix and had played well – scoring 18 points in 36 minutes. But his production as a starter would drop, and the Lakers were not the same defensively.

Looking to bolster the front-line, the Lakers cut ties with point guard Danny Young, allowing his first 10-day contract to expire without signing him to a new one.[224] West didn't look far to find a big body to replace Bowie, luring 36-year-old Kurt Rambis back from retirement to a 10-day contract. Rambis temporarily abandoned his duties as assistant coach to re-join the team on court. In a cruel twist of fate, Bowie had joked with Rambis just two weeks earlier that he was waiting for one of the Lakers' big men to get injured. Why else was he always running the stairs inside the Forum to stay in shape?

The injury bug would claim a major victim on February 3, 1995 when the Lakers lost 88-74 at home against the Denver Nuggets. It was their third straight loss and their equal lowest point total since moving to Los Angeles. Cedric Ceballos left the game with seven minutes remaining in the fourth quarter when he was inadvertently hit on the hand by Dikembe Mutombo's follow-through after the center blocked a shot by Divac. Ceballos winced in pain, went to the locker room a minute later, and was taken to hospital for x-rays. The results weren't good. He had ruptured a ligament in his hand and would require immediate surgery to repair it. He would miss the next 22 games, sidelined until late March.

It was a disaster for the Lakers and for Ceballos. He had been enjoying the best season of his career and was one of the major reasons for the team's sudden turnaround. He was leading the team in scoring with 22.3 points and was second in rebounds with 8.7. Just three days earlier, he had been named as a reserve at the upcoming All-Star Game. It was the first time he had received the honor, and he was the first Laker to make the game since James Worthy in 1991-92. It would have been a perfect story for him too. The All-Star weekend was being held in Phoenix, the city whose team had traded him away just five months earlier. But there would be no triumphant return because he now wouldn't be participating.

The Lakers struggled to a 121-118 win against the 7-37 Los Angeles

---

[224] Danny Young never saw any court time with the Lakers. He never played in the NBA again – his stint with the Lakers closed out his 10-year career.

Clippers at the Sports Arena the following night, barely ending their three-game losing streak. Harris replaced Ceballos by moving Eddie Jones to small forward where he was given 44 minutes and scored a team-high 30 points. Tony Smith got the start at shooting guard, but the injury to Ceballos meant a bigger role for Anthony Peeler, who had averaged only 11.4 minutes to that point. Peeler responded with his best game of the season, scoring 27 points in 33 minutes.

The injury woes continued as Vlade Divac bruised his right thigh in the second quarter and couldn't play the second half. It forced Harris to run with Rambis at center for the entire second half. He held his own, scoring 9 points and getting 5 rebounds in 28 minutes.

Divac was back in the starting line-up three nights later in Denver. A free throw by Threatt gave the Lakers an 85-83 lead with 12.4 seconds remaining, and rookie Jalen Rose missed a 12-footer as the Lakers escaped with the win. "I'm sure we're going to have our doubters," Nick Van Exel said. "A lot of people are going to be waiting for us to fall. Our leading scorer is out, two of our top big men are out. A lot of people think we're going to fold. We're going to have to stay together and play team ball."

The Lakers were back at home the following night against the 30-14 San Antonio Spurs. The Lakers led 57-52 at half-time and David Robinson, who was averaging 28.3 points and 11.0 rebounds, was having a quiet night. He left the game for good midway through the third quarter with a mild sprained right ankle when he landed on Divac's foot. Dennis Rodman was ejected for committing a flagrant foul on Jones, the Lakers went on a run and got their third win in a row, 115-99. Peeler had 26 points and played despite having a stomach virus that made him vomit behind the scorer's table when about to check back into the game during the third quarter.

Most of the Lakers enjoyed a full week off as the schedule paused for All-Star weekend. Though Ceballos was injured and wouldn't be able to take part in the All-Star Game on Sunday, both Jones and Antonio Harvey were involved in events on Saturday. Harvey took part in the Slam Dunk Contest but was eliminated in the first round after failing to complete his third and final dunk. Jones had been selected to take part too, but a bruised hip meant he couldn't compete. He did play in the Rising Stars game though, where he scored a game-high 25 points and was voted MVP.

The Lakers opened their post-All-Star schedule at home against the 34-

12 Seattle SuperSonics, getting two players back from injury but losing another. Bowie was activated from the injured list after missing the last six games.[225] Campbell was cleared to play, though Harris elected to bring him off the bench and keep Harvey in the starting line-up. But Smith, who had started the last three games, didn't suit up because of back spasms. Still surrounded by injuries, the Lakers signed Rambis to a second 10-day contract and Harris decided to move Jones back to shooting guard and start Lynch at the small forward spot.

The Lakers got a 102-96 victory over the Sonics, becoming the first team to beat them three times in a season in two years. It was symbolic of the Lakers' abrupt turnaround from a season earlier when the Sonics swept their season series 5-0. "When they were sweeping us last year, all that trash talking they did, that motivated us. We wanted to beat them bad," Lynch said after scoring 14 points in his first start in a month.

The Lakers saw their four-game win streak come to an end the next night in Sacramento, where they scored only 30 second-half points and lost 98-82 to the Kings.

Following two days off, they were back home against the 26-22 Portland Trail Blazers who five days earlier had traded Clyde Drexler to the defending champion Houston Rockets for forward Otis Thorpe. The trade, which came at Drexler's request, ended his twelve-year run in Portland where he was the all-time Blazers' leader in points, rebounds, and steals. Harris put Campbell back in the starting line-up, and the Lakers tied the game at 78-78 with seven minutes to play on three-pointers by Van Exel and Threatt. Divac then took advantage of foul trouble on center Chris Dudley and scored eight consecutive points to seal a 93-83 victory before a sell-out crowd.

The victory came at a cost though – a big one. Late in the second quarter, Jones took a pass from Van Exel and threw down a driving dunk. He changed direction in mid-air to avoid a defender and slightly twisted his arm when he adjusted for the dunk. He seemed fine after the play but a minute later was rubbing his right shoulder and was subbed out. He didn't return and had his arm in a sling by the end of the night. "It was a twinge at first," Jones said. "But I was trying to move my arm after running down court, then I knew something was wrong." That twinge in his right shoulder was a sprain, one that wouldn't require surgery but

---

[225] The Lakers didn't need to create a phantom injury and move anyone to the injured list to activate Bowie because they had been carrying only 11 players while he was out.

nevertheless would keep him on the sidelines for five weeks. In all, he would miss the next 18 games.

It couldn't have come at a worse time for the Lakers to be bitten again by the injury bug. Jones had played a pivotal role in achieving a 5-1 record since Ceballos went down with his injury. Jones was averaging 14.3 points on the season but had averaged 20.6 points in the last six games. The Lakers would also be without Smith for another three games. After sitting out against Portland with back spasms, Smith played limited minutes in Sacramento but strained his left calf. It left the Lakers with just three healthy guards. "Somebody just doesn't want us to win," said Van Exel.

The Lakers were in Seattle the next night for their second game against the Sonics in five days. They may have been 3-0 against them on the season, but the Lakers were deeply outmatched without their leading scorer, dynamic rookie, and reserve guard. And they were playing on the road against the third best team in the West on the second night of a back-to-back. It was the kind of game that could, and usually would get ugly for the Lakers.

But Van Exel responded by carrying the Lakers' offense, scoring a career-high 40 points on 12-19 shooting, including 7-9 three-pointers. The Lakers led 98-93 with two minutes to go and got clutch baskets every time they needed one. Peeler went one-on-one against Detlef Schrempf with the shot clock running down and made a long two-pointer, pushing the lead out to seven. When Sam Perkins cut the lead to two points with a minute and a half to play, Threatt ran off a screen from Bowie and hit a long two-pointer. When Payton cut the lead down to two again with 35 seconds left, Divac completed a beautiful touch pass to Bowie for a reverse dunk that barely beat the shot clock. They escaped with a 108-105 victory when Nate McMillan's 25-footer missed at the buzzer. "We have an awfully big heart on this team," Harris said. George Karl couldn't understand why his team kept losing to the Lakers, even when they were unfairly shorthanded. "I'm mystified," he said. "They're good, I think they're legit."

Jones was placed on the injured list three days after spraining his shoulder, and the Lakers signed 27-year-old Lloyd Daniels to a 10-day contract to fill the open roster spot. Daniels had overcome a lot to make his NBA dream come true. UNLV head coach Jerry Tarkanian said in 1987,

"They'll write the history of guards and start with Jerry West, Oscar Robertson, Magic Johnson, and Lloyd Daniels.'" And he wasn't kidding. Many considered Daniels to be the best high school player to emerge from New York since Kareem Abdul-Jabbar and Connie Hawkins. He was said to possess Magic's court vision *and* Larry Bird's jump shot. But he never became the NBA star Tarkanian thought he would.

Daniels' mother died when he was three, and he was left in the care of relatives, shuffled from place to place, and attended five high schools in three different states. He quit high school without a diploma and could barely read at a third-grade level. "Any kid like me who doesn't go to school can't read," he said. "How are you going to learn if you aren't there? I wasn't there."

Tarkanian fell in love with Daniel's game the moment he saw him and recruited him to UNLV. One of Tarkanian's assistants, Mark Warkentien, became Daniel's legal guardian and enrolled him at a junior college near Los Angeles to improve his reading and writing. Tarkanian figured he'd be lucky if Daniels stayed in college beyond one year before jumping to the NBA, he was that good. But Daniels never played college ball, for UNLV or anybody else. Before he could even practice with the team, he was arrested for buying crack cocaine from an undercover police officer. He didn't go to jail. Instead, he was placed in a drug rehabilitation program. But the incident led to him being cut from the team.

Instead of potentially starring at UNLV, Daniels spent the next six years bouncing from team to team in professional and semi-professional leagues. He was also in and out of drug rehabilitation and was kicked off a team in New Zealand for reportedly drinking more than a case of beer a day. He applied for the 1988 NBA Draft but went unselected, his checkered past being too much for NBA teams to risk. A year later, he was shot three times in the chest outside his Queens home over a suspected drug debt.

When Tarkanian took over as head coach of the San Antonio Spurs in 1992-93, he threw Daniels a life-line and signed him to a two-year contract. With bullet fragments still lodged in his shoulder, Daniels averaged 14.5 points in 29.2 minutes in the first 20 games of the season. But with the Spurs struggling to a 9-11 start, Tarkanian was fired, and Daniels' role slowly diminished the next two years under new coach John Lucas.

The Spurs waived him prior to the start of training camp, but Lucas, now head coach of the Philadelphia 76ers, signed him days later. But he was waived by the 76ers after playing five games. He signed on with the CBA's Fort Wayne Fury where he averaged 27.2 points in 33 games before the Lakers came knocking.

Daniels had an offer to join the Atlanta Hawks but chose the Lakers instead, in part because of Harris' reputation for rewarding players who work hard. "If you play hard, you're going to get an opportunity," Daniels said. "That's all I ever wanted, an opportunity."

Appropriately, Daniels made his Laker debut against the team that waived him three months earlier, the 15-37 Philadelphia 76ers. Daniels played six scoreless minutes in the Lakers 112-100 win. Van Exel had 20 points, and Divac almost recorded a triple-double with 19 points, 12 rebounds, and 8 assists. But it was Peeler who made the biggest impression. After scoring 21 points when Jones left the game against Portland, he backed that up with another 21 points as a starter against Philly.

Peeler again led the Lakers in scoring two nights later with 27 points, including six three-pointers, in front of a capacity Forum crowd against the Charlotte Hornets. Campbell scored on an eight-foot baseline jumper over Alonzo Mourning with 2.5 seconds left in overtime to give the Lakers a 95-93 win. Divac had one of the best games of his career with 25 points, 24 rebounds, and 8 assists against an excellent defender in Mourning. It was a remarkable win for two reasons. They had already won more games than all last season and broken the franchise record for most three-pointers in a season – all with 31 games remaining on the schedule.

The Lakers had gone 8-1 since Ceballos went down with his injury, and 4-0 since Jones went down with his. And they had done it by holding their opponents to 97.2 points per game, re-discovering the defensive intensity they started the season with but misplaced a month earlier.

It was also a shot in the arm to Harris and a testament to the integrity of the system he had implemented. By developing the system based on the skills and talents of the players, as opposed to enforcing a system upon them, they felt empowered to play their game when called upon. "The interesting thing about this team is that each individual feels like he's a key player," said Divac. "It doesn't matter who's out, and that gives us confidence. Anthony Peeler came off the bench, and he's our best player right now."

The change in culture was also noticeable to Rambis, who was signed for the remainder of the season after being on two 10-day contracts.[226] He was there last year when there was no sense of comradery amongst the players and coaches. "That was worse than the dentist, it was the proctologist," he said. But this season was different. "Guys are laughing, guys are winning, guys are getting along, it's fun."

Divac had 20 points and 20 rebounds, his second consecutive 20-20 game, the next night against the Clippers at the Sports Arena.[227] But the Lakers lost 83-81 to the league's worst team when Van Exel, Threatt, and Daniels each missed hurried shots in the final 11.6 seconds.

It was a bad loss, made worse by the injury bug biting yet again. Lynch played through 22 minutes of pain in his right foot, eventually sitting when it became too much to bear. He underwent x-rays after the game that revealed a stress fracture, an injury that would keep him sidelined for almost six weeks. He would miss the next 23 games. "It was really upsetting to me," Lynch said. "It was the first time this season I had gotten the opportunity to play a lot of minutes."

While he hadn't put up the kind of numbers as a starter that he had the previous season, Lynch had been serviceable since the injuries started to mount. He averaged 7.6 points and 4.5 rebounds in the ten games, but it wasn't his numbers the Lakers would miss. They had now lost their starting *and* back-up small forward to injury at the same time. To make things more difficult, they would also be without Bowie for the next five games. Just weeks after coming back from a sprained thumb, he would have to sit because of a fractured rib.

The Lakers coped with the ludicrous run of injuries the best way they could – with humor. 67-year-old Bill Bertka joked he might finally get his shot to play in the NBA if the injuries continued. Gary Vitti congratulated the team for managing to get from the locker room to the court for their annual team photo without anyone getting hurt. Someone put signs above the locker room door, one read '*M*A*S*H 4077*' and the other '*Enter at Own Risk.*' Chick Hearn gave a preview of what his commentating might be like in a few weeks' time. "Van Exel brings it down, gives it to whats-his-name

---

[226] Rambis was due to join the Magic Johnson All-Stars on their tour of Australia but had to pull out at the last minute when he was signed for the rest of the season.
[227] Divac became the first Laker to record 20-20 games on consecutive nights since Kareem Abdul-Jabbar in December 1975.

on the wing, back out to Sedale Threatt, over to that skinny kid in the corner, lobs it inside to that bald dude we just got from Rapid City, slammmm dunk," he joked.

The Lakers placed Lynch on the injured list and signed forward Randolph Keys to a 10-day contract. Keys was a Mississippi product, playing high school basketball in Collins before playing at the University of Southern Mississippi. He was selected late in the first round of the 1988 Draft by Cleveland and averaged 6.1 points primarily off the bench in three seasons in Cleveland and Charlotte. He spent 1991-92 in France and the 1992-93 season in Italy before returning to the United States with the Quad City Thunder in the CBA.

The Lakers had, justifiably, patted themselves on the back for how well they had played without Ceballos and Jones. But the injury to Lynch would prove to be the straw that broke the camel's back. They simply ran out of bodies. Daniels would go from playing in the CBA six weeks earlier to the starting small forward on a Lakers team simply trying to minimize the damage.

They lost their next two games, both at home against good teams. The first was a 101-95 loss to the Utah Jazz, with Karl Malone feasting on what was left of the Lakers' roster with 32 points. The second was a 101-93 loss to the shorthanded Phoenix Suns without Charles Barkley and Danny Manning. The bug bit again against Phoenix with Threatt missing the game with bursitis in his right foot that would force him to sit out the next two games.

The Lakers avoided a four-game losing streak with a fun 109-104 win at home against the Sacramento Kings in double overtime. It was fun because the Lakers came back from a 15-point deficit, but also because of who was involved in the clutch sequences. Daniels hit a three-pointer with 6.4 seconds remaining to tie the score and send the game into overtime. Keys sent the game into double overtime by rebounding Peeler's miss and hitting a fall-away 10-footer with 2.2 seconds remaining. And Anthony Miller, who had only played in 17 of the Lakers' 48 games before the injuries started, scored the first five points of double overtime to secure the win.

They got their second win in a row two nights later at home against the awful Minnesota Timberwolves behind 17 assists from Nick Van Exel. Divac had 30 points, 14 rebounds, 7 assists, and scored a lay-in with 31.9

seconds left for a 105-102 win.

After two straight wins, the Lakers' schedule got inconveniently tough with a road trip featuring four games in five nights. It opened in Miami where they lost 110-104. True to form, they shuffled the decks of injured players, getting Threatt and Bowie back only to lose Campbell to a sprained left ankle late in the third quarter. It was only a mild sprain, but they would be without their starting power forward for the next two games on the trip.

The next night they were in Orlando where, not surprisingly, Shaquille O'Neal wasn't troubled by a front-line consisting of Divac, Bowie, Rambis, Miller, and Keys. Shaq ran right over the Lakers with 46 points and 11 rebounds, and the Magic handed the Lakers a 114-110 loss. They lost their third straight two nights later in Minneapolis when Isiah Rider lit them up with 33 points leading the Timberwolves to a 109-103 win.

Exhausted and playing their fourth game in five nights, the Lakers traveled to Chicago where the city was abuzz with rumors Michael Jordan was considering a comeback.[228] The bug bit yet again and Van Exel was forced to sit out with back spasms. To make matters worse, Keys left the game after just two minutes with a strained abdominal muscle. He would be lost for the season just one day after he signed a second 10-day contract. The Lakers were so shorthanded that Divac was the lone usual starter, joined by Threatt, Peeler, Daniels, and Bowie. Scottie Pippen scored 40 points and the Bulls led by 14 points in the fourth quarter. But the Lakers outscored them 35-18 in the final quarter for an improbable 108-105 win.

They got another improbable win at home against the 37-23 Indiana Pacers. Divac went to the free throw line with 12.9 seconds remaining and the Lakers trailing 91-89. He made the first free throw but missed the second. Daniels sprinted from behind the free throw line to scoop up the rebound before hitting a twisting two-footer high off the glass and drawing a foul. His free throw gave the Lakers a 93-91 win.

The Lakers traveled to Oakland two days later where they hoped Warriors star point guard Tim Hardaway would elect to end his season by having surgery on a damaged ligament in his left wrist. Instead, he decided to delay surgery for one more game, and had 24 points and 12

---

[228] Jordan of course did eventually come back, but the Lakers missed playing against #45 Jordan by one week. He announced his comeback exactly one week after the Lakers-Bulls game with a fax that simply read 'I'm Back.'

assists in the Warriors' 119-108 victory. "It's too bad he didn't decide to get that thing operated on yesterday," Harris said.

The Lakers were listless two nights later at home against the 24-39 Boston Celtics who outmuscled them to a 55-30 rebounding edge and a 118-92 rout. Sherman Douglas sliced up the Lakers' defense with 33 points, and 35-year-old Dominique Wilkins scored 22 points and 9 rebounds.

They reclaimed some competitive spirit two nights later against the Sacramento Kings at the Forum with a 121-116 win. Most importantly, Van Exel shook off his shooting slump with 35 points, 7 rebounds, and 8 assists. Van Exel had been playing through back pain the last two weeks and would have sat out the game if the Lakers were not so short-handed. And it showed, he had shot just 27% from the field over the previous six games. But against Sacramento, he looked and felt like his old self.

It was late March, and both Ceballos and Jones had been cleared to begin full practices. Ceballos would be activated first and would have to play with a splint on his thumb. Jones would be ready to come back four days later. The nightmare run of injuries looked to be over. "This is obviously good news," said Harris. "They are both very important to us."

After initially surviving the losses of Ceballos and Jones, the Lakers had gone 4-8 since Lynch was sidelined. It had taken a toll, and they had fallen to sixth in the West but were still comfortably in the playoff race. Their excellent run before the injuries had proven an effective buffer to keep them afloat.

Van Exel's shot had been off in patches since the bug began biting, but he had still played well, averaging 15.0 points and 8.0 assists since Ceballos was injured. But the Lakers were mostly carried during this time by Peeler and Divac. Peeler had started the season nailed to the bench but was fantastic when given playing time. He had averaged 17.9 points on 47% shooting in 33.6 minutes since the injuries started. "It's meant a lot to me personally," Peeler said. "I'd been down, but I still came in and worked hard. Then I would leave after games without getting a chance to do anything. So, I wasn't going to let this chance blow past me. I'm just happy I had the chance to play this well."

Like he had done a year earlier, Divac hit a purple patch at just the right time, averaging 19.9 points, 12.4 rebounds, 5.5 assists, and 2.2 blocks while shooting 59% during the run of injuries. "That's the best month of my basketball career," said Divac. "I can't find one game where I played so-so. Almost all have been big games."

The Lakers had found some unlikely heroes too. Daniels had played well enough in his 12 games as the starting small forward, averaging 10.7 points in 30 minutes, to receive a contract for the remainder of the season.

And Miller had gone from missing more games due to coach's decision that he had played to becoming a key part of the rotation. Since Lynch's injury, he had averaged 9.5 points, 6.5 rebounds in 21.3 minutes on 57% shooting, including three double-doubles. It also gave him a chance to become a new favorite with the Forum crowd, who would affectionately chant his nickname, Pig, whenever he checked in or scored. He was first called Pig by his mother when he was a baby because of his hearty appetite, and the name stuck. It sounded like the kind of nickname that was an insult, but Miller was proud of it. "I like it a lot," Miller said. "At State, they just called me Anthony. But I like this better."

With 18 games left, the Lakers would start to put the band back together again for the playoff push. But unlike the last three years, the question wasn't whether they would (or should) make the playoffs. Instead, the biggest unknown was if they would have home-court advantage in the first round.

Just how good was this team? How far can they really go? These were the questions this season. And with those questions came something the Lakers hadn't been bothered by for years – expectations.

Chapter 24
REBUILT EXPECTATIONS

March 22, 1995 to April 22, 1995

H E DIDN'T START, but he was back. After seven weeks on the sidelines, the Lakers' leading scorer was back in uniform at the Forum against Portland. "I wasn't nervous," Cedric Ceballos said. "There wasn't any pressure. If I was coming back in the playoffs, then I'd be nervous. But I knew I had a good team out there. I thought I'd just get my feet wet."

Ceballos checked in five minutes into the game, playing the rest of the first quarter. He missed all four of his shots, made some free throws, grabbed three rebounds. He didn't play in either the second or third quarters before playing all of the fourth. He looked rusty, finishing with 11 points on 3-9 shooting in 19 minutes. But he was back.[229] Most importantly, the Lakers got the 121-114 win.

Two nights later, Vlade Divac recorded his third 20-20 game of the season with 25 points and 20 rebounds, and the Lakers got a 113-103 win over the Washington Bullets at home. Anthony Peeler scored 19 points, knowing his minutes and role would soon diminish now that Eddie Jones was on the verge of coming back. Harris acknowledged Jones would eventually take his starting spot back, but he wasn't going to make Peeler a third-stringer again. "Peeler won't go back to a 10-12-minute player," Del Harris said. "He'll still be a major-minute player, as long as he stays anywhere near where he's played the last 20 games."

Jones was back the next game and just in time for the Lakers to face a

---

[229] The Lakers made room for Ceballos by placing Randolph Keys on the injured list with his strained abdominal muscle. He had been on two 10-day contracts, but the Lakers signed him for the remainder of the season on March 14, 1995, even though they knew at the time his injury would sideline him for the remainder of the season.

big challenge – a home-and-away series against the defending champion Houston Rockets. The Lakers had beaten the Rockets twice in December, but that was before they had swung the blockbuster trade for Clyde Drexler.[230]

The first game was at the Forum in front of a sold out crowd. The Lakers led 91-88 late in the fourth quarter before Sedale Threatt scored six points in a 14-4 run that cemented a 107-96 victory. The Lakers recorded 30 or more assists for the fifth time in six games. Ceballos continued to improve since his return, scoring 20 points in 27 minutes off the bench. But the sight that made Lakers fans happiest was seeing Jones back on the court. He started on the bench and received a warm ovation when he checked in with three and a half minutes to play in the first quarter. He looked rusty in his return, scoring 12 points on 4-14 shooting. But the team was starting to look whole again.

The series switched to Houston two nights later when the Lakers got a break. Neither Hakeem Olajuwon nor Vernon Maxwell played because they were both diagnosed with iron deficiency anemia earlier in the day.[231] For a change, the Lakers were able to wear a short-handed team down by having more talent on the floor and got a 106-96 win, completing a 4-0 season sweep of the defending champions. Ceballos was back in the starting line-up and matched Elden Campbell with a game-high 17 points.

They lost 107-84 the next night in San Antonio but looked more like their old selves when they beat the Atlanta Hawks at home, 121-107. Ceballos led the Lakers with 25 points, and Jones chipped in with 18, both players getting their highest point totals since coming back from injury.

They opened April with a sell-out at home against the Orlando Magic without Anfernee Hardaway who had spent most of the day in the hospital with extreme dehydration. The Lakers were clinging to a 101-100 lead when Van Exel scored five straight points, including a three-pointer which he celebrated by shadowboxing as he ran down court. Ceballos top scored with 33 points and the Lakers won 119-112, overcoming Shaquille O'Neal's 27 points and 12 rebounds.

Jones was back in the starting lineup two nights later in Denver for the first time in six months, but it wasn't in place of Peeler. Harris played

---

[230] The Lakers activated Jones and placed Smith on the injured list with a strained left calf that had made him miss the previous three games.

[231] Apparently both players being diagnosed with iron deficiency at the same time was purely coincidental.

Ceballos off the bench because of a case of food poisoning he got from a shopping mall burger. Despite feeling light-headed and having tunnel-vision-like symptoms, Ceballos played 24 minutes and scored 14 points. Jones and Van Exel each scored 19 points and the Lakers won 104-101 when Dale Ellis missed an open three-pointer in the dying seconds.

With 10 games left on the schedule, the Lakers appeared ready to build momentum heading into the playoffs. They had won eight of their last nine games and were returning to full strength. Both Ceballos and Jones were back, while Lynch was practicing again, due to be activated off the injured list in less than a week. They were 46-26 and had clinched a playoff spot with their win over Orlando, the earliest they had done so since Magic Johnson retired. And they had a four-game lead over Houston for the fifth spot. They seemed like a lock to have the first 50-win season in the post-Magic era.

After being slow to believe these Lakers might be for real, fans started packing into the Forum during the stretch run. It was just like the old days. But instead of charging into the playoffs, they were about to head into an ill-timed tailspin where they would play their worst basketball of the season, just as fans were coming back into the fold.

It started in Dallas where the Lakers gave up the most points they conceded all season and lost 130-111. Ceballos and Jones were both back in the starting line-up, the first time the Lakers had their preferred starters together in nine weeks. Jones scored 22 points but Ceballos, still feeling under the weather, played horribly. He was limited to 19 minutes and shot 1-6 for 2 points. Peeler still got his minutes, but he struggled with his shot, playing off the bench for the first time in six weeks. He finished with 11 points on 3-12 shooting. "It's not fair for a player [Jones] to lose his position because of an injury," Harris said. "And yet, there is no good reason to take Anthony Peeler out of the line-up. The guy is playing marvelously."

They thrashed the Utah Jazz 113-90 in front of a sell-out crowd at the Forum two nights later, making the loss in Dallas appear like a blip on the radar instead of a trend. Ceballos bounced back from his subpar games on the road, scoring 36 points. They raced out to a 31-16 lead at quarter time and never looked back. "That was probably the best I've seen anybody play," Utah coach Jerry Sloan said. "We didn't even belong on the same floor with them."

But it wouldn't last. The Lakers would have a tough schedule to finish the season, with six of their last eight games coming against teams bound for the playoffs in the West. "Every team we're playing is fighting hard for position," Harris said. "So, they'll go all-out to win." It would be a great test leading to the playoffs, but one they would fail miserably.

Ceballos had 26 points, and Divac added 18 points, 17 rebounds, and 7 assists at home against the West-leading San Antonio Spurs. But the Lakers were miserable. They scored 37 points in the first half and trailed by 17 at half-time. They lost 101-87, making the sell-out Forum crowd head for the exits early.

The Lakers kicked off a three-game road trip in Salt Lake City and the Utah Jazz dished out a healthy dose of revenge for the rout they received at the hands of the Lakers four days earlier. The Lakers struggled out of the gate and trailed by 13 at half-time. They lost Nick Van Exel when he was ejected early in the third quarter and lost 100-93.

The loss came despite the fact the Lakers started the game back at full strength for the first time since late December. Lynch scored one point in six minutes off the bench in his first game since late February. Smith scored three points in 24 minutes after sitting out the last eight games with a strained calf muscle. The Lakers made room for them by placing Rambis on the injured list with some well-timed back spasms, and waiving Lloyd Daniels.[232] But the good luck with injuries was short-lived as Threatt strained an abdominal muscle against Utah and couldn't finish the game. The injury wasn't considered serious, but he would miss the remainder of the regular season with the hope he would be ready for the playoffs.

After faltering against two playoff-bound teams, the Lakers fell to one of the few non-playoff teams left on their schedule, losing in Sacramento 109-99 to the Kings. The score was tied 96-96 with less than three minutes to play, but the Lakers turned the ball over on three consecutive possessions, ending any chance for a win. "We didn't perform at the end," Harris said. "We didn't make the big plays, and they did."

The road trip finished three nights later against the Phoenix Suns, who

---

[232] Daniels played the 1995-96 season in the CBA, France, and Italy. He returned to the NBA, playing 28 games from 1996-1998 with Sacramento, New Jersey, and Toronto. He retired from basketball in 2006 after playing the CBA, Greece, Portugal, Puerto Rico, Turkey, Venezuela, as well as the IBL, USBL, and ABA.

were sitting in third place in the West. The Suns were without Charles Barkley who was serving a one-game suspension for committing his sixth flagrant foul of the season, one more than the league limit, two nights earlier against Denver. Ceballos was magnificent, hitting 7-9 three-pointers and scoring 40 points. It was the first time a Laker had scored 40 or more points twice in the same season since Magic in 1986-87. But the Lakers couldn't get any stops in the fourth quarter and lost 119-114. It was their fourth loss in a row, a terrible time of year to have their longest losing streak of the season. But Harris was preaching calm. "We're okay," he said. "There is no reason to panic. There's been a lot of teams that have gotten beaten here by Phoenix."

The Lakers put an end to the rot the next night with a 125-111 win over the Dallas Mavericks in front of another sell-out crowd at the Forum. But they'd immediately get back to struggling once they faced a playoff-caliber team. The Forum was sold out again for the game against the Seattle SuperSonics, who they hadn't lost to all season. But the Lakers hardly seemed to show up for this one at all. They managed just 34 points in the first half and trailed by 30 at the major break. They were out-rebounded by 15, their starters were outscored 76-41, and they lost 113-97. "We were out-energized totally by the Seattle team," Harris said. "Here's a team that played last night and we didn't. That was a playoff job they did on us. Unfortunately, ours was an exhibition job, a pre-season performance."

The Lakers finished the season with a home-and-away series against the seventh-place Portland Trail Blazers. Divac would miss both games, sitting out with a bad case of the flu. After seeming like a lock for a 50-win season, the Lakers would have to win both games to get there. But they would lose them both.

The first game was in Portland, and Bowie replaced Divac as the starter and had 19 points and 15 rebounds. Ceballos top-scored with 36 points but the Lakers faulted from the start.[233] They trailed by 20 at half-time and lost 111-97 while getting hammered 50-33 on the boards.

The final game was back at home where another sold out crowd left disappointed. Unlike their previous two games, the Lakers had a chance

---

[233] Ceballos converted the first 4-point play in Laker history against Portland.

at the end, trailing by three points with 9.2 seconds remaining. But they couldn't find a decent shot and eventually lost 109-104.[234]

The Lakers' best and most exciting season in four years petered out in the final two and a half weeks. They won just two of their last ten games, a troubling sign for several reasons.

They were entering the playoffs with no momentum whatsoever. Instead, they would start the business end of the season with questions being asked about how for real they were. "This is the time you should be getting your game together," said Bowie. "We've got a long ways to go. The way things are going right now, we're going to be one of the worst teams heading into the playoffs from the last part of the season. It's not like you can turn it on and off."

Of greatest concern was the fact they had been a bad defensive team over the last ten games, giving up an average of 109.3 points. And bad defensive teams don't usually make much impact come playoff time.

The let-down coincided with the city of Los Angeles finally getting behind the team. Fans, and the rest of the basketball world, were slow to embrace these Lakers. Interest in the post-Magic Lakers had waned for two years before dropping off a cliff in 1994. They sold out just six of their first 33 home games and finished 23rd in attendance in 1994-95. Evidently, fans weren't coming back just because the Lakers won some games in January. But fans returned in April and the Lakers sold out seven of their last eight home games. But fans mostly saw the Lakers be out-classed by fellow playoff teams. The stars were coming back to the Forum too, just in time for the team to play their worst basketball of the season. "I've gone to see Jack Nicholson and Arnold Schwarzenegger," Harris said. "And they never let me down. And here they were, and we couldn't perform."

The poor finish to the season gave credence to a concern many pundits held about this Lakers team all season – that these Lakers were too young and not mentally tough enough to make a deep playoff run. In late February, they were on pace for a 55-win season, and on pace for 52 as late as early April. They finished with 48. And it was the players' focus on

---

[234] The Lakers honoured the 10-year anniversary of the 1985 championship team, the first Laker team to defeat the Celtics in the NBA Finals, at half-time. Most of the former players – including Magic Johnson, Kareem Abdul-Jabbar, Jamaal Wilkes, and Michael Cooper were in attendance. Pat Riley, who was busy preparing his Knicks for the playoffs, sent a video message.

getting to 50 wins that potentially undid them in the last two weeks. "Maybe we should stop worrying about 50 wins and just play basketball," Ceballos said in late April.

Mark Heisler wrote in the *Los Angeles Times* that the Lakers were a victim of their own rebuilt expectations in the way they finished the season. And he was right. They had all but sewn up the fifth spot in the West by early April with little chance of climbing to fourth. Reaching the 50-win plateau was all they really had left to play for. But if talk of a 50-win season combined with increased interest from fans was too much pressure for them, what would the heat of the playoffs do to them?

While the regular season didn't end well, it was still a success beyond the wildest dreams of even the most optimistic fan. Their 48 wins were a 15-game improvement on the season before, the second biggest improvement in the league.[235]

A big reason for the turnaround was Harris. When introduced to the media as the new head coach of the Lakers in the off-season, he said that he was a flexible coach. And he was true to his word. "I haven't imposed a system on the Lakers," Harris said. "Rather, I've gone with them on a journey to find it." He hadn't made the same mistake Randy Pfund made by trying to re-create Showtime. "A lot of people were living in the past," West acknowledged.

Harris instead found a style of play that suited the team. It was a hybrid of half-court and full-court basketball with a commitment to defense at its core. And it showed in the stats. They were fifth in the league in steals with 9.1 per game and third in blocks with 6.9 per game. Defense was the key driver behind the team. The Lakers played well and got wins when they were working hard and communicating on defense, and they would falter when they weren't.

The defense fueled their offense, and the results, when combined with the young and athletic roster, was at times spectacular. They scored a seventh-best 105.1 points per game and played at the fourth-fastest pace. West and Jerry Buss understood it wasn't enough just for the Lakers to win. If the city was to embrace a new Lakers team, they had to put on a show. "The game has to be played with flair," West said. It wasn't

---

[235] The Dallas Mavericks were the most improved team, going from 13 wins in 1993-94 to 36 wins in 1994-95.

Showtime, it was something unique to these Generation X Lakers. "We call it the Lake Show," said Jones.[236]

The two newest Lakers – Ceballos and Jones – had both exceeded expectations. Though limited to 58 games, Ceballos averaged a team-high 21.7 points, was their second-leading rebounder with 8.0 a game, and was selected to be an All-Star.[237] Not bad for a player no General Manager other than West thought was worth a first-round pick seven months earlier. "The rest of the league were too stupid," Suns coach Paul Westphal said. "I took the best deal I could get."

Jones finished fourth in Rookie of the Year voting, outperforming five of the players selected before him in the draft. He averaged 14.0 points in 64 games and proved to be an excellent defender, finishing sixth in the league with 2.0 steals per game, and leading the league in steal-to-turnover ratio 1.75-to-1.00. And he very quickly became a fan favorite at the Forum.

Divac had turned a corner in the second half of 1993-94, and he carried that momentum into the new season, having the finest year of his career in 1994-95. In his sixth season in the NBA, he averaged 16.0 points, 4.1 assists, 2.2 blocks, and 35.1 minutes – all career highs. All the while grabbing 10.4 rebounds and shooting 51% from the field. He had turned from an inconsistent player in his earlier years to the most reliable low-post scorer on the team. While his unique dribbling and passing skills used to get him in trouble when he tried to do too much, he now played with steadiness and maturity.

Campbell also continued his slow but steady improvement. He increased his scoring average for the fifth straight season and his low-post defense, always a strength of his game, was becoming more consistent.

Peeler had a season of two halves. He had shown considerable improvement in an expanded role in 1993-94 before his season was cut short by injury. He then lost his starting job and started the season glued to the bench. He had nine 'Did Not Play – Coach's Decision' games in the first half of the season and averaged just 4.3 points in 11.4 minutes in his

---

[236] A lot of the team stats were dramatically improved from a year earlier. Their points per game went from 17th in the league to 7th, offensive rating from 17th to 11th, defensive rating from 22nd to 16th, and their field goal percentage from 24th to 7th.

[237] Ceballos was the only Laker to that point to average at least 20 points and 8 rebounds other than Magic, Elgin Baylor, Wilt Chamberlain, and Kareem Abdul-Jabbar.

first 33 games. But injuries gave him an opportunity he made the most of, and he averaged 15.4 points over his final 40 games, including 24 starts. His performance in the second half of the season made him one of the most in-form players on the roster heading into the playoffs.

Van Exel entered training camp wanting to be a better floor leader and more of a distributor. He more than achieved that, becoming one of the league's most promising young point guards. He built on his surprising rookie season by improving in almost every statistical category. He upped his scoring from 13.6 points to 16.9 and his assists from 5.8 to 8.2, good enough for sixth highest in the league. His shot selection was still a work in progress, but he shot the Lakers into far more games than he ever shot them out of. "He had everybody doubting him, doubting his abilities," Ceballos said. "And he's proven them wrong."

Hearn called Van Exel the glue that kept the Lakers together. His fearless approach to the game infused the Lakers with confidence, giving them something they hadn't had for years – attitude. And it rubbed some of the league the wrong way. George Karl called them cocky. Clippers players Pooh Richardson and Loy Vaught claimed these Lakers took trash talk to an unprofessional and immature new level. "We don't like their attitude at all," Charles Barkley said. "They were pretty cocky."

"It comes with youthfulness and winning," Harris said. "A certain amount of it is okay. If you keep it in decent taste, there's nothing wrong with a little exuberance." Ceballos believed the Lakers' attitude came from a lack of respect shown to them by the league. Teams were not willing to anoint these Lakers as 'being back' without proving it first. "Teams come in and say, 'You got no talent in your squad, you're just getting lucky,'" Ceballos said. "We get that a lot. That kind of eggs us on to talk back."

"It's jealousy because the Lakers are back winning again," Van Exel said. The things we went through last year, it's been a big turn-around. Everybody's excited and happy to be out there winning. Whatever little motivation that we can get, it helps us. When we go into other arenas, and the crowd is booing us, I think everybody on the team likes that. It makes us play better."

That cockiness and self-belief was a major reason why the Lakers were able to post 48 wins despite the horrendous run of injuries. They missed a combined 150 games to injury and didn't have their original opening night roster healthy for a single game over their final 56 games.[238] Their December 30, 1994 game in Phoenix was the final time they started and finished a game with their full roster. They had at least one player, often multiple players, out injured for every game they played in the 1995 calendar year. Yet they went 31-25 in their last 56 outings after the injury bug started, showing resilience Laker teams in the post-Magic era rarely showed to that point.[239]

It was also no coincidence the Lakers' best season since Magic retired was the one where he stayed at an arm's distance from the team. Though hardly his intent, his shock retirement three games into the 1991-92 season shattered the team. Likewise, his re-retirement days before the start of the 1992-93 season was almost as disruptive. He criticized the team in the media several times in 1993-94. And it could be argued his foray into coaching late in the season disrupted a team that had been playing its best basketball before he got there. But in 1994-95, he served in his new role as Vice President, doing as promised at the start of the season by keeping a lower public profile.

Magic wasn't the only new face in the management structure of the Lakers. Jeanie Buss, daughter of owner Jerry Buss, became Alternate Governor on the NBA Board of Governors in April 1995. She would eventually become the extremely effective Controlling Owner and President of the Lakers after her father passed away in 2013. Becoming Alternate Governor was her first significant role with the Lakers, empowering her to represent the Lakers at Board of Governors meetings whenever her father was unable to attend.[240] Her first meeting coincided with her posing for Playboy magazine, which must have made the first board meeting interesting. Jerry Buss gave his blessing for the spread and was asked by a reporter if he had seen the layout. "Oh, I'm not looking at that, are you kidding?" he said. "Of course, it's the only Playboy I haven't looked at in 26 years."

---

[238] Ceballos 24, Threatt 23, Lynch 23, Keys 22, Jones 18, Smith 14, Bowie 13, Campbell & Rambis 7, Miller 3, Van Exel & Divac 2.

[239] The Lakers had a horrid run of injuries every year since Magic retired. They missed a combined 104 games due to injury in 1991-92, 142 games in 1992-93 (60 games if you don't include Jack Haley missing all 82 games, which would be considered a relatively healthy season), and a shocking 216 games in 1993-94.

Chapter 25

VAN EXCELIZED

April 27, 1995 to May 4, 1995

D EL HARRIS DIDN'T like what he saw. "Anybody know a good priest?" he shouted at the team during a practice session. "We might need some last rites!"

Harris didn't hold your standard pre-playoff practice sessions in 1995. Not with how poorly the Lakers finished the regular season. Instead, he sequestered the team to Palm Desert for a four-day camp of two-a-day training sessions. There they would try to figure out if their recent poor play was a short detour or the start of a highway leading straight to an early playoff exit.

"It's not back yet, that's all I can tell you," Harris said. "The best I can come up with is where we failed." The coaching staff drilled the team hard on improving their rotations and ball pressure. They focused on getting better at keeping the ball out of the middle, at helping each other out and communicating. Better, basically, at defense. "If we do those things, then we've got a chance," he said. "If we don't, then it's going to be awful tough."

"We feel we can compete with any other team if the Lakers – the Lake Show – shows up," Nick Van Exel said. "If we come out and play like we did when we first started playing this season, we're going to be fine. But if we come out like the second half of the season – timid, too passive, quick shots, a lot of jump shots, no rebounding, trouble in transition defense – it'll kill us."

Fans pinned their hope on the belief that whatever happens in the regular season doesn't necessarily add up to much of anything in the playoffs. "Whether you win all of them or lose all of them, it's still a whole different mindset when you go into the playoffs," Harris said. "It really doesn't affect the playoffs as much as some people think."

The Lakers were the best of the 'rest' in the West. Nobody outside the top four was expected to make much noise in the playoffs.[241] Even though they had beaten them 4-1 in the regular season, few people believed the 48-win Lakers were a serious threat to the 57-win Seattle SuperSonics in the first round.

The Sonics were so talented, they would have been called a Super Team if that term existed in 1995. They were led by three All-Stars who were among the best in the league at their respective positions. Now in his fifth season, Gary Payton had developed into an elite NBA point guard. A terror defensively, he now had an offensive game to match with averages of 20.6 points and 7.1 assists. Shawn Kemp had developed a truly devastating low-post game, was a strong offensive rebounder, and a remarkable athlete. He had averaged a career-high 18.7 points, 10.9 rebounds and 55% shooting in 1994-95. While 32-year-old veteran forward Detlef Schrempf had enjoyed perhaps his finest season, averaging a career-high 19.2 points.

Flanking the three All-Stars was a deep roster of exemplary role players. Shooting guard Kendall Gill possessed the talent to be an All-Star but had yet to find the necessary consistency. Ex-Laker Sam Perkins brought a veteran's calm, good rebounding, and efficient scoring. Their bench boasted two excellent backcourt defenders in veterans Nate McMillan and Vincent Askew. While forward Sarunas Marciulionis had recovered from a knee injury that cost him the entire 1993-94 season and provided even more experience off the bench. 37-year-old center Bill Cartwright may have only played limited minutes throughout the season, but the three-time NBA champion provided a steady head when called upon.

Yet a dark cloud hung over these Sonics all season from their infamous performance in the playoffs a year earlier. They ran roughshod over the entire NBA in 1993-94 with a league-best 63 wins. As the top seed in the West, they matched up with the eighth-seeded Denver Nuggets who won 21 fewer games during the season. It was David vs. Goliath. The Sonics comfortably won the first two games in Seattle, but it all went south from there. They lost both games in Denver and then returned home to lose the

---

[241] The top four teams (San Antonio, Utah, Phoenix, and Seattle) all won more than 55 games. The bottom four teams (Lakers, Houston, Portland, and Denver) didn't win more than 48.

deciding Game 5 in overtime. It was one of the most remarkable upsets in NBA history, and the first time a #8 seed had eliminated a #1 seed.[242]

The team faced a barrage of criticism all off-season, most of it focused on head coach George Karl. Management almost traded Kemp to Chicago for Scottie Pippen but backed out of the deal at the last minute. They recovered to have an excellent 1994-95 season, but they still had their doubters. It made the series difficult to predict. Maybe the Sonics were still scarred from their loss to the Nuggets, and the Lakers could chip away at their fragile confidence. But maybe the Sonics would be highly motivated with something to prove.

The Lakers entered Game 1 at the Tacoma Dome with a completely healthy roster for the first time since December 30, 1994. Sedale Threatt, who hadn't played for almost three weeks with a strained abdominal muscle, was back in uniform. So too was Vlade Divac, who had recovered from his bout of the flu.

Harris made a sudden change to the rotation, starting Anthony Peeler ahead of Eddie Jones. It was a surprise move because Harris had considered the starting spot belonged to Jones all season. But Jones had been struggling since returning from injury, and Peeler, who had played so well as a starter, had seen his production drop since being moved back to the bench. "I think our situation called for a change. A.P. played so well as a starter," Harris said. "Let's get him back in there where he can be an asset. And maybe Eddie can get us some life off the bench." Harris intended to move Elden Campbell to the bench and start Sam Bowie in his place. But his plans changed when Bowie came down with the flu before Game 1. Changes so late in the season could have been perceived as a risky move. But not to Harris. "Not when you've won two of 10," he said.

But the move didn't pay off. Peeler managed just one shot, a miss, in the first seven minutes before being replaced. Jones didn't fare much better, making just one of three shots in the first half. They were hardly the only players to struggle though. Cedric Ceballos, their leading scorer, managed just 2 points on 1-10 shooting. Only Van Exel and Vlade Divac scored in double figures, the Lakers shot 35% and lost 96-71. It was a humiliating loss and the lowest scoring playoff game in franchise history.

The Lakers run of good health proved to be typically short-lived.

---

[242] This was the same Denver Nuggets teams the Lakers were trying to catch for the final playoff spot in 1994.

Threatt made his first appearance in the second quarter and drove the lane for a lay-up when he re-injured his abdominal muscle. "They put me back in the second half," he said. "I couldn't even get back on defense." The injury would require surgery in the off-season and Threatt would miss the rest of the post-season.

One of the Lakers' advantages all season against the Sonics was the strength and length of their frontcourt. But it didn't bother them in Game 1. Kemp, Perkins, and center Ervin Johnson outmuscled the Lakers all night long. "Physically, they outmanned Vlade, myself, and Elden and that was the key to their success," Bowie said. "They received the ball in the paint and our post people, including myself, would receive the ball outside the paint. And that came because they were more physical than we were." It threw the Lakers' offense out of whack. The frontcourt players regularly made soft passes back out to the guards that left the Sonics more than enough time to switch and adjust defensively.

In the day between games, Harris dismissed the idea of another line-up change. Not because he thought it would be risky, but because nobody played well enough off the bench in the first game to justify being promoted to starter in Game 2. Instead, he drilled two basic instructions to the team. The guards were told not to throw the ball in to the big men unless they were in good position, while the big men were told to toughen up and fight for better position.

Signs were ominous prior to tip-off for Game 2 as the Lakers were a tired and sick team. Threatt was in street clothes, and Bowie felt achy and beat up as his flu had gotten worse since Game 1. But he would suit up and try to play. "I can't play any worse than I played [in Game 1]," he figured. All eyes were on Ceballos after his disappearing act in Game 1. But he was sick too and felt nauseous the morning of the game.

After a high-scoring start, Game 2 turned into a grind. The Sonics led 71-69 to start the fourth quarter but came out sloppy. Perkins dribbled the ball off his foot, Gill was called for traveling, they committed a 24-second shot clock violation and an off the ball offensive foul. It would take them more than five minutes to make their first basket, and the Lakers took advantage.

Campbell tied the score at 71-71 with a shot off the glass over Perkins. On the next possession, Van Exel hit a tough fall-away over Payton with the shot clock running down for a 73-71 lead. They barely beat the shot clock on their next possession too, but Divac passed out of a double-team to Peeler for a three-pointer and a 76-71 lead. After four misses on the same possession, McMillian tipped in Schrempf's missed jumper to finally get the Sonics on the board for the quarter. But Ceballos responded by posting Schrempf and hitting a jumper over him for a 78-73 lead. The Lakers got another stop and Jones drove the middle and drew the Sonics' defenders to him. He fired a bullet pass to Ceballos who hit a three-pointer, pushing the Lakers' lead out to 81-73 and capping a 14-2 run.

Just as the Lakers were taking control of the game, the lights went out in Tacoma Dome. Literally. Divac fouled Kemp, who went to the free throw line with his team trailing by eight with four minutes remaining in the fourth quarter. Suddenly a lightning strike caused a power surge outside the building, knocking the electricity out within a five-block radius. Emergency generators kept some concession stands and other areas illuminated, saving the building from being in pitch darkness. But it was too dark to play, forcing a 24-minute delay until power could be restored.

Most of the players desperately tried to stay warm, some shooting around in the darkness. But the delay was good for Ceballos. He took the opportunity to go to the bathroom where he was able to 'alleviate' his stomach bug and returned feeling like a new man.

While waiting for power to be restored, an official sided up to Harris. "I hate to tell you Del, but the league called and said in these situations, you have to reset back to the beginning of the game," he said. "I didn't fall for it."

When play finally resumed, the Lakers lost all momentum. "I knew we wouldn't be ready," Van Exel said. "I knew they would come back." The Sonics immediately went on a 6-0 run that cut the Lakers' lead to 81-79 with three minutes to play.

It was enough to make the Lakers paranoid. "If it never happened before and then it happens in the first round of the playoffs, it makes you go, 'Hmm,'" Van Exel said. "I'm serious. You never know." It was something the Lakers may have expected in Boston, but not in Seattle. "Me and Kurt Rambis were sitting over there thinking about the Boston mystique – putting the lights out on purpose to change momentum," Harris said. "It's an old Indiana trick. Once you're behind, the lights have got to go."

A rejuvenated Ceballos would put an end to the Sonic run. He made a three-pointer with Kemp charging at him to push the lead to 84-79 with just over a minute remaining. Perkins cut the lead back to two when he made a three-pointer ten seconds later. Neither team scored on their next possessions, and the Lakers had the ball and a two-point lead with 16 seconds remaining.

Ceballos attempted a pass to Peeler near the top of the key, but it was intercepted by McMillan. With no fast break opportunities, the Sonics called timeout with 10 seconds remaining to set up a play to either tie or win the game. Payton tried to back Van Exel down on the ensuing play, but he couldn't get past him. Instead, he fired a pass to McMillan who was open for a potential game-winning three-pointer. "Nate had an open one," Karl said. "I thought it was a good play, a wide-open three to win it." But it hit the front of the rim as the buzzer sounded and the Lakers survived, winning 84-82 to tie the series at 1-1.

Ceballos bounced back from his horrible performance in Game 1 to score a game-high 25 points in Game 2. He hit 6-9 three-pointers, tying a franchise record for both makes and attempts.[243] "Not that I have a crystal ball or ESP," Harris said, "but I think I did say that knowing Cedric, he would come back big for this game. He's just one of the best competitive athletes I've ever seen."

With Threatt out injured and Smith seemingly in the doghouse again, Harris played Van Exel all 48 minutes. It was the start of what would be a re-occurring theme for these playoffs, a war of attrition for Van Exel that would physically test him like never before.

Peeler gave the Lakers some life in his 28 minutes, scoring 10 points on 4-8 shooting and hitting two three-pointers. But for the second straight game, Jones was nowhere to be seen. He played 26 minutes and struggled to 2 points on 1-4 shooting. He played so passively, and passed up so many open shots, he all but turned into a wallflower. "He's not playing the same way he played before the injury," Harris said. "If he was playing exactly the same as before he got hurt, I'd have him in the starting line-up."

"I'm going out there to play extremely hard no matter what," Jones said. "I think I'm in a little slump or something. The shot's not falling. Things I do on the court aren't going right like I'm a step too slow. I don't

---

[243] It tied Michael Cooper's record of six three-pointers set in Game 2 of the 1987 NBA Finals against the Boston Celtics on June 4, 1987.

know what it is."

The series returned to Los Angeles for the next two games and the Lakers expected the Sonics, who shot just 31% in Game 2, to come out swinging. Seattle's offense had fallen apart in the second game, but it hadn't been strong in Game 1 either, despite their comfortable win. In response, Karl shook up his starting line-up – benching defensive-minded center Johnson and starting Perkins in his place. "It gives them a little more offense and a little less defense," Harris said. "Well, it gives them *a lot* more offense, as a matter of fact."

The sold-out Forum crowd at Game 3 had to wait almost thirty minutes past tip-off time for the game to start because TNT hadn't finished their coverage of the Knicks-Cavaliers game. But they lost no energy from the wait. The atmosphere was more like a Game 7 of the NBA Finals than Game 3 of the first round. It was so loud nobody heard a whistle on the game's first play when Peeler stole a pass from Schrempf and McMillan fouled him to prevent a breakaway dunk. Officials had to repeatedly blow their whistles and resorted to waving their hands in the air to get the attention of the players to stop play. The city of Los Angeles had been slow to embrace the Lake Show, but the atmosphere in Game 3 proved they had come full circle.

The reception from fans pushed the Lakers to a commanding first-quarter run. Van Exel received a pass from Ceballos for a three-pointer from the corner to give the Lakers a 5-2 lead. Moments later, Peeler drove past Schrempf and launched a pull-up jumper that hit the rim five times before dropping. On their next possession, the Lakers got the Sonics on their heels with some precision ball movement that resulted in an open baseline jumper by Divac.

They then forced a turnover with swarming defense, leading to Van Exel pushing the ball hard in transition. He drew the defense and flicked a perfect pass to Peeler who converted a reverse lay-in for a 12-2 lead. The Sonics called timeout, and the Forum crowd gave the Lakers a standing ovation. Control of the series was swinging, and everybody in attendance could feel it. "Basketball is back at the Great Western Forum," Hearn said over the roar of the crowd.

Following the timeout, Kemp scored on back-to-back possessions to make it 12-6. But Divac drew a double-team and found Peeler wide open for a corner three-pointer to push the lead to 15-6. A few possessions later, Payton scored on a transition lay-in, but the Lakers nullified it seconds later with a length-of-the-court pass to Ceballos for an easy dunk. Holding for the last possession of the quarter, Ceballos missed a tough jumper over Askew. But Jones flew into the lane from the other side, collected the rebound and converted an acrobatic put-back dunk with 0.8 seconds to play for a 34-22 lead.

The first quarter push by the Lakers proved to be one of many runs from both sides. The Sonics responded with an emphatic 18-2 run to close within 46-44. Then the Lakers steadied with a 10-0 run of their own, kick-started by four offensive rebounds on one possession that led to a bank shot by Ceballos.

The Lakers pushed their lead to 15 points late in the third quarter but couldn't put the Sonics away. Seattle went on a 12-4 run in the fourth quarter, getting within 96-93 on a three-pointer by Sam Perkins with less than three minutes to go. From there, the game was decided largely by free throws. Divac hit three of four on back-to-back possessions, and Van Exel's free throws made it a two-possession game with 13.3 seconds to play. A late basket by George Lynch settled it for good, the Lakers winning 105-101 to take a 2-1 series lead.

Ceballos had 24 points, Divac added 20, and Van Exel played the full 48 minutes again, scoring 23 points. Van Exel said he would need some rest at some point to keep his legs strong, but Harris was unsympathetic. "There were 18 timeouts last night, counting your TV timeouts, your 20-second timeouts, and full timeouts," Harris said. "Then you've got your quarter breaks, your half breaks, and these guys are in great shape. They can do this."

The Lakers were on the brink of advancing in the playoffs for the first time since Magic retired, while the Sonics found themselves at death's door in the first round for the second straight season. While it didn't compare to their collapse against Denver, they were down in a series they were expected to win. Seattle was deeper and more talented than the Lakers. They were more experienced, had almost ten more wins during the season, and had home-court advantage. But the ghosts of playoff failure were starting to re-appear. "It's all around us," Karl said. "No question it'll be in front of us until we defeat it. And it might take three years of defeating it until it's behind us."

The voices calling all year for Karl's dismissal became all that much louder, but he was used to the noise. "If the Pope visited Seattle and his hat fell in the lake, and I walked on water to fetch it and slapped it right back on his head," he said, "the headline in Seattle would be 'George Karl can't swim.'"

At the same time Karl was being criticised, Harris was being lauded for his job in turning the Lakers around. He was voted NBA Coach of the Year for the 1994-95 season, dominating the voting for the award.[244] Harris was too focused on the playoffs to appreciate it fully, but the award validated not only his coaching job but Jerry West's decision to break from tradition and hire a veteran coach. "The fact that he's from the old school and is used to coaching guys from the 70s and 80s," Bowie said, "to be able to get a group of guys from the 90s who have a different mental approach and much more money in their pockets, it's been amazing to me the way he's been able to get the guys to believe in him."

Everybody expected Game 4 to be a battle. It was do-or-die for the Sonics, and they fully expected to play their best game of the season. "I had a lot of coaches send a scouting report on us, and one of the tendencies we had was we played best when we had a sense of urgency," Karl said. "We will definitely have a sense of urgency."

The Lakers expected it too. "I think they will come out like mad dogs the first five, six minutes of the game," Bowie said. "If we're able to withstand that initial fight that they have, then I think we'll get an opportunity to end the series here."

Harris received his Coach of the Year trophy prior to tip-off to the sound of raucous applause from the sold-out Forum crowd. Then, like it had been scripted, the Sonics came out fighting. Kemp dominated inside, Payton orchestrated their renewed transition game, and the Sonics led 34-25 at the end of the first quarter.

The Lakers kept coming, making runs that shrunk the lead. But the Sonics responded to every mini-Laker run with a stabilizing run of their own. With their offense ticking along for the first time in the post-season, Seattle held a 90-82 lead at the end of the third quarter. They looked destined to take the series back to Seattle for a fifth and deciding game.

But the Lakers fought back. It started on the first possession of the

---

[244] Harris received 62 votes, 47 votes clear of Cleveland's Mike Fratello.

quarter when Jones blew past Payton, drove baseline and dunked over Kemp. Van Exel and Divac double-teamed Payton on the next possession, forcing him to travel. Divac then took advantage of a size mismatch in the post against Schrempf, attempting a lay-in that was blocked by Kemp, but he was called for goaltending.

Following a free throw by Schrempf, Van Exel pushed the ball in transition. He fired a pass to Jones on the wing who then made a perfect touch-pass to Peeler for a lay-in that cut the Sonics' lead to 91-90.

Payton scored on the next possession before Van Exel made a three-pointer over him a few seconds later, tying the score at 93-93 with nine minutes to play. Schrempf answered with a three-pointer of his own seconds later, but Divac tied the score at 96-96 on an offensive rebound that he converted for a three-point play. The Forum crowd was in a frenzy. "We haven't had crowd reactions like this since the day Magic Johnson made his startling announcement," Hearn said.

Kemp gave the Sonics the lead on the next possession, hitting a turnaround jumper along the baseline. Then the Lakers got their first lead since the first quarter when Divac found Jones for a three-pointer at the top of the key for a 99-98 lead with seven and a half minutes to play. The two teams played tit for tat the next five minutes, with the lead changing hands seven times.

Free throws by Campbell, Ceballos and Divac put the Lakers in the driver's seat. The held a three-point lead with 4.2 seconds when the Sonics were forced to foul Lynch to stop the clock. Lynch needed to make just one free throw to secure the game, but he made the crowd sweat by missing the first. He made the second for a 114-110 lead, Schrempf missed a meaningless mid-range jumper on the buzzer, and the Lakers won.

Van Exel raised his arms in the air with one hand cupped around the ball, with the Forum crowd celebrating behind him. It was the quintessential image of the series, the return of playoff success to Los Angeles. Hearn summarised the scene best by simply saying, "Pandemonium at the Great Western Forum," before going silent to let radio listeners hear all the noise in the building

Defeating the Sonics 3-1 was the most exciting thing to happen in Laker basketball since Magic threw that rebound down court as time expired to knock off the Portland Trail Blazers and advance to the NBA Finals. Four very long years ago.

A fan at the Forum for Game 4 had a home-made sign that read *"GET Van Excelized."* And if anyone in the world had ever been 'Van Excelized', it was these Sonics. Van Exel called most of the plays down the stretch, hammering the ball inside. It resulted in eight free throw attempts down the stretch, enough to seal the win and take the series. "He engineered the game," Harris said. "It was his ballgame all night."

Van Exel played all 48 minutes for the third consecutive game, scoring a game-high 34 points with nine assists. He played with a chip on his shoulder all series, something the Lakers badly needed. "All those doubters, he's calling them out right now," Jones said. "He's letting them know, 'I'm here, I'm going to be here for a while, I'm making my point.'"

He averaged 24.8 points, 5.0 assists, 50% shooting, and 42% on threes in 45.8 minutes for the series. He committed only 8 turnovers in 183 minutes of court time, a remarkable stat for someone who had the ball in his hands so often. And he did all this against three excellent defenders in Payton, McMillan, and Askew. "I thought he did a great job, in a high-pressure situation against a very good team, of controlling the ball," Harris said. "There's a lot of good defense out there against him. It's quite an accomplishment, no question about that."

And he was well supported. Ceballos bounced back from his horrible two-point performance in Game 1 and averaged 22.0 points in the three victories. Divac's play didn't draw a whole lot of attention, but he upped his regular season numbers to 17.8 points and 8.3 rebounds on 54% shooting in the series. Peeler averaged 11.5 points and improved as the series went along, his 16 points a key part of the Game 4 victory. Campbell, who had his hands full at the defensive end against Kemp, averaged 11.3 points and 5.5 rebounds.

The Lakers were heading to the second round for the first time in the post-Magic era. It was territory they never forgot about. Though it felt at times that it had forgotten about them.

Chapter 26
FORGOTTEN TERRITORY

May 6, 1995 to May 18, 1995

T HE LAKERS' REWARD for advancing to the Semi-Finals for the first time in the post-Magic era was a match-up with the #1 seed San Antonio Spurs in the Semi-Finals. "The only thing we were hoping was that we weren't going to face San Antonio in the first round," Van Exel said before the start of the playoffs. Now they couldn't avoid them.

The Spurs were a powerhouse. They finished the season with a league-best 62 wins and won 15 straight games over March and April. They swept the Denver Nuggets 3-0 in the first round with an average winning margin of 15.3 points. They were on a nine-game win streak entering the series with the Lakers and hadn't lost a game in almost a month. "They're the best team in the league," Bowie said.

San Antonio was led by David Robinson, one of the best centers in the league in an era blessed by a plethora of dominant big men. He would be named MVP for the 1994-95 season with averages of 27.6 points, 10.8 rebounds, and 3.2 blocks. And he had an excellent cast of skilled and tough veteran players around him.

The Spurs had pulled off a major coup over the off-season, the culmination of trades tracing back to 1993-94. Back then, they gambled by trading for Dennis Rodman, sending their All-Star small forward Sean Elliot to the Detroit Pistons. Rodman was becoming a household name, but basketball wasn't always the reason. He was becoming better known for being covered in tattoos, dying his hair different colors, regularly being ejected, and showing up to a book launch wearing a wedding dress. But all the outlandishness distracted from the fact he was a truly remarkable defender and rebounder. He led the league in rebounding in 1994-95 for the fourth consecutive season, averaging 16.8 a game.

The coup for the Spurs came before the start of the 1994-95 season.

Elliot hadn't worked out in Detroit, and the Spurs managed to re-acquire him for the draft rights to Bill Curly, who was selected late in the first round of the 1994 draft. [245] It was like Elliot had never left, shrugging off his down year in Detroit by averaging a career-high 18.1 points per game for the Spurs in 1994-95. In the long-run, they had acquired Rodman, one of the all-time greatest rebounders and defenders, for almost nothing.

Rodman and Elliot solidified a frontline that already featured veteran bangers Terry Cummings and J.R. Reid. And then there was Moses Malone, who was in the twilight of his legendary career but was still a crafty back-up at the age of 39. Their backcourt was almost as strong. Veterans Chuck Person, Doc Rivers, Willie Anderson, and Vinny Del Negro were all excellent outside shooters and intelligent players. Pulling it all together was Avery Johnson, a lightning-quick point guard adept at finding seams in the defense. "I don't think they have any glaring weaknesses," said Del Harris. "They are awfully, awfully good."

Home-court advantage was even more meaningful for the Spurs than it was for the average NBA team. They played at the Alamodome, perhaps the most unique NBA arena. Constructed in 1990, it was built primarily for football but would be converted to basketball for Spurs games. Its capacity could be expanded to 35,000 – far and away the biggest in the league. It was also cavernous, lacking the familiar feeling of a traditional NBA arena. Fans were set several feet further back from the basket than usual, causing a problem with depth perception. A giant blue curtain would separate the court area from the rest of the building.

"It's just so wide and spread out," said Ceballos. "Like you're playing outside instead of in a basketball arena. There's no warmth or feel of a gym." While the Spurs were used to playing in the unique conditions, their opponents were not.

The Lakers would start the series as tired underdogs. After finishing off the Sonics in an emotional victory on Thursday in Los Angeles, the team flew to San Antonio on Friday. They landed less than 24 hours before Game 1 was due to tip-off on Saturday afternoon. It only left time for a light work-out the morning of the game. "I thought coming in we were going to play Saturday night, but they gave us a 2:30 game," Ceballos said.

---

[245] The Pistons traded Elliot to the Houston Rockets during the 1993-94 season in exchange for Robert Horry, but the trade was called off when Elliot failed the Rockets' team physical when they uncovered an injury to his kidney.

"It's a tough situation." Meanwhile, the Spurs had spent the last five days at home after finishing their series against Denver on Tuesday.

With little time to prepare and little gas left in the tank, the Lakers frontline was easy prey for Robinson. He registered 33 points and 11 rebounds on 14-23 shooting in Game 1. The Lakers seemed powerless to stop Robinson or the penetration of Johnson, who sliced through the Lakers' defense for 19 points and 12 assists. The Spurs shot 54% and ran out winners 110-94, taking a 1-0 series lead.

But the game was much closer than the score would indicate. If somebody tuned into post-game interviews without having watched the game, they would have been forgiven for thinking the Lakers had won. That was because the Spurs built their win on two short scoring bursts, one in the second quarter and the other late in the game. "The rest of the 40 minutes of the ballgame, we're even," Harris said. Spurs coach Bob Hill lamented his team's frequent defensive lapses and patchy focus. "We did win, but it wasn't the way we wanted to win," he said.

There was a lot for the Lakers to feel good about. They out-rebounded the Spurs 47-40 and committed only 10 turnovers. Their 22 offensive rebounds and a fast-paced attack created 92 shot attempts, 18 more than they averaged in the Seattle series. And their front-line played exceptionally well against San Antonio's physical front-line. Divac had 25 points and 11 rebounds, and Campbell scored a career playoff-high 29 points, mostly against the tough defense of Rodman. "Elden was a monster out there, Vlade was terrific," Harris said. "They worked together well in there."

But Cedric Ceballos, Anthony Peeler, and Eddie Jones all struggled. For the second time in just over a week, the Lakers leading scorer made almost no impact on a playoff game. After scoring two points in Game 1 against Seattle, Ceballos managed just seven points on 3-10 shooting in Game 1 against San Antonio. And three of those points came on a meaningless three-pointer with 39 seconds to play. Harris publicly supported his All-Star forward, saying, "Cedric had wonderful last three games of the Seattle series and just got off to a slow start in that first half." But his actions told a different story as he played Ceballos just 13 minutes in the second half.

Harris focused training the next day on switching up his approach to Robinson. He basically threw every big man he had at the Spurs center and double-teamed him as often as possible in Game 1. But Robinson shrugged it all off and dominated anyway. Harris instead prepared to play Robinson with single coverage for the next game. Campbell and Bowie would be asked to match-up against him from time to time, but mostly the task would fall to Divac. Instead of double-teams, Harris would require Divac to push Robinson out of the post, so he was catching the ball further from the basket. But it would still be a team effort. The guards were tasked with increasing their pressure on the player making the entry pass to Robinson, and not allowing quick, easy passes. A few seconds' delay would give Divac a fighting chance to force Robinson out of his favorite positions.[246]

Game 2 proved to be a ragged, sloppy affair that bordered on unwatchable. But the strategy against Robinson worked. Against single coverage from mostly Divac or Campbell, Robinson struggled to 6-26 shooting.

After trailing by nine at half-time, the Lakers held the Spurs to 34 second-half points and got back in the game with a 25-15 run. They led 83-81 with 26 seconds to play until Rodman tied the score with an unlikely basket. The Lakers milked the clock on their next possession before Divac rolled into the lane for a potential go-ahead basket. Rodman prevented the basket by committing his sixth and final foul, sending Divac to the free throw line with 4.6 seconds remaining.

The Lakers only needed Divac, a 78% free throw shooter, to make one of his two free throws to give them the lead. After that, one strong defensive stand would see them return home with the series tied 1-1. "I was completely sure, 100%, that I was going to make both," Divac said. His first attempt hit the front of the rim, drawing cheers of relief from the crowd. With both benches and 26,127 fans standing in anticipation, Divac took a deep breath, exhaled, then released the ball for his second attempt. It went long. "They gave us back the game," Johnson said.

Elliot grabbed the rebound, and the Spurs called a timeout. They didn't get a good look at the potential game-winning basket, with Robinson air-balling a jumper at the buzzer. The game was going into

---

[246] George Lynch didn't train after suffering a mild concussion when he was inadvertently hit across the face by Robinson in Game 1. But in the days before concussion protocols, he would be back in uniform for Game 2 two nights later.

overtime.

Both teams continued to struggle offensively in the extra period, and the Lakers had a chance to tie the game with two and a half minutes remaining. Divac was trying to inbound the ball from the baseline when he spotted Lynch, who had made several critical shots in the fourth quarter, open near the free throw line. Divac lobbed a pass to Lynch, but he threw it too far, and it sailed over his head. Elliot picked it up, Robinson scored on the next possession, and that kick-started a 7-0 run that gave the Spurs a 97-90 win.

The Lakers had been inches away from tying the series but instead returned home trailing 2-0. The players tried to rally around Divac, but he was inconsolable after the game. "It hurts a lot. I had the game in my hands," said Divac. "I missed the most important free throws of my life. I had it in my hands."

For the young players, it was the most devastating loss of their basketball careers. "The young guys, they were hurt. This loss affected them," Bowie said. "This game beat 'em up."

Divac took responsibility for the loss, but it was hardly all his fault. His defense on Robinson was one of the main reasons the Lakers even had a chance to win the game. And Ceballos continued to struggle. Against Seattle, he bounced back after a bad opening game, but not so after his subpar first game against San Antonio. In fact, he was worse and scored just two points on 1-5 shooting in 27 minutes in Game 2. Having led the Lakers in scoring with 21.7 points per game during the season, he was averaging just 4.5 points on 27% shooting in the two games in San Antonio. Jones bounced back from a poor Game 1 by scoring 20 points in Game 2. But it wasn't enough to fill the void left by Ceballos. For the second straight game, Harris was forced to sit his leading scorer in crunch time – instead playing Lynch for the entire fourth quarter and over-time.

Campbell was excellent for the second consecutive game. He backed up his great performance two nights earlier with 25 points and 18 rebounds. But his performance was nullified by a uniquely brilliant offensive performance from Rodman. Not known as a scorer, Rodman had a team-high 22 points on 10-13 shooting to go along with his 22 rebounds. It was the most he had scored in a game since January 1991. The stars aligning for Rodman offensively was incredibly fortuitous timing for the Spurs, and remarkably unfortunate for the Lakers.

* * * * *

The team flew back to Los Angeles after the game and Divac arrived home after midnight in what was going to be a long night. He tried to sleep but couldn't stop ruminating about those missed free throws. He got out of bed and watched television, finally getting off to sleep at about 5:30am. With three days until the next game, Harris gave the team the day off after the disappointing loss. But it didn't help Divac, who spent the day busying himself at home in the hope of putting the free throws out of his mind. But he couldn't. "I tried to forget, but you can't," Divac said. "Every time I go into bed, I'm just reminded, and my stomach goes. I can't help myself."

The narrative for Game 3 was not about how the Lakers intended to defend Robinson or get Rodman off the boards. Instead, it was about how the team would mentally and emotionally respond to having victory slip through their fingers in Game 2. "There are two ways you can react, strong or weak," Peeler said. "We had our heads down when we lost. There were a lot of guys crying in the locker room, and we've never seen guys take a loss like that before. We know it's going to be a tough game for us, but we have got to be in it emotionally like we were in Game 2."

Harris knew the ghost of the game would hang around the Alamodome for years, that the players would think about the loss every time they played there. He just hoped the ghost hadn't followed them to L.A.

The Forum crowd was as raucous for Game 3 as it had been during the Seattle series. Rivers hadn't seen the Forum rocking like that since Magic Johnson retired and he thought it was maybe louder than during Showtime. "I think it's better because the real basketball fans got to sneak in and get tickets," he said. "All the fickle fans gave up theirs."

The Lakers got off to a perfect start when Campbell was double-teamed on the first possession of the game and found Peeler open for a mid-range jumper. But the first six minutes were sloppy, with both teams turning the ball over regularly. Ceballos worked hard, and the crowd was almost willing him to have a good game. But he was overanxious, fumbling the ball and missing his first few shots. The Lakers would settle though, while the Spurs never really would.

Van Exel hit a pull-up a three-pointer to give the Lakers an 8-4 lead with seven and a half minutes left in the first quarter. A minute later, he pushed the ball up court in transition and found Ceballos wide open in the corner behind the three-point line. He had all the time in the world to settle his shot. He launched the three-pointer and sunk it, the crowd cheering with equal parts joy and relief.

A few minutes later, Ceballos raced up court and found Jones for an easy mid-range jumper, pushing the lead out to 13-8. The Lakers stopped the Spurs on the next possession and Jones, with a rush of blood to the head from the loud cheers he received on his last basket, airballed a three-pointer. Ceballos swooped in from nowhere to collect the ball and no sooner had he caught it than it was off the glass for the easy lay-in.

Robinson missed a short jumper on the other end, and Divac outhustled Rodman for the rebound. He flung a pass to Van Exel who powered the ball up court before hitting a beautiful left-handed scoop shot in the lane. Hill called timeout with the Lakers leading 17-8 and the Forum crowd roaring their appreciation.

The rest of the quarter played out much the same, the Lakers interrupting the Spurs' usual crisp ball movement, forcing turnovers and turning them into easy baskets down the other end. Van Exel hit a long pull-up two-pointer with 30.5 seconds to play in the quarter that gave them a 25-11 lead. Chuck Person missed a three down the other end, and Divac collected the rebound with six seconds to play. He passed to Van Exel, who charged up the court and made a long shot from several feet behind the three-point line at the buzzer. "He pulled up nearly at half-court, shot it and made it," Willie Anderson said. "He was feeling it. The way he was shooting the ball, nobody in the league could stop him." The Lakers led 28-11 at quarter time and again looked like the team who had just stunned the Sonics.

The Lakers kept pushing in the second quarter, and the lead got out to 47-29 when Ceballos hit a three-pointer with less than three minutes remaining in the half. But Rivers led a mini-run by hitting on three consecutive jumpers, including a pair of three-point baskets that got the Spurs to within eight points. Van Exel made a runner in the lane with 2.8 seconds remaining to give the Lakers a 53-43 lead at half-time.

The Spurs kept the pressure on the Lakers throughout the third quarter, getting the lead down to six. But Van Exel took control of the game again. He hit a jumper with the shot clock running down, followed by a three-pointer. He then made a baseline floater over Robinson to push the lead back out to 10.

The Lakers grew the lead to 92-72 with three and a half minutes left in the fourth quarter before taking their foot off the accelerator. The Spurs got closer than they probably should have, but the game was never in doubt during the final minutes. The Lakers won 92-85 and cut the series deficit to 2-1.

Van Exel had his fingerprints all over the game, reminiscent of how he played in the two home games against Seattle. He finished with 25 points on 9-18 shooting and eight assists. Divac bounced back with a solid game with 14 points and 13 rebounds. But the most welcome sight was the return of a far more aggressive Ceballos, who had 15 points at half-time en route to 22 points and 10 rebounds. "It was obvious he'd lost confidence," Divac said. "We were happy to see him shooting like his old self again, like that #23 in Chicago. #45, #23 – whatever his number is now."

Robinson proved single coverage against him wasn't going to work two games in a row, scoring a game-high 34 points with 13 rebounds. But the rest of the Spurs were held to an unsightly 31% shooting.

Chick Hearn was stricken with laryngitis the day of the game, but he insisted on commentating. His voice was so weak by the second quarter he was almost impossible to understand. Bob Steiner, Jerry Buss' longtime public relations adviser, was given the thankless task of telling Chick he couldn't broadcast the second half of the game. Colour commentator Stu Lanz handled play-by-play for the second half and Magic agreed to step in and do the color commentary.[247]

The Lakers avoided an insurmountable 3-0 hole, but the next game would be no less critical. "If we win Game 4, they're in a lot of trouble," Robinson said. They would have to prepare without Van Exel though, who couldn't practice because of back spasms. He had been bothered by tightness in his back all series, and it had only gotten worse. It was a consequence of the heavy minutes Harris had been playing him. After playing all 48 minutes in the final three games against Seattle, he was averaging 46.3 against San Antonio. His back would only recover with rest, which was the one thing Harris couldn't afford to give him.

The Spurs had issues of their own. Rodman played 29 minutes in Game 3, grabbing 12 rebounds. But he got in a shouting match with Coach

---

[247] Chick was livid at Steiner for days after being told he couldn't commentate the second half. He would later say Steiner did the right thing by telling him to go home. It was Chick's 2,781 consecutive broadcast and the streak stayed alive because he had, technically, broadcast the game.

Hill when he was yanked in the second half. He refused to participate in a timeout shortly after, instead taking off his shoes, wrapping a towel around his head, and laying down beside the bench. Following the timeout, he was heard to shout at Hill, "Don't try and put me back in," to which Hill responded he needn't worry about that.

Jack Haley (former Laker, current Spurs benchwarmer, and Rodman confidant) phoned Hill the next day to smooth things over. But Rodman's ranting to the press undid any good Haley had done. "They pay me good money to be a player, they don't pay me great money to be a goodie-two-shoes," he said. "You could buy a robot and program everything the team wanted into his brain, and what's screwed up is they still wouldn't be happy."

It was the kind of distraction the Spurs didn't need in their quest to win a championship. "I wouldn't go so far as to say 'mad,' but we were disappointed in Dennis," Robinson said. "You've got a coach. You've got to pay attention to that coach. You can't be laying on your back, getting a suntan out there."

Hearn was back for Game 4, commentating in full voice. Rodman was back in uniform too, though he never got off the bench. Hill elected to start Cummings in his place and give the remainder of his minutes to Reid. Instead of playing, Rodman entertained himself. He tried to get Jack Nicholson's attention, but he was too focused on the game to notice. He befriended a 12-year-old sitting next to the Spurs bench and chatted to him throughout the game. "He was rooting for us," Rodman said.

In the end, Hill didn't need Rodman because the Lakers were historically bad in Game 4. They shot 36%, committed 18 turnovers, and set a new post-season franchise low by making only 27 shots. They tied the lowest point total by a Laker team in a playoff game for the second time in the one post-season. "We just could not drop it in that hole," Ceballos said.

It was clear from the opening play this wasn't going to be the Lakers' night when Divac missed a dunk. But the Spurs were not exactly shooting lights out themselves, and the game remained close. The Lakers, who shot just 28% in the first half, trailed by only seven at half-time and got within 50-49 midway through the third quarter. But then the wheels fell off. They turned the ball over on four consecutive possessions. When they finally did get a shot off, it was blocked by Robinson and converted down the other end. They'd end up scoring just 12 points on 5-20 shooting for the quarter.

The Spurs won 80-71, the lowest total scoring NBA playoff game since 1945.[248] It was a game of ineptitude, showcasing a combined 38% field goal shooting, 18% three-point shooting, 64% free throw shooting, and 34 turnovers. The unsightly win took the Spurs to a commanding 3-1 series lead, putting the Lakers officially on the brink of elimination. "I'm sure some of their guys are saying it's over," Anderson said

Van Exel played 42 minutes, but his back pain was starting to have a real impact on his game. He finished with just 8 points on 4-16 shooting. Ceballos' return to form in Game 3 proved to be an aberration as he reverted to his passive ways in Game 4, scoring 7 points on 3-11 shooting in 27 minutes.

To stay alive, the Lakers would need to beat the Spurs in Game 5 at the Alamodome, where they had never won a game. And if they were going to break the curse, they would have to do it in front of 35,888 screaming Spurs fans ready to watch their team advance to the Conference Finals for the first time since 1983.

The media continued focusing on the Rodman controversy, speculating whether he would be back in the line-up for the next game. "I want him back," Robinson said. "But with the right frame of mind." But none of the Spurs truly believed they couldn't beat the Lakers without him. In fact, both Elliot and Anderson all but guaranteed a victory. "I'm pretty sure we are going to run away with it," Anderson said. "The Lakers had their day of fame [in Game 3]. Now it's back to reality," Elliot said.

The offense that had eluded both teams in Game 4 re-appeared in the first half of Game 5 and the Lakers took a 55-49 lead into half-time. But it became a grind again in the second half, and the Lakers offense almost completely died. They led 80-71 early in the fourth quarter until going ten minutes without scoring a single field goal. Five straight points by Elliot gave the Spurs an 88-84 lead with one and a half minutes to play, and the Alamodome was celebrating like the Spurs were about to advance.

Van Exel made one of two free throws with 38 seconds left to trim the

---

[248] The 151 combined points by the Lakers and Spurs was the lowest scoring game since the Ft. Wayne Pistons defeated the Syracuse Nationals 74-71 for a combined 145 points on April 7, 1945. This mark would be eclipsed when league offense temporarily died in the 2000s.

deficit to 88-85. Rivers was left wide-open on a three-pointer with 17 seconds remaining, but he missed it badly. Ceballos got the rebound, waived off a request from Harris for a timeout, and charged up the court. He handed off to Van Exel who immediately launched a long three-pointer over Johnson that went in, ending the Lakers' field goal drought and tying the game 88-88 with 10.2 seconds to play. Van Exel was just 4-17 from the field before the basket, his unshakeable confidence in his own shot being another boost at a crucial time for the Lakers. Johnson's potential game-winner barely grazed the front of the rim, and for the second straight game in San Antonio, the teams were going to overtime.

The Spurs broke out to a 96-90 lead with two and a half minutes to play in extra time. But just like the Lakers had done in the fourth quarter, the Spurs went on an ill-timed scoring drought. The Lakers rallied, but made it hard on themselves by missing three of six free throws.[249] A lay-up by Van Exel got the Lakers within 96-95 with a little over a minute remaining. Neither team scored on their next possessions, and when Robinson missed a jumper over Divac, Ceballos got the rebound, and the Lakers called timeout with 18.5 seconds remaining.

Whatever play Harris drew up in the huddle quickly turned into chaos. Van Exel backed Johnson down past the three-point line before Campbell flashed to the post. Campbell received the ball and made a beautiful drop-step, up-and-under move around Robinson. He got a good look at a finger-roll that went in, rolled around the rim and dropped out with 6.7 seconds remaining.

Ceballos tipped the ball back-up before Robinson tapped it out of the key and straight to Johnson. But Divac somehow got a hand on it before it reached him. He secured the ball at the three-point line with 4.1 seconds left and Harris tried desperately to call a timeout. But nobody heard him. Divac found Van Exel with a pass, who gave Johnson a head-fake, stepped around him and launched a high-arching, running three-pointer that hit nothing but net with 0.05 seconds remaining, giving the Lakers a 98-96 lead. The Alamodome crowd, deafening throughout the entire overtime period, fell silent. "I think I put 'em to sleep," Van Exel said.

The Spurs called a timeout, and Elliot got a decent look at a three-pointer on the next possession but with so little time left he had to rush the shot, and it hit the front of the rim. The Lakers had survived.

---

[249] Divac went 1-2, then 1-2 again, then Ceballos went 1-2.

The Lakers also got a much-needed boost from Ceballos, who bounced back from a poor Game 4 with 20 points and 8 rebounds in Game 5. But this was a quintessential Van Exel game. He didn't shoot well on the night, going just 7-22 from the field for 22 points, but he never gave up fighting. In the process he made two clutch three-pointers from almost the exact same spot on the floor, one to send the game into overtime and the other to win the game. "Luckiest man on the earth," Bowie said. "It's just in his nature, it's in the stars. Some people are born with that. Regardless of the game, he always beats the odds. Shooting pool, playing cards, shooting dice – doesn't matter."

Having forged a win out of nothing, the Lakers earned the right for another elimination game in Los Angeles. After playing off the bench in Game 5, Rodman was back in the starting line-up in Game 6. He immediately had an impact, scoring six points and grabbing seven rebounds in the first quarter. The Spurs pushed out to a 30-20 lead early in the second quarter but went on another scoring drought. The Lakers got back in it and trailed 47-44 at half-time.

Ceballos came out hot in the second half, hitting consecutive three-pointers early in the third quarter. The Lakers got their first lead of the game at 62-61 but could only hold it for just over a minute. Then the Spurs went on a 16-4 run to end the third quarter for a 79-68 lead heading into the fourth.

It set up another Laker rally, this one led by Jones and Lynch. Jones swished a long three-pointer to cut the Spurs lead to 84-82 with seven minutes to play, forcing the Spurs into a timeout and the Forum crowd into a long standing ovation. Rodman and Hill got into their nightly shouting match during the timeout, but this time Hill kept him in the game. Rodman came out of the timeout and drained a rare jump shot, sparking an 8-2 Spurs run that proved to be a backbreaker. From that point on, the Spurs simply wore the Lakers down.

Everybody for San Antonio did what they were supposed to do. Robinson dominated with 31 points and 15 rebounds. Elliot made four three-pointers and scored 26 points. Johnson had a tidy 13 points and 11 assists. Rodman scored 12 points, hauled down 16 rebounds, and played tough defense against Campbell down the stretch. It all added up to a 100-

88 victory as the Spurs finally eliminated the pesky Lakers.[250]

"A bad feeling," Divac said of the Game 6 loss. "But I think we had a great season. We showed everybody how good we could be. We showed this can be a championship team."

It was a disappointing series for Ceballos, who saw his regular season averages of 21.7 points, 8.0 rebounds, and 51% shooting fall to 12.3 points, 6.3 rebounds, and 38% shooting against the Spurs. But it was quietly a break-out series for Campbell, long an enigma since entering the league five years ago. Against the tough defensive duo of Robinson and Rodman, he averaged 18.7 points and 8.5 rebounds in the series.

Van Exel played 47 minutes in Game 6 but struggled with his shot for the third straight game. His back spasms continued to be a problem as the grind of heavy minutes took its toll. He scored 13 points, had 11 assists, but shot just 2-13 from the field. But regardless of how it ended, the 1995 playoffs were an outstanding moment for him. For the playoffs, he averaged 20.0 points and 7.3 assists in 46.4 minutes per game. He played in 464 out of a possible 495 minutes in 10 playoff games, committing just 22 turnovers. With his brash competitiveness and clutch shooting, he had stepped forward as the new leader of this young Laker team.

It was the end of a remarkable season. Nobody was paying attention to these Lakers when training camp opened seven months earlier. But after eliminating the 57-win Seattle SuperSonics and pushing the league-leading, 62-win Spurs to six games as the youngest team in the playoffs, people were paying attention again. And not just in Los Angeles.

---

[250] After eliminating the Lakers, San Antonio lost the Conference Finals in six games to the eventual NBA champion Houston Rockets.

PART V:
THE GAP BETWEEN THE AGES

Chapter 27
ACT II

May 19, 1995 to November 2, 1995

F OR THE FIRST time since Magic Johnson retired, the Lakers entered an off-season with the ease only a contented team can have. There would be none of the standard questions fans had been accustomed to asking this time of year. They wouldn't be looking for Magic to come out of retirement to save them, or wondering who would be coaching the team. They wouldn't be wondering if Jerry West would be able to retain the veteran free agents or draft a young savior. The fact they had no cap space and no draft picks hardly seemed to matter since the young core and reigning Coach of the Year were all safely under contract. [251]

There was the sense the franchise was moving in the right direction for the first time in years. There was now something here to be excited about and build upon. West had been named Executive of the Year for the 1994-95 season by making all the right moves to reverse the fortunes of the franchise. He would not be overhauling the roster, searching for answers. Instead, he would only look to make some tweaks here and there. Fans wanted Act II of the Lake Show, and ultimately that is what they would get.

West did make a minor move the day before the 1995 NBA Draft,

---

[251] The Lakers' first-round pick belonged to Phoenix as part of the Ceballos trade. It ended up being the 21st pick and the Suns used it to select Michael Finley out of the University of Wisconsin. The Lakers' second-round pick had been sent to Seattle as part of the Threatt trade, but Seattle had traded it to Golden State in 1994. The Warriors used it to select Martin Lewis who played 25 games with Toronto over two seasons.

acquiring the Washington Bullets' 37th pick in exchange for two second-round picks in 1997. West used the selection on Frankie King, a 6'1 combo guard from West Carolina. King was a virtual unknown, having been scouted only in a post-season all-star tournament in Portsmouth, Virginia prior to the draft. He only worked out with Miami and Portland and was as shocked as anyone when he was drafted. "I thought my chances were next to nothing," he said. "It's always been a dream of mine to be drafted. I was very excited." West had wanted to bring King in for a work-out but didn't want to make it obvious to rival teams he was interested in selecting him. Del Harris, like most people, hadn't heard of King either. But he knew West was excited to have him, which was good enough for the coach.[252]

One thing West liked about King was that he reminded him of Sedale Threatt. Which was handy, because the Lakers knew they might lose the veteran guard in the 1995 Expansion Draft. The Toronto Raptors and Vancouver Grizzlies were entering the NBA in the upcoming season and would select from players on existing contracts with other NBA teams. Each team could protect up to eight players from the draft and West chose to leave Threatt unprotected.

Threatt was a critical part of Harris' rotation, never more obvious than when his injury forced Nick Van Exel to play so many minutes in the playoffs that he physically broke down. But West didn't want to risk losing younger players like George Lynch or Anthony Miller. He was playing the odds that a player like Threatt was more valuable to the Lakers than he was to either the Raptors or the Grizzlies. He hoped an expansion team wouldn't be interested in a 34-year-old veteran due to make $2.4 million in 1995-96. The gamble paid off, with Threatt going unselected in the draft and remaining a Laker. But they did lose Antonio Harvey, who was selected by the Vancouver Grizzlies with the sixth pick.[253]

---

[252] The two 1997 picks the Lakers traded for King were their own as well as the pick they received from New York in exchange for Doug Christie.

[253] Two former Lakers were also selected in the Expansion Draft. Vancouver selected Byron Scott with the 18th pick and Benoit Benjamin with the 22nd pick. Harvey had a long career playing with the Grizzlies, Clippers, Sonics, Trail Blazers and Hawks as well as in Greece, Poland and Spain.

Following the draft, West acquired 26-year-old forward/center Corie Blount from the Chicago Bulls in exchange for 'future considerations.'[254] Blount had been a teammate of Van Exel at the University of Cincinnati before being drafted by Chicago late in the first round in 1993. He averaged 11.7 minutes in his first two seasons in Chicago, never becoming more than a third-stringer. Frustrated with his limited playing time and dejected by the Bulls selecting Jason Caffey, another forward, in the draft, he requested a trade. With Sam Bowie expected to retire and Harvey now in Vancouver, Blount had a real shot at being the Lakers' primary back-up center.

The Lakers acquired Blount on 30 June 1995, and it would be among the last moves any NBA team would make for several months. The Collective Bargaining Agreement (CBA) had expired a year earlier, but the league and players reached a 'no-strike, no-lockout' agreement that protected the 1994-95 season. The agreement expired in June 1995 while negotiations on a new CBA were still ongoing. Consequently, the NBA entered a lock-out on July 1, the first work stoppage in league history. The lockout put a close to all NBA business. No trades, no free agent signings.

In the quiet of the lockout, the only newsworthy happening around the Lakers was Elden Campbell's arrest on drunk-driving charges in Simi Valley in July. Campbell was speeding in the fast lane on California 118 in the early hours of the morning when his car veered to the far right and hit an asphalt beam. He tried to correct the car, but it swung back to the left and flipped. Campbell suffered minor injuries, was assessed on the scene as having a 0.12% blood-alcohol level, and was booked at Ventura County Jail after being treated at an area hospital. He didn't appear at his hearing, instead entering a not-guilty plea through his lawyer. Ultimately, he would be found guilty in late August and sentenced to a $1,850 fine and four days in prison, which he served at Seal Beach City Jail.[255]

Mercifully, the lockout ended without any games being affected. The

---

[254] It appears those 'future considerations' turned out to be nothing. Basketball Reference lists the transaction as Blount being 'sold' to the Lakers.

[255] Campbell was given twice the jail term a first-time drunk driver usually receives. This was at the urging of Ventura County prosecutors, who argued for a harsher sentence because Campbell refused a blood test at the scene of the accident and didn't show up to his hearing.

league and players reached agreement on a new CBA on September 12. It ushered in a suite of new salary cap features, such as the rookie scale cap, that have continued to this day.[256] The agreement saw the salary cap rise from $15.9 to $23 million, though this was of little help to the Lakers. They still owed $5.1 million to retired James Worthy, $4.8 million to the soon-to-be-retired Sam Bowie, and were well over the new cap.

Where the CBA did hurt the Lakers was the removal of the 'salary slot' that allowed teams over the salary cap to replace an out-going player up to half the amount they had earned the previous season. The salary slot was replaced by a $1 million exception that every team was able to use three times over the six-year life of the agreement. This hurt the Lakers because West had planned to chase free-agent forward Anthony Mason with the $2.4 million salary slot they expected to have once Bowie retired. That $2.4 salary slot was now slashed to $1 million – not enough to chase an impact player of the caliber of Mason.

Instead, the Lakers signed 35-year-old back-up power forward Fred Roberts. He had played under Harris in Milwaukee and always got along well with the coach. Roberts had spent the 1993-94 season with FC Barcelona in Spain. He signed with the Cleveland Cavaliers in February 1995 when their starting power forward, Tyrone Hill, was recovering from a fractured right hand. He made Cleveland's playoff roster before being let go at the end of the season.

West also let two free agents walk without offering them a contract. Randolph Keys, who signed two ten-day contracts during the 1994-95 season and then signed for the remainder of the season despite a strained abdominal muscle, was let go. So too was Tony Smith, ending his five-year run with the Lakers after originally being selected in the second round. Smith had struggled to find a spot in the rotation in 1994-95, ultimately becoming a victim of the crowded backcourt.[257]

As expected, Bowie announced his retirement, ending an 11-year NBA career to settle into an idyllic-sounding post-basketball life raising horses in Lexington, Kentucky. Bowie may have been remembered for his long

---

[256] This ended the ability of rookies to stage contract holdouts like Doug Christie, Jimmy Jackson, and Glenn Robinson had infamously done.

[257] Keys spent the 1995-96 season with the Milwaukee Bucks and retired in 1999 after playing three years in Greece and Italy. Smith spent the next three seasons playing in Phoenix, Miami, Charlotte, and Milwaukee. He retired from basketball in 2002 after playing in the ABA, CBA, Italy, and Spain. He currently works as an analyst and studio host for broadcasts of Milwaukee Bucks games on Fox Sports Wisconsin.

run of injuries and for being drafted ahead of Michael Jordan, but with his retirement, the Lakers lost a defensive presence in the paint and a wise, veteran player.

Nothing had been certain when the Lakers opened camp a year earlier. Not the offensive or defensive systems, the starting line-up or the bench rotation. But when they opened training camp on October 6, 1995, the biggest question for Harris was whether Blount or Miller would receive most of the back-up center minutes. Hardly the same kind of drama.

Instead of major changes, the coaching staff wanted continuity, and to build on what worked the previous season. "We have nine players back from last year, and we've all gone through about 100 games together. That kind of experience is a real plus for all of us," Harris said. "That gives us something to build on for this year instead of starting with a blank page. That means training camp should be more productive."

The backcourt still consisted of Nick Van Exel and Sedale Threatt at point guard, and Eddie Jones and Anthony Peeler at shooting guard. The frontcourt included Cedric Ceballos and George Lynch at small forward, Campbell and Roberts at power forward, and Vlade Divac, Blount, and Miller at center.

That left three players fighting for the 12th and final roster spot. The odds-on favorite was the Lakers' second-round draft choice, Frankie King. But he would have to fight off two undrafted rookies – Kareem Townes, a 6'1 guard from La Salle, and Gerald King, a 6'9 forward from Nicholls State University.

The legacy of the injury bug from a season earlier was still being felt, with Lynch unable to take part in camp. After missing 23 games in 1994-95 with a stress fracture in his right foot, he came back for the playoffs before the injury fully healed. His foot hadn't responded to an off-season of rest, and he underwent surgery in the week leading up to training camp. To even out the numbers, the Lakers yet again signed 37-year-old special assistant coach Kurt Rambis to his third playing stint in two years with the team.[258]

During a scrimmage on the third day of camp, Jones badly injured his thumb when he reached in on defense and got it caught in a jersey. It was a bad luck injury that would be costly. He flew back to Los Angeles to

---

[258] At this point, Rambis must have felt like he would never be allowed to retire.

have his thumb examined, where it was determined he tore a ligament. He would be out of action for more than six weeks and miss the remainder of camp, the entire pre-season, and the first three weeks of the regular season. "At least three of the weeks, we don't have games," Harris said, "but that doesn't help him. He needed to get his confidence back after missing those games last season."

The Lakers opened their pre-season campaign in the traditional setting of the Blaisdell Arena in Honolulu with two games in two nights against the Seattle SuperSonics. The rivalry picked up where it left off in the playoffs five months earlier. The more than 6,000 fans in attendance both nights were treated to a pair of exhibition games that felt more like playoff games.

No more than two points separated the two teams in the final six minutes of the first game. Blount blocked a dunk attempt by Shawn Kemp with 31.2 seconds to play to preserve a 101-101 tie before Van Exel scored on a driving lay-up with two seconds remaining to give the Lakers a 103-101 victory. "It was a typical Lakers-SuperSonics game," Harris said. "Hard-fought, well played and down to the wire."

Fans were treated to another nail-biter the following afternoon, with both teams tied at 103-103 in the dying seconds. Van Exel tried to repeat his heroics from the previous night, but his shot from the left side rimmed the basket before falling out. Hersey Hawkins grabbed the rebound and passed off to Gary Payton, who fired the ball down court to Vincent Askew for a buzzer-beating lay-in and a 105-103 Sonics win. "We have a very strong rivalry going," Payton said. "Both teams have excellent players, and we play very well against each other."

Ceballos continued his hot start to the pre-season against Charlotte at the Thomas & Mack Center in Las Vegas. After scoring 27 points in each of the first two games, he scored a game-high 24 as the Lakers beat the Hornets 101-94.

The Lakers won the first game of the annual GTE Everything Pages Shoot-out at the Forum, beating Minnesota by seven, but lost the second 110-109 to Portland when Clifford Robinson made two late free throws. Ceballos again paced the Lakers in both games, scoring 32 against the Timberwolves and 29 against the Blazers.

Three members of the referees' union – Ed Middleton, Bill Spooner, and Greg Willard – picketed one of the entrances to the Forum parking lot before the Portland game. The lock-out was not the only off-court drama that off-season. NBA officials went on strike following a pay dispute with the league and would be replaced by officials from the CBA until a deal could be brokered. It wouldn't happen until midway through the season, and the obviously inferior skills of the replacement officials would cause serious disruption to the quality of play to start the season.

The Lakers lost to Cleveland four nights later on a bank shot by Bob Sura at the buzzer. Lynch, who began light workouts five days earlier, made his first appearance of the season, scoring two points and grabbing three rebounds in eight minutes. But as soon as they got one player back from injury, they lost another. Peeler strained his left shoulder against Cleveland and would sit out the final two games of the pre-season and the first two games of the regular season. The Lakers would have to start the season without either of their two shooting guards.

In a sign Harris and West were not fully satisfied with the play of either Blount or Miller, they reinforced the frontcourt by signing 27-year-old free agent power forward Derek Strong. A former second-round pick of the Philadelphia 76ers out of Xavier University, Strong spent his first three seasons in Milwaukee and Washington. He spent 1994-95 with the Boston Celtics, where he averaged 6.3 points and 5.4 rebounds in 19.2 minutes, mostly off the bench.

Strong was in uniform the following night when the Lakers took on the defending NBA champion Houston Rockets in New Orleans. He scored two points off the bench, but the Lakers were never really in the game, eventually losing 115-103. The loss was worse considering the Rockets were playing without Hakeem Olajuwon and Sam Cassell.

They wound up their pre-season schedule the following night in Dallas against the Mavericks. Van Exel and Divac each had niggling injuries and joined Peeler and Jones on the sidelines. It forced Harris to experiment with Ceballos at shooting guard, starting him in the backcourt along with Threatt and a front-line of Lynch, Blount, and Campbell. The Lakers blew a 23-point lead, Jason Kidd made consecutive baskets in the final minute, and the Lakers lost 102-97.

Ceballos proved to be in excellent form to start the new season, averaging 24.1 points in eight pre-season games. But the loss to the Mavs was their fourth in a row, and they ended the pre-season with a 3-5 record, the first time they finished an exhibition season with a losing record since

1983.

The Lakers trimmed their roster to 13 by making three moves that had been expected since training camp. They waived rookie free agents Townes and Gerard King, who were always considered long-shots.[259] They also waived veteran Kurt Rambis, finally permitting the forward to retire for good.[260] Jones was placed on the injured list to start the season, bringing the roster down to 12 for opening night.

And with that, the Lakers were ready to begin Act II of the Lake Show. Unlike last season, there would be no sneaking up on teams, no more taking the league by surprise. "We had a pretty good year last year," Peeler said. "Everybody's expecting more from us now." It was almost assumed the young Lakers were ready to take the next step forward. The *Los Angeles Times* suggested the team might be good enough to make the Conference Finals. After all, they made the Semi-Finals in 1995 and were expected to be even better this season. But it quickly became evident that nothing was going to be that easy.

---

[259] Townes never played in the NBA. He spent three seasons in Italy and Greece before spending almost nine years in prison for selling crack cocaine to an undercover police officer in Philadelphia. King spent the next three seasons playing in the CBA, ABA, and Italy before signing with the San Antonio Spurs. He won a championship with the Spurs in 1999 before playing the next two seasons with the Washington Wizards.

[260] Rambis wouldn't be called up as an emergency fill-in again. He played a total of nine minutes in four pre-season games, failing to score and only attempting one shot. His final game in a Laker uniform was on October 27, 1995 against Houston in New Orleans. He would go on to have a long career as NBA head coach and assistant. He served as an assistant coach with the Lakers from 1996-2009, becoming interim head coach for 37 games in 1999. He coached the Minnesota Timberwolves for two years and was an assistant in New York.

Chapter 28
TALKING THE TALK

November 3, 1995 to January 2, 1996

A LL THE OFF-SEASON talk about the Lakers building on their success from the previous season quickly turned out to be exactly that – just talk. Very little of it translated to the court in the first two months of the season. By the time the calendar clicked over to the new year, the Lakers were just another middle-of-the-road team struggling for playoff contention.

The schedule didn't do them any favors. They arguably had the toughest schedule in the league over November and December 1995.[261] They would play 31 games in the first two months of the season – the most they had played in the first eight weeks since 1981. Seventeen of those games would be on the road, including a six-game road trip that featured three sets of back-to-back games.

Nick Van Exel suddenly entering an epic shooting slump didn't help, nor that Divac appeared to have regressed after 18 months of steady progress. The Lakers would seem incapable of holding a lead or playing well down the stretch of close games. In the process, the players blamed everyone and everything but themselves, revealing a startling lack of leadership.

The Lakers opened their 1995-96 campaign at the Forum against the Denver Nuggets, only the sixth time in the previous 36 years they started a season at home. With both shooting guards out injured, Del Harris was forced to go with a starting line-up of Van Exel and four frontcourt players, with Cedric Ceballos slotting in at shooting guard. The Lakers

---

[261] No other team played more road games in November and December 1995 than the Lakers. And only three teams played more total games.

held an 18-point lead in the third quarter but lost all of it courtesy of a 28-8 run by the Nuggets. It was the first of many big leads the Lakers would lose in the early months of the season. The score was tied 96-96 with 35 seconds remaining when Van Exel penetrated the lane and passed to Vlade Divac for a game-winning 12-foot baseline jumper. The Lakers escaped with the 98-96 win.

They started a three-game road trip the next night by tying a franchise record low with just 24 field goals, and lost 103-89 to the SuperSonics. After scoring 24 points in the season opener, Van Exel's shooting touch, always unpredictable, disappeared in Seattle. He missed all six of his shots before being ejected in the fourth quarter for arguing with an official. "Horrible refs," Van Exel said. "Two inexperienced refs." Divac didn't make a shot either, scoring two points and being benched the entire fourth quarter.

They were in a tight game in the fourth quarter in Minneapolis where Ceballos was just two free throws away from matching Gail Goodrich's franchise record of 40 consecutive. But he missed five of six in the fourth quarter. "I make the free throws, we win," Ceballos said. He didn't, and the Lakers lost 93-92. Peeler made his season debut off the bench after spending the previous night in jail in Jefferson City, Missouri for failing to turn in two monthly probation reports stemming from his arrest back in 1992.

Harris shuffled the starting line-up the following night in Salt Lake City. He started Fred Roberts ahead of George Lynch, who had underperformed as a starter, shooting just 31%. But the Lakers couldn't protect an eight-point fourth-quarter lead. They went eight straight possessions without scoring and lost 108-98 to the Utah Jazz. Divac finished with six points and was again benched down the stretch. Van Exel blamed the loss on the replacement officials, but Harris wasn't buying it. "We're 1-3, and we don't like it," he said. "There's no reason to make any excuses."[262]

Van Exel struggled again two nights later at home against the Seattle SuperSonics, shooting 1-6 and scoring five points. But the Lakers got a much-needed 100-97 victory when Detlef Schrempf missed a three-pointer at the buzzer. Ceballos had 32 points, including 14 in the fourth quarter. It

---

[262] Threatt played 17 minutes against Utah despite suffering a concussion in Minneapolis that was severe enough that it left him no memory of hitting his head and only scant memories of the game against the Timberwolves.

coincided with his move back to small forward as Harris, still searching for answers, started Peeler at shooting guard for the first time and moved Roberts back to the bench.

Any good feelings from beating the rival Sonics dissipated the next night in Oakland. Ceballos scored 25 points but nobody else played well, and the Lakers lost 123-105. Divac had opened the season in horrible form, averaging just 8.3 points on 35% shooting in the first six games. He was on the court an hour before tip-off, working on basic post moves with assistant coach Michael Cooper. But it didn't help as he shot 4-13 and again spent extended periods on the bench in the second half. Van Exel's struggles continued too, scoring six points on 3-13 shooting. "I know I haven't been playing like Nick," Van Exel said. "I've got to pick it up."

Sitting at a disappointing 2-4, the Lakers finally got their first road win three days later when they beat Sacramento by six. But it felt like a hollow victory because the entire Kings roster had been suspended one game for a bench-clearing brawl with the Indiana Pacers four nights earlier. The suspensions were spaced out over several games to ensure they had enough players each night and they only had a three-man bench against the Lakers. Divac had a welcome return to form, scoring 19 points. But Van Exel's shooting slump continued, finishing with eight points on 3-11 from the field. It was an ugly game, with both teams frequently moaning to the replacement officials. Kings head coach Garry St. Jean was ejected in the third quarter after receiving two quick technical fouls, the crowd chanting, "We want the refs!" as he walked off the floor.

As empty as the victory over the Kings felt, it kick-started a badly needed four-game win streak. The Lakers returned home to get an easy 114-97 win over the struggling Dallas Mavericks at the Forum. Ceballos scored 31 points in each of the last two games, becoming the first Laker since Magic Johnson in 1987 to score at least 25 points in six consecutive games. He would be named NBA Player of the Week for the second time in his career, having averaged 26.0 points and 9.5 rebounds during that stretch.

While Ceballos was thriving, Van Exel continued to struggle, scoring 6 points on 2-9 shooting against the Mavs. The season was two weeks old, and he still hadn't found a way out of his shooting slump. He was averaging 11.5 points on 31% shooting, a dramatic decline from the numbers he put up in the playoffs six months earlier. He had tried everything to turn it around. The ball felt heavy, so he focused on lifting weights. He felt he lacked rhythm, so he did shooting drills to music. He didn't feel fresh in games, so he scaled back his pre-game shooting routine. None of it worked.

But out of the blue, his shot returned two nights later in Vancouver against the expansion Grizzlies. He scored 25 points on 10-16 shooting, and the Lakers ran out to an easy 114-91 win. He then scored 20 points in the Lakers' 109-88 win at home over the Clippers. "I don't think it ever left him," Sedale Threatt said. "You've got to remember, Nick's still a young player."

Momentarily it appeared the Lakers had righted the ship. They were 6-4 and on a four-game win streak. But as quickly as they had stabilized, they fell apart down the stretch in three consecutive brutal losses.

The first was at home against the Portland Trail Blazers. Ceballos scored 38 points, but the end of the game left him still standing on the court with his hands on his hips when the rest of his team had returned to the locker room. Van Exel hit a twisting 10-footer in the lane to give the Lakers a 108-106 lead with 8.8 seconds left. Back-up point guard James Robinson, who airballed a potential game-winner against Sacramento less than a week earlier, nailed a three-pointer on the buzzer to give the Blazers a 109-108 victory. The loss was made more frustrating because Harris had just drawn up a defensive strategy to stop the very play Portland ran to get Robinson the basket. "We saw what the play was and still let it happen," Harris said.[263]

Three nights later they gave up a 16-point lead to the Sacramento Kings at the Forum. Mitch Richmond hit a three-pointer to tie the game at 98-98 with a minute remaining. Then Tyus Edney made one of two free throws to give the Kings a 99-98 lead. Both Van Exel and Threatt missed shots in the dying seconds, and the Lakers lost their second game in a row, each by a single point. "Another tough one to lose," Harris said.

Worse was yet to come. The next night they were in Phoenix where fans began filing out of American West Arena assuming the game was all but over with the Lakers leading 112-103 with 56 seconds left. Kevin Johnson made a contested three-pointer to cut the lead to 112-106. Lynch

---

[263] It was a significant game for the Lakers for two reasons. Kareem Abdul-Jabbar was honoured at half-time to commemorate his induction into the Hall of Fame. And it marked 30 years since Chick Hearn last missed a Laker broadcast.

made one of two free throws, and the Suns got another quick-hitting play when rookie Michael Finley made a three-pointer to trim the lead to 113-109 with 44 seconds to play. Roberts missed a baseline jumper with 27 seconds left, and Charles Barkley hit a transition three-pointer to reduce the Lakers' lead to 113-112 with 19.8 seconds remaining.

Van Exel got the ball just past mid-court but picked up his dribble and found himself trapped by Johnson and Barkley. He assumed Barkley or Johnson would foul him to stop the clock, but no foul was called. Instead of calling a timeout he cradled the ball and pivoted from side to side for nine long seconds. Finally, a jump ball was called with 6.7 seconds left in the game.

Barkley easily won the jump-ball contest at center court against the shorter Van Exel. A.C. Green controlled the tip and passed to Finley at midcourt. Finley frantically drove to the free throw line for a pull-up jumper at the buzzer that was nothing but net – Suns win 114-113. The players mobbed Finley at mid-court, and the fans who did stay to the end went wild having just witnessed a most unlikely comeback.[264]

Instead of taking responsibility for the loss, the Lakers scrambled for excuses. Van Exel said he hadn't been told the Lakers still had a timeout in the dying seconds and blamed his teammates for not calling one. "There are four other players on the court who could have called one," he said. Harris blamed the officiating crew, claiming Van Exel was fouled multiple times by Johnson and Barkley. The only person blaming the loss on the Lakers was Barkley. "That was a stupid play," he said. "He should have called a timeout."

The only good news to come out of the week was the return of Eddie Jones, who made his season debut against the Kings after missing the first 11 games of the season. To make room for Jones, the Lakers placed rookie Frankie King on the injured list with 'back spasms.'[265]

They got a chance at revenge when they hosted the Suns four nights later at the Forum. They built a big lead, getting ahead 79-57 in the third quarter, which they again could not maintain. The Suns pulled to within

---

[264] With their loss to Phoenix, the Lakers joined the 1986-87 Chicago Bulls as the only teams in NBA history to suffer three consecutive one-point losses.

[265] King wouldn't appear in another game for the Lakers, spending the rest of the season on the injured list with those pesky back spasms. He played in six games, averaging 1.2 points in 3.3 minutes.

101-96 on a three-pointer by Finley. But for a change, the Lakers steadied as Divac scored 10 consecutive points down the stretch for a 107-96 win. "I was scared," Divac said. "It was almost like the same scenario that had happened three games in a row." After leading all scorers in Phoenix with 32 points, Ceballos had a game-high 24 points in Los Angeles.[266]

The win against the Suns was the end of an ugly month for the Lakers. When fans wanted Act II of the Lake Show, this wasn't what they were meaning. They were 7-7 and tied with Portland for seventh in the West. Ceballos had been superb, averaging 27.0 points and 9.1 rebounds on 52% shooting over the 14 games. He had stepped his game up a notch from a year ago, but he was the only player on the team to do so. Both Van Exel and Divac had been especially disappointing.

Jones hadn't played well in his first three games since coming back from injury, averaging just 5.3 points on 37% shooting. Peeler had played well as his replacement in the starting line-up, but his 12.1 points in November were down from the 17.4 he averaged as a starter a year earlier.

Needing to get their season back on track, they opened December with a well-timed visit from the struggling expansion Vancouver Grizzlies. Divac looked like a new player, recording 18 points, 13 rebounds, and 7 assists. "I was very aggressive and tried to do a lot of things," Divac said. "I'm just feeling like my confidence is back and I feel more relaxed now." Van Exel also had one of his best games of the season, scoring 14 points and handing out 16 assists. The Lakers shot 53%, the first time they had topped 50% all season, and won easily 113-100.

They picked up a 104-96 win against Indiana at the Forum, but Peeler missed the game with tendinitis in this right foot, an injury that would sideline him for the next five games. It meant Jones was promoted to full-time starter ahead of schedule, and he responded with his best game so far, scoring 15 points on 5-6 shooting.

The Lakers then started a quick two-game Texas road swing starting in San Antonio, and it wouldn't be good. During morning shootaround, some of the Lakers foolishly told a few Spurs players how badly they were going to beat them that night. The Spurs players dutifully returned to their locker room and reported, insult by insult, what they had just heard. It fired them up. In a game Harris called "a mistake from start to finish," the

---

[266] Tony Smith made his first start of the season for the Phoenix Suns, scoring 8 points on 3-10 shooting in 21 minutes.

Lakers shot 30% in the first half, lost every quarter, and were thrashed 117-89. Campbell was ejected four minutes out from half-time for throwing the ball at Will Perdue while he was lying on the ground after attempting to draw a charge. Campbell was asked about it after the game, but he clearly wasn't in the mood. "I ain't got nothing to talk about," he said. "Nothing at all."

Things weren't any better the following night at the Summit. Divac heard a popping noise in his knee the previous night in San Antonio and spent the day limping. He struggled through 22 painful minutes against Houston before having to sit out. The defending champion Rockets gave the Lakers their second thrashing in two nights, this time 112-99. Clyde Drexler top scored with 34 points to go along with 10 rebounds. "I think he was the oldest player on the court most of the time," said Harris. "And he played with the most energy on a consistent basis."

The two losses in Texas dropped them back to .500 on the season with a 9-9 record. But the Lakers received another well-timed visit from a struggling expansion team, this time the Toronto Raptors. Divac sat out with his aching knee, but the Lakers got an easy 120-103 victory with Jones registering 27 points, 7 rebounds, and 11 assists. It had been a slow comeback for Jones, but against Toronto he looked like his old self. "It was a matter of time," he said. "You just can't come right back and play great games. There's just one Michael Jordan."

The Lakers hosted another struggling team two nights later, the 8-10 Detroit Pistons. Divac was back in uniform and looked good, getting 21 points and 13 rebounds. They edged out an ugly 87-78 win on the night James Worthy had his jersey retired at half-time.

Peeler returned to the line-up just in time for the Lakers to head off on a road trip that would see them play six games in nine nights. It started at Madison Square Garden, where NBA officials were mercifully back in action for the first time after a pay deal was struck with the league. It was the end of the replacement officials who had frustrated many players and fans, but none more than the Lakers. "I thought our team did struggle to adjust to them," Harris said. "Being a young team, perhaps we did let some of their calls maybe affect us a little more than we should, especially earlier in the season."

As much as the Lakers had complained about the replacement officials, the lack of them didn't do anything to help them in New York.

They lost 97-82, and Van Exel struggled to 10 points in 36 minutes on 3-13 shooting.

His shooting touch momentarily returned the next night in Detroit, where he scored 30 points and handed out 7 assists. The Lakers built a 16-point lead with ten minutes to play but they, naturally, lost almost all of it. The Pistons had a chance to send the game into overtime with 1.7 seconds remaining. But Jones tipped away Grant Hill's inbounds pass, and the Lakers escaped with a 101-98 win.

The Lakers had a double-digit lead in the fourth quarter in Washington two nights later but again saw it disappear. The Bullets went on a 21-4 run over the last six minutes and stole a 122-114 win. "We continue to make the same mistake," Harris said. "We get rich with a lead, and we feel we have to give money to everybody." To make matters worse, the pain in Divac's knee returned, and he was limited to 24 minutes. "I never thought I'd feel like this," he said. "I'm like an old man."

Struggling at 1-2 on the road trip, the Lakers couldn't have gotten a worse opponent for their fourth game in five days. The Chicago Bulls had raced out to an 18-2 record behind an especially motivated Michael Jordan wanting to prove he was still the game's greatest player after sitting out almost two years. Throw in the off-season acquisition of Dennis Rodman, the development of Toni Kukoc, the all-around play of Scottie Pippen, and the coaching genius of Phil Jackson, and the Bulls were near unbeatable in 1995-96. Jordan dislocated his right index finger in the first quarter, and it affected his shooting. He finished with 20 points on 5-20 shooting, but it didn't come close to mattering. Pippen picked up the scoring slack with 33 points, Rodman grabbed 15 rebounds, and the Bulls got an easy 108-88 win.[267]

Marty Conlon was the biggest thorn in the Lakers' side when they took on the Bucks three nights later. His clutch play in the dying seconds got the Bucks a win when the Lakers visited Milwaukee the previous season. This time he scored 17 points in the fourth quarter, leading a charge that turned an 87-76 Lakers lead into a 109-105 Bucks victory. Conlon was essentially a basketball unknown, but to the Lakers, he was starting to become Larry Bird. "I want to know why Marty Conlon is not on the All-

---

[267] Sam Bowie was considering a comeback after retiring before the start of the season. He had narrowed his choice down to either the Lakers or the Bulls, going so far to as to have talks with Jerry West and working out with the Bulls a week before they hosted the Lakers. Ultimately, he would not come back, choosing instead to stay retired.

Star ballot," joked Harris.

The Lakers concluded their road trip the next night with a 109-98 loss to the Indiana Pacers. Jones sat out the game in Indianapolis after he suffered a broken nose in Milwaukee. After just five minutes of play, he received an inadvertent elbow from Vin Barker while battling for a rebound. "It was excruciating," said Jones. "I had to ball myself up to deal with the pain."

He was cleared to play in the next home game against the Sacramento Kings and had been outfitted for a custom-made face mask. But he almost didn't play because the mask had to be made in Chicago and it was late arriving at LAX. There were further delays when an official from the cargo office wouldn't release the package to the ball-boy the Lakers dispatched to collect it because it was addressed to Gary Vitti. The officer and the ball boy reached an agreement – he would release the package in exchange for Lakers tickets. Jones got his mask just before tip-off and took the floor with the rest of the team for an easy 116-83 win.

Divac fought through 37 minutes, hobbled by knee pain, the next night in Portland. He got 19 points and 10 rebounds, and his baseline jumper and free throws with 25 seconds left sealed a 102-99 win. It was a side of Divac, who was often labeled 'soft' by fans and the media, that the world rarely got a glimpse at. "I get mail and calls from fans saying, 'he's lazy,'" Harris said. "People have no idea who Vlade Divac is. The guy has a heart as big as he is."

The Lakers had three days off before beating the Boston Celtics 102-91 at the Forum on Boxing Day. The win put them a season-high three games above .500 with a 16-13 record. But they would immediately lose their next three games to put them right back at .500.

The first was an eight-point loss at home to a San Antonio Spurs team that, it was safe to say, had the Lakers' number. "We can't beat 'em," Van Exel said. "I guess we're still trying to get over that hill." They were then taken apart bit by bit by the Utah Jazz with a 99-92 loss two nights later in Salt Lake City. They opened 1996 with what should have been an easy win at the Forum against the horrible 5-22 Philadelphia 76ers. The Lakers rushed out to a 23-4 lead, but they were outscored by 20 the rest of the game. Vernon Maxwell's floater in the lane with 46 seconds remaining gave the 76ers a 90-89 lead. The Lakers had two opportunities to win the game, but Van Exel missed a lay-up, and Ceballos' put-back at the buzzer went in and out and the 76ers escaped with the one-point win.[268]

It was early January, and the Lakers were 16-16, and in the sixth spot in the West, hardly the position fans hoped they would be in when the season started. "It's been a long ride," Harris said.

Almost all their offensive numbers were down from the season before. They were averaging four points less a game and their three-point shooting had dropped a full 5% to be dead last in the league. Their backcourt that was so dynamic the previous season had been disappointing. Jones had been slow to return to form, averaging 9.5 points in 20 games, and Van Exel had fought his way through a miserable shooting slump. Meanwhile Divac was banged up and his 12.3 points and 7.7 rebounds over the first two months of the season were a regression to the kind of numbers he averaged earlier in his career.

But it was more than the record and the stats. These Lakers had gone from being one of the biggest surprises of the previous season to a team that looked joyless. They also showed a worrying lack of accountability.

After struggling to 13 points on 4-13 shooting in the home loss to the Spurs, Ceballos was benched in the first five minutes of the fourth quarter. But he didn't blame the loss on himself; he instead called out his coach in the media. "There were times we could have gotten back in the game, but we didn't make right substitutions," he said. Harris shot back at him. "It's up to our team to make a decision where they want to go and where they want to be," he said. "But only by foregoing ego and individual statistics and trying to become a unified team again, which is what made us strong last year."

The relationship between Harris and Van Exel had also become strained behind the scenes. Except for the incident in Portland where Van Exel refused to play the second half, the rift was something the team managed to keep out of the papers the previous season. But word was now starting to seep out. Van Exel was reportedly frustrated by the offense and felt Harris lost confidence in him during his shooting slump. It got to the point where Van Exel was looking distracted and disconnected in the locker room and during timeouts, rarely making eye contact with his coach. "A lot of people are frustrated," Van Exel said. "There are times I want to take over the game, but the coach won't let me. Last year, if I got

---

[268] It was the first time Philadelphia had won at the Forum since 1984 – when Threatt was a rookie with the 76ers.

an opportunity and didn't produce, he didn't take me out. This year, I haven't seen that. Yet."

"We've been to Texas and back, to L.A, to New York and part way back," Harris said. "Eddie Jones has been hurt. Peeler has been hurt. Vlade has been hurt. So, it's a little early to order a tombstone for us."

Harris was right, it was too early to write the team and the season off. But time was running out for them to turn it around.

Chapter 29

EVERYTHING BUT THE WORD

January 5, 1996 to January 29, 1996

L ARRY DREW DIDN'T need to be told. He was now in his fourth
season as Lakers assistant coach. Before that, he was a player with
the team for two years. He saw Magic Johnson play every game in those
two years and practiced against him every other day. In that time, he and
Magic became good friends. So, he didn't need to hear the words. He had
seen enough to know.

"I've been around him enough to know what certain things mean," he
said. "I know when something has caught his attention."

It wasn't simply that Magic had been training with the Lakers for the
last few weeks that made Drew curious. It was *how* he was training. He
was pressing hard, just like he used to. He was hitting, grabbing, holding
players, and demanding they do the same to him. He was making sure he
learned all the offensive sets like he would need to call on them at a
moment's notice.

Magic hadn't said anything to him. That wasn't his style. But Drew
knew what was happening. Magic was going to be a player again. "I've
gotten everything but the word," Drew said.

After a brutal schedule in the first two months of the season, life would
become a whole lot easier for the Lakers to start 1996. Twelve of their next
18 games would be played at the Forum, and two of the 'road games' were
a twenty-minute drive away at the Sports Arena. There would only be two
road trips over the next seven weeks, and they would be relatively short.
It was an opportunity to turn their season around.

They started at home against the Utah Jazz, who had defeated them
by 17 points less than a week earlier. The Lakers built a 16-point lead in
the third quarter and, for once, held on to it. The Jazz never got closer than

12 points in the fourth, and the Lakers won 116-100. Their three most powerful offensive weapons fired at the same time, something that had been rare to that point. Ceballos had 28 points on 11-14 shooting, Van Exel had 26 points and 8 assists, and Jones added 25 points, 7 rebounds, and 8 assists.

It looked like the win may have been only a temporary recovery when they lost at home to the Denver Nuggets 96-93. And they weren't exactly convincing two nights later at home against the lowly Minnesota Timberwolves, needing free throws by Jones with 1.3 seconds remaining to sneak out a 106-104 win. But they then got a 101-100 win over the two-time defending champion Houston Rockets who had roundly beaten them a month earlier. The win again the Rockets, sealed by a late basket and free throw from Divac, was even more impressive because it came without Ceballos who was sidelined with the flu.

Unbeknownst to Lakers fans at the time, Magic Johnson took part in training the day after the win against Houston. And he would be at every session for the next few weeks. When news broke he was training with the team, the question that had been asked so many times over the last few years was, yet again, back out there. Was Magic considering a comeback?

Lon Rosen was quick to downplay it, saying Magic had no plans to play again. "He's just trying to light a fire under the team," Rosen said. "He likes his life too much now, he'll never go back." The players were, publicly at least, singing a similar tune. When asked about it, Van Exel said Magic was simply a constructively critical voice the team needed at practice.

The truth was altogether different. The idea of a comeback had been increasingly on Magic's mind since Michael Jordan came out of retirement in March 1995. After up-and-down performances in his first four games back, Jordan put on a vintage performance at Madison Square Garden. He scored 55 points in the Bulls' win against the Knicks, his first dominating performance since coming out of retirement. Magic watched the game on TV, and something was immediately obvious to him. "It wasn't just that Michael scored all those points," he said. "It was that he looked so happy. You know? He was back in his element. I watched him that night, and I knew that was my element too."

It was the catalyst for Magic to start openly campaigning to be on Dream Team III, the US national team that would compete at the 1996

Summer Olympics in Atlanta.[269] After all, he may have been retired for four years, but he knew he could still play at a high level. He had toured the world with the Magic Johnson All-Stars, playing big minutes, racking up triple-doubles, and leading his team to a 55-0 record. It wasn't against NBA talent, but he knew he still possessed the skills that once made him an all-time great. "I saw him play last summer against our summer-league team," Del Harris said. "I thought he was still probably one of the five best players in the world."

Over the six weeks following Jordan's 55-point game, Magic had watched the Lakers' resurgence in the playoffs. He watched them lose Game 6 to the San Antonio Spurs and knew he could have made a difference. This was no longer the dreadful team he coached a year earlier. The best he could have hoped for out of a comeback then was taking the Lakers from a lottery team to first-round fodder in the playoffs. He wasn't interested in that. But these Lakers, The Lake Show, were different. They had talent, and they sometimes played well together. He could help this team. With him, they just might have a shot at a championship.

During the off-season, Magic accepted an invitation from Jordan, who was in Los Angeles shooting *Space Jam*, to play in a pick-up game. Magic played against Dennis Rodman and scored 9 of his team's 11 points, further evidence he might still be able to compete at a high level.

It was when he was running his fantasy camp in Maui, Hawaii in the off-season that a comeback came front and center in his mind. He even spoke to Steve Chase, a Forum marketing executive, about what jersey number he should wear if he came back. Should he wear his retired #32? Or maybe a different number like Jordan had worn when he unretired? Maybe he could add #3 and #2 together and wear a #5 jersey. He sat next to Chick Hearn on the flight back from Hawaii and talked in specifics of a possible return. "We came back on a Sunday," Hearn said. "And I was convinced he would call on Tuesday to tell me he was doing it."

But the call never came. Shortly after the flight, Magic opened a new business venture and, in the process, had an epiphany about what he should do with the rest of his life. In July 1995 he opened the Magic Johnson Theatres in the Crenshaw District, just a few miles from where the riots broke out in 1992. The 12-screen movie complex represented something more than a business opportunity for Magic. And it meant

---

[269] Like with the original Dream Team, USA Basketball had named a 10-man squad with two spots to be filled closer to the games. Magic wanted one of those spots.

more to the local community than just a new place to catch summer blockbusters. It was something that had proven all too rare in the past – investment and belief in the South-Central region of Los Angeles. It brought employment opportunities to a struggling neighborhood. "If the theatres hadn't opened, I would have come back," Magic said. "People tell me, I've been in this community for 40 years and nothing ever happened like this. Wives were crying, thanking me for creating jobs. I felt God was taking me and saying, 'This is what I want you to do.'"

But like a new year's resolution, Magic's epiphany didn't last long. He was still devoted to his many businesses, but the itch to play again never went away. As the Lakers battled through their tough December schedule, the idea of returning kept re-entering his mind. He spoke to Rosen and Jerry West about training with the Lakers, to test himself against real NBA talent to see, once and for all, if he still had enough left in the tank to come back. But he soured on the idea when he watched the Lakers squander a 19-point lead and lose to the awful 76ers at the Forum. "I don't know how to come back with a team like this," he said. "I'd be fighting with somebody out there."

In what would be the third time he considered a comeback in six months, he again changed his mind when the Lakers put together those wins against Utah and Houston. "You could see the guys are really playing hard and have really pulled together," he said. And with that, he finally took the giant leap of training with the team.

Because he was testing himself, he didn't want it known he was considering a comeback. But he couldn't exactly deny it either. When entering the training facility one day, a reporter asked him if he was planning on playing again. "No, I'm not coming back. I'm just here practicing," Magic replied. The reporter asked if that meant he was never going to make a return. "Well," he said. "I wouldn't say never." It was an exchange Lakers fans met in one of two ways. They either crossed their fingers and hoped this time might be for real, or they rolled their eyes and thought 'yeah, we've seen this play out before.'

With the latest round of comeback speculation still mostly whispers, the Lakers had games to play. They continued resuscitating their season with a 96-88 win in Pat Riley's first game at the Forum as head coach of the Miami Heat. With the win, Harris became just the 25th coach in NBA history to reach 400 career victories. "It's no record, but still, it's nice,"

Harris said. "When I look at the list of names of people who have won 400 games or more, they're awfully good coaches." Jones led the Lakers with 20 points, the third time he had scored at least 20 in three straight games.

Ceballos, who had missed the last two games after being hospitalized with the flu, was back in uniform three days later when the Lakers took on the Clippers at the Sports Arena. He scored 25 points despite having a coughing fit in the middle of the game that he couldn't stop. The Lakers seized control of the game with an 18-8 run to close the third quarter, eventually winning 106-100.

Following an ugly 92-82 loss at home to the Cleveland Cavaliers, the Lakers embarked on their only road-trip of the month, a quick three games in four days out East. It started in Boston where they played at the Celtics' new Fleet Center for the first time. It was a strikingly modern venue and much more comfortable for opposing teams than old Boston Garden. The hot water stayed on in the visitors' locker room, for instance. But long-time assistant coach Bill Bertka still hated it, perhaps demonstrating the psychosomatic toll all the wars in the old Garden had taken on him. "For some reason, it still has the same smell," he said. "That smell. I can't explain it. That rancid, damn smell." The game was never really in doubt in the second half as the Lakers carved up the Celtics' defense, which had become one of the worst in the league. Boston cut the deficit to 60-49 early in the third quarter, but the Lakers responded with an emphatic 17-2 charge that set up the easy 124-107 win.

Appropriately, it was when the Lakers were in Boston that the Magic comeback rumors kicked up a notch. Rosen said he had spoken to the league about Magic needing to sell back his ownership stake in the Lakers if he was to return.[270] He also stated that he expected a decision would be made soon, the first time Magic training with the team had been confirmed to be part of a possible comeback.

The Lakers were playing it safe, careful not to feed the hype or give the impression it was a done deal. Especially after having to deal with dejected fans in 1992 who felt hustled after purchasing season tickets for the 1992-93 season when they expected Magic to play. The players too were protecting themselves from potential disappointment. Jones sounded full of youthful giddiness at the idea of playing with Magic. But

---

[270] League rules dictated a player could not also be an owner, or a part-owner, of an NBA team.

the veterans, especially those who had played for the Lakers for several years, were more cautious. Campbell was asked about the rumors after the game in Boston and gave a curt response. "Whatever," he said. "I'm not commenting on that. I've been through this before. I'll just wait and see what happens." Divac said he hadn't heard anyone from the Lakers talk about it, and the media knew more about it than the players did.

With the rumors heating up, the road trip continued into Philadelphia against the pitiful 7-32 76ers. "We've got a 6'4 guy [Clarence Weatherspoon] out there playing power forward, and a 13-year vet [LaSalle Thompson] who can't jump five inches," said Vernon Maxell. The Lakers enacted some revenge for their embarrassing loss at home to the 76ers at the start of the month, cruising to an easy 100-88 victory.

While the Lakers were in Philly, Magic was in Phoenix preparing to play in a charity game. Lester Conner and Marchell Henry, teammates of Magic's on his exhibition team, were playing against him in practice. They noticed he was far more intense than normal. Instead of running drills, he pushed the players to be more physical with him. He worked harder on defense than they had ever seen, and he spent a long time practicing his hook shot. It was something Conner expected to see in training camp, not in practice for a charity game.

Magic upped the rumors himself when he gave a nationally televised interview with TNT's Craig Sager from Phoenix. He started by saying he wasn't sure if he was coming back and he was just enjoying practicing with the Lakers for now. Sager ended the interview by saying TNT would be ready to cover the game if he chose to come back when the Lakers host the Bulls in a week's time.

Magic looked up to the roof with a smile on his face and nodded slowly in silence. "Yeah," he finally said. "You know, you live for moments like that. What are they, 37-3? They're playing awesome basketball. People don't understand why they're so good. They're the best defensive team in basketball, they're the best passing team in basketball, and they have the most winners in basketball. So, it would be fun just to see, just to play against the best, just to see. It would be great, man."

Like Larry Drew, Sager had seen enough and shook Magic's hand. "Let me be the first to tell you, a week in advance, welcome back Magic," he said, half in jest. Magic wrapped his arm around Sager and laughed with him. "We'll see what happens," he said.[271]

The Lakers completed their quick road trip in New Jersey, where Ceballos led all scorers with 29 points. The Lakers had a 13-point lead with eight minutes left when they went into one of their trademark downward spirals. Guard Greg Graham made two free throws with 4.4 seconds remaining to tie the scores at 98-98. Following a timeout, Jones inbounded to Divac on the right wing. He drove into center Shawn Bradley hoping for a foul but didn't get one. Instead, he forced up a shot that rolled off the hoop. Campbell went up, grabbed control of the rebound and with both hands threw down a thunderous dunk just before the buzzer sounded, giving the Lakers a 100-98 win.

It was the continuation of a kind of comeback for Campbell. Benched for long periods a week earlier against Cleveland and the Clippers, he averaged 20.0 points and 13.7 rebounds on the three-game trip, his best stretch of the season. "He took the weekend off last week [against Cleveland and the Clippers]," joked Harris. "But he's back in business now."

Although they had never said as much publicly, the players knew the true reason Magic was taking part in training. They had been impressed not only by Magic's play but how everybody played better with him on the court. He had been training for several weeks but still hadn't decided. So once back from the short road-trip, the team went about giving him a push.

Harris rang Magic and told him he should come back. So too did Ceballos. But Magic feared they were only telling him what he wanted to hear. Mitch Kupchak then rang him, telling him he didn't think a comeback was a good idea two years ago when the team was still forging its identity. But it was a different story now, it was the best time to do it. Jerry West rang and told Magic his time was running out. He wasn't young anymore and, at age 36, it was getting to a 'now or never' stage. But the clincher came when Van Exel and Jones conference-called him and

---

[271] Another rumor started at this time that Magic had purchased a block of tickets for the Lakers' upcoming games against the Warriors and Jazz at the Forum. It turned out to be a half truth. He hadn't bought tickets for the Warriors game but had purchased 60 for the Jazz game – but they were for participants of the Magic Johnson Foundation, not for friends and family.

said what he needed to hear. They didn't say 'you *should* come back,' they said, 'we *want* you back.'

Magic sold his 5% share in the Lakers back to Jerry Buss, making a $1 million profit in the process. He canceled the Magic Johnson's All-Stars upcoming tours of Australia in March and Japan in May. The Lakers drew up a new player contract for him and met him at the Inglewood offices of Team Physician, Dr. Stephen Lombardo, to avoid a potential media frenzy at the Forum. On January 29, 1996, Magic sat down in the doctor's office with a pen and quickly read over the contract. He sighed, looked up and said, "Forget it, I'm not doing it." After a few seconds of sickening silence from West and Kupchak, Magic broke into his famous smile. "Just kidding," he said. He signed the $2.5 million contract becoming what a few years earlier had seemed impossible – an NBA player again.

From there, Magic joined the Lakers at practice as a member of the team for the first time since the 1992-93 pre-season.[272] And it wasn't like any normal training session, not with the sea of reporters pressed up against one side of the gym waiting for training to finish. The reporters patiently waited as Magic stayed back after practice, just like he always did. After the rest of the team had left, he worked on his three-point shots, then his hook shots, and finally his free throws.

Magic's comeback press conference was a stark contrast to the staged events previously held at the Forum Club. This one was held in the foyer of the Lakers' practice facility at Loyola Marymount. Magic was dressed in yellow shorts, a black t-shirt, and a yellow Lakers practice jersey. Wearing a knee brace and still sweating slightly from the workout, he made his announcement.

"I've been kicking myself too long, I should have been back a long time ago," he said. "I wanted my son and my daughter to see me play. I didn't go out the way I wanted to go out before, and that's the reason I'm back. And I'm also back because the Lakers have put themselves in a position to hopefully do some good things, and I hope that I can be a part of it."

Reporters asked him when he first started contemplating coming out of retirement. Rosen interjected before Magic could reply. "November 7, 1991," he joked. Magic acknowledged that years of frustration were finally ending for him. "You sit in bed at night and watch all these games. I go to

---

[272] Roberts was placed on the injured list with "back spasms" to create a roster spot for Magic.

every Laker home game and sit there. And you struggle, you struggle, you struggle with it. They said playing basketball would kill me. Well, *not* playing basketball was killing me."

He said he wasn't angry at the doctors who told him he should retire in 1991 when, with the benefit of hindsight, he didn't need to. They were providing the best advice they could with the information they had at the time. He wasn't angry at the players who ran him out of the league in 1992 by saying they didn't want to play against him, even though doing so presented so little risk that it wasn't worth thinking about. They were scared because they were uneducated about HIV and AIDS at the time. Instead, he was angry at himself. Angry he didn't force the issue, didn't listen to that voice in him that kept telling him he should still be on the court playing.

Rosen believed Magic was better prepared to deal with negativity than he was in 1992 and was determined not to be run out of the league again. "I'm prepared to take what's going to come," he said. "If there's negativity along the way, I'll deal with that. Having this thing has made me strong. If along the way, people with this same condition can look out on that court and see me smiling and being happy playing ball and maybe feel a little better about things themselves, well, all the better."

The reaction to Magic's announcement was, for the most part, positive. He was put on the cover of *Time*, *Newsweek*, and *Sports Illustrated*. David Stern, always a supporter of Magic, expressed his support yet again, saying he was pleased to have Magic back in the league. Jordan said he was looking forward to competing against him again. Reggie Miller said he didn't think Magic should have retired in the first place, while John Stockton said Magic had a right to play the game if he wanted to. Jayson Williams wasn't worried about contracting HIV from playing against Magic. "You've got about as much chance as Ed McMahon coming to your door," he said.

And then there was Charles Barkley, who threw his support behind Magic with a very Barkley-like statement. "It's not like we're going out to have unprotected sex with Magic on the court, we're just playing basketball," he said. "So, I think we'll be okay."

There was, as expected, some negativity. Nets forward Armon Gilliam said he received contact and scratches all the time in the NBA. "How safe is it?" he asked. "Who can really answer that?" 76ers guard Vernon

Maxwell said he didn't want to be there when Magic got scratched, saying he had a wife and kids to think about. So, what if his coach told him to guard Magic? "I don't know about that," he said.[273] But this time, the negative noise was almost completely drowned out by the deafening sound of positivity coming from the league and its players.

But it didn't really matter what Gilliam and Maxwell said. Or Jordan and Barkley. What mattered the most was the thoughts of Karl Malone, who was the highest profile player to express concerns about playing against Magic back in 1992. "Why don't you do me a favor and sound this to everybody in the league," Malone told the media. "I think it's great. If he wants to come back, I think it's great for the game and great for the organization. Basically, that's it. I have no problem playing against him now, absolutely not." Malone's comments reflected a journey he had been on regarding the prospect of playing against an HIV-positive player, one representative of the journey the entire league had been on.

Magic was in excellent health. Every three months his blood was analyzed at the Aaron Diamond AIDS Research Center in New York. Through a combination of drugs, exercise routine, and positive attitude, the virus had been well controlled. It was, in fact, in the exact same place as it was when he attempted a comeback in 1992. The virus had not progressed in that time.

Due to an intense work out regiment, Magic had bulked up to 250 pounds, about 25 more than his final season in 1990-91. It wasn't all muscle, and he needed to shed a few pounds quickly. "I'm not in NBA shape," he acknowledged. But he was far bigger and more powerful than when he last played in the NBA. He looked like a banger now, like Antoine Carr or Anthony Mason, and was too big and strong to return to his old position of point guard. "Nobody wants to chase around those little guards anymore," he said. "I'm too old for that."

Harris would instead play him primarily at power forward, though he would move him around quite a bit. Magic wouldn't start, he would instead be the Lakers' new sixth man. It was the perfect role for him. Harris could plug him in at either forward spot and occasionally slot him in at point guard when needed. "Because of his flexibility, I think I can put him at any spot," Harris said. "That's a good thing." Magic had no

---

[273] The 76ers wouldn't play the Lakers again that season, something Maxwell probably would have known. So, his concerns really were for nothing.

problem playing off the bench, believing it was better for the team. Just so long as he played in the fourth quarter when it's "winning time."

The role meant the starting unit would remain the same, keeping intact the tenuous good chemistry that had been built over the previous few weeks. Harris' plan was for Magic not to take much playing time from the usual starters, instead carving into the minutes that once belonged to reserves Corie Blount, Derek Strong, George Lynch, and Sedale Threatt. It also meant teams couldn't prepare for defending Magic only at one position. He would play different spots at different times in each game, depending on the need. It would keep the defense on its toes.

Magic's comeback was the biggest news in sports, but the Lakers would try to limit expectations as much as possible. Magic was one of the game's true greats, but there was plenty going against him. He was 36 years old now, and he would be rusty. He had played basketball regularly, all over the world. But it wasn't the same as playing in the NBA. Not even close. "I know I'm five steps slower," Magic said. "But the hook shot's still there, and I have power inside. I know what to do, and I know what not to do. I'm not coming back thinking I'm going to be Magic Johnson at the age of 26 or 25. That would be stupid. But I am coming back with the fact that I still know how to play this game."

He would also be joining the team in mid-season without the benefit of training camp. It was a difficult thing for any player to do, especially one who hadn't played in the league for four and a half years. "Yes, there'll be some rough spots," Harris said. "But I think if you don't make too many demands on him then you'll see steady progress as he integrates himself into our team and they, in turn, become accustomed to playing with one of the greatest players who ever played the game."

The Lakers had quickly reversed the fortunes of their season. Four weeks earlier, they were a disappointing 16-16. But they had gone 8-2 since, playing their best basketball of the season. They were sitting on a 24-18 record, only two games behind where they were at the same time a year earlier.

They were healthier, happier, getting better individual performances, and playing better as a team. Jones was looking far more comfortable since returning from injury, averaging 17.8 points over the last 10 games. Van Exel seemed to have overcome his tumultuous shooting slump and averaged 17.2 points, 7.5 assists and, perhaps most importantly, shot 46% over the last few weeks. Divac and Campbell shook off their inconsistent play of the first two months to become steadier contributors. And all the while Ceballos, easily the most dependable player during the season, had continued his excellent play by averaging 22.8 points over that time.

Things were already looking up before January 29, and now the Lakers had added an historically great player without having to give anything up. Nobody knew what to expect from Magic, but his return was undoubtedly the most exciting thing to happen to Lakers fans in almost half a decade. But no matter what he added on the court, there was little denying what he would bring to the team off it. "People say, 'what does he add to the team?'" Harris said. "A joy for life, a joy for playing, a joy for practice that just can't be duplicated anywhere else."

Chapter 30

THE SECOND COMEBACK

January 30, 1996 to February 16, 1996

M AGIC JOHNSON WAS on the court at the Forum for the first time in four and a half years. It was a sight Laker fans thought they would never see again. He took a few dribbles and launched his first shot of the night, a three-pointer that bounced off the back of the rim. The sold out crowd groaned in unison. He then took a feed from Cedric Ceballos, calmly drove from the right side and threw in a lay-up, his first basket. The Forum exploded in cheers.

There were still 15 minutes to go before tip-off. Magic and the Lakers were just in pre-game warm-ups.

The city of Los Angeles had endured a lot since Magic first retired. The Rodney King verdict and riots. The Northridge earthquake. The Old Topanga Fire. Recession and unemployment. The O.J. Simpson trial. The death of up-and-coming young actor River Phoenix on a Sunset Strip sidewalk. The departure of both the Rams and the Raiders. Promising Dodgers teams who could never go the distance.

Magic's comeback gave the city something to cheer about.

As rumors of Magic's comeback swirled, fans didn't rush to snap up remaining tickets to the game against the Golden State Warriors. After being let down many times by comebacks that never materialized, fans were skeptical. But once the announcement was made they acted quickly, and the remaining 2,300 tickets sold out within hours.

For the first time since they last played in the NBA Finals, a Lakers game felt like an event. Prime Sports got their highest ever ratings, and TNT got the third best they had received for an NBA game. The usually fashionably late-arriving Forum crowd were in their seats by the time the Lakers took the court for warm-ups. A fan held up a hand-made sign that read. *'Laker fans have waited 1,540 days for Magic's return, it's about time!'*

Magic was nervous before the game. Everything felt so familiar yet so new. "It's almost like my first NBA game," he said. Following warm-ups and the national anthem, he took a seat on the bench as the starters took to the floor. It was just the seventh time he had started a game on the bench.[274] The moment fans had waited so long for would have to wait until Harris chose to put him in the game, like the house lights going down before a concert but the band taking another five minutes to hit the stage.

Harris expected to sub Magic in around the mid-point of the first quarter, but his plans quickly changed when Campbell picked up two early fouls. He fouled Joe Smith 90 seconds into the game, then sent Jerome Kersey to the free throw line less than a minute later. Needing to get Campbell out of the game, Harris turned to Magic. "Let's go," he said to him. "Huh?" Magic responded.

With nine minutes and 39 seconds left in the first quarter, Magic stood up and turned towards the scorer's table to check-in. He hardly took a step before the crowd rose to their feet for a standing ovation. He peeled off his warm-ups, revealing the familiar #32 jersey, and waited to be allowed into the game. The ovation continued through Kersey's first free throw, and Lon Rosen became emotional as he watched from the stands. "I don't believe this," he said. "I can still remember the sadness in that first game after he retired. No one thought he would ever play again."

Magic took rebounding position next to rookie Joe Smith, who wore #32 in college and in the NBA because Magic was his favorite player growing up. "It was great," said Smith about matching up with his hero. "Then I realized I had to stop this guy, and that's when it became pretty hard."

The ovation lasted 30 seconds, finishing once Kersey hit his second free throw. The Lakers went right to Magic on his first possession. He backed down Smith and attempted a right-handed hook shot that hit the front of the rim to groans from the crowd.[275] He hardly touched the ball

---

[274] Each time was when Pat Riley was easing him back into the line-up following an injury. The last game he started on the bench was March 25, 1988 at home against the Denver Nuggets when he was coming back from a groin injury.

[275] Rick Reilly described it in his *Sports Illustrated* article as the sound of 17,505 people saying, "Oh god, not Bob Cousy coming out of retirement and averaging 0.7 points for the Cincinnati Royals."

on their next three possessions, the Lakers scoring on all three for a 16-6 lead.

Then Latrell Sprewell tried to force feed Rony Seikaly when the ball was knocked free, falling to Anthony Peeler. He threw an outlet pass to Nick Van Exel that sailed right over his head. Van Exel ran it down, barely avoiding the baseline, and threw the ball back to Magic at the three-point line. Magic fed the ball to Peeler, who caught up with the play and made a three-pointer for Magic's first assist. The Forum crowd erupted as the Warriors called timeout, trailing 19-6.

Following a basket by Sprewell a few possessions later, Vlade Divac inbounded the ball to Magic who charged up the court, not looking much like a power forward at all. He got Smith backpedaling and drove straight to the basket for his first two points. Two possessions later he backed Smith down and hit a left-handed hook shot over him.

Then he almost brought the house down. Left open at the three-point line, he received a pass from Peeler and launched a shot that went in and came out. As the crowd groaned, Divac grabbed the rebound. With only Sprewell between him and the hoop, Magic moved forward and received the ball back from Divac. He made a head and shoulder fake in the direction of Peeler, who was standing unguarded in the corner. Sprewell lunged hard at the ball, taking a full step towards Peeler. Before he could turn his head to see where the ball went, Magic had blown past him and scored a lay-in.

"Sprewell went for it like a carp going after a worm," Hearn said. After the game, Sprewell seemed almost proud to have been fooled so completely by the play. "He got me," he said grinning. "That was a sweet move." It was a quintessential Magic Johnson move that brought the crowd to its feet and a tear to the eye of Pat Riley as he watched the game on TV in Miami.

The Lakers led 35-28 at quarter time, and the game continued to be played at a frenetic pace. Magic played seven more minutes in the second quarter, engineering one fast break after another. The Lakers took a 72-63 lead into half-time and looked like they would turn the game into a blowout in the second half. They led by twenty with seven minutes left in the game, but a lightning-quick Warriors run cut the lead to six points with 45 seconds to play. With the crowd getting nervous, Magic backed Chris Mullin down and drew a double-team from Sprewell. He found Van Exel at the top of the key for a wide-open three-pointer that sealed a 128-118 win. Magic dribbled out the final seconds, throwing his fist in the air as the siren sounded and almost five years of frustration disappeared. He played 27 minutes and had 19 points, 8 rebounds, and 10 assists.[276]

"I can't even begin to tell you how I feel," Magic said. "It was so much fun. When he first put me in, I couldn't feel the game. That was one of the first times in my life I couldn't feel what was going on. I was just out there. And then Joe Smith hit me in my back, Seikaly hit me in my chest, and then I knew I was in a game then."

Nobody knew what to expect from Magic, but not even the most optimistic fan expected him to be just two rebounds short of a triple-double. "I didn't know what was going to happen tonight, I had no expectations," he said. "I didn't care if I didn't score a point or get a rebound or get one assist. All I wanted to do was walk on the court. I just wanted to play."

He had an undeniable impact on his team, with Ceballos the biggest benefactor with 33 points on 15-18 shooting. "Everybody is a better player with him on the team," Divac said. The Lakers played much quicker with Magic, especially with his ability to kick-start fast breaks even after the Warriors would score. And they played unselfishly, with every player making the extra pass. "Great players, when they pass the ball, you want to do the same thing," said Jones. "Even our scorers want to pass the ball."

Magic reported to practice the next day in good shape, with only slight soreness in his lower back. With a night's sleep, he was able to cast a more critical eye over his game. He was disappointed he missed a free throw, turned the ball over a few times, committed an offensive foul and didn't always read the play correctly. A reporter suggested he take it easy on himself because, after all, he barely missed a triple-double. "Yeah," he responded. "But I missed it."

The hype surrounding Magic's first game was intense, but it was nothing compared to the build-up for his second, a home game against the Chicago Bulls. It was billed as *Magic vs. Michael: The Sequel*. They hadn't

---

[276] Because it was the final Laker game in January, those numbers were technically Magic's averages for the month. The Lakers, tongue firmly in cheek, nominated Magic for the NBA's Player of the Month award. "Hey," said assistant PR director Raymond Ridder, "he almost averaged a triple-double for the month." The funny thing? Magic received a vote.

played against each other since the 1991 NBA Finals and Jordan hadn't played at the Forum since November 20, 1992.[277] Neither player was in the league just a year earlier. It was a match-up nobody thought would ever happen again between arguably the two most famous athletes in the world. "Funny how things happen," Magic said. "I never thought I'd be back. And I'm pretty sure he never thought he'd be back."

The Bulls were almost impossibly good. They were 40-3, the best three-loss record in the history of the league. They were the league's highest-scoring team, allowed the second-fewest points, and had a winning margin of 14 points per game. And they were on a seventeen-game win streak.

There were so many reporters from all over the world that many had to watch the game via television under the stands. Tickets had gone on sale on October 8, 1995 and had sold out within 10 days. Now brokers were cashing in, with $5,000 the highest confirmed price somebody paid for a ticket. Prime Sports got their highest ever ratings for an NBA game, the second time in three days, while TNT received their highest ratings ever, estimating the game was seen in 4.7 million homes.

Jack Nicholson had been forced to watch the Warriors game on TV in Miami where he was filming *Blood and Wine*. When director Bob Rafelson took ill and called off the day's filming, Nicholson took advantage and flew back to L.A. just for the game against the Bulls. "This is like a great heavyweight fight," he said. "You don't know what's going to happen, you don't want to miss it."[278]

Chick Hearn called the game "the biggest ever in the regular season for the Lakers." Harris had never seen anything like it outside the NBA Finals. Magic tried to prepare the young Lakers for something, unlike their standard Friday night home game. He feared a let-down from the Lakers, while Chicago coach Phil Jackson expected the hype to elevate the Bulls. And Jordan sounded keen to give the Lakers a dose of reality. "There are some tough teams you have to contend with," he said. "Golden State is not one of them." Meanwhile, Magic was trying to prepare himself for Dennis Rodman, who he expected to be matched up against most of the game. "Am I ready for him?" Magic asked. "Nobody's ever ready for

---

[277] The Bulls had already made their annual visit to the Forum in 1994-95 by the time Jordan came out of retirement.

[278] Nicholson was asked his reaction to Magic's comeback game. He gave a one-word answer – "Thunderstruck." A great quote.

Dennis."

The game was a ton of fun and completely lived up to the hype – for the first quarter anyway. Jones opened the game hot, scoring the Lakers' first eight points. Pippen hit a three-pointer on the game's first possession, and Jones answered with a three of his own. He then stole the ball from Ron Harper and out-sprinted the entire Bulls team for a breakaway dunk. A give-and-go with Campbell ended with Jones soaring for another dunk and a foul for an early 8-3 lead.

Then the Bulls got going. Jordan's first shot, a jumper over Divac, was nothing but net. After a dunk by Campbell, Rodman got two rebounds on the one play, the last resulting in a put-back lay-up. Then Bill Wellington hit a jumper to cut the Lakers' lead to 10-9.

Next to step up was Van Exel. He shook off Jordan with a cross-over and hit a short jumper off the glass. After Jordan missed, he pushed the ball and found Ceballos wide open for a three-pointer. Pippen then missed a finger-roll that led to Van Exel pushing it again in transition, finding Ceballos for a dunk and a 17-9 lead.

Jordan stepped his game up a notch when Magic checked in to a standing ovation with six and a half minutes to play in the quarter. He shook Jones with a hard drive and pulled back to hit a fadeaway jumper along the baseline. On their next possession, he gave Jones a pump fake in the post and drove into an open lane for a dunk that drew cheers from the crowd.

The Lakers went to Magic in the post for the first time against Rodman, and he hit a running skyhook in the lane for his first basket and a 23-17 lead. Then Pippen responded. First, he hit a three-pointer from the top of the key. After Magic turned the ball over trying to feed Campbell, Pippen made an easy jumper in the lane to cut the Lakers' lead to 23-22. A quick Bulls run gave them a 28-25 lead in the dying seconds of the quarter before Van Exel beat the buzzer with a half-court heave that was nothing but net. With the crowd on their feet, the Lakers headed to the break tied 28-28.

Scores were tied 33-33 a minute into the second quarter, but it was the last time the game would be close. The Bulls held the Lakers to just eight points for the rest of the quarter, and took a 54-39 half-time lead. Any hope of a second-half turnaround ended quickly when the Bulls opened the third quarter with an 11-2 run and led by 22 points at the end of the quarter. The Lakers cut the lead back to something vaguely respectable before falling 99-84. The fantasy that Magic's comeback could end in a championship came back to earth with a resounding thud.

For everybody besides the person who paid $5,000, the game was worth the price of admission simply for the sight of Magic and Jordan on the floor at the same time. But the game never fully lived up to the hype, and not just because of the Bulls blow-out. The Magic vs. Jordan match-up never amounted to much. Magic didn't play well, recording 15 points, just 3 rebounds, and 3 assists. He missed several easy shots, was visibly fatigued in the fourth quarter, and lacked the spark that made his comeback game so remarkable. Jordan was quiet too, scoring an efficient 17 points, well below the 30.4 he would average on the season.

Instead, the stars of the show were Pippen, who scored a game-high 30 points, and Rodman, who had a season-high 23 rebounds.[279] Rodman did his bit for AIDS awareness by unceremoniously guarding Magic as tough as he would anyone else in the league – pushing, shoving, and hacking at him all game long. "Who cares if he's got HIV, measles, cancer, whatever," he said. "I'm going to slam him anyway. Anybody's got any balls will do the same thing."

Magic and Jordan held a joint press conference after the game. Magic gushed over how great the Bulls were playing. "They are all what they're built up to be and even more," he said. "A team on all cylinders playing the way basketball is supposed to be played." Jordan said it took him a while to get to the level he wanted to be at when he came back, and it would take Magic some time too. But he wasn't as complimentary about Magic's teammates as Magic was about his. "He has the intensity and the killer instinct in his eyes," Jordan said. "But his team may not have the same."

Two nights after hosting the league-best Bulls, the Lakers hosted the second-best team in the West, the 30-14 Utah Jazz. Fans clearly hadn't forgiven Karl Malone for his comments that helped push Magic into re-retirement in 1992. He was booed loudly during pre-game introductions, and on and off throughout the game. "The fans can boo me," Malone said. "It makes me play better."

Magic checked in for the first time with just under four minutes remaining in the first quarter with the Lakers leading 16-15, and he got

---

[279] Rodman's 23 rebounds were just six less than the entire Lakers team. He outrebounded the Lakers 15-12 by himself in the first half.

straight to work. He played a perfect pick and roll with Divac, looping a pass to him over the defenders for an easy lay-in. The Lakers got a stop on their next possession, Magic pushed the ball up court and fired a no-look pass to Van Exel for a long jumper. Utah then missed another shot, Magic secured the rebound and bolted up the court like a runaway train. He threw another no-look pass, this one an alley-oop to Divac. "He bought his wand tonight, baby," said Hearn. It was vintage Magic, instantly changing the game without taking a single shot, and the Lakers took a 26-20 lead at the first quarter break.

The lead see-sawed for the next two quarters, and the Lakers held a 78-74 lead at the end of the third. They opened the fourth with a 9-2 run giving them a lead they wouldn't relinquish. The Lakers led by 14 when Magic, who was guarded by Antoine Carr most of the night, finally matched-up with Malone in the post. He hit a skyhook over Malone, drawing a huge cheer from the crowd.

The Lakers won 110-101 and Magic had 21 points, 7 rebounds, and 6 assists in 31 minutes. Harris played him at four different positions for the first time. He had wanted to play him at small forward against the Bulls but chose against it because he hadn't learned all the plays yet. He practiced at small forward after the Bulls game and Harris wanted to give him a try. "That's what we want," Magic said. "We wanted that versatility. That makes us one of the best teams."

Magic publicly buried the hatchet with Malone after the game. "He said something maybe everybody else wanted to say," Magic said. "I think he spoke out of not being educated. He didn't know, I didn't know, everybody didn't know. In fact, he probably helped everyone get educated."

The Lakers hit the road with Magic for the first time when they visited the Denver Nuggets who two nights earlier gave the Bulls their fourth loss of the season. It was the start of a two-night test for Magic, his first road game and his first set of back-to-back games.[280]

His comeback hadn't only caused a spike in ticket sales in Los Angeles, but in visiting cities too. The Nuggets rarely sold more than 50 tickets in

---

[280] Unlike when he attempted to come back for the 1992-93 season, Magic intended to play all scheduled games. It's an example of how much had changed. He retired in 1991 because doctors thought the demands of the NBA schedule would be too much. In 1992-93 he tried to come back part-time. By 1995-96, none of that mattered.

one day for a game several weeks away, but after Magic announced his comeback they sold 683 tickets to the Lakers game in one weekend.

Fans at McNichols Arena gave him a standing ovation when he checked in for the first time. The Lakers led 66-61 after three quarters and turned the game on its head with a 10-4 run in the fourth quarter. The Nuggets got as close as nine midway through the quarter, but the Lakers answered with a 7-2 run that sealed a comfortable 99-78 win.[281]

Magic came close to the first triple-double of his comeback, finishing with 16 points, 12 rebounds, and nine assists. He played 33 minutes and more garbage time than expected, especially considering the Lakers had a game back in Los Angeles the next night. He said he wanted to stay in the game to test his endurance in Denver's high-altitude conditions. But Harris was more open about why he was still in the game. "I left Earvin in to get a triple-double," he said. "All he was in for was one more rebound."

Those extra minutes chasing the triple-double in Denver visibly took its toll the next night at home against the New Jersey Nets. Magic came into the game in the first quarter and dutifully made his first shot, a left-handed hook over Armon Gilliam.[282] But he missed seven of his next nine shots. Most of those misses were flat, the tell-tale sign of tired legs. Still, the Lakers led by eleven at quarter time and pushed the lead out further when Sedale Threatt checked-in and immediately hit two three-pointers. A Nets run late in the second quarter got them back to 46-43 before Jones made a three-pointer and Magic made two free throws for an eight-point half-time lead.

The Lakers looked to put the game away when Magic spear-headed an emphatic 17-5 run in the third quarter. He lobbed a pass to Campbell who threw it down and drew the foul. He then made two assists in consecutive possessions to Jones. The first was a lob pass that Jones acrobatically tipped in. The second was a no-look bullet pass through traffic that Jones tossed in with his back to the basket while drawing a foul, pushing the lead out to 78-57 with two minutes left in the quarter.

---

[281] Play was stopped with four minutes remaining when blood from Dikembe Mutumbo was brushed onto teammate Mahmoud Abdul-Rauf. It could have revived fears of playing against Magic, but the incident got next to no media attention.

[282] Gilliam received some boos from the crowd throughout the game for his comments about playing against Magic, but not on the level Karl Malone received.

But the Nets got back in the game with a 12-0 run to end the third quarter. Chris Childs made a three-pointer from beyond half-court to beat the buzzer, cutting the Lakers' lead to 78-69. The run continued in the fourth quarter and the Nets looked like they might steal the game. A jumper by Gilliam got them within 98-94 with less than two minutes to play, and the Forum crowd grew restless.

The Lakers needed a score to temper the storm. Jones blew past a mismatched Shawn Bradley at the three-point line and charged into the lane. He threw a short lob pass to Campbell under the rim, but his shot was blocked from behind by Gilliam. The ball spilled to Ceballos, but he had his shot blocked by Bradley. Jones picked up the loose ball and was swamped by Bradley and Jayson Williams. With three seconds on the shot clock, he flicked a pass to Magic who had no choice but to hoist up a three-pointer. He sunk the three-pointer as the shot clock sounded, sealing a 106-96 win.

"One of the only shots I hit from the outside tonight, and it turned out to be a big one," Magic said. The game was a good challenge for Magic, battling through 31 minutes on the second night of a back-to-back. He was tired, and it affected his shot as he finished 5-16 from the floor, but he collected 18 points, nine rebounds, and eight assists. "I don't think it would have indicated one thing had Magic not had a good game. It was difficult traveling and playing back-to-back after being back in the league only eight days," Harris said. "The fact is he played very well."

The schedule paused for the All-Star break, and unlike last year, not a single Laker would be taking part in any of the festivities. Ceballos wasn't selected to play despite averaging 23.4 points and 7.2 rebounds over the first 45 games of the season, better numbers than a year earlier when he was selected to play.[283] He was likely a shoe-in for the final forward spot, but coaches instead selected three centers to play.[284]

Usually, a team would welcome the mid-season break with open arms,

---

[283] Only five other players in the league were averaging at least 23 points and 7 rebounds at that point in the season – Charles Barkley, Alonzo Mourning, Karl Malone, Hakeem Olajuwon, and David Robinson. Ceballos was the only one on the list not to be named an All-Star.

[284] Dikembe Mutumbo was selected, meaning Ceballos missed out on playing in the All-Star Game twice because of Mutumbo. Ceballos was selected to play in 1995, but couldn't after injuring himself in a collision with Mutumbo. Now Mutumbo was being selected ahead of him in 1996.

but not these Lakers. They had been playing well the last six weeks and wanted to continue the momentum. "We'd rather keep going," Harris said. "When you're just getting started, a break is not what you're looking for."

Both teams looked rusty after a week off when the Lakers hosted the Atlanta Hawks. The game wasn't pretty, with both teams appearing out of synch. But it wasn't short on drama. The Lakers went up 85-83 on a free throw by Magic with 42 seconds to play. But the Hawks gained a one-point lead when Craig Ehlo hit a three-pointer with 25 seconds remaining.

Following a timeout, Magic backed the much smaller Steve Smith down from almost midcourt. He worked his way past the three-point line and spun into the lane. Hawks center Andrew Lang left Divac to double-team Magic, which was exactly what he wanted. Magic fired a pass to Divac who drove to the basket and was fouled by Lang as he scrambled to get back into position.

Divac was at the free throw line with 4.6 seconds left and the game hanging in the balance. "I was waiting for that moment all year long," he said. "I've been waiting since the San Antonio series." Divac made both free throws and the Lakers won 87-86 when Ehlo's three-pointer fell short at the buzzer.

After almost getting a triple-double in several games, Magic got his first since coming out of retirement with 15 points, 10 rebounds, and 13 assists. The game may not have been easy on the eyes, but it was good for the Lakers to grind out a win. "When you're sloppy, when you don't play well, and you can get the victory, that's the sign of a team that's coming," said Magic

If there was ever an example Magic wasn't like any other player in the NBA, it was the kind of questions he got from the media after the Hawks game. He got basketball questions, but was also asked about criticism leveled at him by Speaker of the House Newt Gingrich. Magic had been critical of a recent bill passed by Congress that singled out HIV-positive service members for immediate discharge from the military. Gingrich responded to Magic's criticism, saying he had no understanding of the danger of combat. Magic patiently explained his stance that people who are HIV-positive didn't need to lose their jobs and pension but could be put on non-combat duties instead.[285]

The game two nights later against the Dallas Mavericks was the complete opposite to the Hawks game. Both teams got out in transition regularly, filling up the scoreboard and entertaining the sold-out Forum crowd. The Mavs led 92-87 early in the fourth quarter when Magic did something he hadn't done to that point in his comeback. He completely took over the game.

Mavs coach Dick Motta opened the fourth quarter with David Wood guarding Magic, and Magic took full advantage of the match-up. He scored seven quick points against Wood, tying the score at 94-94. Wood tried to get one back on the other end but launched an ill-advised three-pointer that wasn't close. Ceballos rebounded, and Magic launched a quick three-pointer over Wood that was all net.

Motta changed tack a few minutes later and put George McCloud on Magic. McCloud was much smaller than Magic, and needed help guarding him. Magic scored a hook shot over him on single coverage. When the double teams inevitably came on the next three possessions, Magic made three quick assists.

The Mavs were still alive and trailed by one with three minutes to play. Motta made his third switch of the quarter by putting Popeye Jones on Magic. But Magic made two straight skyhooks over him for a 114-110 lead.

But still, the Mavs hung around. Popeye Jones hit a long jumper to cut the lead to two with a minute remaining. The Lakers went back to Magic in the post, and he ran down the clock. He drew a double-team and threw a pass out to Ceballos, who nailed a three-pointer just before the shot clock expired, sealing the win for the Lakers. Magic and Ceballos ran down court high fiving, the crowd went crazy, the Lakers won 119-114, and the good times were back at the Forum.

Magic finished with 30 points, including 18 in the fourth quarter, to go along with 11 assists and eight rebounds. "I just felt it was the right time to pick it up," he said. "I'm in better shape now. The first couple of games my arms were moving, but my legs weren't. The way it was in the fourth is the way it used to be."

Magic's comeback was two and a half weeks old and proving to be a

---

[285] Magic published an editorial entitled 'Let Us Be All We Can Be' about the issue in the *Los Angeles Times* on March 14, 1996.

hit. He had out-performed even the most optimistic expectations. Over his first seven games, he averaged 19.1 points, 7.7 rebounds, and 9.0 assists in 32 minutes.[286] He was playing so well he started to put a plan in place to continue playing into the next season. "I'm planning on coming back," he said. "I'm setting things up for next season." He withdrew his name from consideration for the Atlanta Olympics, remembering how his younger Dream Team teammates in 1992 felt they didn't get enough rest for the upcoming season. He would instead spend the off-season preparing his body for training camp.

The Lakers were 6-1 since Magic's comeback and 14-3 since their New Year debacle against Philly. They had looked like they would struggle to make the playoffs back in December. Now they were 30-19 and a chance for home-court advantage in the first round. "At this point, we've kind of removed ourselves from the pack," Harris said. "Now you're looking at five teams and then the pack, whereas before it was four teams and then the pack."

A season that looked like it was going to be a let-down had suddenly produced two weeks of incredibly fun basketball. It truly was a *great* fortnight to be a Lakers fan.

---

[286] His Per 36 numbers were better over the first seven games of his comeback than they were for his career. His career Per 36 numbers were 19.1 points, 7.1 rebounds, and 11.1 assists. Over the first seven games of his comeback they were 21.5 points, 8.7 rebounds, and 10.1 assists.

Chapter 31
REALITY BITES

February 20, 1996 to March 19, 1996

O NCE THE BUZZER had sounded on Magic Johnson's comeback game against the Golden State Warriors, fans slowly filed out of the Forum. On the way out the door, a young fan was heard in conversation about the incredible performance Magic had given. "God, what if they're right? What if he's not the player he used to be?" the fan said. "What if he's better?"

It was a fun thought. Magic might just be superhuman, capable of defying Mother Nature and come back a better player after all those years on the sidelines. For two weeks, someone could be forgiven for believing that fantasy. It legitimately looked like it might be true.

But ultimately, reality bit when the Lakers hosted the Los Angeles Clippers in Magic's eighth game back. There the inevitable happened to a player who was 36 years old, not in prime shape, hadn't played in four and a half years, and didn't have the benefit of off-season workouts and training camp. He got hurt. And it would ultimately cost him weeks of productivity on the court.

Magic checked in two minutes into the game when Campbell picked up two early fouls. He lasted two full possessions before calling a timeout and hobbling to the bench. By the time Del Harris finished the timeout, Magic was already back in his warm-ups and heading to the locker room with Gary Vitti. He was quickly ruled out for the rest of the game and diagnosed with a mild to moderate strained right calf muscle.

He first injured the calf while playing on his exhibition team a year earlier and it had been nagging him ever since. It had begun to bother him again in practice the day before, but he was declared fit to play. Magic was frustrated by the injury, knowing he would have to sit out. Vitti recommended rest in the hope they could fix the issue without it turning into a chronic injury that might force him to miss up to six weeks.

Because they were playing the Clippers, the Lakers hardly needed Magic. Vlade Divac, Cedric Ceballos, and Nick Van Exel each scored over 20 points. The Lakers scored 41 points in the third quarter and got the easy 121-104 win.

Magic wasn't in uniform the next night at the Sports Arena when the Lakers took on the Clippers on the second night of a home-and-away series. The Clippers were last in the NBA in attendance but drew their biggest crowd of the season because of Magic's comeback. If it was a crucial game, he would have suited up and tested the calf. But because it was against the Clippers, he sat out.

The Lakers won a close game in odd circumstances when the Clippers didn't foul to stop the game clock. Lamond Murray's dunk cut the Lakers' lead to 109-108 with 26.7 seconds to play. The Lakers ran the clock all the way down until Peeler made a three-pointer from the right corner with 2.9 seconds left to seal the 112-108 victory.

"They were all over the court hollering 'foul, foul, foul,'" Peeler said. Terry Dehere said he grabbed Van Exel with 10 seconds left, but the officials didn't make the call. From there, the Lakers moved the ball, and the Clippers were unable to catch them to foul.

The Lakers then kicked off a two-game, two-night Texas trip against Dallas and Houston. With the chance to see Magic play in Dallas for the first time in five years, the Mavs drew a sell-out crowd. Knowing Magic was unlikely to play, a Mavs official called Lon Rosen and asked if there was any chance Magic could play just a few minutes. Instead, the crowd could only cheer his short walk from the player chase to the bench as he sat in street clothes. Ceballos had 27 points, Divac pulled down 18 rebounds, and the Lakers easily handled the Mavs with a 114-88 win.

The Lakers were one of the hottest teams in the league. The win in Dallas was their eighth in a row, and they had won 14 of their last 16 games.[287] The next night's contest against the two-time defending champion Houston Rockets was a barometer game, a chance to see how good they really were. After playing just one minute in the last ten days, Magic was cleared to test his calf in Houston. The game was too important

---

[287] It was their longest win streak since winning 9 straight just after Magic retired in November 1991.

for him to miss.

Magic checked in with three minutes left in the first quarter and looked unsteady when trying to push off his right leg. He lasted until four minutes left in the second quarter before Harris took him out for good. After lasting a total of 11 minutes, registering 2 points and 3 assists, he wouldn't return in the second half. He didn't aggravate the injury, but it was clear he wasn't ready to play. "It was all right for a minute, then it just tightened," Magic said. "It let me know it's not strong enough yet, so I've got to lay back."

The Rockets had injury concerns of their own. They placed Clyde Drexler on the injured list the day before the game, and he would be out six weeks following knee surgery. And their usual starting point guard, Sam Cassell, was battling the stomach flu.

The Lakers held a nine-point lead with 11 minutes to play when point guard Kenny Smith put on a shooting clinic. After being the starting point guard on back-to-back championship teams with the Rockets, Smith had been in the doghouse. He had hardly played in a month, had requested a trade, but the Rockets couldn't find a deal they liked before the deadline. Rockets coach Rudy Tomjanovich gave Smith a chance in the fourth quarter, who rewarded the decision with 4-4 shooting, all three-pointers. It was enough to give the Rockers a 96-94 victory with Peeler missing a potential game-winning three-pointer in the dying seconds.

The Lakers returned home to host the shorthanded New York Knicks. Patrick Ewing was out with a sprained ankle, Charles Oakley was sitting with a fractured thumb, and J.R. Reid was suspended for breaking A.C. Green's nose with a flagrant foul the night before. The Knicks were fourth in the East but hadn't looked the same all season since Don Nelson replaced Pat Riley as head coach. Magic didn't play, but with the Knicks forced to start Matt Fish at center, the Lakers ran out to a predictably easy 114-96 win behind 27 points from Ceballos.

They shot up to Canada for a one-game road trip in Vancouver. Magic didn't travel with the team, disappointing Grizzlies guard Byron Scott who was looking forward to playing against his old backcourt partner. Instead, he cast his eye to the Grizzlies' visit to the Forum in six weeks' time. "Hopefully I'll get to play against him then," Scott said before breaking out into a smile. "I'll hit him with a couple of elbows and knock a couple of jumpers down."

The Lakers got a methodological 99-80 win despite also being without Van Exel, who sat out with a hip pointer. Harris started Threatt in his place but played him at the two-guard, handing point guard duties to Eddie Jones for the first time. Jones had 18 points, but hoped his stay at the one spot would be short-lived. "I hope Nick's back now," he said. "It's tough. I liked it, but it's tiresome." The Lakers closed out February with the win, finishing the month with a 10-2 record, their best month of basketball since going 15-2 in January 1991.

Van Exel was back when the Lakers hosted the Washington Bullets, who had played most of the season without Chris Webber due to a shoulder injury and were struggling with a 24-32 record. The Lakers sprinted out to a 37-19 lead in the first nine minutes and held on for a 100-95 win behind 27 points from Ceballos.

Most importantly for the Lakers was that Magic was back in uniform against Washington. He played 15 minutes and then only a few seconds of the fourth quarter when Harris briefly subbed him in just to make an inbounds pass. He finished with only 5 points and 3 assists, but it was a welcome sight having him back. It was the first game he had successfully completed in almost two weeks. The leg felt good afterward, and he didn't appear to have lost any conditioning while on the sidelines.

After losing their barometer match in Houston, they got a second chance when they hosted the Rockets a week later. It was a game the Lakers felt they should win. They were at home, Drexler was still injured, and Magic had his warm-up against the Bullets under his belt. But it didn't go to plan. Kenny Smith picked up where he left off a week earlier by hitting his first five shots, and the Rockets led by nine at half-time.

The Lakers opened the third quarter with a 12-2 run, taking a 69-68 lead on a three-pointer by Ceballos with seven minutes remaining in the third. But the Rockets wore the Lakers down in the fourth quarter and built a 105-98 lead with two minutes to play. Two free throws by Van Exel cut the Rockets' lead to four. They got a stop on the next possession, but Peeler missed a three-pointer with 20 seconds left. Free throws settled the game from there, a 111-107 win to the Rockets. Despite their great run over the last seven weeks, the Lakers had twice failed to beat an elite team. Magic managed 26 minutes, scoring 14 points and grabbing 7 rebounds. But he was sluggish, committed seven turnovers, and looked like he was laboring most of the game.

* * * * *

With three full days of rest between games, Magic appeared to move better when the Lakers took on the Kings in Sacramento. The game was tied at 85-85 with five minutes remaining when he backed Michael Smith down in the low post. He drew a double-team from Olden Polynice that left Campbell open below the free throw line. Magic made a short pass to Campbell who flicked in a short jump shot. It was a routine, unspectacular play but it was a meaningful one. It gave Magic his 10,000ᵗʰ career assist, becoming just the second player in NBA history to reach that mark.[288] Play continued until the next dead ball, at which time the achievement was announced to the Arco Arena crowd. An official presented Magic with the game ball, and the crowd gave him a standing ovation. He waived a thank you to the crowd and pointed towards Kings coach Garry St. Jean as a gesture of thanks for allowing the game to stop briefly for the moment. He flipped the ball to the Lakers bench for safekeeping, and the game continued.

The Lakers broke the game open from that point on, comfortably beating the Kings 102-89. They won easily again the next night in Phoenix, cruising to a 119-97 win over the Suns. Magic's workload had returned to its old level just six days after returning from injury. He played 30 minutes in Sacramento, scoring 15 points and handing out 7 assists. He then played 32 minutes the next night in Phoenix, finishing with 12 points and 8 assists. But while surviving the minutes was a good test for his calf, he wasn't playing at the same level as before the injury. After turning the ball over seven times against Houston, he had five turnovers against Sacramento and six more against Phoenix. Magic wasn't the driving force behind either win in Sacramento or Phoenix. Campbell's 29 points, 11 rebounds, and 6 blocks powered the Lakers in Sacramento, while Van Exel's 28 points and 13 assists, combined with Ceballos' 23 points and 10 rebounds, were the catalysts in beating the Suns.

Despite three days off following the road trip, Magic looked unsteady again when the Lakers hosted the Portland Trail Blazers. He struggled

---

[288] It also corrected one of the great statistical injustices in NBA history. Magic finished the 1990-91 season with 9,921 career assists – just 79 short of becoming the first player in NBA history to reach 10,000. Assuming his 1991-92 assist rate would have been similar to that of 1990-91, he likely would have achieved 10,000 just seven games into the season (at home against Houston on November 15, 1991). Magic's assist to Campbell didn't make him the first player with 10,000 (John Stockton got there in 1995), and didn't make him the all-time leader (Stockton had over-taken him), but it did right a wrong.

mightily in 28 minutes, shooting just 1-6 from the field and finishing with 5 points, 5 rebounds, and 8 assists. The Lakers had a five-point lead with three and a half minutes to play when the Blazers steamrolled them. 31-year-old rookie Arvydas Sabonis scored two baskets, both from offensive rebounds, on back-to-back possessions late in the game and the Lakers lost 105-99.

If Magic's first seven games were like something out of a fairytale, his next seven were more like a horror movie by comparison. His calf injury had severely limited him and taken some of the shine off his return. Fans could only hope it was temporary. Over the last seven games, he had averaged just 7.6 points, 3.6 rebounds, 4.9 assists, and 42% shooting in 20.4 minutes. Not exactly the numbers of an all-time great. The Lakers went 4-3 in those seven games and 4-0 with him on the sidelines.

He wasn't expected to play in Oakland two nights later. His calf was still bothering him, and he had also been hampered against Portland by tendinitis in his right Achilles. But he was moving better than expected in morning shootaround and decided to suit up against Golden State. He received a standing ovation from Warriors fans when he checked in and then, out of the blue, looked much more like the Magic from the first seven games of his comeback. He played 34 pain-free minutes and led the Lakers in scoring with 21 points. "My calf finally didn't bother me today," he said with a sense of relief.

Even with Magic playing well, the Warriors played the Lakers tough – like they always seemed to at home. A free throw by Joe Smith got the Warriors within three points of the Lakers with 51 seconds to play. Magic backed Smith down into the paint and dropped the ball off to Van Exel for a lay-in and a 102-97 lead with 33 seconds left. The Warriors had a chance to tie, but Bimbo Coles missed an off-balance three-pointer, and the Lakers won 103-100. It was the Lakers' first win in Oakland in almost three years, ending a seven-game losing streak in that city where they had lost by an average of 20.4 points.

Magic played against a former coach's team for the first time since returning when the Lakers hosted Mike Dunleavy and the Milwaukee Bucks the next night. The two bumped into each other in the hallway outside the visitor's locker room before the game. "How you doing?" Magic asked him. "I've been better," sighed Dunleavy, whose Bucks were 20-40 on the season and just 3-13 since the All-Star break. This, after going

80-164 in the three seasons since he left the Lakers to become their head coach. "I don't think there's any way I would have left if Earvin was still here," reflected Dunleavy when thinking about his departure in 1992.

The Lakers routed the Bucks 117-95 in front of a sold out Forum crowd and Magic looked in form for the second night in a row. He played just 22 minutes but found time to score a game-high 20 points and hand out 8 assists. "I'm running, and I'm moving, and I feel confident," he said. "I'm doing all the things I thought I would be doing after the Dallas game. I am so happy to be where I am now."

Magic was rounding into good form at an opportune moment because the Lakers' schedule, soft since his return, was about to turn brutal. Unable to gain legitimacy when they lost two games to the Houston Rockets, they had three straight barometer games up next. The first would be at home against Shaquille O'Neal and the Orlando Magic, owners of the league's third-best record. Then they had a home-and-away series against the Seattle SuperSonics, who owned the league's second-best record behind Chicago. "Now we'll see what we're made of," Van Exel said.

Unfortunately, the game against Orlando didn't go the way Van Exel would have hoped, as he blew a golden opportunity to win the game in the dying seconds. Orlando was holding a five-point lead with under three minutes to play when Magic led a rally. He rebounded a Van Exel miss for a putback to cut the lead to three. He fed Campbell for a lay-up to make it 95-94 with one and a half minutes remaining. He then fed Divac in the low post where he drew Shaquille O'Neal's sixth foul. Shaq fouled out with 26 points and 10 rebounds, and Divac hit one of two free throws to tie the game 95-95 with one minute to play.

Dennis Scott answered for Orlando, making a three-pointer with 40 seconds remaining to give them a three-point lead. Magic then fed Jones on a quick-hitting alley-oop to cut the lead to 98-97 with 27 seconds left.

Harris gambled and chose not to foul to stop the clock, and it paid off. Anthony Bowie bobbled a pass from Anfernee Hardaway that bounced off his knee and into the hands of Campbell with 8.4 seconds left. Campbell immediately handed off to Van Exel, who charged down court as the Forum crowd rose to their feet in nervous anticipation. Van Exel had nothing between him and the basket except Bowie, who was back-pedaling to try to stay in front of him. He got right under the basket with

4.0 seconds left, but Bowie recovered. Instead of forcing the issue by attempting a lay-up where he likely would have drawn a foul, Van Exel inexplicably dribbled out of the key and bolted to the three-point line. He launched a three-pointer at the buzzer over the outstretched hand of Bowie that hit the front of the rim and bounced off. "I should have taken it to the hole," Van Exel said. "I panicked a little bit, I was out of control, and it was a dumb decision. I should have known better. I blew it."

Divac and Harris got into an argument in the fourth quarter when Divac was called for a technical foul. Divac was frustrated by the technical, claiming the inflammatory comment the official heard wasn't made by him but by a player standing behind him. But Harris erupted, immediately benching Divac and screaming at him on the sidelines. Divac was upset by the way Harris treated him. "Wouldn't you be?" he said. He felt he didn't deserve the technical and Harris' wrath should have been directed at the official who made the call. The rest of the Lakers were bothered by Harris making such a public display of berating Divac. No doubt they hadn't forgotten that Harris had drawn two technical fouls and been ejected less than a month earlier when the Lakers hosted the Clippers.

Magic played well down the stretch against Orlando and, just like in Oakland, the offense looked more stable when running through him down the stretch. But he struggled to have an impact when the ball wasn't in his hands, playing 33 minutes and finishing with 10 points on 4-11 shooting, 4 rebounds, and 5 assists. He struggled defensively and was outplayed by Horace Grant, his power forward counterpart, who had 26 points on 10-15 shooting and 17 rebounds.

He also re-injured his right calf in the second quarter, just two days after he declared himself fully recovered. He left the court but returned and was able to finish the game. He underwent an MRI test the following day that showed no serious damage to the calf. "I thought we had it before," he said. "It's not my age, any young guy would be the same. Anyone who's been out four and a half years, those things are bound to happen."

The Lakers still hadn't got a win against a legitimate championship contender since Magic came out of retirement. They had lost to Chicago, Orlando, and twice to Houston. But they finally got one when they routed the Sonics 94-71 in front of a delirious sold out crowd at the Forum. It was the Sonics' second-lowest scoring game in franchise history and the second-best defensive showing in Lakers history.

Jones put on a spectacular show in the first half, scoring 14 points in the first quarter and six more in the second. "He was dynamite in the first half," Sonics coach George Karl said. "Since Magic came back, he seems to be playing with as much confidence as anybody."

Despite the pain in his calf, Magic had one of his strongest games since the injury. He played 34 minutes and had 14 points and 10 assists, and he bucked a troublesome trend over the last few weeks by not committing a single turnover. But, as always, he was just happy to beat a good team. "I think tonight we proved to ourselves we can win the big game," he said.

On that one night, everything looked bright for the Lakers. The Lake Show was back to beating the talented Sonics again. Chants of *"Ed-die! Ed-die!"* were echoing around the Forum, just like they had done during the playoffs almost a year earlier. They were 41-23, now two wins ahead of where they were at the same stage the previous season.

But the next day things would get weird for the Lakers. Really weird. Something would happen that would end up being the genesis of their undoing. It would be the first step of a process that would turn their promising season into a spectacular train wreck, where they would ultimately throw away almost everything they had built over the last eleven weeks.

Chapter 32

UNDONE

March 21, 1996 to April 21, 1996

W HERE IN THE world is Ceballos?
 That was the headline on the front page of the sports section of
the *Los Angeles Times* on March 22, 1996. It was the question everybody
was asking. Nobody at the Lakers – not the players, coaches, or front office
– knew where the hell their co-captain and leading scorer was.

The afternoon following their impressive win over the Sonics at the
Forum, the Lakers flew to Seattle to take on the Sonics again. But Ceballos
didn't show up for the flight. Neither Ceballos nor his agent, Fred
Slaughter, had called the Lakers to explain where he was. It got to the
point where they couldn't wait any longer for him, and the team boarded
the plane and departed for Seattle without him.

They checked in to their hotel and still hadn't heard from him. They
met the following morning for their routine shootaround, and still
nothing. They arrived at KeyArena for the game in the evening, Del Harris
gave his usual pep talk, and the Lakers trotted out for pre-game warm-
ups. And still, nobody knew where he was.

Jerry West and Mitch Kupchak were back in Los Angeles calling
around to find out if anybody had seen him. At first, they were concerned.
But they realized they hadn't received any calls from worried family or
friends wondering if the Lakers knew where he was. "Our assumption is
that he is fine, and we hope that he is," Kupchak said. They moved on
from being worried, went straight to being angry, and suspended Ceballos
indefinitely.

Back in Seattle, Harris inserted Magic Johnson at the vacant starting
small forward spot, the first start of his comeback. Seattle led the
bewildered Lakers by 13 at half-time and pushed the advantage to 18 in

the third quarter. Nick Van Exel led a comeback, scoring 11 points in the fourth quarter and cutting the lead to 93-88 with two and a half minutes to play. But it would be as close as they would get, and the Sonics would run out 104-93 winners.

Magic played 39 minutes, the most of his comeback so far, scoring 17 points on 7-18 shooting and grabbing 7 rebounds. After the game, he sounded as angry at Ceballos as West and Kupchak were. "I'm not worried about who's not here," he said bluntly. "I don't want to hear about if we had Cedric. Forget Cedric. He's not here. We're going to worry about who's in this locker room."

The press got a tip the next day as to Ceballos' whereabouts when they located a man who had apparently rented him a boat on Lake Havasu in Arizona. "He's on the lake having a good time," the man said. "He's got his family with him, and he's just out having a good time." Ceballos had indeed ditched the Lakers without notice, gone away with his family and some friends, and checked in to the London Bridge Resort. He was spotted waterskiing on Lake Havasu during the day, and dancing and signing autographs at Kokomo's, a local club, at night.

Slaughter phoned the Lakers and informed them Ceballos was safe and working on some personal issues. To West, it was an astonishing act of unprofessionalism, especially from a co-captain. If Ceballos had reached out to West and told him he had personal issues he needed to deal with, West would have been accommodating. Jerry Buss long had a policy allowing players to take leave to sort out off-court problems. But Ceballos never went to West, he just went AWOL.

Ceballos' unannounced and unauthorized vacation couldn't have come at a worse time for the Lakers. They had won 25 of their last 32 games, their delicate psyche starting to come together. They were in the middle of a tough set of games and about to head off on a long road trip. The playoffs were just six weeks away. This was the time of year the team should be coming together, but instead, their co-captain created a huge distraction. "You talk about timing," Magic said. "This is the worst timing it could possibly be."

Word leaked that at least part of the reason for Ceballos' absence was his increasing frustration with Harris' rotations. Though never confirmed publicly, it was likely no coincidence he abandoned the team the night after playing just 12 minutes, scoring two points on 1-7 shooting, against the Sonics.

Ceballos wasn't the only player to have issues with Harris' rotations over the two seasons. Harris, perhaps rightly, believed the Lakers didn't have a go-to superstar on their roster. As a way of compensating, he had an unspoken rule of riding the hot hand – giving minutes to whoever was playing well on any given night. Always a potent scorer, Ceballos often struggled defensively. It was something Harris could overlook a year ago when the Lakers were a rebuilding team. But now the spotlight was on them, and they were expected to go deep into the playoffs. Harris could no longer simply overlook Ceballos' defensive inadequacies.

Ceballos' issue with the rotations had only gotten worse since Magic returned to playing normal minutes after recovering from the calf injury. In Oakland, he had his streak of 67 straight games scoring in double figures snapped, finishing with nine points on just nine shots against Golden State. He appeared to protest the next game by hoisting a series of ill-advised three-pointers against the Bucks, eventually taking a career-high 12 of them, making three. He didn't score a point in the second half against Orlando. And then Magic took most of his minutes at small forward against Seattle. But Ceballos would hear little sympathy from his teammates about being in-and-out of the lineup, not when he was leading the team in minutes and scoring.[289]

Ceballos was still nowhere to be seen at training the day after getting back from Seattle. The players held a meeting following training and voted to strip him of his co-captaincy in absentia. Magic and Van Exel vented their frustration to the media. "He abandoned us," said a flabbergasted Van Exel. "We've got a team captain who just walks out."

Magic had never dealt with anything like this before and admitted he was now questioning his decision to play into next season. "The Lakers don't have problems, they have *a* problem," he said. "We're all upset. We're trying to do something here, we have a great opportunity. He's hurting us."

After five days, Ceballos finally did appear at the Forum, three hours before the Lakers were due to take on the Charlotte Hornets. Ceballos and

---

[289] Ceballos' averages before Magic's comeback: 36.3 minutes, 16.9 shot attempts, and 23.4 points. In the first seven games of Magic's comeback: 35.4 minutes, 15.7 shot attempts, and 22.6 points. In the seven games Magic was either out or limited due to injury: 34.6 minutes, 15.7 shots, and 24.9 points. In the eight games since Magic returned to normal minutes: 30.4 minutes, 12.6 shots, and 15.1 points.

Slaughter met privately with West for about 45 minutes before Ceballos fronted the media at a press conference. "There are a lot of things I put before basketball," he said. "My health, my family, and religion. One of those things came up." He apologized but was guarded, going into few details. He claimed the reason for his absence was a family crisis, and nothing to do with basketball. He said he wanted to put it behind him and move on, but it was telling neither West nor Harris attended the press conference. West answered some questions from the media afterward, while Harris didn't attend at all.[290]

Ceballos left the Forum without speaking to any of his teammates, who a few hours later lost 102-97 to the Hornets.[291] Already shorthanded without their co-captain, the Lakers were also without Vlade Divac who was home with a bad case of tonsillitis. The loss came despite a strong performance from Magic, who started his second straight game. He played 39 minutes and had 28 points, 8 rebounds, and 5 assists.

Ceballos was reinstated the following day, fined $56,657 by the team, and rejoined his teammates as they flew to Orlando to begin their road trip. [292] The team gave him the cold shoulder during the four-plus hours in the air, and he showed an incredible lack of insight when they landed. "It was quiet on the team plane, nobody said anything to me," he said. "So hopefully it's all died down."

The reality was, of course, the opposite. "He has not apologized to the team," Van Exel said. "Some of the guys are still distant from him. If he apologizes, it should be okay. He hasn't said 'I'm sorry.' He hasn't even said 'Hi.'" Ceballos did at least look like he was trying to mend some fences the next day when he was one of only three players who attended a voluntary practice at Orlando Arena the morning of the game.

Harris decided to start Ceballos on the bench against Orlando, something he acknowledged was done both as a continued form of punishment and, in his words, a "concession to the balance of chemistry." He stayed on the bench for almost the entire first half, checking in with

---

[290] Ceballos was due to attend a special assembly at Canoga Park High that week to, ironically, honor students with 95% or better school attendance.

[291] Mike Penner jokingly wrote in the *Los Angeles Times* that Ceballos should have been listed for the game as 'Did Not Play – Skipper's Decision.'

[292] Officially he was fined $54,657 for missing two games and $2,000 for missing two practices and shootaround.

four minutes to play in the second quarter and receiving a chorus of boos from the Orlando crowd. He looked tentative at first, missing a couple of shots badly, but he looked more comfortable when the Lakers kick-started their running game in the second half.

The Lakers led by five points at half-time and blew Orlando out of the water in the second half en route to an emphatic 113-91 victory. It was exactly what Orlando coach Brian Hill was worried would happen, that the controversy over Ceballos would bring the team together for a great performance. The Lakers shot 55% and got contributions from almost everybody. Van Exel top scored with 22 points, Magic added 14 points and 7 assists, and Ceballos scored 15 points in 14 minutes. It was a major victory for the Lakers. Orlando hadn't lost at home in over a year, a streak of 40 consecutive wins.

The Lakers were in Miami the next night where Magic would play against Pat Riley for the first time. "I never in my life thought I would go up against Pat Riley," Magic said. "I'm looking forward to it. And I'm sure it'll be frustrating because I'm sure he'll have some defense ready for me."[293]

The Lakers clung to a six-point lead with less than two minutes to play when Magic took over. He backed down rookie Kurt Thomas and made a right-handed hook shot right in front of Pat Riley on the sidelines. Tim Hardaway, who had been traded by the Golden State Warriors along with Chris Gatling to the Heat a month earlier, made a jumper to cut the lead back to six. Magic then backed Gatling down and hit an identical shot from the same spot to seal the 106-95 win.[294] "I think I'm the last coach to ever be beaten by a skyhook," Riley said. "He buried two right in front of me, just to let me know."

The clutch baskets were the perfect ending to one of Magic's best games of his comeback. He just missed out on a triple-double, finishing with 27 points, 9 rebounds, and 9 assists. The win clinched a playoff berth, a pleasant distraction from the drama created by Ceballos, who scored just 2 points on 1-5 shooting in 21 minutes. After the game Harris said he planned to keep using Ceballos as the sixth man, not for disciplinary

---

[293] Riley presented Magic with a $20,000 cheque for the Magic Johnson Foundation just prior to tip-off to a loud ovation from the fans. Riley made a short speech and the two embraced at midcourt.

[294] Former Laker Tony Smith, who was traded by the Phoenix Suns to the Miami Heat one month earlier, played 11 scoreless minutes without attempting a shot.

reasons but because they had just had two solid road wins with that rotation.

The Lakers flew to Atlanta the next day and were just about to disembark the team bus at their hotel when Ceballos asked for everybody's attention. He only spoke for a few minutes, but he finally apologized for abandoning the team, four days after rejoining them. His apology seemed genuine and was well received by his teammates, who were all too willing to start picking up the pieces of their season.

The Lakers and Hawks wrestled for almost three quarters inside the freezing Omni before the Lakers ramped up their defense to seize control of the game. They closed the third quarter with a 10-0 run to tie the score 70-70 at the final break. They then continued the blitz, outscoring the Hawks 32-19 in the fourth quarter for a 102-89 victory.

Magic had picked up where he left off in Miami, barely missing a triple-double for the second straight game. He had 16 points, 10 rebounds, and 9 assists. But the stat he was most proud of was having only one turnover in 42 minutes. After being turnover-prone following the injury, he had committed just three of them in 117 minutes of playing time so far on the road trip. "I haven't been looking to make the fancy pass," he said. "I'm just trying to hit the open man more. That's probably why my turnovers are down."

The Lakers got their fourth straight win on the road trip two nights later in Toronto against the expansion Raptors. 36,046 fans showed up at the SkyDome, most of them to watch Magic, who had 19 points in 34 minutes. But it was Sedale Threatt who hit the big shot, a jumper with a minute left that sealed the 111-106 win.

The toll of the road trip eventually hit. The weary Lakers shot less than 40% in their final two games. They hung tough against the Charlotte Hornets and trailed by two points with five minutes remaining, but had nothing in the tank to finish the game, losing 102-97. Magic finished with 10 points and 10 assists in 38 minutes, failing to make a basket and doing all his scoring from the free throw line. The next night they were overrun by the Cleveland Cavaliers in the second quarter and never seriously challenged from there, eventually losing 105-89. This time, Magic was the lone Laker to put up decent numbers, scoring a game-high 28 points to go along with 8 rebounds on 8-13 shooting.

Despite dropping the last two games, it had been a successful road trip. They finished it 4-2 and repaired some of the 'chemistry issues' caused by Ceballos' vacation. "So often in life, it takes some sort of problem or crisis or blow up to recommit people to see what's important," said Harris.

Magic had played particularly well on the trip as a starter, averaging 18.7 points, 6.8 rebounds, and 7.5 assists in the six games. Most impressively, he averaged 38 minutes, in no small part because he had shed 10 pounds since the first game of his comeback and increased his stamina. "And I don't hurt afterward now," he said. "That's the key. Before, I was hurting."

But just like that, Magic's Achilles flared up again, and he was rested against the lowly Vancouver Grizzlies as a precaution. Ceballos was temporarily back in the starting line-up, replacing Magic, and was greeted by a mixture of cheers and boos in his first game at the Forum since his vacation. Divac recorded a triple-double with 10 points, 10 rebounds, and 13 assists, and the Lakers got the 104-94 win.[295]

Magic was back in the starting line-up, and Ceballos back to the bench, two nights later when the Lakers hosted the 54-21 San Antonio Spurs. The Lakers had lost nine of their last ten regular season games against the Spurs, including two losses to them in December. David Robinson was unstoppable all night, racking up 40 points and 11 rebounds and the Spurs raced out to a 24-11 lead in the first quarter. But a rally got the Lakers back to within two at half-time, and they led by six midway through the fourth when Peeler hit a three-pointer and Divac converted a lay-up to push the lead to eleven. The Spurs never got close after that, and the Lakers got a 107-97 win.

Magic recorded 15 points, 9 rebounds, and 7 assists against the Spurs, battling through pain in his Achilles for 41 minutes. Despite resting it against Vancouver, the Achilles was sore and swollen after the Spurs game. With eight games left on the schedule, Harris and Vitti decided to put Magic on minute restrictions to ensure he was fresh for the playoffs. It would mean a return to the bench and a commitment to keep his minutes to between 20 to 25 a night for the rest of the season. It also meant Ceballos would be reinstated as a full-time starter, at least until the playoffs began.

---

[295] Byron Scott scored 8 points on 3-10 shooting in 22 minutes off the bench. He never did get to play against Magic during his comeback.

But Magic's Achilles would soon become the least of the Lakers' concerns, and the buzz from the win against the Spurs would quickly fade. That was because Van Exel was about to add to the drama the team had been facing since Ceballos' vacation. It would unfold in the fourth quarter of a seven-point loss in Denver. The Lakers trailed the Nuggets by 10 points with three and a half minutes to play in the fourth quarter when official Ron Garretson called a foul on Denver forward Dale Ellis. Van Exel celebrated the call. "Good call! Good call!" he repeated. Harris called a timeout, and Van Exel reached the huddle when he realized Garretson had just called him for a technical foul. He walked through the Nuggets cheerleaders to midcourt to confront Garretson who was nearing the scorer's table to get a drink. Van Exel demanded an explanation for the technical. After asking him three times, Garretson told Van Exel it was for being a "smart ass." The flimsy excuse for a technical enraged Van Exel, who continued to argue.

Equipment manager Rudy Garciduenas was the only Laker who interjected. He restrained Van Exel and walked him back towards the huddle as the argument between the two continued. Van Exel turned his head and called Garretson a "little midget", resulting in the official whistling him for his second technical foul and his ejection from the game. Van Exel broke free of Garciduenas' hold, and before Magic could get close enough to intercede, he pushed Garretson in the ribs with his left arm. The blow lifted Garretson off his feet and onto the scorer's table, landing him awkwardly on his hip.[296]

Harris threw his arms in the air in exasperation, no doubt immediately aware of the heavy penalty that would follow. Garretson looked stunned, returned to his feet and for a second acted like he wanted to fight Van Exel. He was held back by Magic and quickly calmed down as Garciduenas escorted Van Exel off the court.[297]

The league had never seen this kind of physical contact with an official before this season, and oddly enough, it was the second such incident in just three weeks. Bulls forward Dennis Rodman was fined and suspended

---

[296] On his *Beyond the Glory* episode, Van Exel makes it sound like the shove was accidental, that he bumped Garretson with his arm on the follow through as he yanked it free of Garciduenas' hold.

[297] The game itself was secondary to the incident but, for the record, Magic had 14 points, 8 rebounds, and 2 assists and shot 3-13 from the field in 26 minutes.

six games for making contact with official Ted Bernhardt on March 16, 1996. The Rodman suspension was used as a precedent, with Van Exel's incident considered by the league as being marginally worse. Van Exel was suspended for the final seven games of the season and fined a record $188,195.11.[298] It was the third-longest suspension in NBA history for an on-court incident, behind the 26 games that Kermit Washington got in 1977 for punching Rudy Tomjanovich, and the 10 games issued to Vernon Maxwell in 1995 for going into the stands to fight a fan. An anonymous poll of NBA referees revealed most league officials believed Van Exel got off lightly.

The reaction from the sports world was quick and fierce. Van Exel was painted by the national media as a thug, a brat, and everything wrong with the NBA in the 90s. For many commentators, the incident had been waiting to happen and affirmed the skeptics who said Van Exel had an attitude problem when he entered the league.

Sports Illustrated published an article airing Van Exel's dirty laundry from his years at Trinity Valley Community College. There were details of an alleged 1991 off-court altercation with a teammate that saw him hospitalized after Van Exel repeatedly kicked him in the head while he was lying unconscious on the ground. There were reports he played a part in a break-in of a teammate's room and stole clothes and other personal items that suspiciously reappeared soon after Van Exel was confronted about it. The article claimed the relationship with his girlfriend in 1991 was abusive and he once grabbed her by the throat and threw her down on a bed in a jealous rage.[299]

His teammates were either silent or publicly critical. The most vocal critic was Magic, who sounded world-weary when discussing the matter. "It's inexcusable," he said. "You can't do that, no matter how frustrated you are or what foul has happened." He was especially upset about the timing of the incident. It had been less than three weeks since co-captain Ceballos walked out on the team. The team had begun to put that incident behind them to prepare for the playoffs, and they now got this from their other co-captain. The Lakers would now have to prepare for the playoffs without their starting point guard who led them to their remarkable

---

[298] The breakdown of the fine was $25,00 for the incident, $25,170.73 for each game he would miss ($176,195.11 in total), and $1,000 for the double-technical ejection.

[299] John Black sent a letter to the magazine on Laker letterhead protesting the piece as unfair and one-sided.

playoff run the previous season.

It was especially painful for West. He was never blind to Van Exel's faults, but he identified with him, empathized with his tough upbringing and found him endearing in his own way. But West had no defense for what happened in Denver, and he publicly supported the suspension. "I am embarrassed and apologize to our fans," he said. "This is a low point of the Lakers organization."

Van Exel fronted the media a few days later, acknowledged he had made a terrible mistake by not walking away. He apologized to his teammates, Lakers fans, management, his family, the media, and the little kids who looked up to him. Everybody except Garretson. "I would expect an apology from him also," he said. "If he apologizes to me, then I'll apologize to him." He said Garretson had exaggerated the contact when he landed on the scorer's table, calling it a 'Hollywood job.'

The Lakers had little time to recover as they were in Minneapolis the next night.[300] Magic huddled the team together before the game and implored them to continue playing hard. "Nick is gone, and there is nothing we can do about it," he told them. Sedale Threatt replaced Van Exel in the starting line-up, getting 20 points and 8 assists as the Lakers blew out the Timberwolves 111-90. Magic almost got a triple-double, grabbing 10 rebounds and handing out 11 assists. But he failed to score in double figures, shooting just five times and scoring six points.

They got another win when they hosted Golden State, holding the Warriors to 32 second-half points and winning 94-81. Magic, still on a minutes restriction, scored 10 points and had nine assists in 26 minutes. But it was Peeler who emerged as the go-to player down the stretch. He hit a three-pointer to seal the game and had 12 of his 16 points in the fourth quarter. It was the fifth time in nine games he had scored double figures in the fourth quarter. "A.P. continues to do tremendous fourth-quarter heroics," Harris said.

Just as it seemed things couldn't get any stranger for the Lakers, they got stranger still against the Phoenix Suns two nights later at the Forum. Magic got rolling when he checked into the game at the start of the second

---

[300] The Lakers were without a captain. Ceballos had been stripped of his co-captaincy and Van Exel was suspended. Magic temporarily took over captain duties until the end of the regular season.

quarter. He backed Charles Barkley down on consecutive possessions, scoring a lay-in the first time and firing a no-look pass to Campbell for an easy basket on the second. He then posted up Wayman Tisdale, drew a foul and made both free throws. Minutes later he backed down Barkley for the third time and hit a right-handed skyhook over him. A few possessions later he blew past Barkley near mid-court and hit a tough lay-in over Tisdale.

Magic was feeling it, and he charged into the lane looking to score again. He tried to spin around A.C. Green but appeared to lose his balance, and his lay-in attempt came up short. He thought he was fouled, took a step towards baseline referee Scott Foster and barked his displeasure at the no-call. Foster whistled him for a technical foul and took a step toward the scorer's table while Magic took another step towards him to continue arguing. The two collided, with Magic clearly bumping him, earning him a second technical and an ejection.

Magic stayed on the court for another minute, talking to former teammate A.C. Green who looked as stunned as he did at what had just happened. The fans booed the ejection and threw wadded-up cups, ice, and other debris onto the court after Magic went back to the locker room.

Magic was furious afterward, claiming Foster caused the contact by stopping short. But when he watched the replay, it was obvious he caused the contact. He sent for NBC sideline reporter Hannah Storm and gave a short interview from the locker room. "I tried to get in front of him and accidentally bumped into him," Magic explained. "It was my fault, I should have gotten kicked out, there's no excuse for it. I feel bad for my teammates. I know with Nick being kicked out and Rodman butting heads with the referee earlier, things like that shouldn't happen. I should know better, I've been in this league too long."

The shorthanded Lakers battled on for a 118-114 win. It was their 50th win of the season, the first time they had achieved that mark in five years. But Magic's ejection took almost all the shine off the moment.

The league acknowledged there was a world of difference between the Van Exel and Rodman incidents and what happened with Magic. But it was the third such incident in four weeks, enough for the league to consider it a worrisome trend. The league suspended Magic for three games and fined him a total of $102,463.40.[301] For the second time in five

---

[301] The breakdown of the fine was $10,00 for the incident, $30,487.80 for each game he would miss ($91,463.40 in total), and $1,000 for the double-technical ejection.

days, West spoke to the media about the infractions of one of his players and again supported the sanction against Magic.

Magic and the Lakers were mocked by national sports media. Magic was accused of having a 'do-what-I-say-not-what-I-do' mentality. The team was painted, quite accurately, as being in such disarray that it would be comical if not for the opportunity they were wasting. The Lakers had two of their top players out suspended in the lead-up to the playoffs. There was nothing for Harris to do but make light of the ludicrous situation. "People asked 'will you give the key people a rest before the playoffs?'" he said. "I said 'no', but I stand corrected." [302]

Without Van Exel or Magic, the Lakers still managed to thrash the Dallas Mavericks 113-95 on the road. Two nights later, they held a 19-point lead in San Antonio after three quarters. But they scored just 8 points in the fourth quarter, their lowest output for a quarter since 1977, and lost 103-100. They were down yet another player two nights later at the Forum when Divac sat out with a strained lower back. Fortunately, their opponent was the lowly Minnesota Timberwolves, and they got an easy 106-82 win.

Magic was back for the Lakers' final game of the season in Portland. The Lakers were clinging to a two-point lead with 10.3 seconds left in the game. Following a timeout, James Robinson tried to inbound to Aaron McKie, but Jones intercepted the pass and was fouled immediately. He made both free throws for a 92-88 win. Magic dished out 10 assists in his first game back from suspension but struggled with his shot, scoring six points on ugly 1-7 shooting in 33 minutes.

The win came at a cost though. Peeler was running down the court with seven minutes left in the game when he suddenly clutched the back of his right leg and sat down on the court before play had even stopped. He had never experienced a pain like it and hobbled to the bench. Vitti assisted him to the locker room where he diagnosed Jones with a strained calf and was expected to be on the sidelines for three to four weeks. On top of everything else going on, the Lakers would be going into the playoffs without one of their most reliable fourth-quarter scorers.

---

[302] Looking to add veteran experience for the playoffs, the Lakers activated Fred Roberts and placed Anthony Miller on the injured list with right knee tendinitis.

If somebody hadn't been paying attention the last month, they might have taken a quick glance at the standings and assumed the Lakers' season had been a success.[303] They won 53 games, five more than the previous season. They finished fourth in the West, one spot higher than a year ago, and had home-court advantage in the first round. They had the fourth best-rated offense in the league, and they had Magic Johnson as their sixth man. But it was all surface level. Underneath, this was a team fraying at the edges with deeply fractured chemistry. They would now be tasked with making this patchwork team somehow function in the heated competition of playoff basketball. And they couldn't have been given a first-round opponent more difficult to do that against.

---

[303] The Lakers lost 147 games to injury or suspensions in 1995-96, but only 50 to rotation players. King 61, Roberts 36, Jones 12, Van Exel & Peeler 8, Magic 7, Miller 5, Ceballos 4, Divac & Blount 3.

Chapter 33
THE WRONG MATCH-UP

April 25, 1996 to May 2, 1996

M AGIC JOHNSON WAS ecstatic to be back in the heat of playoff competition for the first time in five years. It was obvious he was so happy because he was in such a bad mood. "I like being moody, crazy," he said. "I like being in this mode."

He told the media he would give no pre-game interviews. If they wanted to talk to him, it would have to be after the game. He sent a memo to all employees of Magic Johnson Enterprises warning them not to call him at home, barring an emergency. He even asked them not to make small-talk with him in the office. Cookie was already getting sick of his irritable mood at home.

The Lakers and Houston Rockets had known for weeks they would likely match-up in the first round, though Del Harris wished they were playing a different team. Harris and Rockets coach Rudy Tomjanovich had been friends for years. They first met in 1976 when Harris was an assistant coach in Houston and Tomjanovich was the Rockets' All-Star power forward. They spent a lot of time together during Tomjanovich's rehabilitation following surgeries stemming from Kermit Washington's punch.[304] They didn't rely on each other for coaching advice, but they were cut from a similar cloth – both unpretentious and both old-school in their approaches.

Their friendship wasn't the only reason Houston was a horrible match-up for the Lakers. The Rockets were reigning back-to-back NBA

---

[304] Harris testified for Tomjanovich in a civil trial against Washington.

champions led by all-time great Hakeem Olajuwon. They were a team that would feast on opponents who were falling apart from within. Teams like these Lakers. The Rockets were a team of shrewd, battle-tested veterans who epitomized professionalism, discipline, and unselfishness. They were everything these Lakers, on the whole, weren't.

Houston had endured an injury-ravaged season and limped into the playoffs as the fifth seed after winning 48 games. But they couldn't be counted out. They won 47 games the previous season and finished in sixth place, only to become the lowest-seeded team in NBA history to win a championship. The Lakers had enough talent to veil their internal strife in the first round against a lesser opponent, but nobody could smoke-and-mirror these Rockets.

Trying to defend the Rockets meant confronting a riddle nobody in the league had ever truly solved. Olajuwon was one of the most effective low-post scorers in league history. No one player could defend him. The best an opposing coach could hope for was to slow him down with double and triple teams. But that only left Robert Horry, Kenny Smith, Mario Elie, and Sam Cassell wide open for three-pointers. All four of them always seemed to shoot better in big games and were tremendous pull up three-point shooters in transition.

Then there was Clyde Drexler, who had arguably been the league's second-best shooting guard from 1988 to 1992. He was 33 years old now, and had lost some of his incredible athleticism. But he was still an effective scorer and was almost always craftier and far smarter than whoever was trying to guard him.

The question hanging over the Rockets leading into the series was their health, which had been awful over the last three months of the season. Drexler sat out 29 games after arthroscopic knee surgery. Cassell missed 20 games following an elbow operation. Elie missed 36 games with a broken arm, and Olajuwon sat out 10 games due to tendinitis in both knees.

They made do with a cast of CBA players nobody had ever heard of until everyone returned, but they still weren't 100%. Drexler was playing through pain, his surgically repaired knee full of fluid, while Horry was hobbled by ankle problems. "We go into the playoffs with a lot of question marks," Tomjanovich said. "Last year we were in a similar situation, but we were trying to find out who we were. This year, the question is, 'how healthy will we be?'"

* * * * *

Harris implemented a media blackout at practices and gave no hint of what starting line-up he'd go with for Game 1. It was gamesmanship, but he genuinely had a lot of options. Three player suspensions in a month had been terribly disruptive to his rotation. He had to change his starting line-up eight times in the last four weeks of the season. But in a twisted way, it gave him something of an advantage – unpredictability. "Houston will find out who we're starting just before game time," he said.

Magic and Van Exel both spouted a series of sports clichés in the lead-up to the series opener. They said the team needed to focus on the present, that all the distractions of the past few weeks were behind them, and the playoffs were a fresh start. But they sounded like they were trying to convince themselves as much as the media.

Van Exel had gone over two weeks without playing in a game. He had been allowed to practice and scrimmage with the team during his suspension, and worked out with Magic's touring team. But it wasn't the same. He'd be rusty, out of synch, and would be coming back with the spotlight on him as the NBA's new leading villain. "I'm hoping it won't affect me. You never know," he said. "Some guys respond great, and some guys don't respond at all. I'm hoping I can respond great. Who knows?"

Bill Walton engaged in his usual charming brand of hyperbole on NBC in the days leading up to Game 1. "This series will be a momentous occasion in the history of the NBA," he giddily said. "I'm the luckiest guy in the world to sit courtside and watch Hakeem Olajuwon and Magic Johnson play. This is going to be a sensational series. I've been so anxious, I can hardly sleep at night. It's just too bad this isn't a best-of-21 series."

Game 1 at the Forum was ugly, with both teams shooting poorly.[305] For a few minutes though it looked like Walton would be right, and the sold out Forum crowd would get to witness a vintage playoff performance from Magic. He scored the Lakers' last eight points of the third quarter to give them a 66-65 lead at the final break. He opened the fourth quarter by backing Horry down from the three-point line, spinning around him and converting a lay-up while drawing a foul. He converted the free throw to give the Lakers a 69-65 lead.

---

[305] For all the mystery before Game 1, Harris went with his standard pre-suspensions starting line-up of Van Exel, Jones, Ceballos, Campbell, and Divac, with Magic as the sixth man.

But then the bottom fell out. The Lakers went scoreless for almost eight minutes, the Rockets forcing them into eight missed shots and five turnovers. The four-point Lakers lead had turned into a 78-69 Rockets lead before Jones finally broke the drought with a three-pointer. They cut the lead back to four before Ellie nailed a three-pointer from the right corner with two and a half minutes remaining that ended any hope of a comeback.[306]

The Lakers lost Game 1 87-83, even though they got what they wanted defensively. Olajuwon was, as usual, unstoppable. He had 33 points and 8 rebounds on 14-26 shooting, but the Lakers held the rest of the team in check. Drexler had 21 points but on 7-18 shooting. Horry went scoreless, missing all eight of his shots. Everybody on the Rockets not named Olajuwon shot just 36%.

It wasn't their defense that the Lakers down, it was their offense. They shot 34%, their worst shooting performance of the season. They committed 22 turnovers, almost eight more than they averaged on the season. Besides 22 points from Ceballos and 19 from Jones, the Lakers got little consistent offense from anybody.

Van Exel was awful in his first game back from suspension, scoring 5 points on 1-11 shooting in 32 minutes. He seemed in his own head, passing up open shots in the second half like he didn't want to shoot – not exactly a trait he was known for. Magic struggled too. He finished with 20 points and 13 rebounds in 36 minutes, good numbers in his first game out of minute restrictions. But other than the stretch over the end of the third and start of the fourth quarters, he never put his stamp on the game. He shot 4-11 from the field and handed out only three assists. Sedale Threatt didn't fare any better. With Anthony Peeler out with the calf injury, Threatt played both guard spots off the bench. He missed all six of his shots and failed to score in 18 minutes.

Magic got into a war of words with Harris after the game that dominated the sports news cycle for the next few days. He complained the Rockets came into the Forum knowing exactly what they wanted to do, while Harris was constantly changing the Lakers' strategy. Magic was irked Harris moved him in and out of the post so much, telling him not to post in the first half but that it was okay to do it in the second. According

---

[306] It was almost from the same spot as his 'kiss of death' three-pointer he made to win Game 7 against the Suns a year earlier.

to Magic, his role switched and changed so much during the game that when he tried to 'turn it on' in the fourth quarter, he couldn't. He wanted the offense to run through him in the post where he could be more assertive as a scorer, while Harris wanted him out on the perimeter as a feeder and driver. "When you make adjustments, you've got to make them and tell me beforehand, not within the game because then my mindset is one way and I have to change," Magic said. "I was coming in ready offensively, and then it was, 'I want you to be a passer.' I didn't know that until I was in the game."

Harris was perplexed as to Magic's confusion. He thought he played Magic the same way in Game 1 as he had over the last 20 games of the season. According to Harris, there had been no change even if Magic thought there had been. He said he wouldn't take something that had been working and change it in the heat of the playoffs with just two days' practice to get it right. The conflict essentially boiled down to Magic wanting to take over the game now it was the playoffs, but Harris wasn't affording him the freedom to do so.

While Magic and Harris bickered through the press, the team got some unexpected good news when Peeler participated in a light workout on the day of Game 2 and was cleared to play. He was still experiencing pain, but it was nothing he couldn't play through. Gary Vitti was astounded by the recovery, which he expected could take up to four weeks but took only five days. He credited the fact Peeler had desperately tried to get back in the line-up, showing up early and staying late for his treatments.

Peeler was relieved because watching Game 1 from the sidelines was like a nightmare, especially since he sat out the 1993 playoffs as a rookie because of injury. "It was tough to sit and watch because I had practiced all year and played 82 games to get to this situation," he said. "And then, you can't go out and play because of an injury that happened in the last game of the season. I couldn't really explain to anybody how frustrated I was."

Game 2 at the Forum was a must-win for the Lakers. "It's do or die basically," Magic said. "You can't go to Houston down 0-2. It's all but over if that happens. The gravedigger is throwing dirt on you."

The first quarter looked like it was going to be a Lakers blowout. The Rockets opened by missing one easy shot after another. They looked slow, flat-footed, and made just three of their first 19 shots. The Lakers led 24-

11 at the end of the first quarter before the Rockets staged a comeback. [307] They made nine consecutive shots and briefly took the lead late in the second quarter. The Lakers then scored the last eight points of the half, including a three-pointer by Magic with 5.4 seconds left, for a 49-42 lead.

The Rockets steadied in the third quarter and threatened to seize control of the game with a 16-2 run, capped off by a vintage transition finger-roll by Drexler, that gave them a 62-56 lead with five minutes to play in the quarter.

It was then that Magic had the final word in his spat with Harris. "I was tired of that run they had. I just said, 'Hey, I'm gonna just go back to me now. I'm tired of this. Give me the ball, everybody get out of the way.'" Magic took over, leading the Lakers on an 18-7 run to finish the quarter.

It started with an assist to Divac for a dunk. On the next possession, he drew a foul on Horry and converted both free throws. A minute later he backed Horry down to the center of the key, made him bite on two ball fakes before hitting a scoop shot that brought the Forum crowd to its feet. Two possessions later he bulldozed through Horry to the basket, had his shot blocked, regathered it and made a left-handed lay-in. Finally, he slithered past Horry for a finger roll with 3.5 seconds to play that gave the Lakers a 74-69 lead at three-quarter time.

The stars aligned for the Lakers just 90 seconds into the fourth quarter when Olajuwon was whistled for his fifth foul when he inadvertently knocked Jones to the floor after a rebound. With his superstar center just one foul away from fouling out, Tomjanovich tried to get Olajuwon out of the game. But his replacement, Sam Mack, didn't reach the scorer's table in time and play continued with Olajuwon still on the court.

The Lakers seized the opportunity. They swung the ball to Peeler at the top of the three-point arc. He exploded down the lane, driving directly at Olajuwon, drawing his sixth and final foul. "I didn't think Hakeem was going to be in at that moment, but when I looked up and started driving I couldn't believe he was under there, it's so early in the game for him to be in with five fouls," Peeler said. The Forum crowd erupted as Olajuwon was forced to head to the bench, the first time he had fouled out all season, and the first time he'd done so in the playoffs since 1987.

---

[307] Magic made a hook shot over Mark Bryant late in the first quarter and landed on Bryant's foot, spraining his ankle and hopping in pain back down court. Harris called a timeout, Magic walked the injury off and received a big ovation from the crowd when he walked back on the court.

Cassell would keep the Rockets close, but the Rockets couldn't maintain a run with Olajuwon on the bench. Magic scored another eight points in the fourth quarter, including a six-foot hook shot over Horry with four and a half minutes left that sealed the game. "That broke our back right there," Cassell said. The Lakers won 104-94, leveling the series at 1-1.

Jones had another strong game, scoring 20 points and grabbing a career-high 11 rebounds. Peeler didn't shoot well in his return, but was steadier in the fourth quarter where he scored nine of his 12 points. Van Exel didn't shoot all that much better than he did in Game 1, hitting 5-14 shots for 15 points, though he looked far more assertive.

But this was Magic's night. He controlled the offense in the second half and finished with 26 points on 7-11 shooting, 7 rebounds, and 5 assists in 31 minutes. He took over the game like he wanted to in Game 1 and learned that he needed to tell his teammates when he was going to do it. "Before, I didn't have to tell anybody. But now, I've got to say, 'Uh-uh. Nobody's taking it but me,'" he said.

The Rockets didn't feel like they lost the game as much as they gave it away. Olajuwon acknowledged the two quick fouls were legitimate calls and were bonehead plays on his behalf. But he disagreed with the previous four fouls called on him and felt he was being targeted by the officials. "The only way I was going to stay in the game today is if I stayed out at the three-point line," he said with a bemused snigger.

Campbell thought it was hilarious that the Rockets were complaining about the officials. "They didn't say that, did they?" he asked. He was bewildered because he had three fouls in 11 minutes in the first half of Game 1, limiting him to 26 minutes overall. He then picked up two fouls in the first quarter of Game 2, eventually fouling out in 27 minutes. "I'm well rested," he said.

The Rockets had other worries besides the officiating. Drexler had 13 points on 6-16 shooting in Game 2, his second bad shooting night in a row. And he was in a world of pain after the game. On top of his knee problems, he had sprained his ankle in the first game and played Game 2 with it heavily taped. But he felt he had no strength in it, causing a lot of his shots to be short. "It only hurts when I push off," he sighed. "And land."

The series moved to Houston for Games 3 and 4, where the Lakers needed to win one game to send the series back to Los Angeles for a fifth and deciding game.[308] Both teams tried to see the move as positive. The Rockets were returning to the comforts of home, while the Lakers often played better on the road than they did at home. After starting the season 3-10 on the road, their away record was second to only Chicago's in the whole league. Sometimes putting some space between them and the pressure of the home fans, especially after Magic's return, meant they could just focus on basketball.

Both teams had shot poorly in Los Angeles and knew that remedying this would go a long way towards winning the series. The Rockets had shot 44% in the first two games and made just 6-31 three-pointers, while the Lakers shot 39% from the field in the two games and just 72% from the line. It wasn't a great indication it was going to change anytime soon when the Lakers were so unfocused in their last practice before heading to Houston that Harris cut it short by 45 minutes. But Harris didn't seem too concerned when asked why the team was so unfocused. "We're playing the same team. There's obviously no need to make any major adjustments," he said.[309]

The Rockets opened Game 3 with a 16-4 run that ignited the Summit crowd.[310] The Lakers got back in it with a 9-0 run when Olajuwon rested in the second quarter, and the game remained close from there. They trailed by five to start the fourth quarter, but a baseline jumper by Campbell and two free throws by Magic quickly cut the deficit to one.

Then Threatt found his shooting touch for the first time in the series. After Drexler scored, Magic found Threatt cutting to the lane for a lay-in. Then after forcing a miss, Threatt made a long-range three-pointer to beat the shot clock, giving the Lakers a two-point lead with nine minutes to play. Two free throws by Olajuwon tied the game until Threatt hit another shot, this one a tough jumper moving left over Cassell, to restore the two-point lead. Mark Bryant made a jumper in the lane and then Threatt, without even looking to pass, used a screen at the top of the key to get open and made another three-pointer. After missing all eight shots he

---

[308] Shirley MacLaine said she believes Jack Nicholson agreed to co-star with her in *The Evening Star*, a poorly received sequel to *Terms of Endearment*, just because it was filming in Houston during the Lakers-Rockets series and he wanted to attend games at the Summit.
[309] Really, Del? You don't want to make adjustments as a playoff series goes on?
[310] It had been five years to the day since Magic last played a playoff game at the Summit when he had 38 points and 7 assists as the Lakers won 94-90, sweeping the Rockets out of the 1991 Playoffs.

attempted in the two games in Los Angeles, he had scored ten consecutive fourth-quarter points in Game 3, giving the Lakers an 89-86 lead with eight minutes to play. "They didn't know what to do with me at that time," Threatt said. "I was in a zone, and they knew it."

But then the game started to look eerily like Game 1. The Lakers went on their second fourth-quarter scoring drought of the series. They went over six minutes without scoring a single basket or free throw. In all, they wasted nine straight possessions, achieving nothing but seven missed shots and three turnovers.

Magic tried to take over as he had in Game 2, but he couldn't get it done. He committed two turnovers during the drought. He airballed a runner in the lane and launched a three-pointer that barely grazed the front of the rim. He got a good look at a hook shot over Horry, but it hit the back of the rim.

The scoring drought in Game 3 was shorter than the one in Game 1, but it was costlier. The Rockets outscored the Lakers 13-0 during the six minutes, giving them a ten-point lead. Peeler finally broke through with a three-pointer with two minutes to play but it was too late, and the Rockets won 104-98 to take a 2-1 series lead, putting the Lakers on the brink of elimination.

Campbell led the Lakers in scoring with 18 points, and Jones again shot the ball well for 16 points. But the attention after the game was on Magic, not for what he did but what he failed to do in the fourth quarter. He played 38 minutes, grabbed 9 rebounds, and handed out 13 assists, but finished with 7 points on 2-9 shooting. "It was like it wasn't my night, it was somebody else's night," he said.

After fouling out in Game 2, Olajuwon stayed out of foul trouble and registered 30 points and 9 rebounds in Game 3. Drexler shot the ball better than he had done in Los Angeles and ended with 16 points, 7 rebounds, and 11 assists. But the biggest difference for the Rockets was Horry, who shot just 17% in the two games in Los Angeles. He vowed before the game to be more assertive and make Ceballos work on defense. "He's basically not playing any defense on me," he said. He broke free in Game 3 with 15 points and 10 rebounds.

The Lakers had plenty of theories for their fourth-quarter breakdown. Jones blamed their lack of movement, saying they stood around too much and watched each other. Threatt thought it was the Rockets' championship-tested composure that got the better of them. Magic credited Tomjanovich's new strategy of doubling him in the post. It took the ball out of his hands, gave him no chance to get into a rhythm, and his teammates didn't know to cut to the basket so he could find them.

Van Exel had a different theory, and it kicked off another round of public bickering amongst the Lakers. Van Exel blamed Harris' rotations. He said it was a mistake to take Threatt out of the game when he was hot to start the fourth quarter. He disagreed with Harris' instruction to get the ball into the post to Campbell and Magic down the stretch. He thought it would have been better to make Jones, who was playing consistently better in the series than any other Laker, the go-to scorer late in the game.

"We've got a lot of coaches on this team, don't we," said Harris after taking a deep sigh. Magic chimed in to the debate, saying Van Exel was the point guard and it was his responsibility to get Jones the ball. "He doesn't have to go to me," Magic said. "If Eddie's hot, go to Eddie. I'm basically the guy who sets picks for Eddie Jones." It was a confusing message from Magic, who the previous game was demanding the ball in the clutch.

The public back and forth with Magic was the final straw for Van Exel. For him, it had been a season from hell. He worked his way through a spectacular shooting slump at the start of the season, and had probably sacrificed more than any of his teammates when Magic came back. He became the NBA's biggest villain in Denver, and wasn't shooting well in the playoffs. Now he was in a public spat with Magic and his coach. When reporters asked him about the dysfunction of the team before shootaround, he broke down sobbing.

Just like they had done the game before, the Rockets came out hot to start Game 4. With their transition game clicking, they shot 64% in the first quarter for the second game in a row and quickly built a double-digit lead. The Lakers would go on several runs for the rest of the game, getting back to within striking distance, but the Rockets would always have an answer, usually a well-timed three-pointer by Smith or Horry to take the wind out of their sails.

The Rockets led 83-76 to start the fourth quarter and Peeler immediately cut the deficit to four by opening with a three-pointer at the top of the key. But the Lakers went on yet another scoring drought, this one lasting almost five minutes and leaving them trailing by 10 points.

Peeler cut the lead back to seven with a three-pointer, then moments later hit a jumper from the top of the key. Ceballos attempted a dunk that would have cut the deficit to three with two minutes to play. But Olajuwon blocked the shot and then scored two straight baskets to put the game out of reach. The Rockets took the game 102-94 and the series 3-1.[311]

Olajuwon was again superb, with 25 points, 11 rebounds, and 7 assists. Drexler was a game-time decision after suffering neck spasms in training the day before. He struggled through 36 minutes for 6 points on 2-11 shooting. But other Rockets players stepped up, including Horry who had 17 points, his second good shooting game in a row.

But it was two Rockets playing the role of unlikely heroes that ultimately ended the Lakers' season. Smith, who had proven to be a Laker-killer all season, scored 17 points in 24 minutes, making all six of his shots, including four three-pointers. And former Laker Chucky Brown, who averaged 5.0 points over the first three games, had the game of his life. Always in the right place at the right time, he slithered around the Lakers' defense to finish with a playoff career-high 16 points on 6-7 shooting. He took one look at the media horde around his locker after the game and smiled. "I'm not used to this," he said. "I can get used to it, though."

Van Exel struggled with his shot again. One year after leading the Lakers to a first-round upset against Seattle, he shot just 29% for 11.8 points in the four games against the Rockets. Magic's numbers weren't pretty in Game 4 – 8 points, 5 rebounds, 5 assists, and 2-8 shooting in 30 minutes. He had little impact on the game, going long stretches without touching the ball. During the most critical six minutes of the season, with the Lakers trying to mount another comeback in the fourth quarter, Magic was watching from the sidelines. Harris took him out with seven minutes to go in the game and didn't sub him back in until the final minute when the game was all but decided.[312]

It was an empty conclusion to Magic's comeback. It started on such a high with a near-triple-double in his first game against Golden State. On that night in January, the Lakers recorded 44 assists – a league high for the season and the most by any NBA team in almost ten years. It was a

---

[311] After eliminating the Lakers, Houston lost the Semi Finals in four games to the eventual Western Conference Champion Seattle SuperSonics.

[312] Magic's stats for the 1996 playoffs: 4 games, 33.8 minutes, 15.3 points, 8.5 rebounds, 6.5 assists, 39% shooting.

picture-perfect example of unselfish basketball, with every player committed to making the extra pass. Few would have thought on that night at the Forum that all this would end with a quick four-game first round exit, and with the team mired in controversy and distrust. "We could never get on the same page," Harris said. "I was spending most of my energy fighting battles within my own team."

It wasn't the way Magic thought his comeback would play out either. He more likely pictured a second battle with Michael Jordan in the NBA Finals in June than he imagined being on vacation a few days into May. "It hurts," Magic said. "Any time you go out this quick, it definitely hurts. We don't trust each other. We don't know how to give. I was just zapped trying to keep this team together."

Following the Game 4 loss, Van Exel changed his clothes in the locker room and walked alone to the team bus. He pulled his luggage off and told assistant coach Larry Drew he wasn't going to fly home with the team. Anthony Miller, who wasn't on the playoff roster, didn't fly back with the team either. The next day the Lakers met at the Forum for the end-of-year tradition of cleaning out lockers and having one final meeting. Neither Van Exel nor Threatt showed up. Neither did Harris.[313] "Boy, I tell you," said an exasperated Magic. "I'm just at a loss for words."

It was during morning shootaround before Game 4 when it dawned on Magic that the Lakers would probably lose the game that night. Instead of preparing for a do-or-die performance, the players were goofing off in shootaround as if the series was already over. The Showtime Lakers used to love playing teams like that in the playoffs. They were easy prey.

He sat quietly next to former Showtime teammate Michael Cooper in the locker room before the game. He looked around and asked Cooper how many of the current Lakers he thought could play for Pat Riley.

"Maybe one? Maybe two?" he said.

"Because Riley wouldn't stand for what's going on around here?" Cooper asked.

"Exactly," Magic said.

---

[313] Harris was reportedly sick.

Chapter 34

THE NEXT DYNASTY

May 3, 1996 to October 9, 1996

T HE LAKERS ENTERED the summer 1996 with an all-too-familiar question needing to be answered – will Magic come back? But unlike in the past, the question almost wouldn't matter in July 1996. That was because Jerry West and the Lakers were about to make two moves that would establish their next dynasty. The moves would come within one week of each other, and they would, finally, shut the door on Showtime without any sense of mourning. They would allow the organization and its fans to accept Showtime was gone. Even though it had been over for years. And they would relegate the previous five years to the dustbin of Lakers history.

For the first time in years, the Lakers were under the salary cap. The $9.95 million they owed James Worthy and Sam Bowie, both long retired, was finally off the books. They had an additional $6.1 million in space from the expiring contracts of six players. Elden Campbell was the only one of those six who the Lakers seriously hoped to re-sign. A temporary oddity in the Collective Bargaining Agreement meant that a generation of young stars were about to become free agents.[314] Armed with cap space, the Lakers were in a prime position to pounce. West had been planning it

---

[314] One of the consequences of the brief lockout before the 1995-96 season was a change to restricted free agency. Before 1995, two completed contracts and a minimum of four years were required to become an unrestricted free agent. Without meeting that criteria, a team had a chance to match any offer made to a player. The CBA that came out of the 1995 lockout eliminated restricted free agency for the first and only time in the salary cap era. It meant any player off contract would now be free to move to whatever team they liked, right in time for the young players from the bumper 1992 draft to be opting out of their rookie deals. Restricted free agency was reinstated in the CBA that was negotiated in 1998, making the summer of 1996 a totally unique time in NBA history.

for a year, it was one of the reasons he elected not to make big roster changes a year earlier.

Every cent of cap space would matter in free agency, something that refocused the question about Magic's playing future. He reiterated his intention to come back immediately after the Game 4 loss to the Rockets, telling reporters it would take something drastic for him to change his mind. But for the first time, whether Magic was wanted was a complicated question.

Fans started to get nervous a week into the off-season when Magic started talking like it was 1986 and not 1996. He said he wanted to be one of the league's highest-paid players, somewhere in the ballpark of what Shaquille O'Neal and Michael Jordan were likely to sign for. It was as if he was unaware that while he was still an effective player, especially at his advanced age, he was no longer one of the league's best players. Plus, he didn't want to play forward anymore and wanted to go back to point guard – even though he was now far too slow to have any hope of guarding the new generation of young, athletic point guards.

If the Lakers were not willing to meet his salary and position demands, he would start talking to the other teams he knew wanted him. He said he wanted to stay in Los Angeles, but maybe he would finish his career with Pat Riley in Miami. "I look forward to playing more at the point next season, whether for the Lakers or for somebody else," he said.

The thought of Magic in a Heat uniform was probably enough to make the average Laker fan physically ill. Almost everybody wanted him back with the Lakers in 1996-97. But if his salary at the age of 37 hampered the Lakers' chances of signing a young superstar in their prime? Well, that was a different story.

But the issue was put to bed on May 14, 1996 when Magic informed the Lakers he was retiring. This time for good. The announcement caught everyone by surprise, even Lakers management, but without the immense sadness that accompanied his two previous announcements.

Wearing a white Lakers t-shirt, Magic sat at his third retirement press conference and gave no indication why he had changed his mind about playing into next season. He said he enjoyed his comeback and was glad his son got a chance to see him play. But it was time to move on, and he wanted to make his plans clear early, so the Lakers had every advantage in planning their future.

He said he would buy back his part-ownership stake in the team and return to a management role. He made it clear this was the end of the story – there would be no more comebacks, no more rumors. He was done. "This is not a sad day or a bad day, it's a good day. I did what I set out to do," he said. "I'm going out on my terms, something I couldn't say when I aborted a comeback in 1992."

Magic wouldn't go so far as to admit his comeback disrupted the team, but he acknowledged he never clicked with his new, younger teammates. He came from a different era, and he had different expectations of them than they had for each other and themselves. Ultimately Magic couldn't bridge the generational divide any more as a player than he could as a coach. He said some of the issues were the fault of their immaturity, but some of them were his fault too. "The gap between the ages, it's a big difference," he said. "Maybe I just came at a different time, that now it's changed, and I can't adjust. Because it's got to be some on me too."[315]

Magic's announcement made the path clearer for the Lakers. They had enough cap space to get themselves a few mid-level NBA players who could complement the existing roster and improve them enough for a deep playoff run. But West was aiming higher. He wanted a tested, transcendent superstar to lead the franchise into a new dynasty. He wanted Shaquille O'Neal.

Shaq was one of the few players who completely lived up to the hype that followed him when he entered the league. In four seasons in Orlando, he had averaged 27.2 points and 12.5 rebounds, and led them to the NBA Finals in 1995 for the first time in the team's short history.

West knew he would have to clear even more space under the cap if the Lakers were to come up with the kind of offer Shaq would seriously consider. One way to do that was to trade an existing player for a draft pick. Their trading partner would absorb the salary of the established player and in return send the Lakers a rookie on a much cheaper contract. The Lakers owned the 24th pick in the first round of the upcoming draft, but West began to look at players expected to be selected much higher. [316]

---

[315] Magic's third retirement was the source of some mocking. XTRA's Jim Rome said Magic now has more retirements than championship rings. It wasn't true, but he had a point.

[316] The Lakers didn't own their second-round pick, the 54rd selection. It was originally sent to Seattle as part of the trade for Sedale Threatt back in 1991 but was traded to Milwaukee in 1995. The Bucks used it to select Jeff Nordgaard, who played 13 games for them in 1997-98.

One of the players he worked-out was a 17-year-old high school kid named Kobe Bryant.

Kobe, the son of former NBA player Joe 'Jellybean' Bryant, played his high school ball for Lower Merion in Philadelphia and had been named the Naismith High School Player of the Year. The fact he was a highly skilled player was never questioned; however, most NBA teams were skeptical about drafting a player straight from high school. Besides Kevin Garnett the previous year, few players had ever made the leap from high school to the NBA. Those who had were mostly big men, not guards like Kobe. "It wasn't in vogue to draft these young kids," West remembers.

Because of this skepticism, Kobe did pre-draft work-outs with an unusually large number of teams. But concerns over drafting an immature teenager were enough to immediately turn most General Managers off the idea of selecting him, no matter how intrigued by his talent they were.

Yet West was blown away by the young player when the Lakers worked him out at the Inglewood YMCA. He watched Kobe's work-out for less than 20 minutes before he knew he wanted to draft him. It wasn't just Kobe's incredible athleticism or scoring ability that impressed West. It was how polished his skills were. He knew no player that young had skills like that unless they had the innate competitive drive that made them work incredibly hard. Always a good judge of talent, West could see in Kobe's eyes the passion, cold-bloodedness, and nastiness all great players needed to have.

Following the work-out, West told Arn Tellem, Kobe's agent, the Lakers would do everything possible to position themselves to draft him. But it wasn't as simple as that. There was no way Kobe would still be available when the Lakers would be picking, not at the 24th spot. West would have to trade up to get him.

Despite his considerable talent, only two lottery teams were seriously considering drafting Kobe – the Philadelphia 76ers and New Jersey Nets. The 76ers were enamored with Kobe and went back-and-forth for weeks behind closed doors about whether to draft him. If they owned the fifth or sixth pick in the draft, it probably would have been a no-brainer to select him. But they didn't. They owned the treasured first pick, and they reluctantly decided it was too much of a risk to use it on such a young player.[317]

---

[317] It may seem like strange logic now, but a fan base would have demanded the head of the GM on a stick if their team used the first pick in the draft on a high school kid in 1996.

That left New Jersey as the likely destination for Kobe. But Kobe and Tellem had no interest in playing there. They desperately wanted to be in Los Angeles, partly because of the bigger market, but mostly because the Lakers had a proven track record of building championship teams. Kobe could be an All-Star in New Jersey, but being one in Los Angeles and winning titles for the Lakers could make him an all-time great.

To get Kobe to the Lakers, it was imperative Tellem convince the Nets that Kobe hated the idea of playing in New Jersey so much he would play in Europe to avoid it. At the same time, West had to be ringing teams to broker a deal to be high enough in the draft to select Kobe without making it obvious he had any interest in him. If word leaked West was looking to move up in the draft to select Kobe, the Nets would know Tellem was just playing hardball.

West eventually did find a deal. By draft night, he secretly had an agreement in place with Charlotte that the Lakers would send them center Vlade Divac if the Hornets selected a player of the Lakers choosing with their 13th pick. West wouldn't tell them who that player was, agreeing only to tell them five minutes before they were due to make their selection.

Kobe and his representatives waited nervously on draft night. They knew if the Nets didn't select him with the eighth pick then he was going to be a Laker. Ultimately, the Nets believed Tellem's threat that Kobe would play in Europe was real. To avoid the drama of having a disgruntled player on their hands, they selected guard Kerry Kittles out of Villanova University.

Unbeknownst to Laker fans at the time, the Nets selecting Kittles all-but activated the trade West had arranged with the Hornets. As agreed, the Hornets selected Bryant with the 13th pick. He dutifully donned a Hornets cap when his name was called and walked on stage to shake David Stern's hand. He did an interview with Jim Grey who presented Kobe with a copy of *Sting*, the official magazine of the Hornets. Grey told Kobe his new coach, Dave Cowens, was on the cover and suggested Kobe do his homework by reading it before presenting to the Hive for the first time. Kobe smiled and said he would, knowing full well he wasn't a Hornet and was never going to be.

The Lakers used their own pick in the draft to select point guard Derek Fisher from the University of Arkansas at Little Rock with the 24th selection. A late first-round selection rarely makes much of a news story, and this one was no different. Nobody was paying any attention to it once news broke the Lakers had traded Divac for Kobe. The deal was an incredibly risky move by West. He knew trading away an established NBA center for a high school player seemed a crazy thing to do. Especially Divac, who had developed into a top ten center. In one move he had cleared an extra $3.3 million to offer Shaq, enough to start a serious conversation with the superstar.[318] But what if Shaq didn't accept the Lakers' offer and Kobe didn't end up being a quality player? There was a legitimate risk West had severely weakened the team.

Then the deal looked like it was going to die almost as soon as it was announced. Just as Kobe had pulled a power play to land in Los Angeles, Divac played one to try to stay. Divac was in Serbia training with the national team when he was informed of the trade.[319] He was blindsided by the trade and declared he wouldn't accept a move to any NBA city except Chicago because of its large Serbian community. He said he would rather retire than accept the trade to Charlotte, and his agent Marc Fleisher informed the Hornets if they complete the trade, they do so at their own risk. He would be walking away from more than $9.5 million of guaranteed money if he retired. But Divac was adamant, saying he had already earned over $16 million from playing in the NBA and didn't need more money. Divac wanted to stay in Los Angeles where he felt at home, and his wife was pursuing an acting career.

On the same day that it was announced Jerry Buss had reached an agreement to build a new sports arena for the Lakers in downtown Los Angeles, Divac opened a dialogue with the Hornets. It would take almost two weeks, but Divac eventually agreed to the trade. His conversations with the Hornets went well. He was made to feel wanted, and he thought about how much fun it was to visit the charged atmosphere at Charlotte Coliseum. The clincher came when his wife told him he couldn't quit basketball when it was something that brought him so much happiness. He even sounded happy to throw himself on the fire to improve the Lakers. "I'm leaving happy," Divac said. "Happy I could help rebuild the

---

[318] The extra $3.3 million was the difference between the $4.2 million they would have paid Divac and the $845,000 rookie salary they would pay Kobe under the rookie wage scale.
[319] The Serbia-Montenegro team was permitted to compete in the 1996 Olympics after being disallowed in the 1992 Olympics. Divac played and won a silver medal.

Lakers if they could bring in Shaq."[320]

But the Lakers landing Shaq sounded like a pipe dream. He was spending the free agency period in Atlanta preparing with Dream Team III for the Olympics. And he didn't sound like a man looking to make a change. "Orlando is my first option," he said. "I've been saying that the whole summer."

He said the money wouldn't be the main issue but, even then, Orlando had the upper hand because they could offer him a bigger contract than any other team. Like today's NBA, teams were permitted to exceed the salary cap to re-sign their own players in 1996. But unlike today, there were no maximum salaries. Orlando could offer Shaq any amount they wanted, while every other team could only offer him whatever they could clear off their books under the cap. Orlando could, if they were willing, offer Shaq a blank cheque. Shaq told his agent Leonard Armato he wanted to stay in Orlando and wanted to get the deal done. Orlando wanted him, Shaq wanted to stay, Orlando could offer him whatever he wanted. It seemed open and shut.

There were rumblings Shaq had issues with head coach Brian Hill and that a rivalry with superstar teammate Anfernee Hardaway had caused a rift in the team. But Orlando looked like they had a budding dynasty that would dominate the NBA once Michael Jordan eventually ended his run. To sign Shaq, West would have to pry him away from one of the most promising teams in the league. And he would likely have to do it with less money to offer. It seemed like a far-fetched idea.

Orlando opened negotiations with Shaq by offering him $54 million over four years. The offer was so far off what Shaq wanted that he felt disrespected. Orlando only made things worse the next day when they engaged in a misguided attempt to create leverage by publicly criticising Shaq's rebounding and defense. To top it off, Orlando told Shaq they needed to be mindful that Hardaway would be a free agent soon and there

---

[320] Divac played two seasons in Charlotte before returning to California when he signed with the Sacramento Kings. He spent six seasons in Sacramento (where he was a teammate of Doug Christie) during which time the Lakers and Kings had a heated rivalry. He was an All-Star in 2001 and eventually had his jersey retired by the Kings. He returned to the Lakers in his final year in the league, playing 15 games in an injury-riddled season in 2004-05 at the age of 36. Divac has run several organisations and programs that supported Serbian refugees, and he became the General Manager of the Kings in 2015.

needed to be enough money to pay him. It was a disastrous way for Orlando to open contract negotiations with their best player, the face of their franchise, and one of the biggest stars in world sports. Low-ball him, criticise him, and then start talking about his teammate instead of him.

The benchmark for what it would cost either the Lakers or Orlando to sign Shaq came early. Alonzo Mourning agreed to a contract with the Miami Heat and Juwan Howard to a nearly identical one with the Washington Bullets – both for $105 million over seven years. These were astronomical numbers in 1996, the type the league had never seen before. But times were changing. Players knew how much revenue they brought in for their teams and now they would be paid their worth. It was a change West and the Lakers understood, and one Orlando clearly didn't. It made Orlando's initial offer appear ridiculous. Armato asked Shaq if he wanted him to investigate options besides Orlando, and Shaq felt disrespected enough to say 'yes.'

West got in contact with Armato minutes after midnight on July 11, 1996 when the NBA moratorium ended, and free agency began. By 3:00am, Armato was at West's Bel-Air home listening to his pitch. It was an in-depth conversation that covered areas from winning championships to the benefits of playing in the profitable Los Angeles sports market. Armato was impressed. "How could Jerry West not make a great pitch?" Armato said. "He's Mr. Clutch, right?"

West swooped into the void by making Shaq an offer of $95.5 million over seven years, with an out clause after three years that would allow him to recoup whatever money he loses by not re-signing with Orlando. West was offering every cent of cap space the team had to Shaq. He didn't reject the offer, but he didn't accept it either. He wasn't going to be rushed into a decision.

The longer West waited, the more of a risk he was running. Every day that went past without Shaq committing saw more and more free agents who the Lakers could have signed instead agree to terms with other teams. West had all his eggs in Shaq's basket, and it cost the Lakers several players. One was forward Dale Davis, an excellent rebounder and tough, physical defender, who agreed to a contract with the Lakers. If West initiated the deal with Davis, he would be taking the Lakers out of the Shaq sweepstakes. He couldn't give up hope of signing Shaq, despite all common sense and logic. Eventually, Davis couldn't wait any longer, and he re-signed with Indiana.[321]

They were also putting the re-signing of Campbell at risk. They wanted him back, and he wanted to remain with the team, but they couldn't sign him until Shaq decided. If they signed Campbell before getting Shaq, they would no longer have enough under the cap to entice him. But they could re-sign Campbell to whatever deal they wanted over the cap after Shaq signed. The Lakers needed to sign Shaq first to make it work. But there was always the risk another team would swoop him up, or even give him a contract offer just to force the Lakers to choose between the two players.

The *Los Angeles Times* started talking about possible consolation prizes for when the inevitable happened, suggesting fans get used to the idea of Chris Gatling and Brian Williams instead of Shaq. "We're not optimistic," said John Black. "But we'll continue to keep our hat in the ring until either he tells us he's not interested in us or he signs with Orlando."

West knew the $95 million offer to Shaq wasn't going to get it done, and he either needed to up the ante or walk away. He decided to continue gambling. After already betting Divac and several potential free agents on Shaq, he put Anthony Peeler and George Lynch on the table too. He agreed to deal both players to the Vancouver Grizzlies in exchange for the right to flip-flop second-round picks in 1998 and 1999.[322] By trading Peeler and Lynch without bringing a player back in return, West cleared an additional $3.63 million in salary cap space to increase the offer to Shaq.

But it was a painful trade. Peeler and Lynch had been the Lakers' reward for suffering two subpar seasons after Magic retired. The Lakers were not getting a first-round pick in return, they weren't even getting additional second-round picks. Instead, they were getting the right to swap picks in the future with Vancouver if they were higher than the Lakers.[323] It would be worth it if Shaq signed. But if he didn't, West had just gutted the Lakers bench for no reason.

Only following the Peeler/Lynch trade did Orlando finally revise their original offer. They now offered Shaq a choice between two contracts –

---

[321] West also had dinner in Los Angeles with Dennis Rodman and his agent during this time, though it isn't clear if a formal contract offer was ever made.

[322] Peeler would go on to play another nine NBA seasons with Vancouver, Minnesota, Sacramento, and Washington before retiring at the age of 35. The 2003-04 Sacramento Kings team featured three former Lakers from this era – Peeler, Doug Christie, and Vlade Divac.

[323] The Lakers did swap picks with Vancouver both years, selecting Ruben Patterson in 1998 and John Celestand in 1999. Neither player spent more than one season with the Lakers.

$64 million over four years or $115 million over seven years with an opt-out after year four. The offer was closer to what Shaq originally wanted, but he and Armato were astounded Orlando was nit-picking on the opt-out year, refusing to give him one after three years like he wanted.

With the extra cap room, West upped his original offer to $121 million over seven years. The offer caused panic with Orlando management, and they immediately flew to Atlanta to meet with Shaq. A decision was obviously imminent.

Then the *Orlando Sentinel* spat out what would have to be one of the most ill-timed publications in the history of sports media. On the day Shaq was likely to make his decision, they printed the results of a poll that asked callers if Shaq was worth the seven-year, $115 million contract the Magic had offered him.[324] Of 4,688 respondents, 91.3% said he wasn't. In fairness, the salaries of NBA players were not discussed with as much nuance in 1996 as they are today. And Orlando fans were hardly the only fanbase at the time who felt alienated from their super-rich superstars. It is hard to know just how much the poll swayed Shaq's opinion one way or the other. But at 2:15 the following morning, he signed with the Lakers.

The press conference to introduce Shaq as a member of the Lakers was hurriedly put together in Atlanta. West described it as one of the biggest days in Lakers history, one that immediately returned the Lakers to championship contenders.

Shaq was pushed by the media to explain why he left Orlando but wouldn't go into details. He said the decision to join the Lakers wasn't about money, it was about feeling appreciated. But he did address the angst that had been building about the incredible amount of money being thrown around that off-season. And he did so with his trademark deadpan humor. "Money was not the main factor here. I think people get tired of hearing money, money, money, money, money, money, money," he said before breaking into a smile. "I just want to be young, drink Pepsi, wear Reebok, and have fun."

For West, the acquisition of Shaq was the crowning achievement of his career, one he expected to look back on as the most important thing he had done for the Lakers. His hard work had paid off. "It really was a gamble," Buss conceded. "We would have been left high and dry. We laid it out

---

[324] There were reports Orlando upped the offer at the last minute to something in the ball park of $130 million over seven years.

there, and we could have lost very easily. From the time we traded Vlade, we knew we were out there on a limb. We were going to either be very sorry or very ecstatic."

West had turned the Lakers around incredibly quickly. Just two years earlier the roster was so bad he couldn't convince Horace Grant to sign. Now he had convinced one of the biggest stars in the league there was enough talent on the team to contend for a championship. It had taken West only three years after suddenly losing Magic to put a new playoff team together. Within five years he had set up another dynasty.

But it all came at a heavy personal cost for West. A few days after returning to Los Angeles, he checked himself into the hospital for nervous exhaustion. In his autobiography, West describes how the stress of the off-season sent him spiraling downward, and he experienced such an emotional let-down that the depression he had dealt with his whole life came back with a vengeance.

The Lakers renounced the rights to six players to officially open the cap space to get Shaq's contract approved by the league. Among them was 34-year-old Threatt, ending his five-year run with the team that saw him arrive as Magic's back-up only to be his replacement and then the back-up to the next generation of Lakers point guards. They also renounced the rights to Derek Strong, Anthony Miller, Fred Roberts, and Frankie King. And, finally, they renounced the rights to Magic, officially severing ties with him for the first time.

They re-signed Campbell just as planned. Trying to recover some of the depth they lost when they moved players for cap space, West targeted veterans who could still contribute but would agree to a minimum salary for a chance to play with Shaq. He signed former Portland Trail Blazers forward Jerome Kersey, and seven-year veteran point guard Rumeal Robinson. [325]

---

[325] Threatt played in France for part of the 1995-96 before signing with Houston in 1996-97, where he played 21 regular season games and 16 playoff games with the Rockets. He played in Greece in 1997-98 and in Switzerland in 2001-02.

King signed with Philadelphia late in the 1996-97 season, playing seven games for the 76ers. Though he never played in the NBA again, he had a long basketball career, playing in Cyprus, France, Germany, Greece, Israel, Spain, Turkey, and Venezuela.

Strong played the next four years in Orlando before finishing his NBA career with the L.A. Clippers in 2000-01. He would go on to be the first NBA player to successfully transition to NASCAR.

* * * * *

The ink was hardly dry on Shaq's contract before Magic once again started talking about a comeback. The day after Shaq's press conference, and just over a month after saying he was done playing for good, he was back at it again. "It definitely gets me thinking I can come back," Magic said. "It gets the juices going. I couldn't sleep last night with the thought of Shaq signing with the Lakers. He always said he wanted to play with me." Because the Lakers renounced him, he wouldn't be able to sign with them until January 1997 under league rules. And they couldn't pay him anything more than the league minimum. "I'll take the minimum," he said.

Shaq was asked what he thought about the prospect of playing with Magic. "It'd be nice," he said. "I need to talk to Magic first. It's his city. Whatever he wants to do, I'm behind him."

A week later, Magic changed his mind. He was happy just being a part-owner. He blamed his suggestion of another comeback on a rush of blood to the head brought on by the excitement of the Lakers being contenders again. Mark Kriegel from the *New York Daily News* published an article detailing each time Magic had either retired or said he intended to come back in the five years since announcing he was HIV positive. He counted 19 such occasions and finished the article by saying 'no one cares anymore.' It would be the last Magic comeback rumor.

Two days before the Lakers opened pre-season against Denver in Honolulu, West signed 35-year-old Byron Scott to back-up Eddie Jones and serve as a mentor for Kobe.[326] For Scott, it was coming back to where he felt he belonged and a chance to end his career where it started. The joy

---

Miller spent the next five years in the league with Atlanta, Houston, and Philadelphia. He spent three years playing in the CBA before returning to the NBA at age 33, playing 2 games in 2004-05 with the Atlanta Hawks. Miller, along with Cedric Ceballos, Vlade Divac, and Del Harris, appeared in the 1996 movie *Space Jam*.

Roberts played 12 games with the Dallas Mavericks in 1996-97 before retiring at the age of 36. By playing in Boston from 1986-1988 and with the Lakers in 1995-96, Roberts was the sole NBA player to be teammates of both Larry Bird and Magic.

[326] Scott played two seasons in Indiana and one in Vancouver before returning to the Lakers for 1996-97 and then retiring. He went on to have a long coaching career, including four seasons with the New Jersey Nets who he coached to back-to-back Finals appearances in 2002 and 2003. He coached in New Orleans and Cleveland before becoming the head coach of the Lakers from 2014-2016.

of being back in a Laker uniform was plainly written all over his face when he was introduced before tip-off two nights later.

Mitch Kupchak sat in the stands of the Special Events Arena in Honolulu watching Shaq score 25 points and 12 rebounds in his first game as a Laker. He looked over at West and Buss and wondered if they were thinking the same thing he was – it's hard to believe Shaq is in a Laker uniform.

EPILOGUE

T HE TRADE FOR Kobe Bryant was one of the deftest moves ever made by an NBA General Manager. It was done to clear cap space for the Lakers to sign Shaquille O'Neal, who would become the league's most dominant big man for the next decade. In doing so, they acquired a young shooting guard who would develop into the best player of his generation and one of the greatest scorers in league history.[327]

Jerry West's vision for a new Lakers dynasty with Kobe and Shaq would be realized, but it would take a few years to get there.

They won 56 games in Shaq's first season in 1996-97, only three more than the season before. They finished fourth in the West, the exact same spot as the previous year. Shaq missed 31 games due to injury but was back just in time for the playoffs. They defeated the Portland Trail Blazers 3-1 in the first round before losing in the Semi-Finals 4-1 to the Utah Jazz. The Lakers won more playoff games in 1995 than they would in 1997.

Shaq missed a further 22 games in 1997-98, but the Lakers won 61 games, their most since 1990, including a franchise record 11-0 to start the season. They finished third in the West and again defeated the Blazers in four games in the first round. They knocked off the Seattle SuperSonics in five games and advanced to the Conference Finals for the first time since 1991. But they were roundly beaten by the Jazz in four games.

The Lakers, and the entire NBA, were a mess in 1998-99. A lockout shortened the season to 50 games, and the Lakers managed a 31-19 record

---

[327] Yes, that is debatable whether Kobe is the greatest player of his generation. And yes, an equally good argument (maybe even a better one) can be made that Tim Duncan is in fact the best of that generation. But to hell with all that. It's Kobe.

(the equivalent of 51 wins in an 82-game season, 10 wins less than a year earlier). They defeated the Houston Rockets 3-1 in the first round, but were swept for the second straight season, this time by the San Antonio Spurs in the second round. Much was made of the fact Shaq had been swept five of the six years he had been in the playoffs.

But that was until the 1999-00 season when they won a league-best 67 games, the second most in franchise history. They would go on to defeat the Indiana Pacers 4-2 in the NBA Finals for their first championship in 12 years.[328] The next year, they beat the Philadelphia 76ers 4-1 for the title.[329] In 2002, they swept the New Jersey Nets to win their third title in a row.

After years of fighting for control of the team, Kobe and Shaq were split up following the 2003-04 season. Shaq was traded to the Miami Heat, and the keys to the franchise were officially handed to Kobe. After a few down years, Kobe and a new cast of teammates won another title in 2009 and backed it up by winning again in 2010 – beating the Celtics for good measure. The only player besides Kobe to be on all five championship teams was point guard Derek Fisher, selected by the Lakers in the same draft from which they acquired Kobe in 1996.

By the time the Lakers finally broke through with their first title in 2000, there wasn't a single player left on the roster from when Magic made his comeback in 1996. All the players who initially survived the roster purge to secure Shaq were gone by 2000.[330]

The first to go was Cedric Ceballos. He blew his knee out in San Antonio during the eighth game of the 1996-97 season. Almost two months later he was practicing and only days away from returning to the

---

[328] 38-year-old Sam Perkins was on the Indiana Pacers team the Lakers defeated in 2000. After five and a half seasons in Seattle, he spent his final two seasons with the Pacers. He averaged 6 points in 21.8 minutes in six Finals games against the Lakers.

[329] George Lynch was on the Philadelphia 76ers the Lakers defeated in the Finals in 2001. He played in Vancouver for two seasons before spending two seasons in Philly and finishing his career playing four years for the Charlotte/New Orleans Hornets. He was limited to 14 minutes of action in two games against the Lakers in the 2001 Finals because of a fractured foot.

[330] A.C. Green was the starting power forward on the 2000 championship team, averaging 5.0 points and 5.9 rebounds in 23.5 minutes per game. After playing three and a half seasons in Phoenix and two and half in Dallas, he was traded to the Lakers for one season at the age of 36. He finished his career the next year with Pat Riley in Miami, playing in an NBA record 1,192 consecutive games to finish his career.

court when he was traded back to the Phoenix Suns on January 10, 1997. The Lakers traded him, along with Rumeal Robinson, in exchange for Robert Horry and Joe Kleine. Horry went on to become a beloved figure to Lakers fans. An unselfish, key contributor to three championships, Horry developed a legendary knack for hitting game-winning shots in the playoffs.[331]

Next to go was Nick Van Exel. He would play well for the Lakers for two more seasons, becoming an All-Star in 1998. But he would continue to be a divisive figure. The final straw for West came right before Game 4 of the 1998 Conference Finals against Utah. Things were bleak for the Lakers. They trailed the series 3-0 and were in a do-or-die game. The players formed their usual huddle before tip-off that would always end with the players chanting '1...2...3...Lakers.' But Van Exel was heard to say '1...2...3...Cancun,' an obvious statement he thought the Lakers were about to go on vacation.

He was moved as part of a draft day trade a month later with the Denver Nuggets on June 24, 1998 in exchange for Tony Battie and the draft rights to guard Tyronn Lue. Battie never played a game for the Lakers. Lue was used sparingly for three seasons before turning 22 minutes of good defense against Allen Iverson in the 2001 NBA Finals into a big contract with the Washington Wizards.[332]

Van Exel's legacy was tarnished by some of his behaviour both on and off the court. But he was important to the Lakers during his time on the team. Ramona Shelburne said it best when she was quoted in Shea Serrano's book. Shelburne said she mourned the loss of Showtime, but she held hope Van Exel could keep Showtime going. "He was never actually able to," she is quoted, "but it was the hope that mattered."

The final three players to go were Eddie Jones, Elden Campbell, and Corie Blount, who were all moved on March 10, 1999. Jones continued to develop into an excellent shooting guard, making the All-Star team in 1997 and 1998. Campbell played well whenever Shaq was out injured but struggled for two and a half years to find his groove next to him.

---

[331] Ceballos would bounce around the league, playing for Dallas, Detroit, and Miami. His last season in the NBA was 2000-01, and he finished his career playing in the ABA, Israel, the Philippines, Russia, and the Harlem Globetrotters.

[332] Van Exel went on to play for Denver, Dallas, Golden State, Portland, and San Antonio. He finished a 13-year NBA career in 2006 with career averages of 14.4 points and 6.6 assists. Not bad for a second-round draft pick. He would go on to become an assistant coach with Atlanta, Milwaukee, and Memphis.

Meanwhile Blount was glued mostly to the bench as a third-stringer playing behind Shaq and Sean Rooks.

Jones and Campbell were traded 20 games into the 1998-99 season to the Charlotte Hornets in exchange for Glen Rice, B.J. Armstrong, and forward J.R. Reid. Blount was waived the same day to make roster space for the incoming players.

The trade was unpopular with Lakers fans who chanted 'Ed-die! Ed-die!' at the first game at the Forum after the trade. Fans speculated as to the reason for the move. Some thought it was to free up minutes for Kobe, even though he and Jones played together a lot that season. Others thought it was because Jerry Buss didn't want to pay both Jones and Kobe big money, and elected to keep Kobe over Jones. Another theory was that Buss regretted giving Campbell a big contract in 1996 and West had to attach Jones to the trade to convince the Hornets to take Campbell. [333] [334] [335]

Armstrong was waived on the same day as the trade, never playing for the Lakers. 18 months later, neither Reid nor Rice was still on the team.

Head coach Del Harris didn't make it to 2000 either. He was fired 12 games into the 1998-99 season after the Lakers opened with a 6-6 record.[336] He was replaced by Kurt Rambis, who served as interim coach for the remainder of the season. Rambis wasn't offered the coaching job the next season, and the Lakers hired former Chicago Bulls coach Phil Jackson before the start of the 1999-00 season. Jackson would steer the Lakers to all five of their titles in the next dynasty.

---

[333] Blount played five more years in the NBA in Cleveland, Phoenix, Golden State, Philadelphia, and Toronto before retiring at the age of 35. He was sentenced to one year in prison in 2009 when arrested for possession of 11 pounds of marijuana. He told the judge it was for personal use, to which the judge said, "Cheech & Chong would have had a hard time smoking that much."

[334] Jones had a 14-year career in the NBA, playing with Charlotte, Miami, Memphis, and Dallas before retiring in 2008 at the age of 36. He played alongside Shaq again with the Miami Heat in 2005 and 2007.

[335] Campbell had a long career, playing with Charlotte, New Orleans, Seattle, Detroit, and New Jersey. He was a 36-year-old back-up center on the 2004 Detroit Pistons team that shocked the Lakers in the NBA Finals, beating them 4-1.

[336] Harris served as an assistant coach in Dallas, Chicago, and New Jersey before retiring from basketball at the age of 72. He was an assistant in Dallas during Van Exel's year and a half playing for the Mavs.

ACKNOWLEDGMENTS

STAFF AT THE Multnomah County Library went above and beyond to find articles from *The Oregonian* covering the 1992 Lakers-Blazers playoff series. Likewise, staff at the Seattle Public Library were of great assistance in sourcing articles from the *Seattle Times* relating to the 1995 Lakers-Sonics series. The chapters covering these two series are infinitely better for the information they provided.

Peter Krieg did a fabulous (that word is yours Peter!) job in copyediting the book, I cannot thank him enough for how much he improved it.

Simon Brown made the beautiful book cover, which exceeded even my wildest expectations.

This book would not have been possible without the support of my partner, Alecia Wright. After all, it was sort-of her idea for me to undertake this project in the first place. She was consistently supportive of me throughout the whole project, patiently dealing with me as I swung between believing I was writing a modern-day sports classic to fearing it was an unreadable mess. The truth is hopefully somewhere in between.

Our daughter Olivia River arrived when I was still working on the first draft, and she has managed to turn our lives upside down ever since. And only in a good way. Among the many things she has already taught me – the virtue of going all-in with everything you do, the meaning to Pearl Jam's 'Sirens', and that it is actually possible to wake up every day with a smile on your face.

Thanks also needs to go to Fletcher, our Border Collie. He never misses a Lakers game and is always curled up beside me whenever I'm watching them. Despite his dedication I suspect he is, in fact, a closet front-running Warriors fan. But I love him anyway.

RESOURCES

Books

Adande J, *Best Los Angeles Sports Arguments*, Sourcebooks, Naperville, 2007

Bird L, Johnson E & MacMullen J, *When the Games was Ours*, Houghton Mifflin Harcourt, New York, 2009

Buss J, & Springer S, *Laker Girl*, Triumph Books, Illinois, 2013

Harris B, *Boom: Inside the NBL*, Pan Macmillan Publishers Australia, Sydney, 1992

Hearn C & Springer S, *Chick: His Unpublished Memoirs and the Memories of Those Who Knew Him*, Triumph Books, Illinois, 2004

Heisler M, *The Inside Story of the Lakers' Dysfunctional Dynasties*, Triumph Books, Illinois, 2004

Johnson, E & Novak W, *My Life*, Random House, New York, 1992

Karl G & Sampson C, *Furious George: My Forty Years Surviving NBA Divas, Clueless GMs and Poor Shot Selection*, Harper Collins, New York, 2017

Lazenby R, *Jerry West: The Life and Legend of a Basketball Icon*, ESPN Books, New York, 2010

Lazenby R, *The Lakers: A Basketball Journey*, St. Martin's Press, New York, 1993

Lazenby R, *The Show: The Inside Story of the Spectacular Los Angeles Lakers in the words of those who Lived it*, McGraw-Hill, New York, 2006

Lazenby R, *Showboat: The Life of Kobe Bryant*, Orion Books, Great Britain, 2015

McCallum, J, *Dream Team: How Michael, Magic, Larry, Charles and the Greatest Team of All Time Conquered the World and Changed the Game of Basketball Forever*, Random House, New York, 2013

Pearlman J, *Showtime: Magic, Kareem, Riley and the Los Angeles Lakers Dynasty of the 1980s*, Gotham Books, New York, 2013

Ridder R & Black J, *Los Angeles Lakers 1992-93 Media Guide*, D.M Steele Company, Fullerton, 1992

Ridder R & Black J, *Los Angeles Lakers 1993-94 Media Guide*, D.M Steele Company, Fullerton, 1993

Ridder R & Black J, *Los Angeles Lakers 1994-95 Media Guide*, D.M Steele Company, Fullerton, 1994

Ridder R & Black J, *Los Angeles Lakers 1995-96 Media Guide*, D.M Steele Company, Fullerton, 1995

Ridder R & Black J, *Los Angeles Lakers 1996-97 Media Guide*, D.M Steele Company, Fullerton, 1996

Serrano S, *Basketball (And Other Things): A Collection of Questions Asked, Answered, Illustrated*, Abrams Image, New York, 2017

Shmelter R, *The Los Angeles Lakers Encyclopedia*, McFarland & Company Inc, Jefferson, 2013

Simmons B, *The Book of Basketball: the NBA According to the Sports Guy*, ESPN Books, New York, 2009

Springer S, *100 Things Lakers Fans Should Know & Do Before They Die*, Triumph Books, Chicago, 2012

Springer S, *The Times Encyclopedia of the Lakers*, Los Angeles Times, Los Angeles, 1998

Streets & Smiths, *Streets & Smiths Guide to Pro Basketball 1994-95*, Ballantine Books, New York, 1994

Streets & Smiths, *Streets & Smiths Guide to Pro Basketball 1995-96*, Ballantine Books, New York, 1995

Travers S, *The Good, The Bad & The Ugly: Heart-Pounding, Jaw-Dropping, and Gut-Wrenching Moments in Los Angeles Lakers History*, Triumph Books, Illinois, 2007

Valenti J & Naclerio R, *Swee'pea: The Story of Lloyd Daniels and Other Playground Basketball Legends*, Atria Books, New York, 2016

West J & Coleman J, *West by West: My Charmed Tormented Life*, Little Brown and Company, New York, 2012

Articles

Anderson K, 'Getting Even: Twenty-four NBA teams passed up Nick Van Exel in the '93 Draft. Now the Lakers' baby-faced killer is happily making them play for it' in *Sports Illustrated*, October 23, 1995

Begley S & Samuels A, 'Back in the Game: The world's most famous HIV patient has lost a step and gained 27 pounds, but he's as joyous as ever. Magic Johnson isn't waiting for a cure, he's too busy living' in *Newsweek*, February 12, 1996

Corry J, *The Inside Story: How the Magic let the Lakers steal Shaquille O'Neal*, CBS Sports, July 21, 2016 [https://www.cbssports.com/nba /news/the-inside-story-how-the-orlando-magic-let-the-lakers-steal -shaquille-oneal]

Deitsch R, *A chat with Charles Barkley about basketball analytics and beyond*, Sports Illustrated, February 15, 2015 [https://www.si.com/more-sports /2015/02/15/charles-barkley-analytics-interview-nba-all-star- weekend]

Dunleavy M, 'Los Angeles Lakers' in *Streets & Smiths Pro Basketball*, 1991-92

Feldman D, David Stern: *Another NBA player besides Magic Johnson, diagnosed after retiring, contracted HIV during my tenure*, NBC Sport, November 8, 2016 [https://nba.nbcsports.com/2016/11/08/david-stern-another-nba-player-besides-magic-johnson-diagnosed-after-retiring-contracted-hiv-during-my-tenure/]

Gilmartin J, 'Pacific' in *Streets & Smiths Pro Basketball*, 1991-92

Gilmartin J, 'Pacific' in *Streets & Smiths Pro Basketball*, 1992-93

Gilmartin J, 'Pacific' in *Streets & Smiths Pro Basketball*, 1993-94

Gilmartin J, 'Pacific' in *Streets & Smiths Pro Basketball*, 1994-95

Gilmartin J, 'Pacific' in *Streets & Smiths Pro Basketball*, 1995-96

Gregory S, *Magic Johnson and HIV: The Lasting Impact of Nov. 7, 1991*, Time, November 4, 2011 [http://content.time.com/time/nation/article/0,8599,2098 685-2,00.html]

Grogan D, 'A Night She Can't Forget' in *People*, July 5, 1993

Harris D, 'Los Angeles Lakers' in *Streets & Smiths Pro Basketball*, 1994-95

Hoffer R, 'Lake Show: Surprising stars, fresh legs and a wily coach have helped lift Los Angeles from its doldrums' in *Sports Illustrated*, January 23, 1995

Hoffer R, 'Welcome to the Club, Big Guy: From George Mikan to Shaquille O'Neal, Lakers centers have been pivotal to the pro game's evolution' in *Sports Illustrated*, November 11, 1996

Hostetler D 'After Midnight: A police report gives disturbing details of a post-playoffs sex party involving some of the Phoenix Suns' in *Phoenix New Times*, June 15, 1994

Johnson E & Johnson R, 'I'll Deal with It: HIV has forced me to retire but I'll still enjoy life as I speak out about safe sex' in *Sports Illustrated*, November 18, 1991

Looney D, 'Legend or Myth? Lloyd Daniels was a storied playground basketball player, but his life – and his once bright NBA prospects – have taken a sorry turn' in *Sports Illustrated*, July 8, 1991

Mack J, *ESPN film on Magic Johnson's 1991 AIDS announcement revives memory of HIV lawsuit against Johnson handled by Kalamazoo judge*, MLive, February 10, 2012, [http://www.mlive.com/news/kalamazoo/index.ssf/2012/02/espn_film_on_magic_joh nsons_19.html]

MacMallum J, 'Memo to Magic: Practice what you preach' in *Sports Illustrated*, May 13, 1996

MacMallum J, 'The Magic is Back: Lakers envision Johnson in sixth-man role' in *Sports Illustrated*, February 5, 1996

MacMallum J, 'The Refs Cry Foul: First Rodman, then Van Exel, now Magic – Why all the official bashing?' in *Sports Illustrated*, April 22, 1996

Markazi A, *L.A Riots: Chaos, hope and hoops*, ESPN, April 26, 2012 [http://www.espn.com.au/losangeles/nba/story/_/id/7859510/1992-los-angeles-riots-chaos-hope-hoops-lakers-clippers]

McCallum J, 'Driving for a Title: Clyde Drexler, now no worse than the NBA's No. 2 player, is gearing up to take Portland to the top' in *Sports Illustrated*, May 11, 1992

McCallum J, 'Eye to Eye: Chicago and Portland should square off for top NBA honors, with the Bulls winning a second straight league title' in *Sports Illustrated*, November 11, 1991

McCallum J, 'His Highness: Michael Jordan and the Bulls soared to a 3-1 lead over L.A. in the NBA Finals' in *Sports Illustrated*, June 17, 1991

McCallum J, 'Let's Play 24 Questions: As the clock ticks down to an NBA season that opens with more questions than answers, here are enough of both to satisfy inquiring minds' in *Sports Illustrated*, November 9, 1992

McCallum J, 'Shining Moment: Michael Jordan dazzled as the Chicago Bulls won their first NBA title' in *Sports Illustrated*, June 24, 1991

McCallum J, 'Show of Shows: For star quality, the Magic and Michael made-for-TV miniseries tops all NBA Finals' in *Sports Illustrated*, June 10, 1991

McCallum J, 'Unforgettable: Magic Johnson, the player nonpareil, was an outsized paragon of style and grace' in *Sports Illustrated*, November 18, 1991

McCallum J & Yaeger D, 'I Know He's Gone Off Before: People who know the Lakers' Nick Van Exel says his recent blowup was merely the latest in a series of disturbing incidents' in *Sports Illustrated*, April 22, 1996

McCallum J, 'Up In The Air: Both teams struggled as the harrumphing Lakers tried to put an early end to the hobbling Rockets' hope of three-peating,' in *Sports Illustrated*, May 6, 1996

Montville L, 'Like One of The Family: When Magic delivered his shocking news, it was, for so many people, the first time the AIDS epidemic had really hit home' in *Sports Illustrated*, November 18, 1991

Newman B, 'Scorecard: Back to Reality' in *Sports Illustrated*, November 9, 1992

Newman B, 'Scorecard: Magic is Back' in *Sports Illustrated*, October 12, 1992

Payne E, *Sterling asked: What has Magic Johnson done? Answer: Quite a lot*, CNN, May 13, 2014 [http://edition.cnn.com/2014/05/13/us/business-of-being-magic-johnson/index.html]

Parham J, *Home Court Disadvantage: The Clippers, the Lakers, and the 1992 Los Angeles riots*, Grantland, April 26, 2012 [http://grantland.com/features/the-clippers-lakers-1992

-los-angeles-riots/]

Pfund R, 'Los Angeles Lakers' in *Streets & Smiths Pro Basketball*, 1992-93

Pfund R, 'Los Angeles Lakers' in *Streets & Smiths Pro Basketball*, 1993-94

Reilly R, 'Welcome Back! Magic Johnson raised goose bumps and took his lumps in an electrifying return to the NBA' in *Sports Illustrated*, February 12, 1996

Serrano S, *Remembering the Wonderful and Captivating 1995-96 Los Angeles Lakers: Post-Showtime and pre-Shaq and Kobe, a fond look back at the exploits of Cedric Ceballos, Nick Van Exel and Magic Johnson (!)*, The Ringer, September 27, 2017 [https://www.theringer .com/nba/2017/9/27/16372552/los-angeles-lakers-1995-magic-johnson-nick-van-exel-cedric-ceballos]

Smith G, 'True Lies: All along, Magic Johnson insisted he wasn't coming back. Was he kidding us, his family – or himself?' in *Sports Illustrated*, February 12, 1996

Smith S, 'Ambushed: The mighty Suns were on the verge of elimination after losing two games to the lowly Lakers' in *Sports Illustrated*, May 10, 1993

Smith S, 'Gut Checks: The Celtics, the Cavs and the Lakers took brutal playoff lickings and came back ticking' in *Sports Illustrated*, May 8, 1995.

Stein M, *Leslie Nielsen lookalike on actor's passing*, ESPN, December 1, 2010 [http://www.espn.com/blog/dallas/mavericks/post/_/id/4671939/nbas-leslie-nielsen-reacts-to-actors-passing]

Stein M, *When Magic defied tragic, 20 years later*, ESPN, November 7, 2011 [http://www.espn.com.au/nba/story/page/magic111107/remember-magic-johnson-hiv-announcement-20-years-later]

Taylor P, '24 Questions: Before our pro basketball package winds down, we take a shot at answering some burning queries about the upcoming season' in *Sports Illustrated*, November 8, 1993

Taylor P, 'Hand It to Magic: After refusing the job for more than a year, Magic Johnson agreed to coach the Lakers – at least for now' in *Sports Illustrated*, April 4, 1994

Taylor P, 'Inside the NBA: No Magic Act' in *Sports Illustrated*, April 25, 1994

Taylor P, 'Kazaam!: In big-bucks bidding, new Laker (and movie genie) Shaquille O'Neal and other top NBA free agents conjured staggering riches' in *Sports Illustrated*, July 29, 1996

Taylor P, 'Magic's Reappearing Act: Earvin Johnson has a right to another NBA comeback – but is it right for him?' in *Sports Illustrated*, July 17, 1995

Taylor P, 'On Spring Break: Cedric Ceballos's unauthorized vacation threatened to destroy the chemistry that had made the Lakers a contender since Magic Johnson's return' in *Sports Illustrated*, April 1, 1996

Taylor P, 'Pacific: The Suns have new talent and the Blazers a new coach, and that rumbling – or grumbling? – sound you hear is the Sonics' in *Sports Illustrated*, November 7, 1994

Taylor P, 'Pacific' in *Sports Illustrated*, November 13, 1995

Taylor P, 'Pacific: The Sonics are bigger up the middle, but the Lakers, with Shaq, have muscled into contention' in *Sports Illustrated*, November 11, 1996

Taylor P, 'The Show Is Closed: The glory days are over in Los Angeles, where the Lakers now dwell in the Pacific Division cellar' in *Sports Illustrated*, January 24, 1994

Taylor P, 'Sonic Soother Sam: Sam Perkin's quite ways are helping settle Seattle in its showdown with Houston' in *Sports Illustrated*, May 24, 1993

Taylor P, 'That Was Then…Then Is Now: Change, a hallmark of the league during its 50 years, will be evident again – though not in the Finals – the golden anniversary season takes off' in *Sports Illustrated*, November 11, 1996

Wolff A, 'The Golden West: Who would have figured - certainly not us - that the retooled Warriors and the Magic-less Lakers would be the big winners in the Pacific Division?' in *Sports Illustrated*, December 2, 1991

Wulf S, 'As if by Magic: After years of exile, Magic Johnson is back to show the world how to live with the AIDS virus' in *Time*, February 12, 1996

Newspapers

More than 1,000 articles from the *Los Angeles Times* were used in researching this book, too many to list individually. Most of the quotes from players and coaches come from these articles. Special mention needs to go to the three main writers who covered the Lakers between 1992 and 1996 - Helene Elliott, Mark Heisler and Scott Howard-Cooper.

Articles were also used from:

The Age, Akron Beacon Journal, Arizona Republic, Asbury Park Press, Atlanta Journal Constitution, Baltimore Sun, Boston Globe, Canberra Times, Chicago Tribune, The Desert Sun, Green Bay Press-Gazette, Honolulu Star-Bulletin, Houston Chronicle, Longview News Journal, The Morning Call, New York Daily News, New York Times, The Oregonian, Orlando Sentinel, Philadelphia Daily News, Philadelphia Inquirer, San Antonio Express-News, Santa Barbara Independent, Seattle Times, Sydney Morning Herald, Star Tribune, Statesman Journal, USA Today.

Articles from the following authors were also used:

David Aldridge, Elliot Almond, Terry Armour, Erin Aubry, Bob Baker, Chris Baker, Jeff Baker, Jesse Barkin, Bill Barnard, Ira Berkow, Andrew D. Blechman, Fran Blinebury, Rachel Blount, Thomas Bonk, Ferd Borsch, Jerry Briggs, Clifton Brown, Clifford Broyles, Conrad Brunner, David Casstevens, John Cherwa, Marlene Cimons, Cary Clack, Bob Cohn, Dan Cook, Bruce Davidson, Hugh Dellies, George Diaz, George

Dohrmann, Mike Downey, Chris Dufresne, Dan Dunkin, William J. Eaton, Stephen Edelson, Kerry Eggers, Paul Elias, Sean Elliot, Steve Fainaru, Jonathan Feigen, Norm Frauenheim, Gordon Edes, Reid English, Michael Fleeman, Mal Florence, Andrea Ford, Mike Freeman, Tom Friend, Sam Goldaper, Alan Goldstein, Bill Goodykoontz, Tom Gralish, Bill Graves, Keith Groller, Earl Gutskey, Amy Harmon, Beth Harris, Buck Harvey, Randy Harvey, Steve Henson, Jim Hodges, Rex Hoggard, Jan Hubbard, Bart Hubbuch, Maryann Hudson, Melissa Isaacson, Bob Jacobson, Phil Jasner, L.C. Johnson, Earvin Johnson, Lanie Jones, Tim Kawakami, Steve Kelley, Peter H. King, Michelle Koidin, Beth Ann Krier, Mark Kriegel, Hugo Kugiya, Bill Kwon, Frank Lawlor, Bernie Lincicome, John P. Lopez, Cindy Luis, Mike Lupica, Michael A. Lutz, Capi Lynn, Jackie MacMullan, Allan Malamud, Peter May, Dave McKibben, James C. McKinley Jr, Corky Meinecke, Ann Miller, Eric Miller, Scott Miller, Malcolm Moran, Mike Morris, Thomas S. Mulligan, Barbara Murphy, Michael Murphy, Jim Murray, John Nadel, Glenn Nelson, Ross Newhan, Blaine Newnham, Bob Nightengale, Robyn Norwood, Kevin O'Keeffe, Lisa Olson, Tom Orsborn, Mike Penner, Ken Peters, Joe Petshow, Eric Pincus, Bill Plunkett, Steve Popper, Tim Povtak, Mack Reed, Dale Robertson, Glenn Rogers, Richard Sandomir, Brian Schmitz, Janny Scott, Eddie Sefko, Kelley Shannon, Lee Shappell, Sam Smith, Steve Springer, Marc Stein, Larry Stewart, W.H. Stickney Jr, Roddy Stinson, Gail Tabor, Pete Thomas, Roger McG. Thomas Jr, Carlton Thompson, Tim Turner, Susan Yerkes, Bob Young, Michael Ventre, Charlie Vincent, Ailene Voisin, Larry Whiteside, Gene Wojciechowski, Mark Wolf, Scott Wolf, Matt White, John Zant.

Most newspaper articles were accessed at www.newspapers.com and High Beam Research.

<u>Films</u>

Announcement, The. (2012). [DVD] USA: Nelson George

Beyond the Glory – Nick Van Exel. (2003). [YouTube] USA: Jason Rem, Anthony Storm, Ronald Krauss [https://www.youtube.com/results?search_query=nick+van+exel+beyond+the+glory]

Dream Team, The. (2012). [DVD] USA: Zak Levitt

Laker Dynasty, The (2004). [DVD] USA: NBA Entertainment

Magic & Bird: A Courtship of Rivals. (2010). [DVD] USA: Ezra Edelman

Once Brothers. (2010). [DVD] USA: Michael Tolajian

This Magic Moment. (2016). [DVD] USA: Gentry Kirby, Erin Leyden

<u>Statistics</u>

All statistics used in this book were sourced from Basketball Reference at www.basketballreference.com.

ABOUT THE AUTHOR

Andrew van Buuren has been an obsessive fan of the Los Angeles Lakers for nearly 30 years. The second-best day of his life was when Jerry West signed Shaquille O'Neal, surpassed only by the birth of his daughter. Andrew is a keen sportswriter, backed by an Honors degree in History. He lives in Adelaide, Australia with his partner Alecia, their daughter Olivia and their dog Fletcher.

Visit www.andrewvanbuuren.com for Lake Show Blog and details of future publications.

Made in the USA
Columbia, SC
12 August 2021